A Practical Approach to
TRAUMA
Empowering Interventions

PRISCILLA DASS-BRAILSFORD
Lesley University

SAGE Publications
Los Angeles • London • New Delhi • Singapore

For information:

Sage Publications, Inc.
2455 Teller Road
Thousand Oaks, California 91320
E-mail: order@sagepub.com

Sage Publications Ltd.
1 Oliver's Yard
55 City Road
London EC1Y 1SP
United Kingdom

Sage Publications India Pvt. Ltd.
B-42, Panchsheel Enclave
Post Box 4109
New Delhi 110 017 India

Printed in the United States of America

Library of Congress Cataloging-in-Publication Data

Dass-Brailsford, Priscilla.
A practical approach to trauma: Empowering interventions/Priscilla Dass-Brailsford.
    p. cm.
Includes bibliographical references and index.
ISBN-13: 978-1-4129-1637-0 (cloth)
ISBN-13: 978-1-4129-1638-7 (pbk.)
    1. Psychic trauma. 2. Post-traumatic stress disorder. I. Title.

RC552.T7D37 2007
616.85′2106—dc22   2006028041

This book is printed on acid-free paper.

07 08 09 10 11   10 9 8 7 6 5 4 3 2 1

Acquiring Editor:	Kassie Graves
Editorial Assistant:	Veronica Novak
Production Editor:	Beth A. Bernstein
Copy Editor:	Diana Breti
Typesetter:	C&M Digitals (P) Ltd.
Indexer:	Sylvia Coates
Cover Designer:	Candice Harman

Contents

Preface

Society, with unmitigated cruelty, has made the Negro's color anathema; every Negro child suffers a traumatic emotional burden when he encounters the reality of his black skin.

—Martin Luther King, Jr. (1967)

The quote from Dr. King brings to life the cruel and harsh reality of the times in which he lived. Emotional trauma has affected the human experience since ancient times. The trauma counseling field exploded after the terrorist attacks of September 11, 2001. As a result, much attention has been devoted to understanding both adaptive and pathological responses to traumatic events. These efforts have generated important clinical advances in both counselor training and professional development programs.

This book captures the information I enjoy sharing with graduate counseling students as well as other professionals and colleagues in the field. In each chapter, I have compiled information based on intervention skills and strategies I have found useful in my work as a psychotherapist in many community and mental health settings. As a practicing counselor, I have used these concepts and skills in several work settings. The empowering model of intervention can be adapted to many situations, and its techniques can be generalized to serve the needs of diverse individuals and communities affected by trauma.

Although written for the beginning counselor, the material included is applicable to a broader audience. It can be used by counselors and paraprofessionals working in mental health agencies or by students taking a college course. When presenting workshops and seminars both nationally and internationally over the past 10 years, I have been struck by three things: First, the growing enthusiasm among counselors to become involved in trauma work. Second, the strong desire of mental health professionals to learn how to conduct effective trauma therapy. Third, the misconceptions that trauma treatment involves an immediate disclosure of trauma details, that all trauma survivors initially present with trauma disorders, and that trauma therapy is vastly different from general psychotherapy. I believe this book will dispel these myths.

To present the material in an engaging format, I have chosen to include case vignettes and clinical material from clients I have encountered in my clinical practice. The case examples illustrate typical client presentations and help clarify diagnoses and different treatment interventions. Pseudonyms have been used to maintain confidentiality; identifying information has been changed to maintain the privacy of the special people I have worked with over the years.

The primary objectives of the book are to provide both a historical overview and theoretical perspectives on trauma; to review symptoms and the clinical picture; and to introduce treatment approaches that provide a stage-appropriate, culture-based paradigm that can be integrated into existing therapeutic orientations. This perspective comes from my belief that psychological and behavioral adaptations to trauma are expressions of pain and efforts to cope with unacceptable environmental demands or stressors. These adaptations are, therefore, not necessarily pathological and are often grounded in cultural systems of meaning-making. It is the counselor's responsibility to locate and use the strength and resilience inherent within individuals, families, and communities and to empower them toward healing and recovery. It is my hope that an understanding of this field will sharpen practice with both traumatized and nontraumatized people and will heighten understanding of the impact of extreme stress and violence while developing a self-reflective stance toward conceptual, ethical, and clinical approaches to trauma.

The book begins with an overview of the trauma field, focusing on intergenerational trauma among several neglected ethnic minority groups in the United States (Native Americans, African Americans, and Japanese Americans). Those readers who want to learn more about the struggles faced by these groups may find the resources offered at the end of Chapter 1 useful. The chapters that follow look at the diagnosis of trauma (Chapter 2) and the different approaches in trauma intervention (Chapter 3). Chapter 4, "Empowering Interventions," describes the model I currently use in my own clinical practice. Although the therapeutic relationship assigns a level of power to the therapist, this chapter is not about the therapeutic power but the power inherent in all clients to change their lives and heal themselves.

An integral role of the therapist is identifying clients' strengths, seeing their promise, and highlighting their power so that they can become independent keepers of their destiny. There is a significant overlap between trauma work and crisis work. Trauma therapists should be familiar with the principles of crisis intervention. Chapter 5 provides this information. Chapter 6 addresses group therapy, which is often used in trauma work either as a stand-alone or adjunctive modality. Trauma interventions with communities are inevitable when one works within an ecological model. Chapter 7 outlines the foundations of community intervention and describes how to conduct a community meeting. The efficacy of debriefing as a form of crisis intervention has been hotly debated in recent years. Chapter 8 reviews the background on debriefing, describes the various debriefing models, and introduces the community debriefing model that supports community empowerment.

In Chapter 9, the focus of the book turns to special populations and situations of trauma, beginning with children and adolescents; Chapter 10 addresses the interpersonal violence of rape and domestic violence as it specifically affects women and children. The chapters that follow look at those affected by political trauma, terrorism, and natural disasters. The book ends with an exploration of secondary trauma in Chapter 14, titled "Helping the Helper."

I hope that this book holds your attention, adequately addresses your major questions, and enhances your ability to recognize, diagnose, and empower individuals, groups, and communities affected by traumatic events.

Acknowledgments

This book would not have been possible without the courage of the many individuals and communities who have touched my life. I remain in awe of their resiliency, courage, and strength. I have been honored to bear witness to their pain as I have listened to their stories of survival in the intimate process of psychotherapy. In addition, a number of experienced, skilled, and devoted clinicians whom I have met in various mental health settings over the years helped inform my trauma practice. My family members cannot be thanked enough for their tremendous emotional support and encouragement: my husband for his undying cheerleading and my son and daughter for their stalwart belief that I could achieve whatever I set out to do.

Special thanks are due to Arthur Pomponio, who worked at Sage, for his acceptance of my initial proposal and his foresight that this book was timely (in the aftermath of September 11, 2001). He passed the baton of support to Kassie Graves, my editor at Sage, who, in her gentle way, has been supportive and critical at the same time. Her guidance and feedback is subtly evident in many aspects of this book. My heartfelt gratitude goes to her. Thanks, Kassie! Veronica Novak at Sage also helped in a multitude of ways. I thank her for her support. My sincere appreciation to production editor Beth Bernstein and copy editor Diana Breti, who both worked tirelessly and graciously to meet important deadlines. I would also like to acknowledge Lesley University for the time provided, through faculty development grants, to work on this book project. I have been able to put this precious time away from teaching to good use. My research assistant, Kimberly Cadden, was with me from the very beginning of this project. She always worked diligently and enthusiastically. Her commitment to the trauma field is evident in the quality of her work. I cannot thank her enough for her help and support. Susannah Buzard and Vanessa Brailsford helped with copyediting. Thank you both so much for doing stellar work under the severe time pressure I placed on both of you. My sincere gratitude to the independent reviewers assigned by Sage for their constructive and critical feedback that helped sharpen the focus of this book.

Finally, my cat Speedy has stood unwaveringly by my side. He was often my morning wake-up call; his gentle nudge and purring was a reminder that it was time to write again. Late at night, he was still by my side, warming me and my laptop and serving as a steady source of both comfort and distraction.

1

Overview of Trauma

On a Friday afternoon in late February, an angry 23-year-old African American man entered a therapist's office. Duane was seeking help because he felt things were "getting out of hand" in his life. He barely slept two or three hours a night; the pains in his legs and his back were excruciating and painkillers were not helping. During his waking hours, he was unable to forget his recent assault. According to Duane, he was driving on the highway when a truck skimmed the side of his car. The driver did not stop but continued driving along the highway. Suspecting that his car was damaged, Duane went abreast of the other car and gestured to the driver to pull over.

The driver eventually stopped on the side of the highway and assertively asked Duane, "What the hell is your problem?" As Duane began to explain what happened, the other man made a call on his cell phone. Duane didn't know that, although the other driver was not in uniform, he was a police officer. A few minutes later, three police cruisers pulled up, and four police officers with their hands over their holsters approached him. Within minutes, he was slammed against a police car as the heel of a boot dug into his rib cage. Racial epithets proliferated and the phrase "you people" currently reverberates in Duane's mind. His girlfriend and grandmother watched in horror as Duane was ruthlessly beaten, thrown into the police car, and taken to the police headquarters. He recalls being beaten in front of his family as the most humiliating aspect of this violent incident.

When asked how the violence unfolded, Duane explained that when he saw the police officers walking toward him with their hands over their guns, he "lost it." He was overcome by a dark rage and hatred for the injustices he has *experienced throughout his life from police officers who, often unfairly or with little cause, "stop and check" the youth in his neighborhood. Additionally, the aggressive posturing of the police officers and his isolation in the group reminded him of lynchings in the South. He had watched many films that captured these racial incidents and the unfair victimization of black men. His aggressive and belligerent response to the police officers' questions was not based solely on the "hit and run" incident but included a history of over 200 years of oppression and disenfranchisement of African Americans in this country. The similarity to the black slave being whipped by the master as his wife and children watched helplessly was apparent. Like many black males, Duane was suffering from multigenerational trauma, which impeded his judgment and influenced his interactions with others.*

In therapy, Duane will have to learn how to manage his anger so that further conflicts do not jeopardize his life. Once he identifies incidents that trigger acts of violence and rage, he can develop effective coping skills before beginning to examine the roots of his rage. In a therapeutic relationship that is attentive to his cultural experience, he will gain a deeper understanding of the origins of the intergenerational trauma he suffers. This understanding can be increased by including other family members, for example his grandmother, in the therapy. The fact that Duane sought therapy on his own is encouraging.

In this chapter, we look at the historical origins of the trauma field. The evolution of the field over the past 20 years will be examined in the context of the experiences of four specific groups: Native Americans, African Americans, Japanese Americans interned during World War II, and Vietnam veterans. This examination includes a chronological discussion of the intergenerational traumas of the Native American genocide, slavery, and the Japanese internment. A discussion of the historical origins of trauma will not be complete without mention of the veterans from the Vietnam War who were the catalyst for the American Psychiatric Association's (APA) adoption of post-traumatic stress as a psychological disorder.

Historical Overview

The English word "trauma" is derived from the Greek word "wound." This word connotes a physical injury and parallels the psychic wounding that can potentially follow a traumatic episode. The earliest records of traumatic reactions appear on cuneiform tablets that describe two events: the death of King Urnamma (2111–2094 B.C.) and the destruction of the city of Ur (2026–2003 B.C.), both of which occurred in Sumeria 4,000 years ago.

According to Ben-Ezra (2004), the tablets explicitly describe elevated anxiety and sleep disturbance experienced by the ancient Sumerians. These reactions are similar to those we find among trauma survivors today, thus showing that psychological reactions to trauma have not changed dramatically across time and culture. It is significant that the ancient Sumerians did not attribute these reactions to supernatural phenomena, as one would expect them to have done at the time. Instead, they identified the traumatic event itself as the cause of the discomfort, indicating that the Sumerians "recognized the concept of psychological trauma" (p. 124).

Until the eighteenth century, references to psychological trauma are largely limited to literary or philosophical writings (Birmes, Hatton, Brunet, & Schmitt, 2003). Homer's epic poems the *Iliad* and the *Odyssey,* dating back to approximately 850 B.C., are literary works that include the heroes Achilles and Ulysses, who experience traumatic reactions. In Greek mythology, the death of Achilles' friend, Patroclus, who was killed in combat, causes him to have recurrent thoughts and ruminations that affect his sleep. Similarly, Ulysses is so overwhelmed by guilt and shame after the death of his fellow soldiers that he wishes he could have also died in Troy (Birmes, Hatton, & Brunet, 2003).

In the West, documentation of post-traumatic reactions appears after the Great Fire of London in 1666. Samuel Pepys, who witnessed this tragedy, describes feeling a great deal of distress, which manifested in difficulty sleeping as well as nightmares, intrusive thoughts, anxiety, and a general feeling of helplessness (Pepys, 1997). In more recent times, Herman (1997) correctly points out that a focus on psychological trauma has surfaced at least three times in public discourse over the past century. The first discourse occurred in the 1870s when the French neurologist Charcot studied women who were victims of sexual violence. He describes these women as suffering from the disorder of hysteria. Charcot's work was continued by Pierre Janet in France and Sigmund Freud in Vienna. In the 1890s, both Janet and Freud independently linked the hysterical symptoms they observed among their female patients to the psychological trauma the patients experienced. They found these traumatic symptoms were significantly reduced when traumatic memories were remembered and discussed in a therapeutic setting. Freud later referred to this recollection as "abreaction and catharsis" while Janet referred to it as "psychological analysis."

Freud began to notice that sexual transgressions against children were just as common among the bourgeois of Vienna, where he had established a practice, as it was among the proletariat of Paris, where he first began to study hysteria. He developed a fear that publicizing his findings would result in a backlash from his supporters, who would withdraw funding. Freud recanted his initial findings, and thus this first opportunity to sustain public attention on psychological trauma was lost (Herman, 1997).

The second resurgence of a discourse on psychological trauma in the public domain occurred after World War I, when the term "shell shock" was used to describe the mental state of many returning soldiers. The development of this disorder was attributed solely to the physical experience of a shell exploding and causing a shock to the nervous system of a soldier. Later, it was discovered that not all soldiers who developed "shell shock" actually experienced a shell exploding. This discovery led to the recognition that other causes explained the soldiers' psychological reactions. By World War II, the concept of "post-trauma syndrome" surfaced as a disorder when Kardiner (1941) described post-traumatic stress disorder (PTSD) as it is understood today. The symptoms included feelings of irritability, outbursts of aggression, an exaggerated startle response, and fixation on the traumatic event. Other diagnostic terms used to describe traumatic stress among combat veterans began to proliferate. These terms included battle fatigue, war neurosis, hysteria, shell shock, post-Vietnam syndrome, and traumatic neurosis (Everly, 1994).

The third attempt to focus on the debilitating effects of psychological trauma occurred during the Women's Liberation Movement of the 1970s (Herman, 1997). Through Betty Friedan's work with the feminist manifesto and her establishment of the National Organization of Women (NOW), Kathie Sarachild's efforts to introduce consciousness-raising as a radical weapon of the Women's Liberation Movement, and Susan Brownmiller's efforts to draw public attention to rape through her feminist writings, the focus on psychological trauma grew. These writers highlighted that it is not war but interpersonal violence directed against women that is the most commonly occurring psychological trauma in Western society. Thus, the plight of many silenced victims of sexual crimes was illuminated.

An acknowledgment of the negative consequences of interpersonal violence occurred in 1975 when the National Institute of Mental Health (NIMH) established the Center for Research on Rape. By focusing on rape, researchers found that childhood sexual abuse and domestic violence were just as prevalent. It would take a few more years for recognition of the syndrome seen in victims of rape, domestic violence, and childhood sexual abuse to be viewed as the same syndrome seen among combat veterans (Herman, 1997).

PTSD was first recognized as a distinct diagnostic entity in 1980 and included in the third edition of the *Diagnostic and Statistical Manual of Mental Disorders;* it was categorized as an anxiety disorder because of the persistent anxiety, hypervigilance, exaggerated startle response, and avoidance behaviors displayed by trauma survivors (APA, 1980). This coincided with research and documentation of PTSD that began in earnest after the Vietnam War. For example, the National Vietnam Veterans Readjustment Study was a major study that found a high prevalence of PTSD among returning Vietnam soldiers (Kulka et al., 1990). The empirical literature investigating traumatic stress among other traumatized groups burgeoned with the recognition of PTSD as a diagnostic category. In 1994, when the fourth edition of the *Diagnostic and Statistical Manual of Mental Disorders* was published, it included findings from many of these empirical studies and field trials (APA, 1994).

Several significant incidents had a major impact, in the form of intergenerational trauma, among several ethnic minority groups living in the United States. The effects of these incidents have been minimally covered in the psychological literature. The next section will focus on these intergenerational and multigenerational traumas as experienced by three ethnic groups: Native Americans, African Americans, and Japanese Americans.

Intergenerational and Multigenerational Trauma

Intergenerational or multigenerational trauma is defined as the cumulative emotional and psychological wounding that is transmitted from one generation to the next (Rakoff, Sigal, & Epstein, 1966). Rakoff et al. first introduced the concept of intergenerational trauma when they described how the effects of the Holocaust were transmitted to future generations. A growing literature based largely on clinical studies and anecdotal reports soon emerged (Portney, 2003).

Violent historical events, discrimination, and oppression experienced by prior generations can potentially affect the lives of future generations in the form of unresolved grief and ongoing trauma. The consequences of these collective traumas continue to be apparent in the oppressive behaviors that are widespread in American society today. Racial profiling and police brutality against black men are examples of institutional violence. The intergenerational accumulation of trauma, the persistence of oppression, and a disadvantaged social status have all had a significant negative impact on minority group members.

The resulting emotional effects of multigenerational trauma can be seen in the high rates of depression, anger, stress, hypervigilance, low self-esteem, and cultural shame as well as loss of language, culture, and traditions. Multiple social ills, including substance abuse, alcoholism, family and domestic violence, high suicide and homicide rates, and frequent incarceration appear to abound disproportionately among ethnic minority groups in the United States.

Three historical and traumatic incidents—the decimation of Native Americans, African American enslavement, and the internment of thousands of Japanese American citizens during World War II—have contributed to the intergenerational trauma found among a multitude of survivor offspring. The impact of these historical traumas are neglected in the trauma literature. The lack of empirical studies of groups who have experienced intergenerational trauma is demonstrative of a selective neglect of disempowered groups in the U.S. One may argue that because the affected groups hold a minority cultural status, studying their histories is not a high priority. It is for this reason that a historical account of trauma among these groups is reviewed in greater depth in this chapter. Several other major traumatic incidents, among them the Jewish Holocaust, have had considerable traumatic impact on many individuals, many of whom later settled in the U.S. The immense suffering of Holocaust survivors and the impact of trauma on their migration, adaptation, and ethnic identity will continue to have a lasting impact. These events are not discussed in this chapter because they did not occur in the U.S.; however, empirical studies of the effects of the Holocaust on survivors have been included for illustrative purposes. A brief account of the traumas that occurred in the U.S. is discussed to acknowledge their existence and to encourage psychotherapists who work in the trauma field to be attentive when treating members of these groups. First among these groups are Native Americans.

The Native American Genocide

The original inhabitants of the U.S. are estimated to have numbered 18 million when Columbus first arrived in the Americas in 1492 (Stiffarm & Lane, 1992). The number was drastically reduced soon after the Natives encountered white colonists. It is estimated that by the end of the nineteenth century, about 95% to 99% of Native people were decimated in battle or killed by diseases brought by European settlers, reducing their population to one million by 1900 (Stiffarm & Lane, 1992). The "Trail of Tears" and the "Long Walk" are examples of violently imposed acts of relocation, which were implemented to create opportunities for additional white settlement at the expense of the Native people. Not surprisingly, many Native Americans view contact with whites as colonialism and genocide (Stamm & Stamm, 1999).

The physical and emotional devastation of the Native people was followed by a cultural devastation, which was caused by the introduction of boarding schools. Boarding schools were initially described as a strategy to control and oppress those who defied "Western ways"; Native children were wrenched from their families in an attempt to force assimilation. Additionally, the practice of Native cultural rituals and traditions was forbidden (Brave Heart, 2003; Weaver, 1998). These acts of oppression resulted in the Native peoples' loss of identity, a sense of cultural shame, and feelings of self-hatred. The self-hatred and severe loss of tradition endured by Native Americans was inevitably carried to future generations and has had a marked effect upon their identities. Native American children who hold negative perceptions of their ethnic group sometimes resort to violence today as an unconscious mechanism to alleviate personal pain.

A 2004 school shooting that took place in Red Lake, MN, was described by Indian tribal leaders as a direct and symbolic consequence of cultural loss and destruction suffered by Native American children. Disharmony, a consequence of intergenerational trauma, has resulted in low self-esteem, cultural shame, and loss of spirit, language, traditions, and culture among Native Americans. In this incident, 16-year-old Jeff Weise, who belonged to the Ojibwa tribe, snatched his grandfather's rifle, then used it to kill both his grandfather and his girlfriend before driving to school to shoot several of his peers and high school teachers.

Native American children experienced other physical, sexual, and emotional abuses in boarding schools, where their trauma was intensified (Morisette, 1994; Weaver, 1998). Even children who were not sent to boarding schools heard of their peers' suffering and were thus not spared the effects of these traumatizing experiences. The intergenerational effects of these traumas are captured in a study conducted by Brave Heart (2003) of the children of Native American parents who attended American boarding schools. Results show that children were exposed to parents who were detached, ineffective disciplinarians, predisposed to alcohol-related violence, and prone to psychiatric problems including depression. Furthermore, parents often engaged in verbal, physical, and sexual abuse of their children.

Additional documentation of the negative sequelae of intergenerational trauma comes from the findings of the U.S. Department of Health and Human Services Substance Abuse and Mental Health Services Administration (SAMHSA; Fox, Becker-Green, Gault, & Simmons, 2005). The SAMHSA report confirms a strong correlation between the high rate of psychological disorders among Native Americans—which include depression, anxiety, substance abuse, violence, psychosomatic symptoms, disturbed interpersonal and family relationships, and suicide—and the failure to address their "historic trauma." The report also highlights continued disregard by mainstream health care providers of the specific cultural needs of Native Americans. SAMHSA considers this disregard a major contributing factor to the many difficulties currently faced by generations of Native Americans.

Rita sought therapy after her brother was murdered "in a drug deal that went bad." At the time, Rita was also abusing several street drugs (crack cocaine, crystal meth). She reports that she and her brother often "used together," and the loss of her brother had a marked impact on her substance abuse history and her decision to "seek recovery." Besides the traumatic loss of her brother and the stressor of recovering from many years of abusing drugs, Rita also disclosed a complicated history of intergenerational trauma, which may have played a significant role in many of her current difficulties.

According to Rita, her father was reclusive and unavailable to Rita and her siblings when they were children. Her father had attended boarding school as a child, and early loss of attachment with his primary caregivers made it difficult for him to connect on a deeper level with those who were close to him. In addition, her father's boarding school experiences inculcated in him a denigration of Indian culture. Rita recalls that he never talked about his experiences, but his feelings about Indian culture were clearly present in their home all the time. He seldom attended Native American traditional ceremonies and attempted to raise his children as "gringos." Rita's mother made some feeble attempts by taking the children to pow-wows, sun dances, and other Native ceremonies. Rita recalls feeling emotionally nurtured and healed in these ceremonies. However, her mother, unable to tolerate the attitude of her father, "disappeared" when Rita was 14 years old. She has not heard from her mother since. Her father was left with the responsibility of taking care of the children, a task he did not enjoy. He apparently went deeper into his shell.

Effective psychotherapy with Rita was multifaceted. To address her issues of substance abuse, attendance in a recovery program that included group work was important. In a trauma-focused individual psychotherapy, she explored the loss of her brother and her mother and a childhood haunted by her father's traumatic memories of boarding school. With encouragement from her therapist, Rita attended several pow-wows and sun dances. As she found the strength within herself, she was able to heal her relationship with her father. He was an older man and she described him as "less angry and more mellow." Eventually she was able to convince him to attend some traditional ceremonies with her.

In the 1950s, new federal legislation required that Americans who identified themselves as Indian had to prove membership by producing a Certificate of Indian Blood. The Certificate, which verified the degree of Native blood an individual possessed, was only legitimate if obtained from the Bureau of Indian Affairs. Unfortunately, many people could not meet these stringent government guidelines, and they lost their claim to Indian ancestry. As a result, they also lost access to benefits and services reserved for Native people. Although the major economic loss for many individuals was obvious, the greater loss of identity and community resulted in major psychological consequences for the Native people (Porter, 1983).

Intergenerational trauma has caused high rates of depression, anger and aggression, and hypervigilance in Native American communities. Social problems of poverty, child abuse, interpersonal and family violence, drug addition, and alcoholism are also prominent (Brave Heart, 2005). The grief and trauma accompanying historical genocide will haunt many Indian clients, but when practitioners acknowledge this trauma and its effects, they can facilitate a client's healing process (Weaver, 1998).

Traumatic healing is also possible through grassroots programs that allow clients to express their culture, language, traditions, rituals, dances, and spirituality. By building and strengthening communities to confront their trauma, a new understanding emerges. This allows a transcendence of trauma, a release of pain, and an embracing of history (Brave Heart, 2005). Witko (2006) strongly suggests that practitioners display cultural competence when working with Native American clients. This cultural competence can be achieved by understanding the impact of multigenerational trauma, forced relocation, attendance at boarding schools, and cultural loss suffered by Native Americans. Witko states that competence is achieved when a therapist simultaneously attends to the vertical stressors that exist within the individual and the horizontal stressors, which exist outside the individual. Vertical stressors are addressed when a practitioner validates the effects of multigenerational trauma by exploring the client's historical and cultural roots. The practitioner addresses horizontal stressors by advocating for Native American clients, helping them obtain resources and access unfamiliar systems. Culturally specific mental health resources for Native Americans can be obtained on the Internet. Some useful links are provided below:

- Association of American Indian Physicians
  o www.aaip.com
- California Rural Indian Health Board
  o www.crihb.org

- Indian Health Services
  o www.ihs.gov
- National Indian Health Board
  o www.nihb.org

Finally, despite the social negation that a history of collective trauma has imposed on Native American communities, Native Americans have survived and empowered themselves in several ways. Since Native American culture tends to follow an oral tradition, Native Americans share their collective suffering while simultaneously gaining communal strength through the telling of stories, poetry, and legends. Arts and crafts such as weaving, jewelry making, pottery, basket making, and beadwork are other outlets Native Americans continue to use to express loss and celebrate life. The National Museum of Indian Americans in Washington, DC, which opened in 2005, has exhibits of valuable Native American artwork. Cultural festivals, dances, and pow-wows are traditional ways Native Americans strengthen their communities and sustain cultural affinity.

Slavery

From the time the first African slaves were brought to American shores they endured severe hardship and suffering. The trauma of these experiences has inevitably been passed down to subsequent generations. In 1619, African slaves were first sold as property or traded into bondage, then shipped to the United States. Although the importation of slaves by United States citizens was outlawed in 1807, the practice continued. By 1860, 3.5 million Africans were enslaved and toiling the fields of the South, sometimes working more than 14 hours a day. According to sociologist Ron Eyerman (2001), slavery and the failure of emancipation created a "cultural trauma" that required African Americans to "reinterpret and represent" their collective identity (p. 4).

Cultural trauma is viewed differently from psychological and physical trauma, as it is more likely to result in a "dramatic loss of identity and meaning, a tear in the social fabric" (Eyerman, 2001, p. 2). Eyerman makes the following point: "Whether or not they directly experienced slavery or even had ancestors who did, Blacks in the United States were identified with and came to identify themselves through the memory and representation of slavery" (p. 14). Collective memory, rather than memory that is directly experienced, is just as capable of producing traumatic reactions. Jewish Holocaust survivors' testimonies further support the idea that trauma is collectively transmitted, creating a second generation of survivors (Kogan, 1993). As Freud (1957) states, time is understood differently in the unconscious, where the past and present merge.

Volkan's (1997) concept of "chosen trauma" refers to the mental representation of an event that causes a large group of people to feel victimized and humiliated and to suffer losses at the hands of another group. These losses, including the loss of self-esteem, help us better understand the implications of collective trauma. The consequences of these wounds on the African American psyche remain noticeable today when we witness the apathy of many inner-city blacks toward the dominant culture, as well as their disillusionment with the prospect of socioeconomic upward mobility.

Mims (2005) refers to the displacement of Africans during the period of the slave trade as the African holocaust and uses the term "post-traumatic slavery disorder" to describe its massive traumatic effects (p. 20). Similarly, Akbar (1996) directly links the current psychological difficulties of many African Americans to the conditions of slavery—not to exonerate them, but rather to draw attention to the ways in which the history of American slavery has played a role in shaping the future actions of those who were victimized. The goal is not to "re-traumatize but to un-traumatize the negative impact of slavery" (Mims, 2005, p. 29). Only by facing the past can current issues be fully understood and overcome by some African American clients who may still be affected by collective trauma.

The federal government has not issued an official apology, nor has it requested forgiveness for permitting the practice of slavery in this country. However, apologies have been made to other ethnic minority groups who were collectively traumatized in the past. In 1993, Congress apologized to Native Hawaiians for overthrowing the Kingdom of Hawaii a century earlier. In 1988, an apology and financial restitution were made to Japanese Americans who were interned during World War II. In 1997, State Representative Tony Hall (D-Ohio) introduced a proposal to Congress for the federal government to apologize for slavery. Three years later his efforts were supported by black Congressional leaders, who also proposed the building of a monument and furthermore explored the feasibility of reparations as part of the apology. Unfortunately, Congress did not pass this proposal (Koch, 2005).

Although slavery officially ended in 1867 (in the U.S.), the racial oppression of African Americans, which is described by Daniel (2000) as "tools of violence," continues. The Los Angeles police brutality against Rodney King in 1991 and the 1998 Texas slaying by three white supremacists of James Byrd, Jr., who was stripped, chained to a pickup truck, and dragged until he was decapitated, are just two horrific examples of the numerous hate crimes that continue to traumatize many African Americans. Conversely, the conviction and sentencing of Ku Klux Klan leader Edgar Ray Killen at the age of 80, which occurred more than 40 years after he orchestrated the killing of three civil rights workers in Mississippi, is an example of a delayed judicial response to the racial injustices of the South. Such an institutional delay in acknowledgment and validation for racial transgressions contributes to the pervasive physical vulnerability and psychological hypervigilance that blacks and other minority groups experience on an ongoing basis (Sanders Thompson, 2002).

The lives of African Americans in the United States have been continuously marked by oppression and the simultaneous fight for freedom and dignity. More than any other population group in this country, they have struggled and continue to struggle with overcoming institutionalized racism and racial oppression. Although racist individuals may change as they grow older, the same cannot be said for racism within institutions. Institutionalized racism lingers for a longer time and is more difficult to exterminate. Members of organizations that practice discrimination tend to redefine racist manifestations as "other issues." The criminal justice system that controls the lives of a disproportionately high number of black males is an example of an institution that does not treat all citizens equally. The lack of resources and qualified teachers in schools that are predominantly African American is another example of institutionalized racism. Counselors who provide services to African American clients must be willing to acknowledge the effects of institutionalized racism and the roles power, privilege, and oppression play in the lives of their clients.

Historical racism and modern-day oppression contribute to the pervasive mistrust African Americans feel toward many institutions that have treated them unfairly. These institutions include the criminal justice system, educational institutions, and other government agencies, which are often viewed with suspicion and cynicism. Mental health institutions are not exempt from this suspicion and mistrust. For these reasons, many African Americans may hesitate to ask for help (Terrell & Terrell, 1984). Sensitivity to the role that cultural mistrust plays in the lives of African American clients is crucial for those involved in the helping professions.

Besides cultural mistrust, institutional racism accounts for the prevalence of feelings of betrayal, high homicide rates among black males and their difficulty in sharing and expressing emotion, internalized oppression, substance abuse, poverty, homelessness, and hypervigilance among African Americans. In order to improve this situation, dominant groups in the U.S. "will need to acknowledge the extent to which the United States was founded on an undemocratic and unfair power structure and attempt to correct it" (Gordon, 2005, p. 32). Simply celebrating cultural differences while political, economic, and education systems continue to perpetuate inequality and discrimination defeats any attempts at coping that African Americans may employ.

However, despite the negating effects of slavery and the sociopolitical disenfranchisement African Americans continue to experience in the United States, they have successfully maintained a sociocultural community that encompasses strong ancestral beliefs and spiritual connections. Their connectedness is evident in the strong imprint of West Africa, the ancestral home of African Americans, in the cultural traditions of the Deep South and the Sea Islands of Georgia and South Carolina.

Through storytelling, poetry, narratives, and other cultural forms of expression, collective traumatic memory is shared by generations of African Americans. Their cultural legacy of pain and suffering has been expressed in a plethora of literary writings, which have become a major genre in American literature. Ralph Ellison's novel *The Invisible Man* addresses many of the social and intellectual issues facing African Americans as they developed an American black identity post-Civil War. The protagonist of the novel attempts to make sense out of his life experiences and his position in American society as he struggles to make himself visible to mainstream culture. Additionally, Richard Wright, James Baldwin, Zora Neale Thurston, Langston Hughes, Maya Angelou, Toni Morrison, Alice Walker, Walter Moseley, and Alvin Hailey are examples of outstanding African American writers who attempt to capture the pain and suffering of African Americans in the United States.

The pain of resistance and the resiliency of the African American spirit are also evident in African American music, which remains one of the most pervasive cultural influences in the U.S. Singing was originally used by slaves to communicate their sadness, contempt, humor, and their clandestine meetings to discuss the secret path to the North. The "hollar" was a musical form used by those working on levees and in the fields, a call-and-response way of relieving the misery of the day (Forcucci, 1984). Many of these early songs inspired American folk music.

After slavery ended, African Americans expressed the pain of continual discrimination and marginalization through their church gospel music, blues, and soul music. They drew on the rhythms and style of their African heritage to convey ongoing struggles. Billie Holliday's 1939 rendition of the song "Strange Fruit" was a powerful response to a lynching that attracted public attention (Margolick, 2001).

Years later, hip-hop music would capture African American disillusionment with urban renewal and growing financial inequities that disrupt their chances to achieve the lifestyle they envision. The lyrics of Rap music, with its subversive cultural themes, fulfill a need for separation from dominant culture and celebrate an alternative that views authority as offensive (Crawford, 2001). Through their critique of public policy and their creative business decision to produce their own music rather than seek endorsements from large corporations, Rap artists including Public Enemy and the Wu-Tang Clan have become forces for social change. In this way, African American youth have found a way to express their resistance and their criticism of mainstream institutions.

Organizations like the Association of Black Psychologists (www.abpsi.org), the National Medical Association (www.nmanet.org), and the National Association of Black Social Workers (www.nabsw.org) can provide helpful information on medical, psychological, and social work resources that positively support the mental health of African Americans.

The Japanese American Internment

Mas Okui remembers being sent, at the age of 10, with his father and two brothers to a Japanese internment camp in California's Sierra Nevada (Song, 2004). He spent three formative years in a military barracks that lacked privacy and the simple comforts of home. During World War II, after the Japanese bombing of Pearl Harbor in 1942, 120,000 Japanese Americans were considered a threat to the national security of the United States. They were gathered hurriedly and forced into military transport vehicles, which relocated them to 10 separate internment camps across the U.S.; this action has been described as "one of this country's most striking examples of social injustice" (Song, 2004, p. 20).

Men, women, and children of Japanese ancestry were held indefinitely without trial. They were ultimately "incarcerated behind barbed wire fences beneath armed guard towers for an average of two to four years" (Song, 2004, p. 20). Only recently were efforts made to acknowledge the suffering of interned Japanese Americans and to memorialize the social injustices they endured. The Manazar camp, which interned Okui, reopened in April, 2004 to allow visitors to view exhibits of the camp and to engage in dialogue regarding issues of civil rights, democracy, and freedom. Okui hopes that white Americans who visit the camp will depart thinking "God, we did this. These people were cruelly treated. And I hope it never happens again" (Song, 2004, p. 20).

The cultural losses caused by the internment experience were immeasurable. Internees were only allowed to take a few personal possessions to the camps. Besides losing their homes, their livelihoods, and their former ways of life, the Japanese Americans also destroyed many objects from their culture in an attempt to appear more "American." The Japanese Americans who were fortunate enough not to be sent to the internment camps were, nevertheless, affected. They quickly destroyed memorabilia including letters, photos, books, and clothing and other evidence that linked them to a Japanese ethnicity; they attempted to assimilate rapidly so a similar traumatic fate would not befall them.

Reintegration after the war was difficult for most Japanese Americans, especially the elderly. Older Japanese Americans felt a deep sense of shame because of the internment. For some who felt shamed by the experience, suicide became an easy option (Commission on Wartime Relocation and Internment of Civilians [CWRIC], 1997). For others, remaining silent about their experience was seen as the only choice, a choice that in itself carried significant meaning. The internment camp experience is often described as an event marked by silences and strategic forgetting (Sturken, 1997, p. 692). This silence displayed by Japanese American internees is often described as similar to the silence Holocaust survivors display toward their children (Auerhahn & Laub, 1998). It is a response reflective of the trauma survivor's post-traumatic stress: Silence is used to avoid thoughts, feelings, and activities associated with the traumatic event.

There are several reasons for survivors' silence. First, silence may have been an attempt by Japanese Americans to protect their children from the horrors of their past internment. Second, Japanese American cultural values do not favor discussing sensitive topics, which may have affected their ability to talk openly about trauma (Sue & Sue, 2003). Third, the social environment at the time dissuaded survivors from verbalizing their traumatic experiences. In this unsupportive environment, it was socially appropriate to forget.

Finally, when trauma stems from racial discrimination, it can have a silencing effect. According to Loo, 1993, the repeated exposure to racial discrimination that often leads to interpersonal and psychological difficulties may be the strongest reason internees remained silent (cited in Nagata & Cheng, 2003, p. 266). Japanese American citizens have suffered a long history of discrimination in this country. Like many other ethnic minority groups, Japanese Americans have endured numerous race-related stressors, including a history of anti-Asian sentiment that predated internment. Racial discrimination was evident in many institutionalized practices prior to World War II: Japanese Americans were denied the right to become landowners, they could not become naturalized citizens, and they were prohibited from marrying Caucasians (Chuman, 1981; CWRIC, 1997). Their internment confirmed what many Japanese Americans already knew: They were perceived as second-class citizens who lacked the rights and privileges of other Americans. Despite their parents' silence, however, the children of internees sensed that something was wrong (Saville-Troike, 1985).

Remembering and recounting the stories of loss and suffering are important aspects of recovering from trauma. The *nisei* are second-generation American-born citizens of Japanese ancestry who reached adulthood at the outbreak of World War II. They never fully developed a historical narrative for their children, the third-generation American-born Japanese who are known as the *sansei*. As a result, the *sansei* have been haunted by their parents' silence and partially articulated memories. These effects have made them indirect victims of the internment. But unlike their parents, the *sansei* have acquired the strong conviction that they have a right to remember and redress past wrongdoings (Sturken, 1997).

To begin this process, the *sansei* have begun to tell stories of survival that illustrate the power of a historical transmission of memory:

> I had never been there, yet I had a memory of it, I could remember a time of great sadness before I was born. We had been moved, uprooted. We had lived with a lot of pain. I had no idea where these memories came from. (Sturken, 1997, p. 699)

The efforts of the *sansei* to redress past wrongs led to the 1980 investigations conducted by the Commission on Wartime Relocation and Internment of Civilians. This Commission concluded that the internment was unjust (CWRIC, 1997). Subsequently, on behalf of all Americans, President Reagan made an official apology in 1988 to the Japanese American internees held in camps during World War II. Each of the 60,000 survivors, about half of the total number of internees, received a payment of $20,000 in restitution (Maga, 1998).

Although the financial restitution did not absolve the U.S. Congress from the act of unfairly interning Japanese Americans, nor did it ameliorate their pain and suffering, it was viewed as a symbolic act of reparation (Sturken, 1997). Holding the memory in public discourse so it can progress from "personal memory" to "cultural memory" allows for the persistence of memory, thus ensuring that injustice and wrongdoing are never completely forgotten. This also allows survivors to always have a personal place in history from which current concerns can sometimes be explained (Hirsch, 1992).

Despite the overt discrimination that Japanese Americans faced during World War II, they are successful in American society. Japanese American culture places a high value on educating children. As a result, the math and reading scores of Japanese American youth on standardized tests exceeds the national average (Lai & Arguelles, 2003). Japanese American internees have also found a way to express resilience through art and poetry. In *Art of Gaman: Arts and Crafts from the Japanese American Internment Camps 1942–1946*, Hirasuna (2005) showcases the artwork of many Japanese American internees who, under the watchful eyes of soldiers, sought solace in creativity. They initially used whatever they could find around the camp but were later able to order material for their creative projects by mail. They whittled and carved, painted and etched, and stitched and crocheted. Their handiwork captures the ability of the human spirit to maintain nobility under adversity.

The collective trauma of some cultural groups in the U.S. has not influenced the formulation of PTSD as it is currently outlined in the *DSM-IV*; the negative effects of these historical traumas continue to affect these groups in both conscious and unconscious ways. Counselors who work with such groups are encouraged to be mindful of these effects and the role they may play in a client's current functioning.

Vietnam: A Special War

The Vietnam War is often differentiated from other World Wars and the Korean War for four reasons: first, it was an undeclared war that became increasingly unpopular in the U.S.; second, guerrilla tactics used frequently by the enemy Vietcong caused U.S. soldiers immense stress; third, soldiers were exposed to a concentration of war atrocities never before encountered; fourth, the soldiers were directly responsible for committing these atrocities (Haley, 1974).

It is for these reasons that psychotherapy with Vietnam veterans can be immensely challenging because the therapist must deal with a client's stressors concurrently. These stressors are individual and environmental. To complicate matters, therapy with Vietnam veterans does not follow the traditional model of war neurosis. This model instead requires those soldiers who committed atrocities to acknowledge their perpetrator role while also working through their own victimization on the battlefield (Haley, 1974).

In comparison to other wars, combat in the Vietnam War forced soldiers to engage in unusually aggressive acts, which increased their suicidal ideation. Since these experiences of violence were seldom discussed on the battlefield, returning veterans unconsciously continued to avoid processing their traumatic experiences, thus negatively affecting their adjustment to civilian life (Bourne, 1970). A sense of isolation and loneliness began to permeate the lives of many soldiers, and some attempted to cope by using illicit drugs (Haley, 1974).

Although war veterans in general hesitate to seek psychotherapy, Vietnam veterans were unique as a group in their prolonged hesitation to seek help. Some soldiers refused treatment until they became desperate and repression as a defense mechanism no longer worked. Many Vietnam veterans were reported as displaying a pattern of delayed reaction. A strong distrust of the helping community, shaped in part by the negative and sometimes hostile reception they were met with upon their return home, was an additional hurdle to overcome. It is for this reason that Haley (1974) describes establishing a therapeutic alliance as "the treatment rather than the facilitator of treatment" for many Vietnam war veterans (Haley, 1974, p. 195).

In the 1970s, when a large number of Vietnam veterans began to seek help for post-traumatic symptoms, the Veteran's Administration (VA) focused its efforts on the assessment and treatment of PTSD. At around the same time, Horowitz's (1975) work on trauma-related reactions within a psychodynamic and information-processing framework was making a major contribution to the discipline of psychiatry. Both these occurrences led to the American Psychiatric Association's (APA) recognition and inclusion of the syndrome of PTSD in the third edition of its *Diagnostic and Statistical Manual of Mental Disorders* (APA, 1980). The formal designation of PTSD was a major milestone for Vietnam veterans seeking treatment. For the professionals who were helping them recover, procuring funding for the National Center for PTSD in the 1980s was considered a major achievement (Kizer, 1996).

Conclusion

Although the inclusion of PTSD as a diagnostic category in the *Diagnostic and Statistical Manual of Mental Disorders* has been fairly recent (*APA,* 1980), psychological trauma has existed for many centuries, and its negative effects pervade all racial, cultural, and socioeconomic groups. Reports of pervasive psychological problems by Vietnam veterans legitimatized the serious psychological consequences of environmental stressors and led to the designation of PTSD as diagnostic category.

Significant time and energy has been invested in the formulation of the post-traumatic stress diagnosis, but it is clear that the diagnosis is incomplete and captures limited features of post-traumatic psychopathology. Not all cultural groups are included in this current formulation; the role of intergenerational and collective trauma remains missing from the *DSM-IV* (APA, 1994). Now that intergenerational and multigenerational trauma has entered the mental health nomenclature, literature in this important area of trauma is growing (Danieli, 1998). We can expect future studies to further explore different types of traumatic transmission, define what is transmitted to future generations, and increase our knowledge and understanding of the genetic traits that make some individuals vulnerable to PTSD. Comparisons between such factors as social vulnerability and resiliency merely broaden our knowledge of the human condition. For full recovery to occur, an acknowledgment of the multigenerational influence of trauma and the generational wounding it has inflicted must be acknowledged. This acknowledgment is invaluable to both victims and American society as a whole.

Although ethnic minority groups have historically experienced hardship and suffering in this country, they have nevertheless also displayed strength and resiliency. This chapter concludes with a list of films and videos that may interest those practitioners seeking to extend their knowledge of ethnic minority groups in the United States.

Resources for Further Understanding

Films on Native Americans

Crazy Horse (1996)

This film tells the true story of Crazy Horse, the Oglala warrior who relentlessly resisted the white man's attempt to take over Indian lands and fought General Custer and his forces at Little Big Horn.

Lakota Woman (1994)

This is a dramatization of the inspiring, true story of the 1973 uprising that united Native Americans in their fight for survival. One woman rises from ignorance and fear to meet the challenge of her proud heritage during a bloody siege in which 2,000 Native Americans stood their ground and vowed never to be silent again.

Naturally Native (1998)

This drama follows the lives and relationships of three sisters of American Indian ancestry as they attempt to start their own business. Adopted by white foster parents as young children, each sister has unique identity issues. The film interweaves a subtle but strong wake-up call regarding the treatment of Native people in corporate America and provides some insight into tribal infrastructure and gaming issues.

The Last of the Mohicans (1992)

The love of Hawkeye, rugged frontiersman and adopted son of the Mohicans, and Cora Munro, aristocratic daughter of a British colonel, blazes amidst a brutal conflict between the British, French, and Native American allies in colonial America.

Sioux City (1994)

This drama is about a Native American surgeon who was given up for adoption as an infant. Returning to the Nebraska reservation where he was born to locate his natural mother, he learns that she died in a suspicious fire. He soon finds himself in a dangerous confrontation with local police.

Smoke Signals (1998)

Two Coeur d'Alene Indians travel from their Idaho reservation to Phoenix, Arizona, to retrieve the remains of a dead father. They discover some truths about themselves along the way. This movie offers a refreshing Native American viewpoint.

Films on Slavery

Amistad (1997)

This epic film is a historical example of man's inhumanity to man. African captives aboard the slave ship *Amistad* free themselves and take over the ship. A lengthy court battle ensues in which the Africans have to prove that they were rightfully freed individuals. The film depicts the horrors of slavery.

Beloved (1998)

A middle-aged former slave in rural Ohio is haunted by the painful legacy of slavery years after her emancipation from a Kentucky plantation.

Daughters of the Dust (1991)

Five women of a Gullah family (descendants of West African slaves) living on the Sea Islands off the coast of Georgia in the early twentieth century contemplate moving to the mainland in this emotional tale of change.

Eyes on the Prize (1987)

This documentary series uses archival footage to record the growth of the American Civil Rights movement from 1954 to 1965, with a special focus on the ordinary people who effected change.

Mississippi Burning (1988)

This film explores the story of three civil rights movement activists who were murdered in Mississippi. It reveals the extent of Southern white violence against those (black or white) who agitated for black rights, almost one century after emancipation.

Roots (1977)

An epic panorama of America's past is covered in this saga of a black man's search for his heritage. This milestone film dramatizes the shared heritage of millions of African Americans.

Films on the Japanese Internment

After Silence: Civil Rights and the Japanese American Experience (2002)

Frank Kitmoto of Bainbridge Island, Washington, was among the first of 110,000 West Coast Japanese Americans forced to leave his home during World War II. He describes his three years of internment and discusses the importance of safeguarding civil rights for future generations.

Children of the Camps (1999)

In this documentary film, six Japanese Americans who were incarcerated as children in the internment camps discuss their experiences. The cultural and familial issues that arose during incarceration, the long internalized grief, the shame they felt, and the effects of this early trauma in their adult lives is also covered.

Of Civil Wrongs & Rights: The Fred Korematsu Story (2000)

Fred Korematsu was probably never more American than when he resisted, and then challenged in court, the forced internment of Japanese Americans during World War II. Although Korematsu lost this landmark Supreme Court case in 1944, he did not relinquish his indignation and resolve. This is the untold history of the 40-year legal fight to vindicate Korematsu—one that finally turned a civil injustice into a civil rights victory.

Time of Fear (2005)

This film traces the lives of 16,000 Japanese Americans who were sent to camps in southeast Arkansas, one of the poorest and most racially segregated places in America. The film explores the impact of this historical event on the civil rights movement and social justice issues today.

Rabbit in the Moon (1999)

This documentary/memoir covers the lingering effects of the World War II internment on the Japanese American community. Visually stunning and emotionally compelling, this film examines issues that ultimately created deep rifts, revealing the racist subtext of the loyalty questionnaire and exposing the absurdity of the military draft in the camps. These testimonials are linked to the filmmakers' own experiences in the camps and are also placed in the larger historical context.

Who's Going to Pay for These Donuts Anyway? (1992)

The profound effect of the Japanese American internment on generations of individuals is chronicled in the director's own search for her father. She eventually finds him in a halfway house.

When You're Smiling (1999)

The first comprehensive account of the resettlement of the Japanese American community after internment during WWII, this film tells the story of the filmmaker's family's struggle during the harsh post-camp years. Even though the community appeared to put their unjust incarceration behind them, in reality class, race, religion, stereotyping, lack of ethnic values, and emotional and familial distance caused a serious identity crisis.

References

Akbar, N. (1996). *Breaking the chains of psychological slavery*. Tallahassee, FL: Mind Productions & Associates.

American Psychiatric Association. (1980). *Diagnostic and statistical manual of mental disorders* (3rd ed.). Washington, DC: Author.

American Psychiatric Association. (1994). *Diagnostic and statistical manual of mental disorders* (4th ed.). Washington, DC: Author.

Auerhahn, N. C., & Laub, D. (1998). Intergenerational memory of the Holocaust. In Y. Danieli (Ed.), *International handbook of multigenerational legacies of trauma* (pp. 21–41). New York: Plenum Press.

Ben-Ezra, M. (2004). Trauma in antiquity: 4000-year-old post-traumatic reactions? *Stress and Health, 20,* 121–125.

Birmes, P., Hatton, L., & Brunet, A. (2003). Stress and health. *Journal of the International Society for the Investigation of Stress, 19*(1), 17–26.

Bourne P. G. (1970). *Men, stress and Vietnam.* Boston: Little Brown.

Brave Heart, M. Y. H. (2003). The historical trauma response among natives and its relationship with substance abuse: A Lakota illustration. *Journal of Psychoactive Drugs, 35*(1), 7–14.

Brave Heart, M. Y. H. (2005). From intergenerational trauma to intergenerational healing: A teaching about how it works and how we can heal. *Wellbriety! White Bison's Online Magazine, 6*(6), 3–8.

Chuman, F. (1981). *The bamboo people: The law and Japanese Americans.* Chicago: Japanese American Research Project and the Japanese American Citizen League.

Commission on Wartime Relocation and Internment of Civilians. (1997). *Personal justice denied: Report of the Commission on Wartime Relocation and Internment of Civilians.* Seattle: University of Washington Press.

Crawford, R. (2001). *America's musical life: A history.* New York: W.W. Norton & Company.

Daniel, J. (2000). The courage to hear: African-American women's memories of racial trauma. In L. C. Jackson & B. Greene (Eds.), *Psychotherapy with African-American women: Innovations in psychodynamic perspectives and practice* (pp. 126–144). New York: Guilford.

Danieli, Y. (Ed.). (1998). *International handbook of multigenerational legacies of trauma.* New York: Plenum Press.

Everly, G. S., Jr. (1994). Psychotraumatology. In G. S. Everly & J. M. Lating (Eds.), *Psychotraumatology: Key papers and core concepts in post-traumatic stress* (pp. 3–8). New York: Springer.

Eyerman, R. (2001). *Cultural trauma: Slavery and the formation of African American identity.* Cambridge: Cambridge University Press.

Forcucci, S. (1984). *A folk history of America: America through its songs.* Englewood Cliffs, NJ: Prentice Hall.

Fox, K., Becker-Green, J., Gault, J., & Simmons, D. (2005). *Native American youth in transition: The path from adolescence to adulthood in two Native American communities.* Portland, OR: National Indian Child Welfare Association.

Freud, S. (1957). Thoughts for the times on war and death. In J. Strachey (Ed. & Trans.), *The standard edition of the complete psychological works of Sigmund Freud* (Vol. 14, pp. 275–302). London: Hogarth Press. (Original work published 1915)

Gordon, M. (2005). *Ten common myths in American education*. Brandon, VT: Holistic Education Press.

Haley, S. A. (1974). When the patient reports atrocities: Specific treatment considerations of the Vietnam veteran. *Archives of General Psychiatry, 30*, 191–196.

Herman, J. L. (1997). *Trauma and recovery*. New York: Basic Books.

Hirasuna, D. (2005). *Art of Gaman: Arts and crafts from the Japanese American internment camps*. Berkeley, CA: Ten Speed Press.

Hirsch, M. (1992). Family pictures: Maus, mourning and post-memory. *Discourse, 15*(2), 8.

Horowitz, M. (1975). Intrusive and repetitive thoughts after stress. *Archives of General Psychiatry, 32*, 1457–1463.

Kardiner, A. (1941). The traumatic neurosis of war. *Psychosomatic Medicine Monograph, 1*(2–3), x–258.

Kizer, K. W. (1996). Progress on post-traumatic stress disorder. *Journal of the American Medical Association, 275*(15), 1149.

Koch, W. (2005). *Senate apologizes for not enacting anti-lynching law*. Retrieved July 12, 2005, from http://www.usatoday.com/news/washington/2005–06–13-senate-ynching_x.html

Kogan, I. (1993). Curative factors in the psychoanalyses of Holocaust survivors' offspring before and after the Gulf War. *International Journal of Psychoanalysis, 74*, 803–814.

Kulka, R. A., Schlenger, W. E., Fairbank, J. A., Hough, R. L., Jordan, B. K., Marmar, C. R., et al. (1990). *Trauma and the Vietnam war generation: Report on the findings from the National Vietnam Veterans Readjustment Study*. New York: Brunner/Mazel.

Lai, E., & Arguelles, D. (Eds.). (2003). *The new face of Asian Pacific America: Numbers, diversity and change in the 21st century*. San Francisco: Asian Week.

Maga, T. P. (1998). Ronald Reagan and redress for Japanese-American internment, 1983–1988. *Presidential Studies Quarterly, 28*(3), 606–619.

Margolick, D. (2001). *Strange fruit: The biography of a song*. New York: HarperCollins.

Mims, S. (2005). Introduction to post traumatic slavery disorder. In O. G. Reid, S. Mims, & L. Higginbottom (Eds.), *Post traumatic stress disorder* (pp. 9–46). Charlotte, NC: Conquering Books.

Morisette, P. J. (1994). The holocaust of first nation people: Residual effects on parenting and treatment implications. *Contemporary Family Therapy, 16*, 381–392.

Nagata D. K., & Cheng, W. J. Y. (2003). Intergenerational communication of race related trauma by Japanese American former internees. *American Journal of Orthopsychiatry, 73*(3), 266–278.

Pepys, S. (1997). September 1666. In T. Griffith (Ed.), *The concise Pepys* (pp. 429–447). Ware: Wordsworth Editions.

Porter, F. W., III. (1983). *Non-recognized American Indian tribes: A historical and legal perspective*. Occasional Papers, Series 7. Chicago: Newbury Library.

Portney, C. (2003). *Intergenerational transmission of trauma: An introduction for the clinician.* Retrieved April 3, 2006, from http://www.psychiatrictimes.com/p030438.html

Rakoff, V., Sigal, J. J., & Epstein, N. B. (1966). Children and families of concentration camp survivors. *Canada's Mental Health, 14,* 24–26.

Sanders Thompson, V. L. (2002). Racism: Perceptions of distress among African-Americans. *Community Mental Health Journal, 38*(2), 111–118.

Saville-Troike, M. (1985). The place of silence in an integrated theory of communication. In D. Tannen & M. Saville-Trioke (Eds.), *Perspectives on silence* (pp. 3–18). Norwood, NJ: Ablex.

Song, S. (2004, February 16). The Japanese camps: Making the 9/11 link. *Time, 163*(7), 20.

Stamm, B. H., & Stamm, H. E. (1999). Trauma and loss in Native North America: An ethnocultural perspective. In K. Nader, N. Dubrow, & B. H. Stamm (Eds.), *Honoring differences: Cultural issues in the treatment of trauma and loss* (pp. 49–69). Philadelphia: Brunner/Mazel.

Stiffarm, L. A., & Lane, P., Jr. (1992). The demography of native North America: A question of American Indian survival. In M. A. Jaimes (Ed.), *The state of Native America: Genocide, colonization, and resistance* (pp. 23–53). Boston: South End Press.

Sturken, M. (1997). Absent images of memory: Remembering and reenacting the Japanese internment. *Positions, 5*(3), 687–702.

Sue, D. W., & Sue, D. (2003). *Counseling the culturally different: Theory and practice* (4th ed.). New York: Wiley.

Terrell, F., & Terrell, S. L. (1984). Race of counselor, client sex, cultural mistrust level, and premature termination from counseling among black clients. *Journal of Counseling Psychology, 31,* 371–375.

Volkan, V. D. (1997). *Bloodlines: From ethnic pride to ethnic terrorism.* New York: Farrar, Straus, & Giroux.

Weaver, H. N. (1998). Indigenous people in a multicultural society: Unique issues for human services. *Social Work, 43*(3), 203–211.

Witko, T. M. (2006). *No longer forgotten: Addressing the mental health needs of urban Indians.* Washington, DC: APA Books.

2

Assessment of PTSD, ASD, and DESNOS

Ellen, described as "challenging" by several therapists at a trauma program, was assigned a new therapist. The team of clinicians had struggled for many years with understanding and helping Ellen, a client with multiple diagnoses (bipolar disorder, major depressive disorder, post-traumatic disorder, and dissociative identity disorder) who was frequently admitted as an inpatient at various local hospitals. Both of Ellen's prior therapists were interns. The intake coordinator concluded, quite wisely, that forming a therapeutic relationship with a staff person over a longer period of time might improve Ellen's stabilization. When the therapist initially read her two-volume file, she learned a great deal of basic information about Ellen. It soon became apparent that it would be difficult, at best, to develop a clinical formulation that could be used as a road map for future therapy sessions.

Since Ellen began treatment in the program three years ago, she had developed a pattern of requiring inpatient treatment at least once every six months. There did not appear to be any definable triggering event to these recurrent admissions. Each time Ellen was discharged, some well-meaning psychiatrist would give her a slightly different diagnosis and several new medications to try.

Ellen attended therapy once a week for a period of six years. In the final two years of her therapeutic engagement, Ellen was not once admitted as an inpatient. Furthermore, she was employed part-time at a department store so she would not have to rely solely on her Federal Disability grant. After getting married, she considered relocating to another state so she could live closer to her daughter and granddaughter.

What factors contributed to Ellen achieving such an improved level of functioning? In describing the factors, the process of her treatment is described. First, it was important for Ellen to be psychologically tested in order to exclude concerns of neurological disorders and frontal lobe malfunctioning. Other personality and trauma screens, some of which are outlined later in this chapter, helped provide objective data on her functioning.

Second, the therapist attempted to understand Ellen's perspective by exploring the role her hallucinations may have served and the underlying causes of her mood fluctuations. Often, new therapists are afraid to examine the inner workings of a client's psychoses. As Ellen began to develop trust in the therapeutic relationship, she started to engage more fully. The recollection soon emerged that she had been sexually abused by her maternal uncle from the age of five until her teenage years. This trauma explained the origin of her mixed moods; her recollection also gave some clarity to her report of hearing negative internal voices. Ellen claimed that for the first time in her life, she felt heard and understood. Early in her treatment, when Ellen was hospitalized, the therapist attended Ellen's discharge meetings so she could advocate for her. At these meetings, the health care providers involved in discharging Ellen were informed about treatments that had already been tried without success. By advocating for Ellen, the therapist served as the container that temporarily held Ellen's world together.

This chapter begins with a brief discussion of the challenges inherent in assessing PTSD and acute stress disorder (ASD) and then focuses on the factors affecting recovery from trauma. Common reactions to trauma are reviewed along with the diagnostic criteria for PTSD and ASD. This is followed by a discussion of the effects of trauma on the brain and the body. Complex PTSD and other concepts such as co-morbidity (substance abuse), triggers, and dissociation are discussed because they often arise in trauma work. Finally, the second part of the chapter concludes with an overview of assessment tools that can sometimes provide practitioners with objective data and, therefore, increase their understanding of a traumatized client.

Assessment Challenges

Assessing trauma survivors can be a challenge for many reasons. Trauma is seldom the presenting issue that brings clients to therapy. It is often not until much later in the therapeutic relationship that a therapist discovers an underlying history of trauma in a client's life. Discovering this painful history illuminates a possible source for a client's current difficulties. In Ellen's case, treatment was sought for severe mood fluctuations; Ellen also wished "to get rid of the voices that tell me I am no good." The client was correctly diagnosed with manic depressive disorder. Later, as her visual and auditory hallucinations became more debilitating, Ellen was given the diagnosis of schizoaffective disorder. However, merely assigning these diagnoses without understanding her symptoms at a deeper level failed because it neglected to fully address the underlying cause of her difficulties. For clients who may possess multiple psychiatric diagnoses, knowing the area on which to focus during a therapy session can be a challenge for the therapist. One possible strategy is to allow the client's mood to dictate the focus of a particular session. This method of conducting therapy can also help the client maintain a sense of control and competency.

The majority of individuals exposed to trauma do not develop a posttraumatic disorder. The *DSM-IV* cited prevalence rates of PTSD between 3% and 58% in 1994. More recent findings indicate that only about 25% of individuals who experience trauma develop PTSD (Brady, 2001). Therefore, it is useful to explore the factors that enable the other 75% of trauma victims to survive, and even to psychologically recover, despite their traumatic experiences. Resiliency is the term applied to those individuals exposed to severe risk factors who nevertheless thrive and excel (Werner, 2001). It is an ability to successfully overcome physical and psychological trauma that defines resiliency.

In what is now considered a classic study on resiliency, Werner (2001) found that in spite of extreme disadvantages and multiple risk factors, resilient children manage to succeed and contribute to society. Werner followed 505 individuals from birth to adulthood, on the island of Kauai (Hawaii), to study the impact of various biological and psychosocial risk factors, protective factors, and stressful life events on their development. The group comprised individuals from many different ethnic groups, including Japanese, Hawaiian, and Filipino. Results of Werner's study indicated that one in three of these high-risk children developed into confident, capable, and caring young adults.

Individual differences partly accounted for resiliency among some children. The presence of grandparents or mentors who provided children with consistent nurturing and support emerged as an additional factor that ameliorated suffering and buffered responses to constitutional risks and stressful life events (Werner, 2001). Besides innate and environmental circumstances that support resiliency, several other factors also influence an individual's ability to recover from trauma. By becoming familiar with these factors and the intensity at which they are likely to occur, a practitioner is better equipped to determine the direction of a therapeutic relationship.

Factors That Influence Recovery From Trauma

- *Intensity.* Obviously, the more intense and chronic the trauma, the more damaging are its effects.
- *Chronicity.* Chronic PTSD, described as Type II trauma, is more difficult to treat than acute, or Type I, trauma (Terr, 1991). Previous experiences of victimization can severely compromise an individual's ability to recover. PTSD symptoms of more than 16 to 18 months' duration tend to be classified as chronic (Friedman & Rosenheck, 1996). Chronic PTSD is usually characterized by fluctuations in symptom severity with periods of remission, but rarely is more than partial recovery achieved (Ronis, Bates, Garfein, Buit, Falcon, & Liberzon, 1996).
- *Pre-existing condition.* A pre-existing mental illness, substance abuse, or chronic medical condition decreases an individual's ability to recover from trauma, leading to co-morbid disorders.
- *Personality.* The personality, including a positive self-concept, high self-esteem, high self-confidence, and an extraverted personality style, influences resiliency and recovery from trauma (Werner, 2001). In a study conducted among college students, those with trauma histories reported more trait anxiety, lower self-esteem, higher neuroticism, more introversion, and reduced emotional stability than non-traumatized subjects (Bunce, Larsen, & Peterson, 1995).
- *Cognitive style.* The individual's cognitive style can also influence recovery. Traumatized individuals reported more cognitive disturbances. They display cognitive styles that are associated with an increased risk for depression (Bunce et al., 1995). In contrast, resilient individuals tend to possess higher cognitive ability, which provides a protection against PTSD (Werner, 2001). Positive self-talk when under distress is an example of such an ability.
- *Relationship to perpetrator.* The relationship between the victim and the perpetrator influences a traumatized individual's recovery. The closer the relationship between the victim and the perpetrator, the greater the effects of the trauma. For example, abuse inflicted by a father or stepfather tends to be more traumatizing than those trauma acts perpetrated by less familiar individuals (Ray & Jackson, 1997).

- *Social support.* The reaction of family, friends, and colleagues also contributes to a victim's ability to recover from a traumatic experience. Strong social support can act as a safeguard against the development of PTSD (McNally, Bryant, & Ehlers, 2003).
- *Continued exposure.* Continued exposure to danger puts an individual in a chronic state of trauma, and such situations severely compromise opportunities for recovery.
- *Physical injury.* A physical injury suffered during a traumatic experience may be a constant reminder of the trauma. This may impede complete recovery.

Common Responses to Traumatic Exposure

Emotional, cognitive, behavioral, and physical reactions are often experienced by individuals affected by trauma (see Appendix I). These reactions are not necessarily unhealthy or maladaptive, but rather are normal responses to abnormal events. While most people recover within a few months, some victims' problems may persist. Over time, it is also common for symptoms to vary in intensity. Some individuals may not experience any significant reactions for a long period of time and then relapse when faced with a major life stressor. On rare occasions, symptoms may not appear for months or years after the trauma has occurred.

When traumatic reactions interfere with social and occupational functioning within four weeks of an incident, ASD is a likely diagnosis. If these reactions persist beyond one month, a diagnosis of PTSD may be more appropriate. Trauma reactions impair several areas of functioning, as outlined below:

Emotional Response. Frequently observed emotional responses to trauma include shock, numbness, anxiety, panic, fear, feelings of aloneness, hopelessness, helplessness, uncertainty, horror, irritability, depression, grief, and guilt.

Cognitive Response. Impaired concentration, confusion, disorientation, difficulty in making a decision, and a shortened attention span are examples of cognitive reactions that trauma survivors often display. Those affected by trauma also report an increased sense of vulnerability, more frequent blaming of self and others, lowered self-efficacy, loss of control, and a heightened state of hypervigilance. Perseveration, or internally recounting and constantly replaying the event, is a symptom often experienced by individuals in the aftermath of a traumatic event.

Behavioral Responses. Traumatic exposure may manifest itself behaviorally in withdrawal, noncommunication, and erratic or repetitive movements (i.e., pacing, impulsivity, an exaggerated startle response, irritability, a sense of aimlessness, and an increase in antisocial and high-risk behaviors).

Physical Responses. Responses that may also be termed physiological reactions include an elevated heart rate and blood pressure, difficulty breathing, hyperventilation, chest pains, muscle tension, fatigue, excessive perspiration, dizziness, headaches, and stomachaches.

Individuals affected by trauma may experience several of these reactions. It is not unusual for traumatized individuals to feel as if they are on a rollercoaster. They may find their reactions temporarily abating or suddenly increasing in intensity. Reassurance that these reactions are to be expected and an affirmation that other traumatized individuals report similar reactions can provide survivors with validation. Traumatic experiences can cause severe physical damage with long-term effects that impair the functioning of the brain and the body.

Effect of Trauma on the Brain and Body

Research shows that those who develop PTSD experience significant changes in their brain structure and neurological functioning (Bremner & Bryant, 2001; Debiec & LeDoux, 2004; LeDoux, 2000). For many survivors, and especially for those who are chronically traumatized, trauma becomes the principal lens through which sensory input is processed in the brain. Brain imaging studies have shown a hyperactivation of the amygdala and a hypoactivation of the medial prefrontal regions in response to fearful stimuli (Shin et al., 2004). The constant activation of the amygdala leads to hypertrophy of the amygdala, which results in the growth of new neuron branches. This may explain the trauma survivor's enhanced emotional responsiveness and perception of everything as fear-inducing (Ledoux, 2000; Vyas, Mitra, Rao, & Chattarji, 2002).

In contrast, chronic exposure to stress leads to an atrophy of the hippocampal neurons. The hippocampus mediates the frontal cortex and memory functioning (LeDoux, 2002). Research indicates the trauma symptoms of amnesia are caused by atrophy of hippocampal neurons (McEwen, 1999). Those diagnosed with PTSD exhibit a decrease in hippocampal volume (Stein, Koverola, Hanna, Torchia, & McClarty, 1997). Deficits in hippocampal memory function have been strongly associated with cortisol dysregulation and impairment in neurogenesis, which is the ability to replace damaged neurons in the hippocampus (Bremner, Randall, & Vermetten, 1997). Other studies demonstrate a failure of activation in the frontal cortex, the part of the brain involved in shutting off the fear response, by inhibition of the amygdala (LeDoux, 1996).

Since the release of hormones in the brain and body triggers the flight or fight response in the human species, hormones are critical for survival. Norepinephrine (adrenaline) acts like a fire alarm in the human body. When danger is present, norepinephrine raises an individual's level of fear by increasing the heart rate and blood pressure; norepinephrine also mobilizes the body to meet the challenge of a stressful situation. However, when the adrenal gland constantly releases high levels of norepinephrine, the effects on the immune system can be detrimental (LeDoux, 1996; Nelson, 2000).

Adrenaline keeps the body in a constant state of alertness, causing high blood pressure and constricted arteries. Perry (1997) studied persistent physiological hyperarousal and hyperactivity among children and found that the younger the child at the time of the trauma, the more severe the damage to the brain. Experiencing the chronic stress of witnessing domestic violence or assaults and experiencing violence (such as physical abuse) first hand produces a fear that lingers far beyond the event itself. These feelings of fear affect the brain and increase an individual's vulnerability to future traumas (Webb, 2004). Similar studies were conducted with victims who experienced violence as children. As adults, these victims found that they experienced greater biological and behavioral reactions to stress (Yehuda, Spertus, & Golier, 2001).

The norepinephrine secreted by the sympathetic nervous system is balanced by the secretion of cortisol by the hypothalmic-pituitary-adrenal (HPA) axis. Cortisol acts as a counterbalance to adrenaline and plays an important role in redistributing energy when a person is under stress. In this way, high cortisol levels benefit individuals in the short term. A high secretion of cortisol on a consistent basis, however, occurs at the expense of an individual's long-term survival because high cortisol levels can cause gastric ulcers, bone thinning, and possible brain damage.

In contrast, low levels of cortisol secretion among individuals who are under stress means that cortisol will be ineffective in balancing the secretion of adrenaline, which plays a role in the imprinting of horrific and intrusive memories (Yehuda, 2000). Low levels of cortisol allow adrenaline to act unopposed. Thus, individuals with low cortisol levels may find themselves unable to relax. Decreased levels of cortisol were found among individuals who suffer from chronic PTSD (Yehuda, 2000; Yehuda, McFarlane, & Shalev, 1998). This may explain the hyperarousal reactions of sleep impairments and flashbacks that survivors often report (van der Kolk, 1988).

Positron Emission Tomography (PET) imaging studies suggest that lower levels of norepinephrine stimulate brain activity in the prefrontal cortex, while very high levels discontinue it (Bremner, Innis, Salomon, 1997; Schmahl, Vermetten, & Elzinga, 2003). These high levels of norepinephrine may explain why trauma survivors have difficulty remembering their trauma. The flooding of the hippocampus, which plays a major role in the storing of memories, in conjunction with the adrenaline and cortisol, may contribute to impaired recall, as reported by trauma survivors (LeDoux, 1996). In addition, a marked reduction in the size of the corpus callosum has been observed among children with abuse histories (DeBellis et al., 1999; Teicher, Ito, Glod, Anderson, Dumont, & Ackerman, 1997). The corpus callosum is responsible for carrying messages between the two sides of the cerebral cortex. This malfunction may also explain the traumatized individual's difficulty recalling traumatic memories (Schiffer, Teicher, & Papanicolaou, 1995).

Trauma can affect the body and the mind over the long term in many ways. In addition to the physiological effects just described, a trauma survivor can also be more susceptible to physical disease. Psychologically, a trauma survivor may engage in risky and self-destructive and addictive behaviors, which may include gambling, smoking, drinking, and overeating. Ultimately, the physiological and psychological responses to trauma can cause early death.

Relationship Between PTSD and ASD

Both national classifications, which appear in the *DSM-IV*, and international classifications, which appear in *The ICD-10 Classification of Mental and Behavioural Disorders* (World Health Organization [WHO], 1992) currently designate two specific categories of psychopathology following an individual's exposure to trauma: acute stress reactions and PTSD. In 1980, the American Psychiatric Association listed PTSD under the category of anxiety disorders because marked symptoms of persistent anxiety, hypervigilance, an exaggerated startle response, and phobic-like avoidance behaviors were noted among trauma survivors (Meichenbaum, 1994). The diagnosis includes intrusive episodes of re-experiencing the trauma, avoidant behaviors, and increased physiological arousal as other possible symptoms of PTSD.

Acute stress reactions usually occur in the first month after traumatic events. If these reactions persist beyond a month, the diagnosis of PTSD is made (*DSM-IV*; World Health Organization, 1992). Since ASD and PTSD share some symptoms, it is helpful for a practitioner to know the separate diagnostic criteria for each. Below are the diagnostic criteria for ASD and PTSD, as stated in the *DSM-IV*.

Since ASD is a relatively new diagnosis, extensive research has not been conducted on this disorder. Several studies support the rates of ASD among trauma survivors as ranging from 6% to 33% of the population,

Acute Stress Disorder (ASD)	Post-Traumatic Stress Disorder (PTSD)
A. The person has been exposed to a traumatic event in which both of the following were present: (1) The person experienced, witnessed, or was confronted with an event or events that involved actual or threatened death or serious injury or a threat to the physical integrity of self or others. (2) The person's responses involved intense fear, helplessness, or horror. B. Either while experiencing or after experiencing the distressing event, the individual has three (or more) of the following dissociative symptoms: (1) a subjective sense of numbing, detachment, or absence of emotional responsiveness; (2) a reduction in awareness of his or her surroundings (e.g., "being in a daze"); (3) derealization; (4) depersonalization; (5) dissociative amnesia (i.e., inability to recall an important aspect of the trauma). C. The traumatic event is persistently re-experienced in at least one of the following ways: recurrent images, thoughts, dreams, illusions, flashback episodes, a sense of reliving the experience, or distress on exposure to reminders of the traumatic event. D. Marked avoidance of stimuli that arouse recollections of the trauma (e.g., thoughts, feelings, conversations, activities, places, people).	A. The person has been exposed to a traumatic event in which both of the following were present: (1) The person experienced, witnessed, or was confronted with an event that involved actual or threatened death or serious injury or a threat to the physical integrity of self or others. (2) The person's response involved intense fear, helplessness, or horror. B. The traumatic event is persistently re-experienced in one (or more) of the following ways: (1) recurrent and intrusive distressing recollections of the event, including images, thoughts, or perceptions; (2) recurrent distressing dreams of the event; (3) acting or feeling as if the traumatic event were reoccurring; (4) intense psychological distress on exposure to internal/external cues that symbolize or resemble an aspect of the traumatic event; (5) physiological reactivity on exposure to internal or external cues that symbolize or resemble an aspect of the traumatic event. C. Persistent avoidance of stimuli associated with the trauma and the numbing of general responsiveness (not present before the trauma), as

Acute Stress Disorder (ASD)	Post-Traumatic Stress Disorder (PTSD)
E. Marked symptoms of anxiety or increased arousal (e.g., difficulty sleeping, irritability, poor concentration, hypervigilance, exaggerated startle response, motor restlessness). F. The disturbance causes clinically significant distress or impairment in social, occupational, or other important areas of functioning, or impairs the individual's ability to pursue some necessary task, such as obtaining necessary assistance or mobilizing personal resources by telling family members about the traumatic experience. G. The disturbance lasts for a minimum of two days and a maximum of four weeks and occurs within four weeks of the traumatic event. H. The disturbance is not due to the direct physiological effects of a substance (e.g., a drug of abuse, a medication) or a general medical condition, is not better accounted for by Brief Psychotic Disorder, and is not merely an exacerbation of a pre-existing Axis I or Axis II disorder.	indicated by three (or more) of the following: (1) efforts to avoid thoughts, feelings, conversations about the trauma; (2) efforts to avoid activities, places, people associated with the trauma; (3) inability to recall an important aspect of the trauma; (4) markedly diminished interest or participation in significant activities; (5) feeling of detachment from others; (6) restricted range of affect; (7) sense of foreshortened future. D. Persistent symptoms of increased arousal (two or more of the following): (1) difficulty sleeping, (2) irritability, (3) difficulty concentrating, (4) hypervigilance, (5) exaggerated startle response. E. Duration at least one month. F. The disturbance causes clinically significant distress or impairment in social, occupational, or other important areas of functioning.

depending upon the type of trauma experienced. In a study conducted among assault survivors, 19% were diagnosed with ASD (Brewin, Andrews, Rose, & Kirk, 1999), while 13% of survivors who experienced other traumas such as assaults, burns, and industrial accidents were found to suffer from ASD (Harvey & Bryant, 1998). In a study conducted among victims of robberies and assaults, 25% met the criteria for ASD (Elkit, 2002), while a study done with survivors of a mass shooting incident found that 33% of the participants showed symptoms of ASD (Classen, Koopman, Hales, & Spiegel, 1998). These studies suggest that the frequency of ASD among trauma survivors is contingent on the type of trauma experienced.

Among trauma survivors, a diagnosis of ASD appears to be a strong predictor that they will develop PTSD. In a study conducted by Harvey and Bryant (1998), more than three quarters of individuals involved in motor vehicle accidents who met the diagnostic criteria for ASD later developed PTSD. This evidence is consistent with other findings that more than 80% of trauma survivors diagnosed with ASD developed PTSD six months later (Brewin et al., 1999; Bryant & Harvey, 1998).

Complex Trauma

Despite several revisions to the *DSM-IV*, the diagnosis for PTSD excludes the effects of prolonged and repeated trauma on some individuals (Perrin, Smith, & Yule, 2000). For this reason, the APA, even while the *DSM-IV* was still under construction, began investigating the psychopathology of complex and chronic trauma (van der Kolk & Courtois, 2005). Complex PTSD, or Disorders of Extreme Stress Not Otherwise Specified (DESNOS), was proposed as this new diagnosis (Herman, 1997).

The Complex PTSD or DESNOS category was viewed by those in the field as better capturing the effects of prolonged, repeated trauma (Herman, 1992). Four particular groups of victims are reportedly affected by complex trauma: prisoners, hostages, battered women and children, and victims who are held in captivity and under the control of the perpetrator. Prolonged sexual abuse perpetrated during an individual's childhood is one example of DESNOS. The case vignette described below is that of a client who could be diagnosed with DESNOS.

Molly was first raped by her father when she was six years old. He warned her not to tell anyone about their "secret time" together. His nocturnal visits were followed by gently caressing her until she fell asleep and buying her expensive gifts when he came home after a business trip. Molly recalls that her father "visited" her at least once a week and more frequently during family vacations. The abuse inflicted on Molly lasted for more than eleven years.

When she turned 17, Molly ran away from home. She first lived in a commune and then a crack house as her addiction to heroin increased. Sometimes she offered her body in exchange for drugs; she recalls being sexually molested on several occasions while she was "drugged out." At age 45, she participates in a substance abuse recovery program and has three children by three different men. Molly is currently in a relationship with a man "old enough to be her father." She states that she feels "totally confused" about relationships and she does not believe she has ever been in love. She finds herself constantly ruminating about the violation she experienced as a child. A likely diagnosis for Molly might be DESNOS. Trauma-focused treatment with a client like Molly who exhibits complex trauma should initially focus on stabilization and a reduction in symptoms. By closely monitoring her participation in a substance recovery program, the therapist ensures that she does not relapse. Other stabilization techniques may include teaching her to identify her triggers and developing effective coping skills. As Molly's trust in the therapeutic relationship grows, she can be slowly encouraged to process her traumatic memories and emotions. A final phase of treatment will focus on an integration of her past trauma into her current life.

Broad areas of disturbance are noted among those who suffer from complex trauma or DESNOS. First, the symptoms are usually "more complex, diffuse, and tenacious than in simple PTSD" (Herman, 1992, p. 379). DESNOS is formally defined by 27 symptoms arranged into 7 categories often described by survivors of complex trauma (Pelcovitz, van der Kolk, Roth, Mandel, Kaplan, & Resick, 1997; van der Kolk, Roth, Pelcovitz, Sunday, & Spinazzola, 2005). The following seven categories of symptoms were not addressed in the original *DSM-IV* categorization of PTSD but are included in the complex PTSD conceptualization (van der Kolk & Courtois, 2005):

1. Altered affect or impulse regulation

2. Altered identity and sense of self

3. Alterations in ongoing attention or consciousness

4. Altered perception of the perpetrator

5. Alterations in relationships with others

6. Alterations in physical and medical issues, which manifest as somatization

7. Alterations in systems of meaning

Dissociation involves the altering of consciousness to cope with an unbearable reality; it is a response that commonly occurs among individuals who experience complex trauma (Herman, 1997). Changes in the functioning of personality are also the result of the traumatic exposure. When repeated exposure to trauma occurs early in a victim's life, the survival response becomes complex and inevitably shapes the development of personality. For example, children who have matured in an environment where terror and helplessness are endemic tend to become introverted and unassertive adults who lack self-esteem. Another effect of trauma is the survivor's increased vulnerability to repeated self-harm and harming others. Self-mutilation or para-suicidal behaviors commonly occur among those who have been abused for an extended period of time (Briere & Gil, 1998; van der Kolk et al., 2005). The risk of rape, sexual harassment, and battering increases steadily among those who have been abused as children.

Although DESNOS is often used by mental health professionals as a trauma-related diagnosis, only a few published reports of its use in clinical settings exist (Pelcovitz et al., 1997; Zlotnick et al., 1996). A strong appeal has been made to expand the definition of trauma from a single acute episode to complex disorders of extreme stress (DESNOS). The latter definition better captures the experience of those who live through several similar situations over an extended period of time. Unfortunately, for survivors who experience cycles of trauma throughout their lives, the disorder can become pervasive; for example, the child who was emotionally and physically abused by a parent may become an adult who lives with a controlling and abusive partner and is harassed by a supervisor at work.

Findings from both developmental psychopathology and neuroscience provide additional support for DESNOS. Developmental research indicates that many brain and hormonal changes occur as a result of early, chronic trauma. These changes contribute to an individual's difficulties with memory, learning, and regulating impulses and emotions (Yehuda, Schmeidler, & Wainberg, 1998). Combined with a disruptive and abusive home environment that discourages healthy interaction, these brain and hormonal changes can lead to severe behavioral difficulties such as impulsivity, aggression, sexual acting out, eating disorders, alcohol and drug abuse, and other self-destructive actions. Emotional difficulties such as intense rage, depression, and panic are also possible. Mental difficulties include scattered thoughts, dissociation, and amnesia (van der Kolk & Courtois, 2005).

As adults, individuals who experience complex traumas are often diagnosed with depressive, personality, or dissociative disorders. Treatment with such survivors may progress at a slower rate and may take a longer time. Furthermore, treatment with those who experience complex trauma requires a sensitive therapist whose interventions are structured in their delivery.

DESNOS best captures the multidimensional nature of trauma. Since this classification was not included as a distinct category in the *DSM-IV*, post-traumatic criteria that are not included in the current PTSD diagnosis have been relegated to co-morbid conditions, which are viewed as secondary to post-traumatic psychopathology (van der Kolk & Courtois, 2005). They include affective, anxiety, dissociative, somatic, and substance abuse disorders. Treatment for complex PTSD/DESNOS is usually long term (individual and group therapies), focusing on relationships, social and vocational skills training, and substance abuse rehabilitation. Dialectical behavior therapy (DBT), a comprehensive, balanced, and flexible cognitive behavior therapy approach, has been proposed as an effective adjunctive treatment for complex PTSD (Koerner & Linehan, 2000). DBT focuses on skills to reduce chronic impulsive behavior, suicidal behavior, relational issues, and frequent psychiatric admissions.

Co-Morbidity

Epidemiological data indicate that PTSD rarely occurs on its own (Solomon & Davidson, 1997). Rather, it often coincides with other disorders. Approximately 84% of those diagnosed with PTSD have another lifetime diagnosis (Kessler, Sonnega, Bromet, Hughes, & Nelson, 1995); major depression has been shown to exist in 48% of the PTSD population and alcoholism in 52% (Creamer, Burgess, & McFarlane, 2001). Research indicates that the risk for suicidal ideation is significantly higher among those with PTSD than in any other anxiety disorders (Ballenger et al., 2000).

Co-morbidity of PTSD and other disorders is more likely to occur when an individual is exposed to repeated or long-standing trauma and lives in an atmosphere of ongoing threats or unpredictability (Goenjian et al., 1995). Psychiatric disorders that are typically concomitant with PTSD include depression, alcohol and substance abuse, panic disorder, and other anxiety disorders (Kessler et al., 1995). Although any crisis that threatens the safety of the survivor must be addressed first, the best treatment results are achieved when both PTSD and the other disorder(s) are treated simultaneously rather than consecutively.

Substance Abuse and Trauma

The most common disorder concurrent with PTSD is substance use disorder. Many trauma survivors attempt to manage the intrusive and arousal symptoms of PTSD by resorting to alcohol and other addictive substances (Amaro, Larson, Gampel, Richardson, Savage, & Wagler, 2005; Najavits, Weiss, Shaw, & Muenz, 1998; Triffleman, Carroll, & Kellogg, 1999).

Studies have found that individuals who suffer from both PTSD and substance use disorder (SUD) have more frequent inpatient admissions, longer stays for addiction treatment, and higher readmission rates compared to patients who suffer from SUD alone (Ouimette, Ahrens, & Moos, 1997; Ouimette & Brown, 2003).

Whether the SUD or the trauma disorder should be treated first or whether they should be treated concurrently is a complicated question. Questions that explore a client's history will clarify whether substance abuse preceded the trauma or vice versa. If the substance abuse followed the trauma, it is possible that the client may be using the substance to alleviate traumatic symptoms. In this case, it may not be cogent to ask the client to give up a crutch before developing alternative coping strategies.

Traditional treatments that address only SUD may have to adapt their focus, given the high incidence of PTSD among those who abuse substances (Najavits, Sullivan, & Schmitz, 2004). Similarly, programs that focus on PTSD may have to adapt their focus to admit clients with current SUD. Support for a combined treatment approach derives from many experts in the field of PTSD/SUD treatment (Brady, Back, & Coffey, 2004; Najavits et al., 2004; Ouimette & Brown, 2003; Triffleman et al., 1999). Although patients frequently show a preference for a combined treatment approach, only individual psychotherapy appears to focus on both diagnoses at the same time (Najavits et al., 2004).

Although a clinical decision on which disorder to treat first should be based on a range of factors, substance abuse must (at the very least) be under control so that a client can attend treatment sober. Socioeconomic factors such as social vulnerability, racial and ethnic differences, exposure to community violence, and criminal justice and child welfare involvement must be included in the decision on which disorder to treat first (Amaro et al., 2005). There are advantages to consulting clients about the type of treatment they prefer while maintaining clinical oversight at the same time. An empowered client is likely to be more committed to his or her treatment. Educating clients about the different types and preferences of treatment is a first step toward their empowerment.

Triggers and Retriggering: A Case Example

Triggers are events, objects, or people that cause survivors to recall traumatic memories. Often, survivors will attempt to avoid anything associated with the trauma. However, events that remind them of the trauma may retrigger feelings initially triggered by the trauma itself. The concepts of triggers and retriggering often come up when doing trauma work. Traumas that are sidestepped and not processed always create the potential to retraumatize an individual. This is especially likely to occur when another incident similar to the original occurs.

Danny, a young Latino male, was referred for counseling after he was discharged from a local hospital. He had spent three months recovering from chest wounds incurred in a shooting by an unknown assailant and was suffering from insomnia and severe weight loss. At home, he was obsessed with locking doors and looking out the window. He sometimes piled furniture behind the front door at night as a deterrent to intruders. These behaviors were causing conflicts between him and his family. Danny described a tough life of growing up on the streets, where he had come to accept gang membership and street violence as a normal way of life. When asked whether he had experienced other significant traumatic incidents, he leaned forward, looked directly into my eyes, and asked whether our conversation was confidential. He informed me that he had not told anyone what he was about to say to me.

He proceeded to disclose in detail a history of childhood sexual abuse by a maternal uncle over a six-year period. As he narrated his story, Danny's rage and sense of violation increased steadily. His jaw tightened and he hoped that he could see his uncle again so that he "could kill him." I was relieved when he later revealed that his uncle had passed away several years ago. Danny had pushed thoughts and memories of the violation he experienced as a child to the back of his mind. In some ways, his tough street demeanor had always masked the suffering he experienced as a child. However, his current trauma resulting from the shooting had clearly triggered this past incident, filling him with intense feelings of anxiety, vulnerability, and helplessness. The trauma therapist will initially focus on helping Danny control intense feelings of anxiety and helplessness, which interfere with his daily functioning. It may be necessary to refer Danny to a psychiatrist for a medical evaluation to assess whether there are any physical concerns underlying his symptoms. Medication may improve his sleep and appetite and reduce his paranoid behaviors. Several cognitive-behavioral techniques (relaxation training, deep breathing, and thought stopping) can help Danny regain control of his life. Finally, once a trusting relationship is established, he will be able to discuss his childhood trauma fully and explore how to release painful memories so that he can go on with his life.

Dissociation

"I heard someone screaming; it was me" is a statement made by a rape survivor and an example of dissociation, which is often used by rape victims as the psyche tries to cope with overwhelming trauma. In its simplest definition, dissociation is an adaptation and emotional numbing, which causes the body to shut down when it feels too much pain. In its broadest definition, dissociation includes disconnections from self, world, emotions, and memories (Herman, 1997). The French psychiatrist Pierre Janet characterized this disorder as dissociation from conscious memories and an escape from personal awareness and control (Janet, 1907). When clients display complex and pervasive dissociative symptoms with a separation between processes that are normally integrated, the disorder is diagnosed as dissociative identity disorder (DID; *DSM-IV*). The Dissociative Experiences Scale (DES) is a 28-item self-report questionnaire that assesses psychological dissociation. It has adequate test-retest reliability, good internal consistency, and clinical validity (Carlson, Putnam, & Ross, 1993).

Alexithymia is a form of dissociation in which an individual has difficulty accessing emotional experiences (Grabe, Rainermann, Spitzer, Gaensicke, & Freyberger, 2000). Dissociation that manifests in disturbances of sensation, movement, and other bodily function is referred to as *somatoform dissociation* (Nijenhuis et al., 1999). Somatoform dissociation is the "partial or complete loss of the normal integration of somatoform components of experience, reactions, and function" (Nijenhuis et al., 1999, p. 512). It involves the transformation of unacceptable memories into somatic symptoms that cannot be explained medically (Nijenhuis, Spinhoven, van Dyck, van der Hart, & Vanderlinden, 1998). A most extreme form of dissociative amnesia, a failure to recall one's entire life, is described as *generalized amnesia* (van der Hart & Nijenhuis, 2001). The following case described by Modai (1994) captures the case of a client with generalized amnesia:

A child survivor of the Holocaust was referred for depression, which included symptoms of low self-esteem, lack of concentration, suicidal ideation, and feelings of guilt. A cousin provided the details of the survivor's childhood. She was born in Hungary, the only child of a Jewish couple. When she was eight years old, both her parents were arrested by the Germans. She was left with her grandmother, who died a few days later. Ultimately, she immigrated to Israel, where she suffered total amnesia regarding her childhood and the events of the Holocaust. When she spoke of her past, she spoke in a tone completely devoid of emotion; she intellectualized her past and her feelings. Additionally, she did not dream about any of her childhood difficulties. Her childhood was completely dissociated from her life.

Individuals who inhabit environments that are chronically traumatic or that do not validate their experiences may adapt by dissociating. Through dissociation, individuals can isolate information that is cognitively dissonant from their awareness (Goldsmith, Barlow, & Freyd, 2004). For this reason, dissociation is often described as the incest survivor's "internal wisdom" (Herman, 1997). Internal wisdom deems the resultant amnesia more of an adaptive strategy than a pathological phenomenon. However, merely repressing memories from awareness can be problematic for individuals in the long term. Repressed material impedes psychological functioning in many ways, which include disallowing an individual's conscious access to past experiences. Furthermore, an individual can potentially recover repressed memories without warning; when this painful material emerges, the impact can be debilitating for the individual.

Julie is a survivor of multiple sexual traumas. At the age of 12, she was raped by two male teenage cousins. In high school, Julie was molested by a teacher. As a young woman, she was repeatedly sexually assaulted and beaten by a boyfriend over a span of several years. Julie reports that she copes with these painful experiences by "escaping in her mind." In therapy, she finds talking about her traumatic feelings very difficult because she claims she "was not there." Although dissociating helped Julie cope during the immediate aftermath of the physical and sexual violations she suffered, this coping mechanism has become problematic in the long term. Whenever Julie feels distress, she "escapes into her mind."

The other day she walked out of the supermarket where she packs shelves as a part-time stock clerk. Her supervisor had yelled at her because she had not priced the canned goods correctly. She fled, as she usually did, into her own world to calm herself down. The screeching of tires drew her out of her reverie. With a gasp, she realized she had walked into the middle of the street without checking for traffic.

Once a client with a history of dissociation enters counseling, the practitioner must carefully weigh when and how to access and process the dissociated memories. It may not be in the survivor's immediate best interest to uncover memories that serve an unconscious purpose without first understanding that purpose. Research has found that the traumatic memory of some trauma survivors who are abused under a severe state of arousal, where fear and shock dominate, may be irretrievable (van der Kolk, 1996). A primary characteristic of a traumatic experience is that it challenges an individual's capacity to create and integrate a narrative of that experience (van der Kolk, 1996). Furthermore, traumatic experiences tend to consist of intense emotions and sensory impressions that challenge an individual's capacity to relate the experience through language. It is this challenge that often makes an individual's recollection of traumatic memories appear to be incoherent.

Hypnosis and guided imagery are two therapeutic techniques therapists use to assess a client's dissociated memories. "Because some victims of sexual abuse repress memories by dissociating them from consciousness, hypnosis can be a very valuable tool for retrieving these memories. For some victims, hypnosis may be the only successful option" (Brown, Scheflin, & Hammond, 1998, p. 647). However, Barber (1997) cautions that clients should recall traumatic memories in an alert and conscious state through a gradual recollection process so that the client always maintains control over the recovered material.

Conclusion

The defining characteristic of a traumatizing event is that it is uncontrollable and inescapable; trauma is a stressor that requires a response outside the usual range of adaptation (Foa, 1992). Several major traumatic events in recent years, including the 2001 attack on the World Trade Center, the 2004 tsunami in Southeast Asia, and Hurricane Katrina in 2005, have made terms like hypervigilance, flashbacks, and triggers part of the public vernacular.

This chapter examined the challenges in assessing PTSD. These challenges are complex because most clients do not initially present with issues of trauma when they enter therapy. In addition, research evidence indicates that many individuals who experience trauma are resilient in the face of stress. However, assessment of clients is ethically required and necessary for effective mental health treatment. Counselors are encouraged to conduct a thorough assessment that includes a complex understanding of trauma and its symptoms (see also Appendix X). This is important when working with any client, but it is particularly important when working with clients from diverse groups. Counselors who consider all aspects of clients' culture together with past and present life circumstances avoid misdiagnoses or unnecessary diagnoses. Accurate assessment of clients will help counselors avoid potentially destructive and enduring labels that may expose clients to invasive treatment practices.

References

Amaro, H., Larson, M. J., Gampel, J., Richardson, E., Savage, A., & Wagler, D. (2005). Racial/ethnic differences in social vulnerability among women with co-occurring mental health and substance abuse disorders: Implications for treatment services. *Journal of Community Psychology, 33*, 495–511.

American Psychiatric Association. (1994). *Diagnostic and statistical manual of mental disorders* (4th ed.). Washington, DC: Author.

Ballenger, J. C., Davidson, J. R. T., Lecrubier, Y., Nutt, D. J., Foa, E. B., Kessler, R. C., et al. (2000). Consensus statement on posttraumatic disorder from the International Consensus Group on Depression and Anxiety. *Journal of Clinical Psychiatry, 61*, 60–66.

Barber, J. (1997). Hypnosis and memory: A hazardous connection. *Journal of Mental Health Counseling, 9*, 305–318.

Brady, K. T. (2001). Co-morbid post-traumatic stress disorder and substance use disorders. *Psychiatric Annals, 31*(5), 313–319.

Brady, K. T., Back, S. E., & Coffey, S. F. (2004). Substance abuse and posttraumatic stress disorder. *Journal of American Psychological Society, 13*(5), 206–209.

Bremner, A., & Bryant, P. (2001). The effect of spatial cues on infants' responses in the AB task, with and without a hidden object. *Developmental Science, 4*(4), 408–415.

Bremner, J. D., Innis, R. B., & Salomon, R. M. (1997). Positron emission tomography measurement of cerebral metabolic correlates of tryptophan depletion-induced depressive relapse. *Archives of General Psychiatry, 54*(4), 364–374.

Bremner, J. D., Randall, P., & Vermetten, E. (1997). Magnetic resonance imaging-based measurement of hippocampal volume in posttraumatic stress disorder related to childhood physical and sexual abuse: A preliminary report. *Biological Psychiatry, 41*(1), 23–32.

Brewin, C. R., Andrews, B., Rose, S., & Kirk, M. (1999). Acute stress disorder and posttraumatic stress disorder in victims of violent crime. *American Journal of Psychiatry, 156*, 360–366.

Briere, J., & Gil, E. (1998). Self-mutilation in clinical and general population samples: Prevalence, correlates and functions. *American Journal of Orthopsychiatry, 68*(4), 609–621.

Brown, D., Scheflin, A. W., & Hammond, D. C. (1998). *Memory, trauma treatment and the law*. New York: Norton.

Bryant, R. A., & Harvey, A. G. (1998). The relationship between acute stress disorder and posttraumatic stress disorder following mild traumatic brain injury. *American Journal of Psychiatry, 155*, 625–629.

Bunce, S. C., Larsen, R. J., & Peterson, C. (1995). Life after trauma: Personality and daily life experiences of traumatized people. *Journal of Personality, 63*(2), 165–188.

Carlson, E. B., Putnam, F. W., & Ross, C. A. (1993). Validity of the dissociative experience scale in screening for multiple personality disorder: A multicenter study. *American Journal of Psychiatry, 150*(7), 1030–1036.

Classen, C., Koopman, C., Hales, R., & Spiegel, D. (1998). Acute stress disorder as a predictor of posttraumatic stress symptoms. *American Journal of Psychiatry, 155*, 620–624.

Creamer, M., Burgess, P. M., & McFarlane, A. C. (2001). Posttraumatic stress disorder: Findings from the Australian National Survey of Mental Health and Well-Being. *Psychological Medicine, 31*(7), 1237–1247.

DeBellis, M. D., Keshavan, M. S., Clark, D. B., Casey, B. J., Giedd, J. N., Boring, A. M., et al. (1999). A. E. Bennett research award: Developmental traumatology, Part II: Brain development. *Biological Psychiatry, 45*(10), 1271–1284.

Debieic, J., & LeDoux, J. (2004). Fear and the brain. *Social Research, 71*(4), 807–818.

Elklit, A. (2002). Acute stress disorder in victims of robbery and victims of assault. *Journal of Interpersonal Violence, 17*, 872–887.

Foa, E. (1992). Treatment of PTSD in civilian contexts. *British Journal of Clinical Psychology, 31*(4), 505–506.

Friedman, M. J., & Rosenheck, R. (1996). PTSD as a chronic disorder. In S. Soreff (Ed.), *The seriously and persistently mentally ill* (pp. 369–389). Seattle, WA: Hogrefe & Huber.

Goenjian, A. K., Pynoos, R. S., Steinberg, A. M., Najarian, L. M., Asarnow, J. R., Karayan, I., et al. (1995). Psychiatric comorbidity in children after the 1988 earthquake in Armenia. *Journal of American Academy of Child Psychiatry, 34*, 1174–1184.

Goldsmith, R. E., Barlow, M. R., & Freyd, J. J. (2004). Knowing and not knowing about trauma: Implications for therapy. *Psychotherapy: Theory, Research, Practice, Training, 41*(4), 448–463.

Grabe, H. J., Rainermann, S., Spitzer, C., Gaensicke, M., & Freyberger, H. J. (2000). The relationship between dimensions of alexithymia and dissociation. *Psychotherapy and Psychosomatics, 69*, 128–131.

Harvey, A. G., & Bryant, R. A. (1998). The relationship between acute stress disorder and posttraumatic stress disorder: A prospective evaluation of motor vehicle accident survivors. *Journal of Consulting and Clinical Psychology, 66*, 507–512.

Herman, J. L. (1992). Complex PTSD: A syndrome in survivors of prolonged and repeated trauma. *Journal of Traumatic Stress, 5*(3), 377–391.

Herman, J. L. (1997). *Trauma and recovery.* New York: Basic Books.

Janet, P. (1907). *The major symptoms of hysteria.* London: Macmillan.

Kessler, R., Sonnega, A., Bromet, E., Hughes, M., & Nelson, C. (1995). Posttraumatic stress disorder in the national co-morbidity survey. *Archives of General Psychiatry, 52*, 1048–1060.

Koerner, K., & Linehan, M. M. (2000). Research on dialectical behavior therapy for patients with borderline personality disorder. *Psychiatric Clinics of North America, 23*, 151–167.

LeDoux, J. (1996). *The emotional brain* (2nd ed.). New York: Touchstone.

LeDoux, J. (2000). Emotion circuits in the brain. *Annual Review of Neuroscience, 23*, 155–184.

LeDoux, J. (2002). *Synaptic self: How our brains become who we are.* New York: Viking Press.

McEwen, B. S. (1999). Stress and hippocampal plasticity. *Annual Review of Neuroscience, 22*, 105–122.

McNally, R. J., Bryant, R. A., & Ehlers, A. (2003). Does early psychological intervention promote recovery from posttraumatic stress? *Psychological Science in the Public Interest, 4*(2), 45–79.

Meichenbaum, D. (1994). *A clinical handbook/practical therapist manual for assessing and treating adults with post-traumatic stress disorder (PTSD).* Waterloo, ON: Institute Press.

Modai, I. (1994). Forgetting childhood: A defense mechanism against psychosis in a Holocaust survivor. *Clinical Gerontologist, 14*, 67–71.

Najavits, L. M., Sullivan, T. P., & Schmitz, M. (2004). Treatment utilization by women with PTSD and substance dependence. *American Journal on Addictions, 13*(3), 215–224.

Najavits, L. M., Weiss, R. D., Shaw, S. R., & Muenz L. R. (1998). Seeking safety? Outcome of a new cognitive-behavioral psychotherapy for women with posttraumatic stress disorder and substance dependence. *Journal of Traumatic Stress, 11*, 437–456.

Nelson, R. J. (2000). *An introduction to behavioral endocrinology* (2nd ed.). Sunderland, MA: Sinauer Associates.

Nijenhuis, E. R. S., Spinhoven, P., van Dyck, R., van der Hart, O., & Vanderlinden, J. (1998). Degree of somatoform and psychological dissociation in dissociative disorder is correlated with reported trauma. *Journal of Traumatic Stress, 11*(4), 711–730.

Nijenhuis, E. R. S., van Dyck, R., Spinhoven, P., van der Hart, O., Charou, M., Vanderlinden, J., et al. (1999). Somatoform dissociation discriminates among diagnostic categories over and above general psychopathology. *Australian and New Zealand Journal of Psychiatry, 33*, 511–520.

Ouimette, P. C., Ahrens, C., & Moos, R. H. (1997). Posttraumatic disorder in substance abuse patients: Relationship to 1-year treatment outcomes. *Psychology of Addictive Behaviors, 11*(1), 34–47.

Ouimette, P. C., & Brown, P. J. (Eds.). (2003). *Trauma and substance abuse: Causes consequences and treatment of comorbid disorders.* Washington, DC: American Psychological Association.

Pelcovitz, D., van der Kolk, B., Roth, S., Mandel, F., Kaplan, S., & Resick, P. (1997). Development of a criteria set and a structured interview for disorders of extreme stress (SIDESNOS). *Journal of Traumatic Stress, 10*, 3–16.

Perrin, S., Smith, P., & Yule, W. (2000). Practitioner review: The assessment and treatment of post-traumatic disorder in children and adolescents. *Journal of Child Psychology and Psychiatry, 41*(3), 277–289.

Perry, B. (1997). Incubated in terror: Neurodevelopmental factors in the "cycle of violence." In J. D. Osofsky (Ed.), *Children in a violent society* (pp. 124–149). New York: Guilford Press.

Ray, K. C., & Jackson, J. L. (1997). Family environment and childhood sexual victimization: A test of the buffering hypothesis. *Journal of Interpersonal Violence, 12*, 3–17.

Ronis, D. L., Bates, E., Garfein, A., Buit, B., Falcon, S., & Liberzon, I. (1996). Longitudinal patterns of care for patients with posttraumatic stress disorder. *Journal of Traumatic Stress, 9*, 763–781.

Schiffer, E., Teicher, M. H., & Papanicolaou, A. C. (1995). Evoked potential evidence for right brain activity during the recall of traumatic memories. *Journal of Neuropsychiatry Clinical Neuroscience, 7*, 169–175.

Schmahl, C. G., Vermetten, E., & Elzinga, B. M. (2003). Magnetic resonance imaging of hippocampal and amygdala volume in women with childhood abuse and borderline personality disorder. *Psychiatry Research: Neuroimaging, 122*(3), 193– 198.

Shin, L. M., Orr, S. P., Carson, M. A., Rauch, S. L., Macklin, M. L., Lasko, N. B., et al. (2004). Regional cerebral blood flow in the amygdala and medial prefrontal cortex during traumatic imagery in male and female Vietnam veterans with PTSD. *Archives of General Psychiatry, 61*, 168–176.

Solomon, S. D., & Davidson, J. R. T. (1997). Trauma: Prevalence, impairment, service use, and cost. *Journal of Clinical Psychiatry, 58*(9), 5–11.

Stein, M. D., Koverola, C., Hanna, C., Torchia, M. G., & McClarty, B. (1997). Hippocampal volume in women victimized by childhood sexual abuse. *Psychological Medicine, 27*, 951–959.

Teicher, M. H., Ito, Y., Glod, C. A., Anderson, S. L., Dumont, N., & Ackerman, E. (1997). Preliminary evidence for abnormal cortical development in physically and sexually abused children using EEG coherence and MRI. *Annals of the New York Academy of Science, 821*, 160–175.

Terr, L. C. (1991). Childhood traumas: An outline and overview. *American Journal of Psychiatry, 148*(1), 10–20.

Triffleman, E., Carroll, K., & Kellogg, S. (1999). Substance dependence posttraumatic stress disorder therapy: An integrated cognitive-behavioral approach. *Journal of Substance Abuse Treatment, 17*(1–2), 3–14.

van der Hart, O., & Nijenhuis, E. (2001). Generalized dissociative amnesia: Episodic, sematic and procedural memories lost and found. *Australian and New Zealand Journal of Psychiatry, 35*, 589–600.

van der Kolk, B. (1988). The trauma spectrum: The interaction of biological and social events in the genesis of the trauma response. *Journal of Traumatic Stress, 1*, 273–290.

van der Kolk, B. A. (1996). Trauma and memory. In B. A. van der Kolk, A. C. McFarlane, & L. Weisaeth (Eds.), *Traumatic stress: The effects of overwhelming experience on mind, body and society* (pp. 279–302). New York: Guilford Press.

van der Kolk, B. A., & Courtois, C. A. (2005). Editorial comments: Complex developmental trauma. *Journal of Traumatic Stress, 18*(5), 385–388.

van der Kolk, B. A., Roth, S., Pelcovitz, D., Sunday, S., & Spinazzola, J. (2005). Disorders of extreme stress: The empirical foundation of a complex adaptation to trauma. *Journal of Traumatic Stress, 18*(5), 389–399.

Vyas, A., Mitra, R., Rao, B. S. S., & Chattarji, S. (2002). Chronic stress induces contrasting patterns of dendritic remodeling in hippocampal and amygdaloid neurons. *Journal of Neuroscience, 22*(15), 6810–6818.

Webb, N. B. (2004). Ongoing issues and challenges for mental health professionals working with survivors of mass trauma. In N. B. Webb (Ed.), *Mass trauma and violence helping families and children cope* (pp. 347–359). New York: Guilford.

Werner, E. E. (2001). *Journeys of childhood to mid-life: Risk, resilience and recovery.* New York: Cornell University Press.

World Health Organization. (1992). *The ICD-10 classification of mental and behavioural disorders diagnostic criteria for research.* Geneva: Author.

Yehuda, R. (2000). Biology of post-traumatic stress disorder. *Journal of Clinical Psychiatry, 61,* 14–21.

Yehuda, R., McFarlane, A. C., & Shalev, A. Y. (1998). Predicting the development of posttraumatic stress disorder from the acute response to a traumatic event. *Biological Psychiatry, 44,* 1305–1313.

Yehuda, R., Schmeidler, J., & Wainberg, M. (1998). Vulnerability to posttraumatic stress disorder in adult offspring of Holocaust survivors. *American Journal of Psychiatry, 155*(9), 1163–1171.

Yehuda, R., Spertus, I. L., & Golier, J. A. (2001). Relationship between childhood traumatic experiences and PTSD in adults. In S. Eth (Ed.), *PTSD in children and adolescents* (pp. 117–158). Washington, DC: American Psychiatric Assoc. Press.

Zlotnick C., Zakriski, A. L., Shea, M. T., Costello, E., Begin, A., Pearlstein, T., et al. (1996). The long-term sequelae of sexual abuse: Support for a complex posttraumatic stress disorder. *Journal of Traumatic Stress, 9*(2), 195–205.

3

Models of Trauma Treatment

A 35-year-old financial executive sought therapy after starting a new job. Michael, a graduate of an Ivy League institution, described his new position as a dream job with one major challenge. It involved visiting the company's branches in other states. Michael stated that he needed therapy to help him with his flying phobia. He recounted that when he was 14 years old his father was killed in an air crash. As a result, any mention of planes and flying plunged him into a state of panic. However, with therapy he was able to keep his panic under control. His new employment was bringing up intense anxieties, and he was helpless in the face of them.

In further discussion with Michael, and by prioritizing his problems, the therapist and Michael decided to use systematic desensitization to help him with his flying phobia. Relaxation training is a first step in systematic desensitization, and Michael was already familiar with progressive muscle relaxation and deep breathing. The next step was to help Michael create an anxiety hierarchy (packing luggage, making reservations, driving to the airport, checking in, etc.). The third step was to have Michael engage in activities outlined in his anxiety hierarchy, beginning with the least anxiety provoking. As soon as his distress increased, he was encouraged to stop the activity and practice relaxation.

This phase of treatment took several months, but Michael was able to manage his fears and take short trips. At this point, the therapist suggested the next phase of treatment should focus on the issues underlying Michael's flying phobia. Using a stage-oriented trauma treatment approach, Michael was gradually able to discuss his underlying thoughts and memories when his phobia began. He *reported being close to his dad and missing him terribly after he died. As the oldest of three children, he felt that he had to be stoic to support his mother and to watch over his younger siblings. He felt that he could not express his loss at the time. Since his father's remains were never identified, he lacked closure in an important relationship. In therapy, Michael was able to mourn his loss fully for the first time.*

This chapter will examine the different models used in trauma-focused therapy with adult survivors, from the cognitive-behavioral to stage-specific and self-trauma models. Most of these models are theoretically integrative and focus on the healing that is possible in a therapeutic relationship. Eye Movement Desensitization Reprocessing and psychopharmacology are also outlined as treatment options. Specific strategies are provided for the beginning psychotherapist interested in working with traumatized populations. Trauma treatment with particular populations, such as victims of rape, domestic violence, and political trauma, will be covered in later chapters.

Therapeutic Approaches

Many effective therapeutic approaches and techniques have been used with trauma survivors. Most practitioners use a combination of approaches depending on their training and background. The client's needs, however, should be the final determinant of the approach the therapist chooses to use to support recovery. When shaping interventions, the therapist must consider the client's cultural and social background. The therapist's awareness of these factors inevitably affects the progress of treatment. If practitioners are not familiar with the culture of the client, they should make every effort to gain this cultural understanding. Attending professional conferences and workshops and reading independently are ways to increase one's cultural repertoire. However, when the cultural differences between client and therapist become insurmountable even after a therapist has worked at cultural understanding, it is reasonable for the therapist to refer the client to more appropriate services. The therapeutic relationship is not the venue for negotiating cultural differences.

In addition to, and sometimes concomitant with, cultural differences is the role of empowerment and disempowerment within a therapeutic session. As a professional with expertise, the practitioner holds a position of power.

The client who seeks services does not share the same privilege and may feel disempowered as a result. If racial and cultural differences exist in the client-therapist dyad, issues of power and privilege are highlighted. Racial and cultural differences can significantly impact therapy, and a culturally competent practitioner does not hesitate to raise the issues appropriately.

Finally, it is important to remember that trauma work is often integrated into therapeutic work with clients. Often, trauma material does not surface until much later in the therapeutic process. Establishing rapport and trust should be critical goals of any therapy, especially those that are trauma-specific. For some practitioners, these goals remain the primary focus of therapy with their clients for several years.

Brief Psychodynamic Psychotherapy

Brief psychodynamic psychotherapy is an abbreviated form of psychodynamic therapy in which the emotional conflicts caused by the traumatic event are the focus of treatment, particularly as they relate to the client's early life experiences (Horowitz, 1997; Horowitz, Marmar, Krupnick, Wilner, Kaltreider, & Wallerstein, 1997; Krupnick, 2002). The rationale of brief psychodynamic psychotherapy is that a client's retelling the traumatic event to a calm, empathetic, compassionate, and nonjudgmental therapist will result in greater self-esteem, more effective thinking strategies, and an increased ability to manage intense emotions successfully (Marmar, Weiss, & Pynoos, 1995). Throughout the process, the therapist helps the client identify current life situations that trigger traumatic memories and exacerbate PTSD symptoms. In this model of treatment, the therapist emphasizes concepts such as denial, abreaction, and catharsis (Horowitz, 1997; Horowitz et al., 1997).

By using a psychoanalytic approach, Burton (2004) found that clients were able to reenact their trauma. He concluded that these reenactments serve several purposes. First, reenacting a trauma is validating since it confirms for the client that the trauma really happened. Second, a reenactment helps the client gain mastery over the situation that was once an experience of helplessness. Finally, reenactments present the possibility of reversing prior outcomes, controlling what was uncontrollable in the past, and dealing with the trauma in different and more hopeful ways.

Cognitive-Behavioral Therapy

Cognitive-behavioral therapy (CBT) combines two very effective kinds of psychotherapy: cognitive therapy and behavior therapy. Behavior therapy, based on learning theory, helps clients weaken the connections between troublesome thoughts and situations and their habitual reactions to them. Cognitive therapy teaches clients how certain thinking patterns may be the cause of their difficulties by giving them a distorted picture and making them feel anxious, depressed, or angry (Beck, 1995). When combined into CBT, behavior therapy and cognitive therapy provide powerful tools for symptom alleviation and help clients resume normal functioning.

A cognitive approach has been found to be a suitable framework for trauma therapy because traumatic experiences usually impede the emotional process by conflicting with pre-existing cognitive schemas (Jaycox, Zoellner, & Foa, 2002). Cognitive dissonance, which occurs when thoughts, memories, and images of trauma cannot be reconciled with current meaning structures, causes distress. The cognitive system is driven by a completion tendency: a psychological need "to match new information with inner models based on older information, and the revision of both until they agree" (Horowitz, 1986, p. 92).

The fluctuation between symptoms of hyperarousal and inhibition commonly seen among trauma survivors is well described by van der Kolk (1996). During the acute phase of the trauma, in an attempt to comprehend and integrate the traumatic experience, the trauma survivor normally replays the event that has been stored in active memory. Each replay, however, distresses the traumatized individual, who may inhibit thought processes to modulate the active processing of traumatic information. This observable inhibition gives the appearance that the traumatized individual has disengaged from processing the traumatic memory. Thus, some trauma survivors, as a result of excessive inhibition, display withdrawn and avoidant behaviors. However, when an individual is unable to inhibit traumatic thoughts, the intrusive symptoms are expressed in the hyperarousal symptoms of flashbacks during the waking states and nightmares during sleep states (van der Kolk, 1996). For this reason, researchers commonly observe trauma survivors as oscillating between denial and numbness, or intrusion and hyperarousal (Lindy, 1996; van der Kolk, McFarlane, & van der Hart, 1996). Once clients can reappraise the event and revise the cognitive schemas they previously held, the completion tendency is served. These common reactions and cognitive processes seen among trauma survivors can be explained using the framework of cognitive theory. However, the therapist's central focus on the client's internal cognitive mechanisms and how the client processes information may result in a neglect of contextual and sociocultural factors in cognitive theory.

CBT primarily involves working with a client is cognitions to change emotions, thoughts, and behaviors (Meichenbaum, 1977, 1997).

CBT techniques used by trauma therapists focus on the following:

- Learning skills for coping with anxiety (such as breath retraining or biofeedback)
- Using cognitive restructuring to change negative thoughts
- Managing anger
- Preparing for stress reactions (stress inoculation)
- Handling future trauma symptoms
- Addressing relapse prevention and other substance abuse issues
- Communicating and relating effectively with people (social skills)
- Addressing thought distortions that usually follow exposure to trauma
- Relaxation training and guided imagery

Additional information on CBT can be obtained from www.cognitive therapy.com. Several specific CBT approaches are outlined below:

1. *Exposure Therapy.* In exposure therapy, clients are encouraged to confront the fear-inducing thought or memory in varying levels of exposure that can be imaginal or in vivo (Cook, Schnurr, & Foa, 2004; Foa, Zoellner, Feeny, Hembree, & Alvarez-Conrad, 2002; Jaycox et al., 2002). Gradually and repeatedly, clients are guided through a vivid and specific recall of traumatic events until emotional reactions decrease through a process of habituation. The safe, controlled context of the therapeutic relationship helps clients face and gain control of the fear and distress that they previously experienced as overwhelming. For example, issues of safety dominate the lives of sexual assault victims. As the clients recount their narratives in exposure therapy, practitioners are able to identify possible risk areas. Making these distinctions can later be used to help clients discriminate unsafe situations from safe ones (Foa & Meadows, 1997).

   In some cases, the therapist may encourage clients to confront all their memories or reminders of trauma at once. This technique is referred to as *flooding.* It is critical that a practitioner discuss this technique with a client carefully, and it is also imperative to offer the client the option to refuse treatment. Clients should be aware of the technique's negative consequences; they should also be aware that it may not work. In general, exposure therapy has been found to be an ineffective and unsuccessful treatment modality with veterans who have experienced chronic combat-related PTSD (Schnurr, Friedman, & Foy, 2003). In fact, it was so poorly tolerated by this population that most participants chose to drop out of treatment (Foa, Keane, & Friedman, 2004; Keane, Fairbank, Caddell, & Zimmering, 1989). However, strong empirical support exists for the efficacy of exposure therapy with other trauma-affected groups (Foa & Meadows, 1997). Studies conducted among rape survivors, for example, suggest that exposure therapy may actually be an effective treatment for PTSD (Foa et al., 2002; Hembree & Foa, 2000).

2. *Systematic Desensitization.* Systematic desensitization, developed by Wolpe in 1958, is an effective form of treatment for individuals who prefer gradual

recall rather than immediate total recall of traumatic memories. When using systematic desensitization, clients are supported through deep muscle relaxation techniques and diaphragmatic breathing (see Appendix VI and Appendix VII). These techniques are taught to clients before treatment is administered; they are used during therapy whenever a client's anxiety increases. Once clients have established a hierarchy of fear-inducing stimuli and gained competence in using relaxation techniques to overcome these situations, the least upsetting situation is recalled. The client proceeds to systematically recall the least distressing aspects of the traumatic experience. If negative reactions ensue, relaxation is induced. Otherwise the client ascends up the hierarchy to recall the next distressing stimuli. In this systematic method, clients work toward overcoming and integrating their worst fears.

3. *Anxiety Management.* From an anxiety management perspective, the practitioner attributes the client's anxiety to a lack of skills in managing anxiety when faced with situations that provoke it. The aim of client treatment is to develop skills in managing anxiety. Clients are taught specific anxiety-reduction skills: relaxation training, positive self-talk, and distraction techniques. Anxiety management has been successfully used to treat PTSD in rape survivors (Foa, Rothbaum, Riggs, & Murdock, 1991).

4. *Stress Inoculation Therapy.* One of the most commonly used anxiety management treatments for PTSD is stress inoculation therapy (SIT). Originally developed by Meichenbaum (1994) for anxious individuals, SIT incorporates psycho-education and skill-building techniques such as relaxation, thought stopping, breath retraining, problem solving, and guided self-dialogue. When used with female rape victims, SIT has yielded encouraging results (Foa et al., 1991).

Positive client outcomes have been achieved by combining treatments. In a sophisticated controlled study, a combination of prolonged imaginal exposure, SIT, and supportive counseling was found to significantly reduce symptoms (Foa et al., 1991).

Eye Movement Desensitization and Reprocessing

In Eye Movement Desensitization and Reprocessing (EMDR), the goal is to help the client desensitize to traumatic stimuli through saccadic eye movements (Shapiro, 1995). The treatment procedure follows a structured sequence. Clients are first asked to perform bilateral eye movements while recalling a disturbing image or memory. The therapist then waves a finger repeatedly across a client's visual field while he/she tracks it with his/her eyes (Shapiro, 1995).

The treatment involves a combination of exposure therapy elements and eye movements, hand taps, or sounds to distract clients' attention. After each sequence, clients indicate their subjective units of distress (SUD). If the SUD is high, the client practices relaxation techniques. When the client is ready, EMDR is resumed. Shapiro (1989, 1995) maintains that EMDR, with its brief exposures to associated material, external/internal focus, and structured therapeutic protocol, represents a distinctly different and new paradigm in therapy.

However, EMDR is a controversial therapeutic approach for several reasons. Some argue that EMDR lacks a theoretical foundation, empirical data, and sound methodology (Resick, 2004). Claims that EMDR is a rapid and effective treatment have been subjected to many empirical studies and much scientific scrutiny. More specifically, 12 controlled randomized studies, which investigated the efficacy of EMDR with PTSD-diagnosed participants, were conducted (Maxfield & Hyer, 2002).

With Vietnam veterans, Devilly, Spence, and Rapee (1998) compared EMDR to control conditions using two different forms of EMDR and psychotherapy. Although the EMDR groups showed some improvement, they found that at six-month follow-up, these treatment gains had not been maintained. Another study done by Devilly and Spence (1999) compared EMDR with a combination of exposure, SIT, and cognitive therapy techniques in a mixed sample of trauma survivors with PTSD. While EMDR was effective, cognitive therapy was found to be superior because treatment gains were maintained at three-month follow-up.

Some researchers suggest the effectiveness of EMDR derives mostly from its cognitive behavioral aspects, which include exposure, cognitive restructuring, anxiety desensitization, and breathing (Lohr, Tolin, & Lilienfeld, 1998; McNally, 1999). In fact, Lohr, Lilienfeld, Tolin, and Herbert (1999) state that if EMDR had been presented as a form of exposure therapy, "much of the controversy . . . could have been avoided" (p. 201). EMDR forces the client to think about the trauma, to think about the negative cognitions associated with the trauma, and to replace them with positive cognitions. Without the lateral eye movements, EMDR is similar to cognitive and exposure therapy methods, which facilitate a client's processing of traumatic memory. Any efficacy demonstrated by EMDR likely derives from a client engaging with and processing the traumatic memory, rather than from eye movements. Resick (2004) points out that EMDR treatments with a more extensive behavioral and imaginal exposure, as well as cognitive therapy, are likely to be more effective.

Despite ongoing scientific scrutiny, the originator of EMDR, Francis Shapiro, claims that even a single session of EMDR produces positive results (Shapiro, 1989). While the theory and research continues to evolve, there is some evidence that attentional alternation, which is unique to EMDR, may actually facilitate the accessing and processing of traumatic material in adults (Chemtob, Tolin, van der Kolk, & Pitman, 2000; Hyer & Brandsma, 1997; Sweet, 1995). The aggregate evidence of research results demonstrates that EMDR is an effective treatment for civilian PTSD (Maxfield & Hyer, 2002; Perkins & Rouanzoin, 2002). EMDR demonstrates greater efficacy and requires less time to achieve positive results. However, several sampling and methodological flaws and the lack of control groups make it premature to draw any solid conclusions about the generalizability of these findings until they are replicated to confirm their reliability. Additional information on training and certification in EMDR can be obtained from www.emdr.com.

A Stage-Specific Model

Herman (1997) describes trauma recovery as unfolding in three broad stages. The first stage focuses on establishing a client's safety and stabilization. Once these goals are reached, the client proceeds to the next stage of remembering, exploring, and mourning past traumas. The third and final stage of recovery is described as one of reconnection. This stage focuses on expanding and revitalizing the relational world of the client. The therapeutic alliance is described as a collaborative relationship with the client in charge of recovery; the therapist's role is described as that of witness, consultant, and ally (Herman, 1997). A more comprehensive discussion of Herman's specific stage model is described below.

1. Safety

According to Herman (1997), trauma causes disempowerment and disconnection. The focus of the first stage of recovery is empowerment and connection. Effective therapy shifts unpredictable danger to reliable safety, dissociated trauma to acknowledged memory, and stigmatized isolation to restored social connection (Herman, 1997). A healing therapeutic relationship restores a survivor's trust in others by validating the client's experience. Practitioners of this model are described as

- allowing clients to ultimately have control in the therapeutic setting;
- acting as assistants, allies, and advocates in the role of bearing witness;
- exercising care in not resorting to dysfunctional rescuing and patronizing, both of which can take control away from client;
- adopting a neutral stance and not taking sides in the client's interpersonal conflict.

The timing and focus of treatment is paced to suit the client's needs. Recovery is viewed like running a marathon, with the therapist acting as coach and the client determining the pace. Therapists who share their diagnosis and treatment plans with their client early in treatment can actually empower the client because knowledge is power. In some circumstances, to help clients re-establish control and reduce anxiety and hyperarousal, psychopharmacology may have to be used.

2. Remembrance and Mourning

The second stage of Herman's (1997) model is referred to as remembrance and mourning. It focuses on past issues, in particular the traumatic event that causes a client's difficulties. Clients are encouraged to recall traumatic memories so that they are transformed from a snapshot to a full picture. The goal of this stage is to tell the full story of the trauma with the therapist in the role of witness and ally. The survivor determines how much is shared in each therapy session. The subtle balance between facing the past and preserving safety is constantly negotiated between clients and therapists. Clients who avoid their traumatic memories may stagnate and not improve in therapy. On the other hand, those clients who recall their traumatic memories too quickly can become overwhelmed and may compromise their safety.

A full recall of the traumatic memory includes the participation of all five senses so that all aspects of the memory are available to consciousness. Two techniques help the recall of traumatic memories: flooding and testimony. Flooding is a behavioral technique. The client is taught relaxation techniques before directly recalling traumatic material. However, flooding has been found to be effective only with those individuals who have experienced a single incident of trauma (Herman, 1997). The testimony method involves a detailed record of the traumatic experience. This record is created from the clinical material that emerges in the therapy sessions. The testimony method has been found to be successful with those who have experienced political trauma (Herman, 1997). Both these techniques involve an active collaboration between client and counselor. The outcome is the construction of a detailed trauma narrative in which the client relives the intense experience of the trauma in a safe and trusting therapeutic relationship.

Hypnotherapy is another technique that Herman (1997) recommends for those client's whose gaps in memory disallow them from fully recalling traumatic events. She cautions practitioners on several aspects of this therapeutic method. First, she notes, hypnotherapy requires a high degree of therapeutic skill. Second, it requires adequate preparation of the client. Third, once a memory is uncovered, the practitioner must ensure that it is carefully reintegrated into the client's life.

Mourning is an inevitable outcome of traumatic loss. Sometimes clients resist mourning in order to "deny victory to the perpetrator" (Herman, 1997, p. 188). Ultimately, mourning is a necessary aspect of healing. The therapist helps the client accept grief as an act of courage rather than defeat. Mourning can have a restorative power by helping clients come to terms with fantasies of revenge. However, clients never discard the quest for justice and tenaciously hold perpetrators responsible for their immoral acts.

3. Reconnection

In the third stage, Herman (1997) describes clients reconnecting as they create new selves, reconcile with the past, and repudiate those aspects of the self that may have been imposed by the trauma. She notes that for those victims recovering from childhood sexual abuse, the new identity may feel like a second adolescence. Clients transition from victims to survivors by taking concrete steps to increase their sense of power and control, by protecting themselves from future danger, and by deepening their alliances with those whom they have learned to trust (Herman, 1997, p. 197).

The goal of reconnection is to remain autonomous while simultaneously developing connections. In this way, the ability to trust both self and others becomes more possible. Individuals who come from abusive families may consider confronting their families, the perpetrator, or those who were silent about their trauma. These confrontations can be emotionally useful if they are carefully planned and executed.

Some clients, in the reconnection stage of recovery, choose to become social activists and commit to a survivor mission pursuing the eradication of violence. In joining such groups, the survivor satisfies a yearning for connection while creating opportunities to ally with others who share a common purpose. Herman (1997) describes joining survivor groups as a constructive way of transforming the meaning of personal tragedy. Sarah Buel, a victim of domestic violence, is a survivor who overcame personal challenges by creating new meaning out of a traumatic experience. Buel attended school at night while raising a son as a single parent. After earning a law degree from Harvard University in 1990, she drafted the first abuse-prevention law in New Hampshire. The law allows abuse victims without a lawyer to petition the court for a restraining order; it also specifies other ways that abuse victims can maintain safety. Buel has become an accomplished and sought-after public speaker on domestic violence. In her legal practice, she concentrates on legally protecting abuse victims.

A Self-Trauma Model

The trauma model developed by Briere (1996) is a blend of humanistic, psychodynamic, and cognitive-behavioral theories. Important principles of Briere's treatment model include respect, positive regard, and the assumption of growth. Key concepts for practitioners to follow are safety, support, therapeutic feedback, and working through the trauma.

Safety and Support

Through extended and intensive psychotherapy, clients build a positive source of identity. They become better able to regulate affect and monitor internal states, they begin to rely on inner resources in times of stress, and they maintain internal coherence in their interactions with others. The support and care shown by the therapist is an important aspect of treatment. A stable and optimistic therapeutic environment supports a client's positive sense of self. Such an environment also allows clients to transition from a state of hypervigilance regarding their external environment to one that focuses on their internal psychological environment. A consistent, caring, and nonjudgmental therapist demeanor helps clients develop an ability to explore their inner landscape safely.

Therapeutic Feedback

According to Briere (1996), therapeutic feedback is an important aspect of client-therapist interaction because it increases clients' self-understanding. With the therapist's encouragement, clients examine illogical thoughts and compare these thoughts to their actual experiences. Therapists act as a positive mirror, by illuminating avoidant and dissociative client responses (Kohut, 1977). As clients learn more about themselves, self-defeating and self-destructive behavior decreases. A state of helplessness is replaced with a greater sense of control. Most importantly, clients develop increased self-nurturance, self-confidence, and an improved ability to self-support.

Working Through

Since the therapeutic relationship carries the potential to elicit needs, projections, and responses that are abuse-related, it is possible that clients may experience boundary confusion. When this occurs, the effective therapist uses the opportunity to help the client rework old relationships in which boundaries may have been violated. Clients are able to recover "missed" stages of development while in an environment of unconditional positive regard.

With therapeutic support, clients can test their autonomy by attempting behaviors they previously considered risky. They may assertively confront a boss or an abusive parent. An important and useful idea described in the self-trauma model is the concept of the "therapeutic window." Briere (2002) describes this as the psychological area that has the upper limit of clients feeling overwhelmed by exposure to abuse-related material and the lower limit of excessive avoidance of traumatic material. The therapist strives to work within the area demarcated by the therapeutic window so that sessions are tolerable in intensity. At the upper limit of the therapeutic window, the experience is likely to become an "insurmountable affective task" (p. 185). On the other hand, interventions that are not psychologically demanding can result in minimal psychological growth or "a surmountable affective task" (p. 185). Therapists constantly monitor the amount of abuse-related distress that clients can tolerate, with the aim of balancing exploration and consolidation of traumatic material.

The self-trauma model of treatment requires the active involvement of client's in order for healing to occur. It is based on the premise that to overcome pain and fear, both of these elements must be directly confronted in the safety of the therapeutic setting (Briere, 2002). The therapist is cautioned to maintain sight of the clients' courage and strength in attempting to achieve this goal.

A Stage-Oriented Treatment Model

Chu (1998) describes a stage-oriented trauma treatment model that includes self-care, acknowledgment of the trauma, improving functioning, expression of affect, and relationship building. It is summarized and represented by the acronym SAFER:

S = Self-Care

A = Acknowledgment

F = Functioning

E = Expression

R = Relationships

These five stages of treatment can be further differentiated into early, middle, and late stage categories.

Early Stage Treatment

1. Self-Care

Behaviors that are self-destructive and high risk commonly occur among trauma survivors and increase their vulnerability to revictimization. A focus on self-care eradicates a trauma survivor's feelings of unworthiness and instills a positive sense of identity. The control of traumatic symptoms, especially those that interfere with current functioning, reduces a client's sense of helplessness (Chu, 1998). Grounding and self-soothing techniques such as deep breathing, squeezing a ball, or rubbing a stone can help clients overcome intrusive thoughts and re-orient to the moment.

2. Acknowledgment

Acknowledgment of abuse is a central concept in trauma recovery. Clients are constantly reassured they were not responsible for the abuse. By acknowledging abusive experiences, counselors tacitly avoid colluding with a client's denial of abuse and flawed beliefs of personal defectiveness.

3. Functioning

In this stage of treatment, clients are guided toward normal functioning in the current reality of their lives. To avoid dwelling on past trauma issues and to ameliorate distress, clients are encouraged to establish and maintain a routine while developing supportive relationships.

4. Expression

To relinquish the unspeakable aspects of the trauma, clients must find other outlets for expression. Several expressive therapy techniques, including poetry writing, drawing, and movement, can potentially capture the unspeakable aspects of trauma in constructive ways.

5. Relationships

Establishing mutually beneficial and collaborative relationships is an important task of early recovery. Since the client is likely to reenact early abusive relationships within the therapeutic setting, the therapist may find that the therapeutic alliance has to be constantly renegotiated. The process of disconnection and reconnection is likely to repeat itself, but by continuing to provide support and care, the therapist models a corrective emotional relationship for a client.

Middle Stage Treatment

Once clients master the tasks of early treatment, they can begin to tackle the tasks of the middle treatment stage. Exploration and abreaction are the major tasks of this stage. Chu (1998) cautions that abreaction and exploration can only take place when clients have achieved a position of strength; exploration of traumatic material should not be done with clients who display vulnerability or with clients who find themselves in a new crisis. Although the direction of abreaction differs among clients, several common features are evident:

- An increase in symptoms
- Intense internal conflict
- Acceptance and mourning
- Mobilization and empowerment

Abreaction frees the client from the fears instilled by past trauma (Chu, 1998). Clients can then develop a personal narrative of understanding that allows them to continue with their lives.

Late Stage Treatment

Chu (1998) describes the last stage as the consolidation stage of trauma treatment. In this stage, the client continues to develop new skills while stabilizing gains. With a newly empowered sense of self, the client can participate in interactions that were earlier viewed with anxiety. Although clients may achieve good ego strength, continuing treatment may be a necessary option as the client inevitably encounters new challenges.

The stage-oriented model was primarily developed for treating clients who experienced childhood trauma. It may therefore be limited to use with this specific group.

Pharmacotherapy

Medication can reduce the anxiety, depression, and insomnia that often accompany PTSD. In some cases, medication may also relieve the distress and emotional numbness caused by traumatic memories. Several antidepressant drugs have yielded mostly positive results in clinical trials. Antidepressant drugs used to control PTSD symptoms include tricyclic antidepressants (TCAs), monamine oxidase inhibitors (MAOIs), and selective serotonin reuptake inhibitors (SSRIs).

Other classes of drugs have shown some promise. For example, Clonidine reduces hyperarousal symptoms, while Clonazepam regulates anxiety and panic symptoms. The SSRIs have good outcomes in globally and effectively treating all categories of PTSD. This class of drugs is currently the most widely used and best studied (Sutherland & Davidson, 1998).

Currently, no particular drug has emerged as a definitive treatment for PTSD, although medication has been clearly successful in providing immediate relief of traumatic symptoms. Once clients are able to control their symptoms through pharmacotherapy, it becomes possible for them to participate more effectively in psychotherapy. As a sole treatment, pharmacotherapy will not help clients recover from trauma (Vargas & Davidson, 1993). It can, however, stabilize clients so that psychotherapy and other interventions are possible.

Cultural factors should be an important consideration when psychopharmacology is used as a treatment option. Clinical trials are seldom done on every population group. Caution is necessary when medicating individuals from groups who may not have been tested for a particular drug. For example, it has been suggested that the dosage of medication should be reduced with traumatized Southeast Asian refugees. Indochinese people regularly eat food rich in tyramine and/or use herbal remedies, which can exacerbate the side effects of TCA and MAOI (Demartino, Mollica, & Wilk, 1995). In some cultures, the sharing of medication is common practice. Before dispensing medication to such clients, the practitioner should fully discuss side effects of the medication and the dangers of sharing it with those for whom it was not prescribed (Demartino et al., 1995).

In some cultures, there may be a cultural stigma associated with taking medication. For example, an ethnographic study of psychiatric patients in hospital care in East Malaysia, where traditional healing continues to be a popular alternative to biomedicine, found that few patient rights are recognized (Crabtree, 2005). The researcher found that the medical culture remains embedded in a paternalistic and custodial attitude that does not acknowledge issues of spirituality or alternative healing practices that are important to hospitalized patients. Modernization of services has not included patient participation or an appropriate inclusion of cultural responses. The researcher concludes that until this takes place, treatment resistance will continue to be exhibited.

Marotta (2000) describes the key role that counselors play with clients who use psychopharmacology as an adjunctive treatment. Counselors see clients more often than the professionals who prescribe medications and can monitor potential side effects of medication. By communicating with the prescribing physician on a client's behalf, practitioners become strong advocates for their clients. For these reasons, counselors are encouraged to familiarize themselves with the different medications used to treat PTSD, especially the SSRIs, which are prominent in the treatment of PTSD. Counselors can help wary clients who may not be convinced about the benefits of pharmacotherapy to better understand the consequences of using medication. Finally, counselors play an important role in improving clients' compliance with medication. This can be achieved by planning adjunctive sessions with family members or significant others.

Determining Which Approach to Use

Several approaches to trauma treatment have been outlined. The approach that a therapist adopts depends on several factors. First, the specific training of the therapist determines the approach used. Second, the client's phase of recovery guides treatment. The most effective mental health intervention in the immediate aftermath of a traumatic event is psychological first aid, which includes the provision of basic needs (food and shelter) and safety and security. Psycho-educational approaches help in stabilization and increasing one's knowledge about a traumatic event. Cognitive-behavioral approaches, which include relaxation techniques, assist in the reduction of physiological arousal. Co-morbid disorders are treated before beginning trauma-focused therapy, which involves in-depth exploration of traumatic material.

Clinicians often combine treatment methods. Psychopharmacology is often combined with individual therapy to reduce clients' physical symptoms associated with PTSD; this also makes clients more psychologically available for individual treatment. Other adjunctive treatments are family therapy and group therapy. However, when combining treatments, it is important to introduce one treatment at a time and evaluate its effectiveness before introducing another modality.

For therapists who have expertise in multiple approaches, the clients' needs take precedence over the therapeutic approach utilized. Discussing one's training with clients, especially if a client is seeking a particular model of therapy, is important early in the therapeutic relationship. For example, a client may have unsuccessfully tried cognitive therapy approaches and may be seeking an insight-oriented approach to therapy; being clear about therapeutic expertise helps clients establish clarity about their own needs. Finally, a consideration of cultural factors is a crucial determinant of the approach used and will influence clients' compliance.

Conclusion

Several models of treatment are currently used in trauma therapy. These include cognitive-behavioral therapy, EMDR, stage-oriented, and self-trauma models. Thus far, cognitive-behavioral therapy has been shown to be most successful (Cook et al., 2004; Foa et al., 2000). Other treatments, such as exposure therapy and EMDR, have received widely divergent evaluations from the scientific and professional community. Pharmacotherapy may be a necessary adjunctive treatment for clients who experience intense traumatic symptoms. The counselor can play a salient role in helping clients understand the effects of medications and in ensuring medication compliance.

Since trauma affects all aspects of an individual's functioning, treatment approaches that are holistic, comprehensive, and biopsychosocial are the most rational approaches; this is exemplified by the stage-oriented models proposed by Herman (1997), Briere (1996), and Chu (1998). These models are clinically sequenced according to three primary phases, each with a variety of healing tasks. Symptom reduction and stabilization appears to be the first goals of all three models. After these goals are reached, the client focuses on processing trauma memories and emotions. The final stage focuses on life integration, rehabilitation, and reconnection (Ford et al., 2004). Since these stage models of treatment illustrate a major overlap in terms of goals, areas of focus, and steps in treatment, it is quite likely that counselors can use any them to achieve similar results.

References

Beck, J. S. (1995). *Cognitive therapy: Basics and beyond.* New York: Guilford.

Briere, J. (1996). *Therapy with adults molested as children* (2nd ed.). New York: Springer.

Briere, J. (2002). Treating adult survivors of severe childhood abuse and neglect: Further development of an integrative model. In J. E. B. Myers, L. Berliner, J. Briere, C. T. Hendrix, C. Jenny, & T. Reid (Eds.), *The APSAC handbook on child maltreatment* (2nd ed., pp. 175–203). Thousand Oaks, CA: Sage.

Burton, K. B. (2004). Resilience in the face of psychological trauma. *Psychiatry, 67*(3), 231–234.

Chemtob, C. M., Tolin, D. F., van der Kolk, B. A., & Pitman, R. K. (2000). Eye movement desensitization and reprocessing. In E. B. Foa, T. M. Keane, & M. J. Friedman (Eds.), *Effective treatments for PTSD: Practice guidelines from the International Society for the Traumatic Stress Studies* (pp. 139–154). New York: Guilford.

Chu, J. A. (1998). *Rebuilding shattered lives: The responsible treatment of complex post-traumatic and dissociative disorders.* New York: Wiley.

Cook, J. M., Schnurr, P. P., & Foa, E. B. (2004). Bridging the gap between post-traumatic stress disorder research and clinical practice: The example of exposure therapy. *Psychotherapy: Theory, Research, Practice, Training, 41*(4), 374–387.

Crabtree, S. A.(2005). Medication, healing and resistance in East Malaysia. *Mental Health, Religion and Culture, 8*(1), 17–25.

Demartino, R., Mollica, R. F., & Wilk, V. (1995). Monamine oxidase inhibitors in posttraumatic stress disorder. *Journal of Nervous and Mental Disease, 183,* 510–515.

Devilly, G. J., & Spence, S. H. (1999). The relative efficacy and treatment distress of EMDR and cognitive behavioral trauma treatment protocol in the amelioration of post-traumatic stress disorder. *Journal of Anxiety Disorders, 13*(1–2), 131–157.

Devilly, G. J., Spence, S. H., & Rapee, R. M. (1998). Statistical and reliable change with eye movement desensitization and reprocessing: Treating trauma with a veteran population. *Behavior Therapy, 29, 435–455.*

Foa, E. B., Keane, T. M., & Friedman, M. J. (2000). *Effective treatments for PTSD: Practice guidelines from the International Society for Traumatic Stress Studies.* New York: Guilford.

Foa, E. B., & Meadows, E. A. (1997). Psychosocial treatments for post-traumatic stress disorder. *Annual Review of Psychology, 48,* 449–480.

Foa, E. B., Rothbaum, B. O., Riggs, D. S., & Murdock, T. B. (1991). Treatment of posttraumatic stress disorder in rape victims: A comparison between cognitive-behavioral procedures and counseling. *Journal of Clinical and Consulting Psychology, 59*(5), 715–723.

Foa, E. B., Zoellner, L. A., Feeny, N. C., Hembree, E. A., & Alvarez-Conrad, J. (2002). Does imaginal exposure exacerbate PTSD symptoms? *Journal of Consulting and Clinical Psychology, 70*(4), 1022–1028.

Ford, C. V., & Ebert, M. H. (2004). Remembering trauma. *Journal of Clinical Psychiatry, 65*(11), 1580.

Hembree, E., & Foa, E. B. (2000). PTSD: Psychological factors and psychosocial interventions. *Journal of Clinical Psychiatry, 61*(Supp. 7), 33–39.

Herman, J. L. (1997). *Trauma and recovery.* New York: Basic Books.

Horowitz, M. J. (1986). *Stress-response syndromes* (2nd ed.). New York: Jason Aronson.

Horowitz, M. J. (1997). *Stress response syndromes* (3rd ed.). Northvale, NJ: Jason Aronson.

Horowitz, M. J., Marmar, C., Krupnick, J., Wilner, N., Kaltreider, N., & Wallerstein, R. (1997). *Personality styles and brief psychotherapy* (2nd ed.). New York: Basic Books.

Hyer, L., & Brandsma, J. M. (1997). EMDR minus eye movements equals good psychotherapy. *Journal of Traumatic Stress, 10, 515–522.*

Jaycox, L. H., Zoellner, L., & Foa, E. B. (2002). Cognitive behavior therapy for PTSD and rape survivors. *Psychotherapy and Practice, 58*(8), 891–906.

Keane, T. M., Fairbank, J. A., Caddell, J. M., & Zimmering, R. T. (1989). Implosive (flooding) therapy reduces symptoms of PTSD in Vietnam combat veterans. *Behavior Therapy, 20,* 149–153.

Kohut, H. (1977). *The restoration of the self.* New York: International Universities Press.

Krupnick, J. L. (2002). Brief psychodynamic theory and PTSD. *Journal of Clinical Psychology, 58*(8), 919–932.

Lindy, J. D. (1996). Psychoanalytic psychotherapy of posttraumatic stress disorder: The nature of the relationship. In B. A. van der Kolk, A. C. McFarlane, & L. Weisaeth (Eds.), *Traumatic stress: The effects of overwhelming experience on mind, body and society* (pp. 525–536). New York: Guilford Press.

Lohr, J. M., Lilienfeld, S. O., Tolin, D. F., & Herbert, J. D. (1999). Eye movement desensitization and reprocessing: An analysis of specific versus nonspecific treatment factors. *Journal of Anxiety Disorders, 13,* 185–207.

Lohr, J. M., Tolin, D. F., & Lilienfeld, S. O. (1998). Efficacy of eye movement desensitization and reprocessing: Implications for behavior therapy. *Behavior Therapy, 29,* 123–156.

Marmar, C. R., Weiss, D. S., & Pynoos, R. S. (1995). Dynamic psychotherapy of posttraumatic stress disorder. In M. J. Friedman, D. S. Charney, & A. Y. Deutch (Eds.), *Neurobiological and clinical consequences of stress: From normal adaptation to post traumatic stress disorder* (pp. 495–506). Philadelphia: Lippincott-Raven.

Marotta, S. A. (2000). Best practices for counselors who treat posttraumatic stress disorder. *Journal of Counseling & Development, 78*(4), 492–495.

Maxfield, L., & Hyer, L. (2002). The relationship between efficacy and methodology in studies investigating EMDR treatment of PTSD. *Journal of Clinical Psychology, 58*(1), 23–41.

McNally, R. (1999). EMDR and mesmerism: A comparative historical analysis. *Journal of Anxiety Disorders, 13,* 225–236.

Meichenbaum, D. (1994). *A clinical handbook/practical therapist manual for assessing and treating adults with post-traumatic stress disorder (PTSD).* Waterloo, ON: Institute Press.

Meichenbaum, D. (1997). *Treating post-traumatic disorder.* Chichester, England: Wiley.

Meichenbaum, D. (1977). Dr. Ellis, please stand up. *Counseling Psychologist, 7*(1), 43–44.

Perkins, B. R., & Rouanzoin, C. C. (2002). A critical evaluation of current views regarding eye movement desensitization and reprocessing (EMDR): Clarifying points of confusion. *Journal of Clinical Psychology, 58*(1), 77–97.

Resick, P. A. (2004). *Stress and trauma.* Philadelphia: Taylor Francis.

Schnurr, P. P., Friedman, M. J., & Foy, D. W. (2003). Randomized trial of trauma-focused group therapy for posttraumatic stress disorder: Results from a

Department of Veterans Affairs cooperative study. *Archives of General Psychiatry, 60*(5), 481–489.

Shapiro, F. (1989). Eye movement desensitization: A new treatment for post-traumatic stress disorder. *Journal of Behavioral Experimental Psychiatry, 20,* 211–217.

Shapiro, F. (1995). *Eye movement desensitization and reprocessing: Basic principles, protocols, and procedures.* New York: Guilford Press.

Sutherland, S. M., & Davidson, J. R. T. (1998). Pharmacological treatment of post-traumatic stress disorder. In P. A. Saigh (Ed.), *Posttraumatic stress disorder: A comprehensive text* (pp. 95–115). Boston: Allyn & Bacon.

Sweet, A. (1995). A theoretical perspective on the clinical use of EMDR. *The Behavior Therapist, 18,* 5–6.

van der Kolk, B. A. (1996). Trauma and memory. In B. A. van der Kolk, A. C. McFarlane, & L. Weisaeth (Eds.), *Traumatic stress: The effects of overwhelming experience on mind, body and society* (pp. 279–302). New York: Guilford Press.

van der Kolk, B., McFarlane, A., & van der Hart, O. (1996). A general approach to treatment of posttraumatic stress disorder. In B. A. van der Kolk, A. C. McFarlane, & L. Weisaeth (Eds.), *Traumatic stress: The effects of overwhelming experience on mind, body and society* (pp. 417–440). New York: Guilford Press.

Vargas, M. A., & Davidson, J. (1993). Post-traumatic stress disorder. *Psychopharmacology, 16,* 737–748.

Wolpe, J. (1958). *Psychotherapy by reciprocal inhibition.* Stanford, CA: Stanford University Press.

4

Empowering Interventions

When I began to see Trina, a middle-aged African American woman attending weekly psychotherapy, she presented with several diagnoses of PTSD, Dissociative Identity Disorder, Schizophrenic Disorder and Major Depressive Disorder. To say that I did not know where to start was putting it mildly. My approach was to set these diagnoses aside and to make my own unbiased assessment. A male family member sexually abused Trina when she was a child. The abuse began when she was seven years old and continued until she left home as a teenager. Although Trina informed her mother about the abuse, her mother dismissed it as a fabrication. To complicate her experience of trauma, Trina reported that incidents of severe physical abuse inflicted by both her mother and grandmother occurred on a regular basis. At the age of 45, she still carried scars from these beatings.

It is no wonder that as a child suffering repeated and pervasive abuse she began to "escape" into a "safer world of dissociation" when experiencing distress. Rather than dismantling a defense mechanism that seemed to be working for the client, I engaged with her so that dissociative episodes were not completely disallowed in therapy sessions. For example, there were times when it was clear that Trina "was not in the room"; I would have to repeat my questions and struggle to obtain answers from her. I eventually learned that she "communicated" with "three ladies" who were constantly present in her life, sometimes distracting her focus during a therapy session. Over time, "the ladies" also became part of treatment, and Trina would communicate her ideas, needs, and wishes indirectly *through these imagined women. In turn, I was able to use "the ladies" as vehicles to encourage her to consistently take medication (she was inconsistent in the past), regularly attend therapy, and decrease the frequency of psychiatric hospitalizations from once every three months to zero in two years.*

In this chapter, the practitioner learns how to work within a framework that is ecological and empowering. This process involves viewing clients and their difficulties in the context of their life experiences, culture, social background, and history. Practitioners identify, assess, and utilize clients' strengths and resources to guide them toward resiliency. I believe this approach is the most helpful, respectful, and least pathologizing to use when working with trauma survivors.

Empowerment as a Construct

Over the past decade, some practitioners have embraced psychological empowerment as a way to increase client recovery (Abrahamson, 1996). Empowerment is defined as helping individuals, families, and communities to discover and use the resources and tools within and around them (Kaplan & Girard, 1994). The goal of empowerment is to cultivate individuals' awareness of oppressive tensions and conflicts in their lives, to help them find ways to be free of these constraints (Pinderhughes, 1994).

As a result of working in organizational settings and understanding empowerment from the viewpoint of the individual employee, Menon (1999) defines psychological empowerment as "a cognitive state characterized by a sense of perceived control [and] perceptions of competence" (p. 161). In empirically supported studies conducted in organizational settings, empowerment was found to be an important construct because it offered the potential to positively influence individual change (Liden, Wayne, & Sparrowe, 2000; Spreitzer, Kizilos, & Nason, 1997). Improved job performance and positive organizational commitment were improvements attributed to empowerment.

Additionally, Zimmerman and Warschausky (1998) view empowerment as a key principle in working with individuals with disabilities. These researchers cite the success of the independent living movement as illustrative of the benefits of empowerment. Researchers who study empowerment distinguish between its socio-structural and psychological aspects. It is the psychological aspect of empowerment that is important in trauma therapy.

Therapists focused on empowering clients help them gain mastery and control over destabilizing issues.

Simon (1994) proposes that empowerment is based on five important principles: collaborating with clients, expanding clients' strengths and capacities, focusing on individuals in the context of their environment (family and community), assuming that clients are active agents, and focusing on the historically oppressed and disenfranchised.

In an empowering therapeutic relationship, clients participate in all the decision making that affects their lives. The psychotherapist strives to make client participation a central aspect of treatment. The goal of the therapeutic environment is to provide clients with opportunities to develop and practice skills that allow control and increase competence. In this way, clients become "more self-reliant and self-governing and less controlled by external forces" (Zimmerman & Warschausky, 1998, p. 6). These goals are achieved by encouraging health, adaptation, and competence rather than deficiency and by focusing on wellness rather than illness.

Empowerment insists that people (especially those who experience oppression) must engage in persistent, frequent, and sometimes prolonged efforts to negotiate benefits, resources, and support that may be more easily available to less oppressed groups (Simon, 1994). The empowering therapist recognizes the burden of oppression and the challenges race, class, sexual orientation, and other differences can present. Empowering clients involves increasing and strengthening their personal effectiveness; in doing so, clients are able to take advantage of opportunities while reducing negative outcomes and barriers (Bandura, 1997). The empowered client proactively works to resolve issues and to achieve desired outcomes. This action, according to Webb and Glueckauf (1994), involves attending to the following:

- Self-efficacy is a belief in one's ability to successfully perform desired behaviors in specific contexts.
- Mastery is the belief that one can act on one's environment and achieve a desired outcome.
- When clients perceive themselves as capable of becoming agents for change in charge of individual destiny, then they can act upon the environment to achieve a realistic outcome.
- Control allows the client to take actions that prevent potentially harmful situations and solve problems. It motivates the client to gain knowledge about what reduces empowerment.

In studies where adults were actively involved in setting the goals for their treatment, a two-month follow-up study conducted after the intervention showed that the gains were maintained.

The empowering therapist must be attentive to the power difference inherent in the therapeutic relationship. When these differences arise in a therapy session, the therapist and the client must together reflect on these differences so that both can agree on a mutually acceptable direction. Ultimately, the therapist and client collaborate to determine the pace and content of psychotherapy. By offering survivors choice, control, empathy, and respect, therapy repairs and restores the negative aspects of the traumatic experience and facilitates healing and empowerment.

Important Principles of an Empowering Intervention

Constructivist Perspective

Therapeutic philosophy influences how a therapist defines and approaches a clients difficulties. This, in turn, will influence a clients perception of therapy as well as the progress that is established and sustained through the therapeutic encounter. Although it is important to be aware of the role of trauma in a clients' life, conversely, it is imperative that not all aspects of a client's functioning are viewed through the trauma lens. In overemphasizing the role of trauma, practitioners are likely to make errors in judgment. Additionally, the therapist may use a minimal set of causal explanations and neglect to assess other contributing circumstances and experiences.

Several years ago, I was asked to evaluate a five-year-old child for possible ritual abuse. Tanya was in foster care with her grandmother after Department of Social Services (DSS) substantiated allegations of her mother's parental neglect. After hearing the child describe events that contained suspect elements of "ritual abuse," the case manager made the referral.

The concerned case manager immediately removed the child from the care of her grandmother, where the abuse had allegedly occurred. She placed the girl in a temporary foster home before referring her to me. After seeing the child for several sessions, I began to discuss with Tanya the "events" that were described in her referral. As I explored the reported incidents more carefully, it became clear that the experiences the child described to her case manager did not derive from abuse, but instead from watching "cult-like" movies late at night with her grandmother. Clearly, the case manager had based her allegations on scanty information and had caused unnecessary upheaval in the child's life as a result.

The well-meaning case manager evidently made assumptions about an already disempowered child on very weak evidence. Had she questioned the child a little more carefully, the child could have been spared the additional challenge of transitioning to a foster home.

The empowering therapist defines concepts by taking a constructivist rather than reductionist perspective. Such a therapist does not assume that trauma leads to PTSD in all cultures and individuals. Silove (2000) encourages viewing trauma in broader social terms of safety, grief, injustice, and faith rather than the distinct, clinical terms of PTSD. When the traumatic response is viewed as a disruption in the normal process of stress recovery, the survivor is imbued with hope because the trauma is viewed as less permanent. Such a perspective can direct healing and promote the client's empowerment, safety, mental health, and well-being.

Ecological Perspective

Bronfenbrenner (1979) defines the ecological view of human development as the mutual accommodation between human beings and the immediate environment inhabited by them. The interaction between individuals and their environment is considered bi-directional and reciprocal. For example, while an infant's development is shaped by the parents, family, and community, the infant, in turn, influences the behavior of each of these groups.

Bronfenbrenner (1979) conceptualizes the ecological environment as a complex interconnection of different settings that are both broad and differentiated. The individual's perception of and relationship to the environment are crucial factors in understanding a response. Bronfenbrenner (1979) originally described the ecological environment as four nested systems: *microsystem* (e.g., immediate family, preschool), *mesosystem* (linkages between two or more settings, such as day care and family), *exosystem* (parent's workplace and extended family), and *macrosystem* (customs, values, and laws). Bronfenbrenner (2001) later included the *chronosystem* to incorporate the dimension of time and its effects on human development. For example, the family structure that a child experiences is temporaneously different from the one experienced by the child's parents. Parents who came of age during the Depression may be financially conservative in spending habits, whereas children who were raised during the economic boom of Silicon Valley may have a different perception of financial resources.

Taking an ecological perspective requires observing the interaction of individuals in their surrounding communities: the communities from which they draw meaning, a sense of identity, and a sense of belonging (Harvey, 1996). Community resources are ecological assets while violence and traumatic events threaten an individuals ecological well-being. A community's ability to foster health and resiliency among its members is always handicapped when violence and trauma occur; the effects are even more negative when violence and trauma are recurrent (Norris & Thompson, 1995).

As an ecological threat, violence affects every person it touches. Racism, poverty, and prejudice are examples of ecological pollutants that promote violence and threaten the capacity of communities to promote health. Since these violent and traumatic events affect multiple systems, interventions also require a concordant multi-system perspective. For example, psychosocial healing cannot take place in situations of abject poverty with little access to jobs, education, and health care. Embedded in the macrosystem are the preliminary steps that need to be changed. Only by working holistically and systemically to bridge macrosystems and microsystems can psychosocial healing be achieved (Wessells, 1999).

In contrast, community values, beliefs, and resources can offer protection; they can bulwark the effects of negative stressors to promote resilience in the aftermath of violence. The ecological perspective reminds people that they do not have to always rely on their own resources. A healthy community with adequate resources can sometimes support the recovery of its members. Community outreach and intervention programs can offer havens that enhance the dignity of its members.

Helpers who adopt an ecological perspective assume that mental health issues are influenced by multiple intersecting factors, which include individual characteristics, family, school, community, and other contexts (Bronfenbrenner, 1979; Mowbray, Bybee, & Collins, 1998). Several years ago, Felner, Brand, and DuBois (1995) proposed an ecological-mediational model to explain urban youth adjustment in response to a broad range of contextual factors. In specifically evaluating poverty, this model identified three proximal experiences—school, family, and life stress—that significantly predicted child adjustment.

Adopting an ecological perspective involves evaluating symptoms and problems in both the historical contexts in which they developed and the current contexts that maintain them. Being attentive to these contexts is important because they determine responses to trauma and shape how recovery takes place.

Needs-Based Perspective

In order to empower clients to achieve success, it is important to help them prioritize their needs. According to Maslow (1962), needs are organized hierarchically so that basic needs, such as security or stability, must be satisfied before more abstract needs, such as interpersonal connectedness and self-respect, are met. Traumatic experiences diminish the psychological and physical health of an individual. More specifically, traumatic experiences potentially diminish individuals' attainment of basic needs. According to Maslow (1962), an individual has the following five basic needs:

1. *Physiological.* At the physical level, humans need oxygen, water, sleep, and food in order to survive. Those affected by trauma often report a dysregulation in this area, such as an increase or decrease in sleep and appetite. This first level must be fulfilled in order to continue to the next.

2. *Safety and Security.* The next level in Maslow's hierarchy of needs is safety and security, a level at which trauma victims often report feeling physically unsafe and vulnerable. Hypervigilance is a common reaction to trauma. Survivors are often described as always trying to preempt another attack. Some victims spend much time and energy securing their property by repeatedly locking doors, by installing expensive alarm systems, and by making other elaborate efforts at self-protection.

3. *Social.* According to Maslow, all individuals possess an inherent need to maintain positive relationships with family and friends. When a connection to one of these groups is lost, one's sense of social stability may become fragmented.

4. *Self-Esteem.* Trauma survivors sometimes feel that they have contributed to their trauma. They may harbor the belief that they could have better handled the situation. Such beliefs, together with common reactions of shame and guilt, contribute to decreased self-esteem.

5. *Self-Actualization.* According to Maslow, all human beings strive toward self-actualization and the realization of one's full potential. For trauma survivors, this self-actualizing tendency becomes "frozen," and their development of selfhood is arrested.

When working with trauma survivors, an evaluation of needs is crucial. Several trauma treatment models advocate focusing on the basic needs of safety, stability, and security in the early stages of treatment (Briere, 1997; Chu, 1998; Herman, 1997). To test the validity of Maslow's theory, Eastmond (1998) conducted a study that compared two groups of Bosnian refugees from a concentration camp who were relocated to Sweden. One group was offered temporary employment immediately upon resettlement, while a second group was offered psychotherapy. The individuals who worked immediately fared much better psychosocially than those who were offered psychological help rather than employment. Clearly, attention to the provision of basic needs is an important first step in healing. Similarly, Summerfield (1997) proposes that recovery from trauma does not occur without the rebuilding of social worlds, which may have been decimated. Finally, Kaniasty and Norris (1999) suggest that an individual's psychological reaction to traumatic experiences cannot be understood without considering an individual's functioning prior to and after his or her interaction with the political, cultural, environmental, and social realities of the surrounding ecosystem.

Multicultural Perspective

Counselor cultural sensitivity has received a great deal of attention since the American Counseling Association, the accrediting body of counseling, and the American Psychological Association, the accrediting body of psychology, mandated that curricula include multicultural training for all counselors, especially those who work with culturally diverse populations. All experiences originate from a particular cultural context; the counselor must be attentive to this context and the role that cultural identity plays in a client's life (Sue & Sue, 2003). Three principles are important in cultural competence (Sue, Arredondo, & McDavis, 1992; Weaver 1998):

1. The counselor must be knowledgeable about the cultural group.

2. The counselor must be self-reflective and recognize personal and professional biases.

3. The counselor must be able to integrate multicultural knowledge with practical skills.

While counseling and psychotherapy offer opportunities for psychological healing to most individuals in the U.S., especially those who belong to the dominant culture, not all cultural groups favor this approach to healing. Counselors trained in Western systems of healing should be prudent when working cross-culturally because "the imposition of Western, decontextualized views marginalizes local voices and cultural traditions, disempowers communities, and limits healing" (Wessells, 1999, p. 269). For the most part, people of color have not been involved in the development of the DSM. As a result, the significant role ethnicity and culture play in mental disorders and the development of the diagnostic system has been severely neglected (Velásquez, Johnson, & Brown-Cheatham, 1993).

Since culture influences the duration, course, and outcome of mental illness (Castillo, 1997), it is important for the therapist to ask the client several questions when completing an assessment. Specifically, questions that provide information about the client's worldview are necessary to make an accurate diagnosis and for counseling to be meaningful (Lonner & Ibrahim, 2002). Information about a client's cultural identity and level of acculturation are critical for therapeutic effectiveness. In the U.S., there are multigenerational immigrants, as well as new immigrants, who bring their original cultural perspectives, values, practices, and beliefs to this country. This requires practitioners to learn as much as they can about people in their communities in order to respond more appropriately in any kind of helping context. It is important to remember that culture as a concept is not stagnant but always evolving. Based on different levels of acculturation, family members may hold differing cultural perspectives.

The complexity of cultural differences is illustrated in the example of Japanese *nisei* parents. For cultural reasons, this group of parents had difficulty discussing their internment experience with the next generation, the *sansei*. This reluctance was partly due to tremendous feelings of shame about their experiences and losses. In contrast, their U.S.-born children believed they, along with the rest of the world, had a right to know of these past wrongdoings. The *sansei* were not afraid to talk about the injustices experienced by their parents. Their efforts resulted in an acknowledgment and apology from the U.S. government in 1988.

What clients perceive as the cause of their problems, the effect of these problems on others, and what they hope for in terms of courses of treatment are variables that help inform and guide assessment and treatment. In some cultures, people view problems as being caused by spirit possession or bad luck (Castillo, 1997). In such cases, it may be necessary to collaborate with other colleagues (faith healers, shamans) who clients perceive as helpful.

Socioeconomic status, education, and employment status also contribute to the prevalence of mental disorders. These factors may help explain the variance in the prevalence of mental illnesses among different racial, ethnic, and economically diverse groups. It is difficult to determine how social conditions, such as discrimination and stereotyping, specifically influence disorders featuring paranoid, depressive, and antisocial symptoms. However, low socioeconomic status and education, regardless of ethnicity, has been found to contribute to the onset of certain disorders. Yet, these circumstances become lost as the *DSM* focuses on attributing disorders to individual factors (Kress, Eriksen, Rayle, & Ford, 2005).

Many cultural groups, particularly Native Americans, prefer indigenous healing approaches, such as shamanic healing, instead of Western-based

treatments (Sue & Sue, 2003). Combining indigenous and Western interventions can facilitate a client's involvement and participation in treatment
(Fong, Boyd, & Browne, 1999). Manson (1986) describes three traditional
healing practices that have been incorporated into contemporary
approaches to mental health treatment:

1. *Four circles* is a structural concept of self-understanding that develops from the
   construction of concentric circles of relationships between client, Creator,
   spouse, and nuclear and extended family.

2. *Talking circle* is a forum for expressing thoughts and feelings in an environment of total acceptance, free of time constraints, with the use of sacred objects.

3. *Sweat lodge* is a ritual that emphasizes the relationship between human
   beings and Creation. The ritual provides an opportunity for physical and
   spiritual self-purification.

To be effective, therapists must readily identify and embrace crucial
aspects of a client's culture and recognize the ways the culture explains illness
and wellness (Heinrich, Corbine, & Thomas, 1990). For example, mind,
body, spirit, and nature are perceived as one process in Native culture. A cultural shift on the part of the therapist will prevent counseling from becoming
a cultural compromise for clients who feel caught between cultures. Several
authors provide valuable information for practitioners who work with clients
from different cultural backgrounds (Arredondo & Perez, 2006; Comas-
Diaz, 2005; Sue & Sue, 2003).

Normalization Perspective

Therapists who normalize clients' experience do not condone violence
and abuse but communicate that the abuse was not deserved, nor was it the
clients' fault. This normalization is achieved by therapists repeatedly and
gently rejecting clients' self-derogation and self-blame, consistently using
therapeutic reframing, and introducing clients to psycho-educational literature. Normalization also assures clients that most people would respond
similarly when faced with a traumatic experience.

Solution-Focused Perspective

The foundation of a solution-oriented approach rests on emphasizing
strengths and solutions rather than problems and dysfunction (Corcoran,
1997). Solution-focused therapy is a systemic, strengths-based, collaborative
approach to supporting clients in therapy (Dermer, Hemesath, & Russell,
1998). Since the systems a client inhabits are interconnected, change in one

domain influences other domains. Thus, even modest changes in one area can effect substantial change overall. Solution-focused therapy is based on the assumption that change is constant; it emphasizes solutions and possibilities, which facilitate change. This therapeutic approach emphasizes that there are always new ways to view problems. Because there is not "one right way" to view things, one does not need to know a lot about a problem in order to solve it (De Shazer, 1985). In addition, individuals and families are competent to choose their goals and solutions, which can evolve through conversation and interaction with others. Solution-focused therapists achieve change by encouraging clients to adjust their own behavior instead of blaming their problems on others (Hudson & O'Hanlon, 1991). This model is criticized for its emphasis on behavior rather than insight (Kiser, Piercy, & Lipchik, 1993). Although solution-focused therapists acknowledge that insight and emotion are important, behavioral change receives more attention. Interventions concentrate on clients' actions rather than the cognitive and emotional domains that underlie them (Dermer et al., 1998). Solution-focused therapy focuses on the internal locus of control of clients, based on the belief that people have strengths and areas of expertise. Although this can be empowering for clients, it also risks obscuring power differences between clients and therapists. In addition, there are no mechanisms within the framework of solution-focused therapy to deal with issues of power, nor are these issues overtly discussed in the model. However, the emphasis on relieving symptoms, highlighting strengths, and assuming competency makes solution-focused therapy a useful model of treatment.

Strengths-Based Perspective

Dennis Saleebey (2006), a proponent of the strengths-based perspective, points out that the mental health field has overly focused on "the impediments and injuries, the deficits and desolation, rather than people's compensating and transformative responses to challenges" (p. 77). Recognizing strength in clients involves giving credence to the way clients experience and construct their social realities. It also involves an acknowledgment of the unique and distinctive social circumstances of each client. According to Saleebey, there are other important principles that guide the strengths-based perspective:

- The therapist enters the client's life-world authentically and respectfully by developing a relationship that affirms the client's goals and places the client's needs at the core.
- Genuine dialogue, in which clients are asked what they would like to see happen in therapy, overtly conveys the belief that clients have strengths, resources, and abilities to improve the quality of their lives.

- Forming positive expectations of clients is the basis of a strengths-based perspective. In recent years, positive psychology has emphasized the importance of identifying client strengths rather than focusing on pathology.
- The therapist helps clients participate more fully in their communities.
- The therapist identifies clients' resources and strengths by simply identifying client interests, talents, and competencies.
- The therapist learns from clients by listening carefully to their narratives and the way they construct their social realities. An appreciation of context and construction acknowledges the unique social situation of each client.

In a review of studies that investigated constructive change in psychotherapy, Assay and Lambert (1999) concluded that strengths and resources within the individual, the family, and the environment account for the greatest change in individuals. The empowerment model of trauma treatment is derived from the strengths-based perspective. A strengths-based model assumes that clients are capable of solving their own problems; the counselor perceives the client as the source of solutions and the expert in what works best for him or her (Peterson & Nisenholz, 1999). Therefore, early in therapy the counselor identifies situations from the client's past when the client successfully solved problems. These proven examples of the client's past successes are later used to encourage, motivate, and strengthen the client when new problems occur. When these experiences of past successes are depleted, skill building becomes the new focus of treatment (Corcoran, 2005). The therapist collaborates with the client to teach these skills. Skills are always relevant to the client's unique circumstances, and the therapist holds client self-determination as the guiding principle. The following are examples of skills that can be developed:

- Self-reflection
- Problem solving and decision making
- Effective communication
- Authentic listening

Therapists who adopt a strengths-based perspective define the helping relationship as purposeful, reciprocal, friendly, trusting, and empowering (Rapp, 1999).

The strengths-based perspective is based on Adlerian psychology and regards people as capable of changing their own lives (Dinkmeyer & Sperry, 2000; Fall, Holden, & Marquis, 2004). It is not the events and circumstances of clients' lives that are important, but the behavioral choices that individuals make (Fall et al., 2004). The focus on a client's strengths and resources places this model in the category of resiliency-based rather than deficit-based treatment. In the former, competence and positive developmental outcomes are identified and promoted (Masten & Coatsworth, 1998). By drawing on inner resources and acting independently, the client soon learns the therapeutic environment is a collaborative one that focuses on positive change. As Saleebey (1996) contends, "capitalizing on a client's resources, talents, knowledge, and motivation" becomes an opportunity to obtain "environmental collateral" that can be used to promote the client's recovery (p. 302). As a success-oriented model, strengths-based therapy involves small and incremental changes; client self-exploration is done carefully, and the assumption of the client as authority is always paramount.

The strengths-based perspective reframes reality and develops a language of possibility and opportunity for the client. Identifying a client's strengths expands choices and increases the possibility of growth and change (Saleebey, 1996). The empowered client perceives himself or herself as possessing sufficient resources to manage challenges and meaningfully change his or her life direction.

An Empowering Model of Individual Intervention

The empowering model borrows from relational, cognitive-behavioral, and solution-focused therapies and is framed by an ecological, empowering, and multicultural perspective. The focus is on exploring the role of ecological and multicultural factors as shared meaning is established and a collaborative relationship develops between therapist and client. Promoting empowerment means believing that clients are capable of making their own choices and decisions. The empowering therapist helps clients identify their individual and community strengths and resources while simultaneously encouraging clients to articulate their issues and the solutions they perceive as holding positive outcomes.

Collaboration begins with clients (rather than therapists) defining traumatic experiences and the challenges these experiences present in their lives. Subjective questions focus on understanding clients' trauma histories, rather than therapists making a decision on their own regarding clients' functioning. Much of professional practice as it is currently conducted shifts the focus of attention from oppressive social systems to individual deficits (Dietz, 2001). A collaborative client-therapist relationship avoids such pitfalls. The therapist who attempts to conceptualize client issues from a client-centered perspective has a better understanding of the client, one that usually includes the client's ecological environment.

This model has emerged from many years of doing community and crisis work. Structurally, each therapy session begins with the client and counselor operating within a cognitive phase before proceeding to an affective phase that includes a deeper processing of emotional material. Before the therapy session is concluded, the therapist returns to the cognitive phase and engages in a discussion of how to manage the time until the next therapy session. The advantage of such a structured and predictable format is that it offers a client safety and control while making the therapeutic relationship less mysterious (see Figure 4.1).

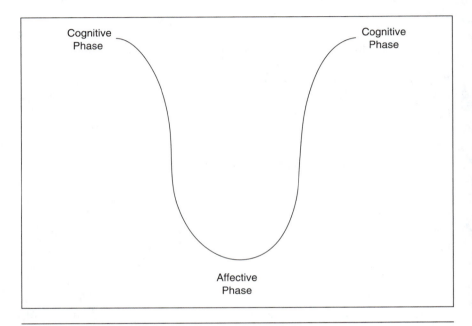

Figure 4.1   Empowering Intervention Model

Initial Cognitive Phase

Check In. Each session begins with the therapist "checking in" with the client to acquire factual information regarding the client's functioning. The first interview with a client may run longer than a usual session as the therapist seeks to obtain as much background information as possible. Guidelines about confidentiality and the pacing of future sessions are discussed.

Setting an Agenda. A level of organization and structure for both the client and the therapist is accomplished by beginning each session with an agenda. It also avoids what I regard as "doorknob" disclosures, in which the client presents material that may require extensive discussion just as the session is about to end. The following case example, taken from the early years of my career, describes a client who had a tendency to make these doorknob statements.

Rhonda entered therapy as a result of an allegation that she had physically abused her two-year-old son in a shopping mall. Her commitment to therapy was weak at best. However, she appeared to be making tentative progress in discussing her past as well as current abusive relationships. After six sessions, her progress remained tentative and minimal. As she was about to leave a session one afternoon, Rhonda calmly told me that she had obtained a restraining order against her abusive boyfriend. We had just spent an entire session exploring the academic difficulties of her older son and her challenges in addressing these difficulties with his teacher. Upon realizing Rhonda's doorknob pattern, it became important to set an agenda with Rhonda for future sessions. Setting an agenda can be a reassuring strategy to encourage clients like Rhonda who are anxious, emotionally distressed, and unable to effectively delineate between urgent and less urgent issues.

Although the client always has the freedom to specify the issues he or she considers require immediate attention, the therapist and client collaborate to negotiate the agenda. It is the therapist's responsibility to keep the client's larger treatment goals in mind when collaborating with the client to ensure that agenda items lead toward these goals. Once the client has an opportunity to check in and negotiate an agenda with the therapist, treatment can proceed to affective processing of clinical material.

Affective Processing

Using open-ended questions, the therapist gently guides the client to a deeper exploration of affective functioning. During this phase, the therapist can focus on a particular therapy technique. For example, with a client who has negative beliefs and irrational fears that the trauma will recur, cognitive restructuring may be a useful technique to employ. The client must first gain awareness of these beliefs and recognize distortions. The bulk of a session (and additional sessions, if necessary) focuses on exploring the client's awareness (or lack thereof) of these beliefs. When the client is ready, the therapist helps the client replace the distortions with more accurate beliefs.

If memory exploration is part of treatment, the safety, trust, and connection inherent in a positive therapeutic relationship can provide necessary client support as these painful memories are accessed. Traumatic memories are often incomplete. Although it is important to fully recall traumatic memories for complete recovery to occur, the counselor should remain cautious throughout this process and place client safety as most important. Furthermore, the counselor should consider that escaping overwhelming traumatic memories through dissociation may be adaptive for some clients because this defense protects a vulnerable ego from dissolution (Burton, 2004). The client's psychological readiness, sense of control, and competence dictates when and how dissociated memories are explored. After memory exploration, the remaining 10 to 15 minutes of the session reverts to the cognitive phase of treatment.

Final Cognitive Phase

The focus in this phase is on self-care and the assignment of a homework activity. Predictions are made and planning is established to anticipate what will occur between therapy sessions. During this final phase, the therapist reviews and summarizes the current session and briefly examines how the current session fits into the context of the overall treatment goals. The concept of self-care is introduced during a client's initial session, and the concept is reviewed in ongoing sessions. If a therapist introduces self-care strategies for the first time, enough time should be set aside to fully explain and practice these strategies in session. Self-care techniques always relate to a client's particular traumatic reaction; the techniques are tailored to fit the client's comfort level.

Self-Care Techniques

- Grounding techniques are useful for clients who use dissociation to cope with their traumatic memories. The purpose of these techniques is to help clients "ground," or stabilize themselves, and get in touch with their bodies and surroundings. One of the fastest ways to ground, or to bring clients back from the past mentally, is to shock their bodies by placing an ice cube in their hands. Asking them to drink cold water, or splash it on their face, or suggesting that they take a shower are other methods that ground clients in the present.
- Distraction techniques help clients control repetitive flashbacks and engage in more absorbing activities. The goal is to have clients redirect the focus of their attention. Watching television, taking a walk, and calling or visiting a friend are examples of distracting activities.

- Self-induced relaxation techniques can be used to calm anxious clients. Guided imagery can be effective in soothing clients who feel out of control by refocusing thoughts and emotions. This technique involves asking clients to first close their eyes and take a few deep diaphragmatic breaths, in through their noses and out through their mouths (see Appendix VI). Second, clients are asked to think of a place that is safe and imagine themselves being there. They are directed to picture as much detail as possible. The more details that are imagined, the greater the chance of the guided imagery relaxing the individual. The possibilities stretch as far as imagination takes them. An example of a guided imagery scene is the following: Imagine walking along the shore of the ocean. Feel the warm sand squish between your toes. Hear the waves crash and the seagulls rush past you as you walk toward the water. Just as a wave crashes by your ankles, you feel the cool water rush over your feet and gush between your toes. Clients use their imagination to create similar scenes as they consider what feels safe to them.

- Positive self-talk is a self-supporting and self-soothing technique that assists clients who have a diminished sense of self-reference. When feeling distressed, clients recall positive statements that make them feel better about themselves. Clients who may have difficulty remembering positive statements can generate a list of positive statements when feeling more stable and less distressed.

- Journal writing helps clients concretize thoughts and emotions. Writing thoughts down on paper reduces their power and ability to evoke intense emotions that distract clients. When clients experience flashbacks or experience nightmares of traumatic memories, writing down everything they remember can be useful. Clients should write exactly what they think and feel, leaving nothing out no matter how "improper" or "negative" it may appear. The objective is to record every emotion on paper. One of the advantages of journal writing is that the written material remains the property of clients and does not have to be edited.

Homework

Finally, I find it helpful to assign a client a small task to occupy the time between sessions. Such a task can be an effective way for clients to practice new behaviors and to keep a record of their activities (Peterson & Nisenholz, 1999). To avoid homework becoming a source of conflict or frustration between the therapist and client, it should be assigned with discretion. The therapist should stay alert to client cues; if a client displays resistance to completing a homework activity, it should be postponed or abandoned altogether. Depending on the magnitude of the task, enough time should be allocated during a session to clearly outline the task so the client feels competent to execute it. The following vignette illustrates how a homework exercise can be used effectively to empower a client toward healing (see also Appendix V).

Linda was in her third month of recovery from a cocaine addiction that had lasted 18 years. She was living in a sober home for women when she engaged in individual therapy. One of her major presenting symptoms was insomnia. She had difficulty falling asleep. She would only manage to get four hours of sleep at most before she would wake up again. In an exploratory discussion, I learned that ruminations of past traumatic memories kept her awake: her mother stabbing an abusive boyfriend, her father beating her brother "within an inch of his life," violent fights with women "on the street," and an undisclosed number of sexual assaults and rapes.

Linda felt a failure as an adult. She was irritable and impatient with her sobriety. It became clear that Linda had to find a way to contain her thoughts so that they did not dominate her life. Linda's homework was to write down these memories and bring them to her next session. In the subsequent weeks, a notebook began to brim with memories. Additionally, we made a little paper origami box where she stored the information. The box was kept in my office, and she would choose a page from the box and make it the focus of clinical discussion. In this way, she maintained control over her traumatic memories; unsurprisingly, her distressing thoughts decreased dramatically after participating in this type of therapy.

Each individual session follows a format that initially focuses on cognitive issues before transitioning to a discussion of affective issues. The session concludes by refocusing on cognitive issues. In addition, the client's overall treatment takes a similar inverted bell shape (see Figure 4.1). During the first stage of therapy, the cognitive stage, sessions focus on gathering information about the client's background, history, presenting problems, resources, and strengths. After these sessions, client-therapist rapport and a working relationship will have been established. At this point, the client can embark on the next stage of treatment, the affective stage, which involves a deeper exploration of affective issues. This stage can vary in duration, depending on how much time the client may need to resolve or integrate his or her traumatic issues. A client's financial resources will also determine the length of this stage. Once a termination date has been established, the therapist moves toward the final stage of treatment, the cognitive stage, which focuses on summarizing the overall treatment, reviewing gains and self-care strategies, and exploring termination issues.

Conclusion

Trauma can be conceptualized as an open wound in the human psyche. If untreated, it carries the potential to fester, causing long-term problems for individuals. The helplessness and fear a traumatic experience often engenders can change a client's internal world, tainting his or her future with feelings of uncertainty, anxiety, and despair. Despite treatment, when a client experiences a new traumatic event or old traumas are retriggered, there is a risk that past scars will manifest themselves. Clients who are empowered to heal, however, develop effective coping skills and resilient capacities. They are able to take control of their lives in the face of new challenges. Psychological scars never diminish entirely, but the empowered client learns how to function effectively in spite of them.

A model of therapy that places the sociocultural experience of a client at the core views the clinical relationship as an intersubjective process. The emphasis is on the co-construction of meaning between therapist and client. Strengths-based (rather than problem-based) therapy is the most effective way to invest in the healing and recovery of a survivor of trauma.

References

Abrahamson, E. (1996). Management fashion. *Academy of Management Review, 21,* 254–285.

American Psychological Association. (2003). Guidelines for multicultural education, training, research, practice, and organizational change for psychologists. *American Psychologist, 58,* 377–402.

Arredondo, P., & Perez, P. (2006). Historical perspectives on the multicultural guidelines and contemporary practice. *Professional Psychology: Research and Practice, 37*(1), 1–5.

Assay, T. P., & Lambert, M. J. (1999). The empirical case for the common factors in therapy: Qualitative findings. In M. A. Hubble, B. L. Duncan, & S. D. Miller (Eds.), *The heart and soul of change: What works in therapy* (pp. 33–56). Washington, DC: APA Press.

Bandura, A. (1997). *Self-efficacy: The exercise of control.* New York: W. H. Freeman.

Briere, J. (1997). *Psychological assessment of adult posttraumatic states.* Washington, DC: American Psychological Association.

Bronfenbrenner, U. (1979). *The ecology of human development experiments by nature and design.* Cambridge, MA: Harvard University Press.

Bronfenbrenner, U. (2001). Developmental ecology through space and time: A future perspective. In P. Moen, G. H. Elder, Jr., & K. Luscher (Eds.), *Examining lives in context: Perspectives on the ecology of human development* (pp. 619–647). Washington, DC: American Psychological Association.

Burton, K. B. (2004). Resilience in the face of psychological trauma. *Psychiatry, 67*(3), 231–234.

Castillo, R. J. (1997). *Culture and mental illness: A client-centered approach.* Pacific Grove, CA: Brooks Cole.

Chu, J. A. (1998). *Rebuilding shattered lives: The responsible treatment of complex post-traumatic and dissociative disorders.* New York: Wiley.

Comas-Díaz, L. (2005). Becoming a multicultural psychotherapist: The confluence of culture, ethnicity, and gender. *Journal of Clinical Psychology, 61*(8), 973–981.

Corcoran, J. (1997). A solution-oriented approach to working with juvenile offenders. *Child and Adolescent Social Work Journal, 14*(4), 277–288.

Corcoran, J. (2005). *Building strengths and skills: A collaborative approach to working with clients.* New York: Oxford University Press.

Dermer, S. B., Hemesath, C. W., & Russell, C. S. (1998). A feminist critique of solution-focused therapy. *The American Journal of Family Therapy, 26,* 239–250.

De Shazer, S. (1985). *Keys to solutions in brief therapy.* New York: W. W. Norton.

Dietz, C. (2001). Working with lesbian, gay, bisexual, and transgendered abuse survivors. *Journal of Progressive Human Services, 12*(2), 27–49.

Dinkmeyer, D., & Sperry, L. (2000). *Counseling and psychotherapy. An integrated, individual psychology approach* (3rd ed.). Englewood Cliffs, NJ: Prentice-Hall.

Eastmond, M. (1998). Nationalist discourses and the construction of difference: Bosnian Muslims in Sweden. *Journal of Refugee Studies, 11*(2), 161–181.

Fall, K. A., Holden, J. M., & Marquis, A. (2004). *Theoretical models of counseling and psychotherapy.* New York: Brunner-Routledge.

Felner, R. D., Brand, S., & DuBois, D. L. (1995). Socioeconomic disadvantage, proximal environmental experiences, and socioemotional and academic adjustment in early adolescence: Investigation of a mediated effects model. *Child Development, 66*(3), 774–792.

Fong, R., Boyd, C., & Browne, C. (1999). The Gandhi technique: A biculturalization approach for empowering Asian and Pacific Islander families. *Journal of Multicultural Social Work, 7,* 95–110.

Harvey, M. (1996). An ecological view of psychological trauma and trauma recovery. *Journal of Traumatic Stress, 9*(1), 3–23.

Heinrich, R. K., Corbine, J. L., & Thomas, K. R. (1990). Counseling Native Americans. *Journal of Counseling & Development, 69,* 128–133.

Herman, J. L. (1997). *Trauma and recovery.* New York: Basic Books.

Hudson, P. O., & O'Hanlon, W. H. (1991). *Rewriting love stories: Brief marital therapy.* New York: W. W. Norton.

Kaniasty, K., & Norris, F. (1999). The experience of disaster: Individuals and communities sharing trauma. In R. Grist & B. Lubin (Eds.), *Response to disaster: Psychosocial, community and ecological approaches* (pp. 25–62). Philadelphia, PA: Brunner/Mazel.

Kaplan, L., & Girard, J. L. (1994). *Strengthening high-risk families: A handbook for practitioners.* New York: Lexington Books.

Kiser, J. K., Piercy, F. P., & Lipchik, E. (1993). The integration of emotion in solution-focused therapy. *Journal of Marital and Family Therapy, 19*, 233–242.

Kress, V. E. W., Eriksen, K. P., Rayle, A. D., & Ford, S. (2005). The DSM-IV-TR and culture: Considerations for counselors. *Journal of Counseling & Development, 83*, 97–103.

Liden, R. C., Wayne, S. J., & Sparrowe, R. T. (2000). An examination of the mediating role of psychological empowerment on the relations between the job, interpersonal relationships, and work outcomes. *Journal of Applied Psychology, 85*(3), 407–416.

Lonner, W. J., & Ibrahim, A. A. (2002). Appraisal and assessment in cross-cultural counseling. In P. B. Pedersen, J. G. Draguns, W. L. Lonner, & J. E. Trimble (Eds.), *Counseling across cultures* (5th ed., pp. 355–379). Thousand Oaks, CA: Sage.

Manson, S. M. (1986). Recent advances in American Indian mental health research: Implications for clinical research and training. In M. R. Miranda & H. H. L. Kitano (Eds.), *Mental health research and practice in minority communities: Development of culturally sensitive training programs* (pp. 51–89). Rockville, MD: NIMH.

Maslow A. H. (1962). *Toward a psychology of being*. Princeton, NJ: Van Nostrand.

Masten, A., & Coatsworth, D. (1998). The development of competence in favorable and unfavorable environments. *American Psychologist, 53*, 205–220.

Menon, S. T. (1999). Psychological empowerment: Definition, measurement and validation. *Canadian Journal of Behavioral Science, 31*(3), 161–164.

Mowbray, C. T., Bybee, D., & Collins, M. E. (1998). Optimizing evaluation quality and utility under resource constraints. *Evaluation and Program Planning, 21*(1), 59–71.

Norris, F., & Thompson, M. P. (1995). Applying community psychology to the prevention of trauma and traumatic life events. In J. Freedy & S. Hobfoll (Eds.), *Traumatic stress: From theory to practice*. New York: Plenum Press.

Peterson, J. V., & Nisenholz, B. (1999). *Orientation to counseling*. Boston: Allyn & Bacon.

Pinderhughes, E. (1994). Empowerment as an intervention goal: Early ideas. In L. Gutierrez & P. Nurius (Eds.), *Education and research for empowerment practice* (pp. 17–31). Seattle: University of Washington School of Social Work, Center for Policy and Practice Research.

Rapp, R. C. (2006). Strengths-based case management: Enhancing treatment for persons with substance abuse problems. In D. Saleebey (Ed.), *The strengths perspective in social work practice* (4th ed., pp. 128–147). Boston: Allyn & Bacon.

Saleebey, D. (1996). The strengths perspective in social work practice. *Social Work, 41*(3), 296–306.

Saleebey, D. (Ed.). (2006). *The strengths perspective in social work practice* (4th ed.). Boston: Allyn & Bacon.

Silove, D. (2000). A conceptual framework for mass trauma: Implications for adaptation, intervention and debriefing. In B. Raphael & J. Wilson (Eds.), *Psychological debriefing: Theory, practice and evidence* (pp. 337–350.). New York: Cambridge University Press.

Simon, B. L. (1994). *The empowerment tradition in American social work.* New York: Columbia University Press.

Spreitzer, G. M., Kizilos, M. A., & Nason, S. W. (1997). A dimensional analysis of the relationship between psychological empowerment and effectiveness, satisfaction, and strain. *Journal of Management, 23,* 679–704.

Sue, D. W., Arredondo, P., & McDavis, R. J. (1992). Multicultural counseling competencies and standards: A call to the profession. *Journal of Multicultural Counseling and Development, 20*(2), 64–88.

Sue, D. W., & Sue, D. (2003). *Counseling the culturally different: Theory and practice* (4th ed.). New York: Wiley.

Summerfield, D. (1997). The impact of war and atrocity on civilian populations. In D. Black, M. Newman, J. Harris-Hendriks, & G. Mezey (Eds.), *Psychological trauma: A developmental approach* (pp. 148–156). London: Gaskell.

Velásquez, R. J., Johnson, R., & Brown-Cheatham, M. (1993). Teaching counselors to use the DSM-IIIR with ethnic minority clients: A paradigm. *Counselor Education and Supervision, 32*(4), 323–331.

Weaver, H. N. (1998). Indigenous people in a multicultural society: Unique issues for human services. *Social Work, 43*(3), 203–211.

Webb, P. M., & Glueckauf, R. L. (1994). The effects of direct involvement in goal setting on rehabilitation outcome for persons with traumatic brain injury. *Rehabilitation Psychology, 39,* 179–188.

Wessells, M. G. (1999). Culture, power and community: Intercultural approaches to psychosocial assistance and healing. In K. Nader, N. Dubrow, & B. H. Stamm (Eds.), *Honoring differences: Cultural issues in the treatment of trauma and loss* (pp. 267–280). Philadelphia: Brunner/Mazel.

Zimmerman, M. A., & Warschausky, S. (1998). Empowerment theory for rehabilitation research: Conceptual and methodological issues. *Rehabilitation Psychology, 43*(1), 3–16.

5

Crisis Interventions

Sherry was a sophomore at an Ivy League institution when she committed suicide. Her parents, who amidst great hardship had emigrated from China, were devastated by their loss. They could not understand what they had done wrong and continued to blame themselves for the death of their daughter. With encouragement from Sherry's college counselor, the family eventually agreed to attend family counseling, although they did not have much confidence that it would help. Working from an empowering and ecological framework, the therapist's encouragement was successful.

The family identified what they had done well for their children, the social stressors prevalent in their upper-middle-class suburb, and ways to support their surviving children. Receiving information about the progression of grief reactions and what they could anticipate in the future helped the family feel that they could conquer a hopeless situation. Eventually, the parents were willing to attend a suicide survivors' group in a neighboring community to address their family trauma. They were determined to be better parents to their surviving children.

This chapter reviews effective principles and guidelines in crisis intervention. Detailed procedural steps inform the reader how to act immediately, make appropriate assessments of crises, conduct successful interventions, and make referrals. Different models of crisis intervention that assess the severity of a crisis from a multidimensional perspective are explored.

Finally, the chapter discusses how to assess suicidal ideation, how to determine suicidal intent, and how to work with survivor families.

Definition

Caplan (1964) initially defined a crisis as occurring when individuals are confronted with problems that cannot be solved. These irresolvable issues result in an increase in tension, signs of anxiety, a subsequent state of emotional unrest, and an inability to function for extended periods. James and Gilliland (2005) define crises as events or situations perceived as intolerably difficult that exceed an individual's available resources and coping mechanisms. Similarly, Roberts (2000) defines a crisis as "a period of psychological disequilibrium, experienced as a result of a hazardous event or situation that constitutes a significant problem that cannot be remedied by using familiar coping strategies" (p. 7). The Chinese translation of the word "crisis" consists of two separate characters, which paradoxically mean danger and opportunity (Greene, Lee, Trask, & Rheinscheld, 2000). Crisis intervention thus provides opportunities for clients to learn new coping skills while identifying, mobilizing, and enhancing those they already possess.

The following are characteristics of crisis events:

- The event precipitating the crisis is perceived as threatening.
- There is an apparent inability to modify or reduce the impact of stressful events.
- There is increased fear, tension, and/or confusion.
- There is a high level of subjective discomfort.
- A state of disequilibrium is followed by rapid transition to an active state of crisis.

The following are examples of crises:

- An accident (automobile or in home)
- Death/loss of a loved one
- Natural disaster
- Physical illness (self or significant other)
- Divorce/separation
- Unemployment
- Unexpected pregnancy
- Financial difficulties

The difficulty in discriminating whether the events listed above constitute crises or traumas may be obvious. A crisis is distinguished from a trauma by timing and by how quickly it is resolved. Most crises develop into traumas; conversely, most traumas begin as crises. Socioeconomic status, availability of emotional support, and the nature of the crisis will dictate how soon the individual can resolve it and resume regular functioning. In the aftermath of Hurricane Katrina in September, 2005, two individuals I worked with epitomized the differences between a crisis and a trauma:

Amelia had moved from New York City to New Orleans to seek employment. She was unable to evacuate the city before the hurricane hit. She temporarily stayed at the shelter where I worked as a disaster responder. Although Amelia was deeply affected by the pain and suffering that surrounded her, she had a clear plan of action. She was resolved to return closer to her family and chalk up her material losses in New Orleans to fate. Once her check came in from the American Red Cross, Amelia rented a car and drove to her home state. Her former company assured her that a new job awaited her. Amelia's crisis would soon be over.

Kenny also found himself at the shelter where I worked. However, Kenny, in contrast to Amelia, had lost everything including his childhood home, a parent and a sibling, and his pet dog. Kenny sat on the edge of his cot for hours, wearing a forlorn countenance as he tried to make sense of what had happened. He was overwhelmed and unclear about the direction his life would take in the following few months. He also anticipated the check from the American Red Cross, though he already knew that it was not going to entirely solve his problems. In the face of this crisis, he displayed complete hopelessness and helplessness, and a crisis therefore became a trauma for him.

Background on Crisis

Presumably, crises have always occurred, yet the movement to help individuals in crisis did not begin until 1906, when a suicide prevention center called the National Save a Life League was established in New York City. Several years later, the catalyst for contemporary conceptualization of crisis work occurred when Lindemann (1944) and his colleagues from the Massachusetts General Hospital introduced the concepts of crisis reactions and intervention in the aftermath of the Coconut Grove fire. This fire occurred in a nightclub in Boston in 1943. The concepts are based on the acute and delayed reactions of the fire's survivors and the family members of its victims.

Expanding on Lindemann's work, Caplan (1961) describes the four stages of a crisis reaction as follows:

1. An initial rise in tension occurs in response to an event.
2. Increased tension disrupts daily living.
3. Unresolved tension results in depression.
4. Failure to resolve the crisis may result in a psychological breakdown.

In the past 10 years, crisis intervention surged as a specialized field. The focus on this field began with the rise in school and community violence as well as the higher frequency of natural and national disasters. The trademark of a crisis is its unpredictability: The crisis itself is unpredictable, and its ability to affect people is unpredictable as well. Crises happen suddenly, unexpectedly, often to arbitrarily chosen victims. A full understanding of the cultural context in which the crisis occurred will help the responder comprehend how the affected community perceives it. This understanding will influence and inform the design of an appropriate intervention.

Currently, more people are aware that attending to crisis reactions immediately potentially prevents them from developing into serious psychological problems. When crises occur, this awareness motivates administrators to invite crisis responders to the workplace on a more regular basis (Thompson, Smith, & Bybee, 2005). Through the support of Employee Assistance Programs, employers appropriately support employee mental health needs; thus, crisis intervention can prevent the development of serious mental disorders.

Why Crisis Work?

The common motivation for doing crisis work, whether a person is a trained professional or a volunteer, is the need to help and care for others. Unfortunately, this altruistic motivation is not enough. Appropriate training is crucial and can determine whether a crisis worker will become a help or a hindrance to a community in crisis. In addition to altruism, the following are often-cited reasons for doing crisis work:

- Recognition that such work is important in ensuring the survival of the species
- Gratification that comes from helping others
- Bearing witness to others' experience
- Personal and professional validation
- Community and personal connections that result from crisis
- Desire to make a difference

Crisis Intervention Guidelines

Every crisis is different, but all crises require immediate intervention to interrupt and reduce crisis reactions and restore affected individuals to precrisis functioning. Crisis interventions provide victims with emotional first aid targeted to the particular circumstances of the crisis (Rosenbluh, 1981). Several guiding principles are involved in crisis intervention; some key principles are outlined below (Shapiro & Koocher, 1996).

- Making an accurate assessment is the most critical aspect of a crisis response because it guides the intervention. A wrong decision in response to a crisis can be potentially lethal. Although situations may be similar, each person is unique; therefore, care must be exercised to avoid overgeneralizing.

- The ability to think quickly and creatively is crucial. People under crisis sometimes develop tunnel vision or are unable to see options and possibilities. The crisis responder must maintain an open mind in order to help explore options and solve problems in an empowering manner with those affected. People in crisis already feel out of control; when opportunities to restore control present themselves, they should be grasped quickly.

- The responder must be able to stay calm and collected. Crisis work is not suitable for everyone. It requires the ability to maintain empathy while simultaneously avoiding subjective involvement in the crisis.

- Crisis intervention is always short term and involves establishing specific goals regarding specific behaviors that can be achieved within a short time frame. For example, in response to a suicidal client, a therapist may increase the frequency of therapy sessions until the client's ideation subsides. Management, rather than resolution, is the objective of crisis interventions.

- Crisis intervention is not process-oriented. It is action-oriented and situation-focused (Aguilera, 1998; Pollin, 1995). Crisis interventions prepare clients to manage the sequelae of a specific event. Therapists help clients recognize an event's impact and anticipate its emotional and behavioral consequences. Furthermore, clients learn to identify coping skills, resources, and support available to them. They learn to formulate a safety plan in an effort to cope with the current and anticipated challenges the event presents.

- A crisis is characterized by loss of control and safety. This loss makes it incumbent on the helper to focus on restoring power and control in the client's internal and external environment (Yassen & Harvey, 1998).

- The goal is not to ask exploratory questions, but rather to focus on the present ("here and now"). The crisis responder merely acts as an emotional support at a time when self-direction may be impossible (Greenstone & Leviton, 2002). Therapists do not attempt to change clients, but serve as catalysts for clients' discovery of their own resources, which they can then use to accomplish their goals (Saleebey, 1997).

- Since crisis intervention is the first intervention that a client may encounter after a calamity, the goal is always to reestablish immediate coping skills, provide support, and restore pre-crisis functioning.
- Crisis intervention requires responders to possess familiarity with the work setting. The ability to direct people to local shelters and other safe places and to offer help in locating loved ones is crucial in this work.
- Viewing the client holistically, rather than isolating the individual's emotional and cognitive functioning, will provide insight into the resources and support available to the victim.
- A solid training in crisis intervention (with a focus on identifying suicidal and homicidal ideation) as well as experience in counseling is indispensable.

Finally, although crises are universal and affect people from all cultures, culture mediates how individuals and communities express crisis reactions and how they ask for and accept help (Dykeman, 2005). Since culture defines individuals' pathways to healthy adjustment and how they reconstruct their lives after a crisis, the crisis responder has to be multiculturally competent.

Multicultural Competence

Self-knowledge and awareness of one's cultural biases are integral to effect culturally appropriate interventions. Flexibility and openness in using alternative strategies better suited to the cultural background of victims is an asset in responding to crisis. The responder has to be able to consider the worldview of the client to prevent making erroneous interpretations, judgments, and conclusions, which cause clients further harm (Arredondo, 1999; Sue & Sue, 1999).

A crisis can be culturally universal or culturally specific. For example, the mudslides in California and the tsunami in Asia were universal because either could happen to anyone, and neither occurrence was dependent on the cultural background of its victims. Teen pregnancy, on the other hand, is an example of a culturally specific crisis. Socioeconomic resources and religious as well as other cultural beliefs determine whether a crisis develops. In the case of teen pregnancy, these factors determine whether a woman has a choice in the outcome of her pregnancy. Awareness of biases within oneself and one's culture is indispensable when working with cultural groups that differ. For therapists working with culturally different groups, it is always advisable to ask for clarification rather than base conclusions on previous assumptions.

Assuming an understanding of the nonverbal communication of a client can be misleading, unless one is quite familiar with a client's culture.

Finally, crisis responders should be careful not to impose their personal values and coping strategies on clients. Instead, responders should always maintain openness to the client's coping strategies. If a client's method of coping is strongly faith-based, for example, and the responder's is not, tolerance and taking a nonjudgmental stance are strongly suggested. A crisis is neither the time nor the place to explore different cultural perspectives.

Factors Affecting Long-Term Recovery

Several factors are likely to affect the long-term recovery of those affected by a crisis. Some of these factors depend on individual characteristics and coping responses, while others depend on an individual's ecological environment and the support and resources inherent in this environment:

- Frequent triggers may remind people of the traumatic event and/or their losses (e.g., living in a chronically violent area);
- A second assault occurs when the media reports the traumatic event, when court appearances are made, or when the anniversary of the event approaches;
- Developmental factors, such as the victim's age, will play a role in the recovery process. Younger children and the elderly may need a large amount of additional support;
- Trauma history and the number of prior losses experienced will compound or intensify a person's current reactions;
- The availability of environmental support or lack of support will determine how the survivor experiences the traumatic event.

Working under conditions that are time-limited, the crisis responder will have to make a swift determination of the factors outlined above. A crisis intervention should not be approached as a psychological intervention; referrals for counseling or other help often follow crisis intervention.

Crisis Phases

Individuals affected by a crisis event experience reactions that may change over time. Individual characteristics, the event itself, and the ecological environment that the individual inhabits affect these changes. Researchers have identified three primary phases of crisis reactions (Herman, 1997; Horowitz, 1986; Yassen & Harvey, 1998). These phases are outlined below. However, these phases show a cyclical progression; when individuals are reminded of the crisis event, they appear to return to the acute phase.

Acute Phase

Initial crisis reactions in response to a traumatic event usually encompass the physiological and psychological realm. Reactions include overwhelming anxiety, despair, hopelessness, guilt, intense fears, grief, confusion, panic, disorientation, numbness, shock, and a sense of disbelief. In this acute stage of crisis, the victim may appear incoherent, disorganized, agitated, and volatile. Conversely, the victim may present as calm, subdued, withdrawn, and apathetic.

Outward Adjustment Phase

For some people, the outward adjustment phase can begin within 24 hours of the trauma. The individual may then attempt to gain mastery by resuming external control through engaging in routine activities (Yassen & Harvey, 1998). However, this should not preclude the possibility that victims who outwardly appear to be "back to normal" may inwardly remain "deeply affected." Other victims isolate themselves from sources of support; they may appear to have withdrawn from society completely. The tension and fluctuating reactions involved in this phase should be noted as an attempt to return to normal while still processing the trauma.

Integration Phase

In this phase, the victim attempts to make sense of what has happened. An important task of this phase is to resolve one's sense of blame and guilt. Individuals who can recognize and identify the assumptions about their world and others that have changed because of the trauma develop a sense of integration sooner. Most importantly, clients should begin to make the changes necessary to minimize the recurrence of a crisis.

Some clients will cycle and recycle through these phases as they attempt to come to terms with their trauma. There are also those clients who cycle through phases too quickly or even skip a phase altogether. It may come as no surprise to find these clients later overwhelmed.

Several years ago, I worked with a community in the aftermath of a shooting. The high-school–aged young man was walking with his girlfriend when a rival gang member shot him in the chest. People in the community described his girlfriend, Juliette, as "doing very well." She returned to school a few days after the shooting. She was determined to collaborate with a few community leaders on a project aimed at ending violence in her urban environment. Though she appeared to be coping well, it came as no surprise when six months later I learned she had been brought into the psychiatric emergency room at the local hospital. She cried constantly and she had not slept in days. Furthermore, she was no longer attending school. Juliette had recycled from outward adjustment to the acute phase of crisis.

Models of Crisis Assessment and Intervention

There are three primary methods of assessing clients in crisis: standardized inventories, general personality tests interpreted in the light of the crisis, and client interviews. The interview is the most commonly used method. The models of crisis assessment and intervention outlined below, therefore, use the interview as a primary assessment tool.

Gilliland's Six-Step Model

Gilliland's Six-Step Model, which includes three listening and three action steps, is a useful crisis intervention model. Attending, observing, understanding, and responding with empathy, genuineness, respect, acceptance, nonjudgment, and caring are important elements of listening. Action steps are carried out in a nondirective and collaborative manner, which attends to the assessed needs of clients as well as the environmental supports available to them (James & Gilliland, 2005).

1. Listening
   o defining the problem
   o ensuring client safety
   o providing support

2. Action
   o examining alternatives
   o making plans
   o obtaining commitment

Triage Assessment System

The Triage Assessment System was developed by Myer (2001), who posits that it is necessary to assess crisis reactions in three domains: affective (emotional), cognitive (thinking), and behavioral (actions). According to Myer, an assessment based on these three domains captures the complexity of crises. Affective reactions include anger, hostility, anxiety, fear, sadness, and melancholy. Cognitive reactions include transgression, threat, and loss. Behavioral reactions include approach/avoidance and immobility, and can be constructive or maladaptive. In addition, Myer (2001) describes four life dimensions that are affected by a crisis: physical, psychological, social, moral, or spiritual.

Seven-Stage Model of Crisis Intervention

This model, developed by Roberts (1990), contains seven stages:

1. Plan and conduct a thorough biopsychosocial and crisis assessment. This also includes assessing suicidal and homicidal risk, need for medical attention, drug and alcohol use, and negative coping strategies. Assessing resilience and protective factors as well as family and other support networks is helpful.

2. Make psychological contact and establish rapport. By conveying respect and acceptance, the responder develops a solid therapeutic relationship with the client. Displaying a nonjudgmental attitude and neutrality are important in crisis work.

3. Examine and define the dimensions of the problem or crisis. Identifying any issues and challenges the client may have faced, especially the precipitant to the crisis, will provide valuable insight into the presenting problem.

4. Encourage an exploration of feelings and emotions. This can be achieved by actively listening to the client and responding with encouraging statements. Reflection and paraphrasing can also help this process.

5. Explore past positive coping strategies and alternatives. Viewing the individual as a resourceful and resilient person with an array of potential resources and alternatives can help this process (Roberts, 2000). Crisis workers should be creative and flexible in resolving crisis situations.

6. Implement the action plan. At this stage, identify supportive individuals and contact referral sources. The client should be able to implement some coping strategies.

7. Establish a follow-up plan. It is important to follow up with clients after the initial intervention to determine the client's status and ensure that the crisis has been resolved.

An Empowering Model of Crisis Intervention

In my many years of responding to communities and individuals in crisis, I have found the following steps to be helpful. These steps are an integration of the models outlined above, but also borrow some important principles from community psychology. The model consists of three steps: pre-intervention, assessment, and disposition.

Pre-Intervention

Before responding to a community or individual in crisis, find out as much as possible. Individuals in a crisis have difficulty remembering details, and asking questions for which they may not have answers may be perceived as disempowering. It is usually feasible to get background information from the person who initiates the crisis intervention. To prevent oneself from becoming overwhelmed by the crisis, alert supportive people such as supervisors, family, and colleagues about the crisis in order to introduce stress-reduction procedures immediately. By taking preliminary action, the responder appears stable and supportive when interfacing with distressed individuals or communities.

Assessment

Identify the victim's current concerns and triggers or precipitants to the crisis. Make the evaluation quick, accurate, and comprehensive. Gathering information about how similar crises were handled in the past is essential for problem solving. In addition, establishing what worked and what did not is useful in designing current interventions.

An ecological chart may be helpful in identifying sources of help and support. This chart is constructed with the affected individual or community in the middle, encircled by significant groups that are named as important by the client or the client's community. Exploring which groups can provide ongoing support is also informative when planning termination with the client.

Disposition

Allow the client to talk as little or as much as possible about the event. The telling and retelling of a trauma can assist in the healing process. Psycho-educational information on what actions can be taken to maintain safety and stabilization are valuable in empowering clients. Information helps them know what to expect so they will not be later taken by surprise. Decisions on how to handle the crisis are made by exploring options with clients, an action that supports client empowerment. Additionally, decisions that include active client participation promote client compliance. Thinking creatively with clients can resolve most problems. Since crisis intervention requires short-term involvement, it is important to refer a client to other sources of help as soon as stability is established. Finally, responders should be aware that not all clients need mental health support in order to overcome a crisis.

Referral and Resource List

Keeping a referral and resource list is an important aspect of crisis work. The effective crisis responder researches and maintains information regarding agencies and programs in a client's community that can be sources of future help. If time allows, it might be helpful to visit these agencies before referring a client to them. Such visits increase the responder's familiarity with the services of the referral resources. Knowing whether they have a waiting list, sliding scale of payment, or whether they give priority to crisis victims is important additional information. Once a list is generated, make sure that phone numbers, addresses, and names of contact persons are constantly updated. It can be frustrating for clients in crisis to call a disconnected number for help.

Information about potential resources should be clearly printed on a card and carefully reviewed with clients. Clients are better informed if they have some knowledge about the process involved before services are sought. Remember, one of the challenges for people in crisis is the ability to concentrate and remain focused; short-term memory can often be seriously impaired. The crisis responder should have clients review their next steps before departing. It is a good idea to call clients after a few days to get an update on how they are feeling.

Helping Children and Adolescents

While the emotional effects of a crisis can significantly affect children and adolescents, most victims in this age range make a full recovery. The following crisis responses are likely to manifest in younger children (AAETS, 1999).

- Regressive behaviors are likely to occur among toddlers, preschool, and elementary school children. Thumb-sucking, bed-wetting, fear of the dark, and other past problematic behaviors can recur.
- Fears and anxiety are likely to be exhibited in separation anxiety and clinging behaviors. Children may have difficulty leaving a parent's side.
- Although school phobia and anxiety may develop, parents are encouraged to continue sending children to school to maintain routine. Children who are kept at home experience greater anxiety when they later return to the classroom.

Adolescents display generalized anxiety rather than the specific fears observed in younger children.

- As adolescents' anxiety increases, a decrease in academic performance and poor concentration may become evident. However, as with younger children, maintaining the routine of school attendance surpasses the benefits of staying at home.
- An increase in aggressive and oppositional behavior is possible. Controlling anger and frustration becomes a challenge for adolescents in crisis. Adolescents are also likely to display an increase in rebellious and risk-taking behaviors. They tend to defy rules both at home and at school. Antisocial behaviors of substance abuse and alcoholism may become prominent in this group.
- A general sense of sadness, loss of interest, and increase or decrease in appetite and sleeping can occur. Adolescents are likely to display moodiness and social withdrawal. Since adolescents are at risk for suicide, caregivers should be alert for suicidal ideation in this group.
- Denial is an effort to cope with the reality of the crisis. Adolescents are likely to deny that something bad happened; they may continue to use denial as a coping mechanism. It may be necessary to confront them in a sensitive but direct manner.

Understanding the responses of children and adolescents is a first step in helping them. This understanding will also help identify those children who may need professional assistance. Schools and homes are the places that children and adolescents are likely to spend most of their time. Teachers and caregivers become critical resources to help children cope with a crisis. The crisis worker can teach parents how to set boundaries and limits without shaming the child. Supportive and warm parenting can buffer adolescents from suicidality (Kaplan, Pelcovitz, Salzinger, Mandel, & Weiner, 1997; Perkins & Hartless, 2002). Similarly, researchers have found that adolescents who report a close relationship with their parents, positive family communication, and the receipt of adequate support and affection from their parents have a lower risk for later suicidality (Ferguson, Woodward, & Horwood, 2000; Prinstein, Boergers, Spirito, Little, & Grapentine, 2000).

An on-site school mental health program is an effective vehicle for engaging children and adolescents in treatment. When mental health assistance has to be provided quickly to a large number of students, school-based services are ideal. Receiving services in school is also less stigmatizing than receiving them in hospitals (Waxman, Weist, & Benson, 1999).

However, in order to make school interventions successful, strong collaboration between schools and mental health professionals must exist (Brock, Sandoval, & Lewis, 2001; Johnson, 2000). Within a school community, there can be debate about who is primarily responsible for assisting with crisis intervention (Brock et al., 2001; Johnson, 2000). The American School Counselor Association (ASCA) designates the professional school counselor as this individual, with the primary role of providing direct counseling service during and after a traumatic incident (ASCA, 2000). School counselors are expected to serve students and school personnel during times of crisis by providing individual and group counseling. Consulting with administrators, teachers, parents, and professionals, as well as coordinating services within the school and in the community, are additional tasks for the school counselor (ASCA, 2000; King, Price, Telljohann, & Wahl, 2000; Riley & McDaniel, 2000). School counselors' training should be aligned with the demands of their profession to ensure solid preparation for responding to children's emotional needs during a crisis (Perusse, Goodnough, & Noel, 2001).

Suicide Assessment Issues

Working with a suicidal client in crisis is a scenario many counselors face. The American Association of Suicidology (2002) reports the following statistics in the United States:

- 31,655 individuals completed suicide in 2002, which equates to 86.7 people each day and one person approximately every 17.2 minutes.
- Suicide is the 11th leading cause of death in the United States; however, it is the third leading cause of death for youth (ages 15–24), exceeded only by accidents and homicides. Homicide is the 14th leading cause of death overall, indicating that more Americans kill themselves than are killed by others.
- Annually, 790,000 Americans attempt to kill themselves.
- The elderly (ages 65+) have the highest rate of completed suicides: Approximately 5,548 elders completed suicide in 2002. For every four older adults who attempt suicide, one successfully completes the act.
- Youth have the second highest rate of completed suicide: For every 100–200 young people who attempt suicide, one successfully completes the act.
- Women are three times more likely to attempt suicide than men, but men are four times more likely to complete it.
- Firearms are the most commonly used method for completing suicide (54% of all suicides were completed with a firearm); approximately 17,108 individuals used firearms in 2002.
- Each suicide intimately affects at least six other people; thus, for each suicide there are six new survivors.

Risk Factors

The first step in preventing suicide is to identify and understand risk factors. The Department of Health and Human Services (1999) identifies the following as risk factors:

- Previous suicide attempt(s)
- History of mental disorders, particularly depression
- History of alcohol and substance abuse
- Family history of suicide
- Family history of child maltreatment
- Feelings of hopelessness
- Impulsive or aggressive tendencies
- Barriers to accessing mental health treatment
- Loss (relational, social, work, or financial)

- Physical illness
- Easy access to lethal methods
- Unwillingness to seek help because of the stigma attached to mental health, substance abuse disorders, or suicidal thoughts
- Cultural and religious beliefs, for instance, the belief that suicide is a noble resolution of a personal dilemma
- Local epidemics of suicide
- Isolation or a feeling of being disconnected from other people

Determining Suicidal Intent

With approximately one million people committing suicide worldwide each year (WHO, 2000), there is little doubt that suicidal behavior of a client is a crisis situation many counselors will encounter (Rosenberg, 1999). Assessing and determining suicidal intent is, therefore, a valuable skill to develop. Attention to the following guidelines will help counselors determine the suicidal intent of a client.

- Assessing the persistence of suicidal thoughts and the client's ability to control them and differentiating between active, passive, or compulsive suicidal thoughts are important first steps for determining intent. Understanding a clients reasons for living or dying, establishing specific motivating forces and their bases (i.e., feeling worthless), and determining the contributing psychosocial factors can shed more light on a clients' level of intentionality.
- Assessing the degree of planning involved, the method contemplated for use, its lethality, and the individual's access to weapons or other means can help a therapist determine the likelihood that the client will carry out the suicidal act.

For example, a client who has already rehearsed exactly how to carry out a suicidal plan, and who anticipates staying at home alone for an extended period, should be regarded as high risk. Specificity in planning, opportunity, and a sense of "capability" to execute the attempt should be significant warning signals. The terms, intent, and lethality allow for an objective assessment of a client's level of suicidal ideation. Is the suicidal ideation a precursor of actual lethal intention? Is it a subjective means of gesturing? Is it merely a signal used to draw attention to one's inner pain?

Suicidal gesturing (also known as para-suicidal behavior) refers to individuals' use of less than lethal means to harm themselves; this gesturing can be complicated and confusing to the novice counselor. Those who "attempt" suicide may be ambivalent about dying, and their suicidal behavior could be perceived as a "cry for help."

- It is critical to assess the deterrents in the client's environment, such as family or religion, that may help prevent implementation of the suicidal plan. Identifying deterrents will help assess clients' ability to maintain safety once they leave the therapy session.
- It is helpful to ascertain prevailing co-morbid symptoms. When making an assessment, the crisis responder must know whether a client is actively abusing substances or suffering from depressive symptoms. This includes knowing whether the client takes any psychiatric medications, whether these medications have been recently changed, or whether a client has recently stopped taking the medication altogether.
- The specific characteristics of the suicidal ideation also provide helpful information. How often (frequency) does the client think about suicide and for how long (duration)? Does the client have control over suicidal thoughts?
- When a client has made actual preparation for suicide, or when a suicide note is written, the responder should proceed with great caution. Final acts in anticipation of death, such as cashing life insurance, securing a will, and distributing one's possessions as gifts, are a significant forewarning of serious intent. Additionally, a deception or concealment of a contemplated attempt (failure to communicate ideation) also serves to warn the crisis responder that a client is a high suicide risk.

How to Help

Several protective factors can buffer individuals from attempting suicide (Department of Health and Human Services, 1999):

- Effective clinical care for mental, physical, and substance abuse disorders
- Easy access to a variety of clinical interventions and support
- Family and community support
- Support from ongoing medical and mental health services
- Skills in problem solving, conflict resolution, and nonviolent handling of disputes
- Cultural and religious beliefs that discourage suicide and support self-preservation

Outpatient Issues

In outpatient treatment, it is crucial for all therapists to ask clients about a suicide history on their first visit. If the history is notable or active, a therapist must commit to assessing a client's suicidal ideation in every subsequent session. To gain additional information, previous treatment records should be requested from other agencies/institutions that may have served the client. This documentation offers the therapist an opportunity to cross-check information that the client has already provided. It may also indicate how past crises were resolved.

Issues of confidentiality are discussed ahead of time, especially if the therapist anticipates communicating with family members or other supportive individuals when a client's suicidal ideation accelerates.

It is essential to assess clients' level of compliance and whether they will follow through with a safety plan that instructs them to go to an emergency room when suicidal feelings increase. Medication for clients with a suicide history has to be actively monitored. Large prescriptions carry the risk of providing clients with a means to end their lives. Finally, therapists who treat suicidal clients have to obtain adequate coverage during periods of leave or vacation.

Working With Survivors of Suicide

Approximately 30,000 completed suicides occur annually in the U.S., leaving behind many family survivors (Kaslow & Aronson, 2004). Research illustrates the following:

- Partners who lose a loved one to suicide display more psychological distress and impairment than those whose partners die naturally (Farberow, Gallagher-Thompson, Liewski, & Thompson, 1992).
- Parents whose child commits suicide experience more shame than parents who lose their child in an accident (Seguin, Lesage, & Kiely, 1995).
- Mothers who lose a child from suicide are more likely to stay depressed than mothers who lose a child from an accident (Saarinen, Viinamäki, Hintikka, Lehtonen, & Lönnqvist, 1999).
- Children who lose a parent to suicide persistently reminisce about the loss, engage in self-destructive behavior, and are more likely to display behavioral and academic problems (Saarinen, Hintikka, Viinamäki, Lehtonen, & Lönnqvist, 2000).

When notifying a family of a loved one's suicide, a therapist should be clear, sympathetic, and offer immediate but continuing support. During the meeting, address their concerns directly. In response to questions such as, "Why did this happen?" explain the multi-causal nature of suicide and appreciate the relevant stages of grief (anger, blame, bargaining, depression; see also Appendix III). Demystify "If only . . ." statements that are usually present among those who lose a family member to suicide, but accomplish this with sensitivity to the family's needs.

Avoid defensiveness and do not apologize. It is especially important to avoid a discussion of any wrongdoing. Maintain appropriate boundaries while showing caring and compassion. When a therapist expresses shock, family members may question the therapist's competence, yet a stoic therapist may be regarded as uncaring.

While working with survivors, it is recommended that therapists use techniques consistent with their own theoretical training; they should remember to consider the role of family traditions and other contextual or cultural factors. An awareness of the family's death and mourning rituals can be useful. Encourage family members to honor the dead by observing anniversaries and other important holidays or special family days. Establishing or following previously established traditions fosters the healing process and gives people permission to grieve.

Empowering interventions encourage family members to seek support from each other and their social network. Teaching the family about the stages of the grieving process and predictable responses to suicide can restore control. Some families also become concerned about inheriting a predisposition to suicidal behavior and may need additional support in this area (Brent, Oquendo, & Birmaher, 2002).

Although a therapist may be tempted to first work with child survivors, it is important to give adult survivors adequate support so that they, rather than strangers, can be psychologically available to their children. Informing them of available resources and educating them about what grief reactions they can expect their children to display can be initial steps in helping adults cope. Children should be encouraged to talk about their loss and be actively involved in memorializing the dead (see Appendix IV). They should be encouraged to resume normal peer, school, and extracurricular activities (Kaslow & Aronson, 2004).

Finally, client records and other documentation, such as termination and discharge summaries, should be completed as soon as possible. If family members request these records, regulations regarding confidentiality should be reviewed. A signed release form is needed from the administrator of the estate before any records are released to family members.

Conclusion

The high frequency and indiscriminateness of violent acts make many individuals vulnerable to crises. During a crisis, normal ways of dealing with the world are suddenly interrupted. Although reactions and responses to crises are time-limited, they may persist as symptoms of post-traumatic stress. Crises are universal and can affect people from all cultures; however, culture plays a strong role in how an individual interprets and reacts to a crisis. The recovery process and support individuals are offered by their communities is culture-bound.

For all these reasons, crisis intervention strategies should be structured and considerate of a culturally diverse and dynamically changing world. Crisis interventions are usually brief, and counselors can expect to have only a single session to work with a client. Although this time may appear to be limited, an effective counselor conveys an expectation that change will occur, that small changes can be sufficient to solve problems, and that the client's abilities and strengths are central to problem solving (Rosenbaum, Hoyt, & Talmon, 1990). The satisfaction of seeing people resume control after their lives have been shattered can be quite rewarding.

Resources for Further Understanding

The following books may be used as bibliotherapy for families bereaved by suicide. Counselors interested in increasing their understanding of suicide may also find these titles helpful.

Cammarota, D. (2001). *Someone I loved died by suicide: A story for child survivors and those who care for them.* Palm Beach Gardens, FL: Grief Guidance.

Fine, C. (1999). *No time to say goodbye: Surviving the suicide of a loved one.* New York: Broadway Books.

Hsu, A.Y. (2002). *Grieving suicide: A loved one's search for comfort, answers and hope.* Downers Grove, IL: Intervarsity Press.

Jamison, K. R. (1999). *Night falls fast: Understanding suicide.* New York: Knopf.

Kolf, J. C. C. (2002). *Standing in the shadow: Help and encouragement for suicide survivors.* Grand Rapids, MI: Baker.

Stimming, M. T., & Stimming, M. (Eds.). (1999). *Before their time: Adult children's experience of parental suicide.* Philadelphia: Temple University Press.

Wertheimer, A. (2002). *A special scar: The experiences of people bereaved by suicide.* London: Taylor & Francis.

References

Aguilera, D. (1998). *Crisis intervention: Theory and methodology* (8th ed.). St. Louis, MO: Mosby.

American Academy of Experts in Traumatic Stress. (1999). *Teacher guidelines for crisis response.* New York: Author.

American Association of Suicidology. (2002). [Summary data]. Unpublished raw data, Indiana University South Bend.

American School Counselor Association. (2000). *Position statement: Critical incident response.* Alexandria, VA: Author.

Arredondo, P. (1999). Multicultural counseling competencies as tools to address oppression and racism. *Journal of Counseling and Development, 77*(1), 102– 108.

Brent, D. A., Oquendo, M., & Birmaher, B. (2002). Familial pathways to early-onset suicide attempt. *Archives of General Psychiatry, 59,* 801–807.

Brock, S. E., Sandoval, J., & Lewis, S. (2001). *Preparing for crises in the schools: A manual for building school crisis response teams* (2nd ed.). New York: Wiley.

Caplan, G. (1961). *An approach to community mental health.* New York: Grune & Stratton.

Caplan, G. (1964). *Principles of preventive psychiatry.* New York: Basic Books.

Department of Health and Human Services. (1999). The Surgeon General's call to action to prevent suicide. Washington, DC: Author.

Dykeman, B. F. (2005). Cultural implications of crisis intervention. *Journal of Instructional Psychology, 32*(1), 45–48.

Farberow, N. L., Gallagher-Thompson, D. E., Liewski, M. J., & Thompson, L. W. (1992). The role of social support in the bereavement process of surviving spouses of suicide and natural deaths. *Suicide and life threatening behavior, 22,* 107–124.

Ferguson, D. M., Woodward, L. J., & Horwood, L. J. (2000). Risk factors and life processes associated with the onset of suicidal behavior during adolescence and early adulthood. *Psychological Medicine, 30,* 23–39.

Greene, G. J., Lee, M., Trask, R., & Rheinscheld, J. (2000). How to work with clients' strengths in crisis intervention. In A. R. Roberts (Ed.), *Crisis intervention handbook: Assessment, treatment and research* (pp. 31–55). Oxford, UK: Oxford University Press.

Greenstone, J. L., & Leviton, S. C. (2002). *Elements of crisis intervention: Crises and how to respond to them.* Pacific Grove, CA: Brooks/Cole.

Herman, J. L. (1997). *Trauma and recovery.* New York: Basic Books.

Horowitz, M. J. (1986). Stress-response syndromes: A review of posttraumatic and adjustment disorders. *Hospital & Community Psychiatry, 37*(3), 241–249.

James, R. K., & Gilliland, B. E. (2005). *Crisis intervention strategies.* Belmont, CA: Thomson.

Johnson, K. (2000). *School crisis management: A hands-on guide to training crisis response teams* (2nd ed.). Alameda, CA: Hunter House.

Kaplan, S. J., Pelcovitz, D., Salzinger, S., Mandel, F., & Weiner, M. (1997). Adolescent physical abuse and suicide attempts. *Journal of the American Academy of Child & Adolescent Psychiatry, 36,* 799–808.

Kaslow, N. J., & Aronson, S. G. (2004). Recommendations for family interventions following suicide. *Professional Psychology: Research and Practice, 35*(3), 240– 247.

King, K. A., Price, J. H., Telljohann, S. K., & Wahl, J. (2000). Preventing adolescent suicide: Do high school counselors know the risk factors? *Professional School Counseling, 3,* 255–263.

Lindemann, E. (1944). Symptomatology and management of acute grief. *American Journal of Psychiatry, 101,* 141–148.

Myer, R. A. (2001). *Assessment for crisis intervention: A triage assessment model.* Pacific Grove, CA: Brooks/Cole.

Perkins, D. F., & Hartless, G. (2002). An ecological risk-factor examination of suicide ideation and behavior of adolescents. *Journal of Adolescent Research, 17,* 3–26.

Perusse, R., Goodnough, G. E., & Noel, C. J. (2001). A national survey of school counselor preparation programs: Screening methods, faculty experiences, curricular content, and fieldwork requirements. *Counselor Education and Supervision, 40,* 252–262.

Pollin, I. (1995). *Medical crisis counseling: Short-term therapy for long-term illness.* New York: Norton.

Prinstein, M. J., Boergers, J., Spirito, A., Little, T. D., & Grapentine, W. L. (2000). Peer functioning, family dysfunction, and psychological symptoms in a risk factor model for adolescent inpatients' suicidal ideation severity. *Journal of Clinical Child Psychology, 29,* 392–405.

Riley, P. L., & McDaniel, J. (2000). School violence prevention, intervention, and crisis response. *Professional School Counseling, 4,* 120–125.

Roberts, A. R. (Ed.). (1990). *Crisis intervention handbook: Assessment, treatment and research.* Belmont, CA: Wadsworth.

Roberts, A. R. (Ed.). (2000). *Crisis intervention handbook: Assessment, treatment and research.* New York: Oxford University Press.

Rosenbaum, R., Hoyt, M. F., & Talmon, M. (1990). The challenge of single-session therapies: Creating pivotal moments. In R. A. Wells & V. J. Giannetti (Eds.), *Handbook of the brief psychotherapies* (pp. 165–189). New York: Plenum Press.

Rosenberg, J. I. (1999). An integrated training model using affective and action-based interventions. *Professional Psychology: Research and Practice, 30*(1), 83–87.

Rosenbluh, E. S. (1981). *Emotional first aid.* Louisville, KY: American Academy of Crisis Interveners.

Saarinen, P. I., Hintikka, J., Viinamäki, H., Lehtonen, J., & Lönnqvist, J. (2000). Is it possible to adapt to the suicide of a close individual? Results of a 10-year prospective follow-up study. *International Journal of Social Psychiatry, 46,* 182– 192.

Saarinen, P. I., Viinamäki, H., Hintikka, J., Lehtonen, J., & Lönnqvist, J. (1999). Psychological symptoms of close relatives of suicide victims. *European Journal of Psychiatry, 13,* 33–39.

Saleebey, D. (Ed.). (1997). *The strengths perspective in social work practice* (2nd ed.). New York: Longman.

Seguin, M., Lesage, A., & Kiely, M. C. (1995). Parental bereavement after suicide and accident: A comparative study. *Suicide and Life Threatening Behavior, 25,* 489–492.

Shapiro, D., & Koocher, G. (1996). Goals and practical considerations in outpatient medical crises. *Professional Psychology: Research and Practice, 122,* 109–120.

Sue, D. W., & Sue, D. (1999). *Counseling the culturally different: Theory and practice* (3rd ed.). New York: Wiley.

Thompson, S. E., Smith, B. A., & Bybee, R. F. (2005). Factors influencing participation in worksite wellness programs among minority and underserved populations. *Family & Community Health, 28*(3), 267–273.

Waxman, R. P., Weist, M. D., & Benson, D. M. (1999). Toward collaboration in the growing education-mental health interface. *Clinical Psychology Review, 19,* 131–135.

World Health Organization. (2000). *Mental and behavioral disorders.* Geneva: Author.

Yassen, J., & Harvey, M. R. (1998). Crisis assessment and interventions with victims of violence. In P. M. Kleespies (Ed.), *Emergencies in mental health practice* (pp. 117–143). New York: Guilford.

6

Group Psychotherapy for Trauma Survivors

Karin's teacher referred her for group therapy to work on her anger issues. Her teacher reported that the 14-year-old was constantly getting into fights with other students at school. She was suspended from school several times. Karin joined an open group, which meant that group membership was ongoing.

During the first few group sessions, Karin huddled in her winter coat, slumped in her chair as she constantly scanned the group and rolled her eyes at some of the remarks made by other group members. It was clear that Karin was trying to figure out whether she could trust other group members. Several sessions later, she felt more comfortable and slowly began to talk about her difficulties at home.

Karin and her younger brother were in foster care with her maternal aunt. Her biological mother, who had lost custody of her children because of her substance abuse, was in recovery and living in the aunt's home. Karin experienced authority figures as confusing mostly because her mother and her maternal aunt had different parenting styles. In the safety and cohesion provided by this long-term group, she was able to explore her confusion with authority figures as well as her confusion about her sexuality. She had become sexually active two years ago after a male cousin raped her. Her perpetrator was currently incarcerated for larceny. Although Karin had disclosed the rape to her aunt, charges were not pressed against the perpetrator. The group listened attentively to Karin's experience, providing appropriate feedback and validation. Her disclosure opened up an intense discussion on sexuality by other group members. To the group leader, it was clear that such an animated discussion would have been unlikely in individual therapy.

Participation in a therapeutic group helps participants change the way they think about themselves and provides a sense of community and identity. It can be an effective modality for individuals who, by virtue of race, ethnicity, class, sexual orientation, or immigrant status, occupy a marginalized position in U.S. society (Pack-Brown, Whittington-Clark, & Parker, 1998). Group participation can reduce distress while empowering group members to think innovatively about their options.

While some trauma survivors experience individual interventions as too intense and prefer a group format, others opt for both modalities in their healing and recovery. This chapter looks at trauma groups that are based on different theoretical models: support and psycho-educational, psychodynamic, and cognitive-behavioral groups. Guidelines on conducting groups with children and adolescents are reviewed. Finally, a protocol is provided for conducting cognitive-behavioral groups with adolescent girls who have experienced sexual abuse.

Benefits of a Group Modality

Group participation is an ideal therapeutic modality for trauma survivors. In a group setting, survivors are able to share traumatic material. The safety, cohesion, and empathy other survivors provide is experienced as supportive. The assumption underlying group therapy with trauma survivors is that survivors who have experienced similar traumatic events will bond. This is conducive to recovery and adjustment (Solomon & Johnson, 2002). The supportive, secure, and intimate social environment of the group rebuilds positive relationships and repairs damage to group members' sense of control and self-esteem.

In addition, group members provide each other with feedback based on their similar experiences. As group members achieve a greater understanding and resolution of their trauma, they become more confident and develop an ability to trust again. Erikson (1968) describes trust as a foundational building block in human development. When children are infants, primary caretakers fulfill basic needs. If this caretaking is consistent, children develop a sense of trust in both themselves and their environment.

One of the most profound consequences of trauma is the betrayal of trust. Some victims are unable to socialize and meet new people because their core belief that people can be trusted is shattered. Others trust too quickly because the alternative of being alone may be too overwhelming. As a defensive strategy, some victims repress details of the traumatic event. An inability to remember traumatic detail is a consequence of repression and distrust in one's abilities. Group therapy can restore faith in both self and others.

As group members share experiences of trauma-related shame, guilt, rage, fear, doubt, and self-condemnation, they prepare themselves to focus on the present rather than the past. In describing the trauma narrative and directly facing the grief, anxiety, and guilt it evokes, survivors cope with traumatic symptoms and memories.

The trauma narrative plays a valuable role in promoting a cathartic effect. Catharsis is a crucial feature of trauma recovery, and some groups encourage participants to unburden themselves. For example, Hanscom (2001) describes a model of treatment with survivors of torture and war trauma in Guatemala. Threats of death or imprisonment by the repressive Guatemalan government silenced these victims. This intimidation caused victims to withdraw from society and to choose isolation as a survival strategy. However, group participation allowed individuals to communicate confidentially with each other, thus undoing the impact of political repression and forced isolation. Through group support, they were able to manage their lives and cope adequately. For those with limited social support, group contact helps maintain connection with others and provides opportunities for commonality. Social support can "tap into and nourish an individual's innate resilience" and coping (Mapp & Koch, 2004, p. 100). It can also play a protective role by offering traumatized individuals a network of relationships. These new relationships can be strengthening, can offer direction and support, and thus promote recovery.

An example of a project that provides opportunities for social, psychological, and emotional support for children between the ages of 7 and 18 is the Mural Project. It began as an art project in New York City for children who experienced traumatic responses after the terrorist attack on the World Trade Center in September, 2001 (Mapp & Koch, 2004). The researchers conceptualized mural drawings as a therapeutic process that would provide social support and help children cope with stress. Through the group process of creating murals, children and their mentors from the Big Brother/Big Sister program worked together, combining images of hope, optimism, and love against those of fear, stress, and anxiety.

Group participation helps clients cut through their denial and face their feelings more quickly than they would through individual therapy (Foy, Eriksson, & Trice, 2001; Solomon & Johnson, 2002). In individual therapy, the responsibility of client confrontation rests solely on the therapist. In a group setting, other group members share this important role. Promising group therapy practices, which relied on cognitive or experiential therapy, were identified in a study conducted among low-income, chemically dependent women treated at community agencies (Washington & Moxley, 2003). These interventions focused on strengthening self-efficacy and helping participants think in empowering ways. The researchers found that group participation facilitated the cutting of denial, the confrontation of feelings, and the facing of fears.

Models of Group Intervention

Group treatment for post-traumatic disorders has a long tradition (Foa, Keane, & Friedman, 2000; Foy et al., 2001; Foy, Ruzek, Glynn, Riney, & Gusman, 2002; van der Kolk, 1993). It is discouraged for survivors who are in the acute phase of treatment and those who have dissociative disorders (Chu, 1998; Putnam, 1989). A detailed discussion of past abuse can trigger other group members' memories of abuse; listening to traumatic details is not advisable in the acute phase of recovery (Chu, 1998). Groups with psycho-educational and skill-building foci are better suited for such clients. In addition, groups that involve some form of activity may be more appropriate for clients who prefer nonverbal modalities; such groups are useful in cross-cultural settings. Effective models of group treatment for trauma survivors include the following:

- Support groups
- Psycho-educational groups
- Psychodynamic groups
- Cognitive-behavioral groups
- Groups for children and adolescents
- Cultural groups

Support Groups

The primary goal of support groups is to increase the coping skills of group members. This is accomplished by focusing on current life issues. Support groups achieve the intrinsic goal of therapy groups: establishing normalization and cohesion (Yalom, 1995). There is little attention given to the content of group members' traumatic experiences. Instead, the group validates the impact of the traumatic event and develops positive cohort relationships (Foy et al., 2001). Support groups are frequently used in PTSD treatment programs to help clients achieve stability.

Although the group leader encourages an exploration of emotional reactions to the trauma, the group environment is kept at a comfortable level. The group format is open and new members can join the group at any time. Groups usually meet weekly for 10 to 15 weeks. Support groups can be used as a primary form of treatment while group members wait for individual therapy; additionally, support groups can be an adjunctive treatment to individual therapy (Foy et al., 2001).

Interactive Psycho-Educational Groups

The interactive psycho-educational group model is an empirically validated model for treating traumatized individuals (Johnson & Lubin, 2000). The general objectives of this group model are to inform participants about the impact of traumatic experiences and to assist group members to reorganize their thoughts and feelings after a trauma.

The group leader helps participants differentiate between traumatic schemas and unimpaired aspects of the self. This ability to discriminate between traumatizing and nontraumatizing stimuli becomes a resource for individuals threatened by distressing reactions.

Psychodynamic Trauma Groups

These groups are informed by psychodynamic theory. The focus of psychodynamic groups is to uncover traumatic material so that an accurate trauma narrative can emerge. Psychodynamic groups have been widely expounded by Yalom (1995), who has published extensively on group modalities in psychotherapy.

In psychodynamic groups, the meaning of symptoms is uncovered and examined in the context of past and current functioning. Group members carefully explore conscious and unconscious material evoked by the trauma. The task of group leaders is to closely monitor the group to ensure that a participant's traumatic material does not emotionally overwhelm the entire group.

Groups can be conducted weekly for a minimum of 10 weeks. A longer-term model, however, will probably remain within the purview of the independent psychotherapist because it is unlikely that third-party reimbursement will occur for such an extended treatment (Scheidlinger, 2004).

Cognitive-Behavioral Groups

Group leaders who primarily use cognitive-behavioral techniques as a model of intervention usually use systematic prolonged exposure and cognitive restructuring techniques to help group members process traumatic experiences (Foa et al., 2000; Foy et al., 2001; Solomon & Johnson, 2002). Through systematic prolonged exposure, group members recount their trauma stories. The processing of the traumatic experience occurs on two levels: directly through group members retelling their traumatic experience, and indirectly as group members listen to the traumatic experiences of others. This technique emphasizes the strength of the personal narrative shared in the atmosphere of a supportive group. Cognitive restructuring encourages group members to examine their irrational beliefs and illogical thoughts and replace them with more practical and realistic thoughts.

Exposure techniques were included in a trauma-focused group conducted with individuals suffering from combat-related trauma (Foy et al., 2002). The researchers felt that the cognitive-behavioral technique of imaginal exposure to traumatic memories would reduce trauma-related fears and desensitize group members to reminders of their trauma. Group participation was based on several factors, which included an agreement to participate in exposure work and a willingness to disclose their trauma memories and previous group experiences. In addition, participants could not have paranoid or sociopathic symptoms, nor could they have suicidal or homicidal thoughts. The researchers found that using CBT techniques had a positive impact on group members. They concluded that trauma-focused group therapy was an alternative modality for individuals who do not favor individual trauma therapy.

Cultural Groups

Modern psychotherapy is often criticized as being ethnocentric, culture bound, and based on middle-class, individualistic values. As the U.S. population becomes more culturally diverse, psychotherapists must adopt a multicultural perspective (Nader, Dubrow, & Stamm, 1999; Sue & Sue, 2003). It is important for therapists to understand the worldview of clients in any counseling interaction. This is especially important when clients belong to non-Western cultural groups. Group leaders who attempt to view the world through a client's eyes develop trust and rapport and achieve a rich connection with their clients.

Based on her work with Salvadoran refugee women living in North America, Jenkens (1996) criticizes the individual trauma model as ineffective with ethnic minority groups, especially groups who have experienced collective trauma. She suggests that a group modality allows for a more comprehensive examination of collective trauma. Since group therapy focuses on healing within a social context, it may be a preferable format for some cultural groups. In addition, the group setting provides members with opportunities for social interaction, which benefits later reintegration into society.

The inclusion of culturally appropriate traditional ceremonies can enhance the therapeutic process. Research has shown that group leaders who integrate cultural traditions with professional practice obtain positive results with culturally diverse clients (Mapp & Koch, 2004; Nader et al., 1999; Wessells, 1999). Using a group modality, Guatemalan survivors of political torture were taught Buddhist mindfulness (Hanscom, 2001). Group members were first taught relaxation techniques of deep abdominal breathing, followed by sensory focusing techniques to make them more mindful of their daily surroundings. Since the women who participated in this group often used water in their household chores, water was used as a cue to practice deep abdominal breathing. Women who preferred to pray or sing spiritual hymns were encouraged to use these alternate coping skills.

Researchers have found indigenous healing practices to be effective with two ethnic minority groups: Native American Vietnam veterans and Southeast Asian refugees (Hurdle, 2002; Wilson, 1988). Cultural practices provide both groups with a culturally meaningful explanation of pain and healing, which they are more apt to understand and accept. The practice of rituals and ceremonies provide ethnic minority communities with sources of security and opportunities to connect with others (Weeks, 2001). Rituals also serve two other purposes: enhancing healing (e.g., the use of a sage stick is believed to clear the space of negative energy) and sustaining cultural traditions (for ethnic minority groups who may be at risk of cultural loss).

Counselors who work with culturally diverse clients should be aware of their underlying cultural assumptions and biases. Even the most well-intentioned counselor can alienate clients through a lack of cultural awareness. Counselors must first see clients as people seeking help; reducing their pain and suffering is a priority. This requires modifying therapeutic techniques to meet the needs of the client; the primary task of a group leader is to create and maintain a group culture that meets the needs of all clients (Yalom, 1995). A flexible and open therapeutic style helps to achieve this goal.

The Kaffa ceremony (coffee ceremony) described by Loewy, Williams, and Keleta (2002) is an example of culturally sensitive group therapy that effectively combines Western group therapy principles with East African cultural practices. This group modality is described below.

The Kaffa Ceremony

The Kaffa ceremony was developed specifically for six Eritrean and Ethiopian women living in the U.S. Eritrea is an East African country that fought a 30-year war for independence from Ethiopia. These refugee women with histories of rape and torture were experiencing transitory maladjustment. All six participants displayed symptoms of PTSD, which included nightmares, flashbacks, depression, and somatic complaints.

The Kaffa ceremony, similar to the tea ceremony practiced in Japan, has a 3,000-year-old history in East Africa. In its traditional format, the ceremony possesses healing properties. In its adaptation as a therapeutic group activity, the Kaffa ceremony was co-led by an African American and an Eritrean therapist. The ceremony was held in the home of one of the group members. The group leaders and members of the group initially negotiated issues of confidentiality and whether the group would be open or closed.

At each session, the women sat in a circle, serving each other coffee while discussing their traumatic experiences. The format of a circle created a sense of equality among members. The client-centered approach adopted by group leaders contributed to participants feeling heard, understood, and appreciated. Through careful questioning, by asking participants to clarify their thoughts and feelings, group leaders promoted healing.

Over a six-week period, group members transitioned from feeling fear and isolation to empowerment. Participants shed past feelings of shame, recognized their strength and resiliency, and ultimately achieved a level of safety and well-being. A number of factors account for the dramatic progress made by participants. The group leaders practiced effective group counseling techniques. The inclusion of a culturally appropriate ceremony created a safe and familiar forum in which group members shared their traumatic experiences. The comfortable atmosphere created by serving and drinking coffee, and the altruism inherent in such actions, provided group members with much-needed support. This support was especially valuable for those women who had lost their entire families through war and dislocation. The innovative design of this group encouraged the narration of pain and suffering, bringing relief to women who may not otherwise have sought therapy.

Group Therapy for Children and Adolescents

The safety and sharing that is possible in group therapy provides a positive therapeutic environment for children and adolescents who have experienced violence and trauma. Children are generally interested in social interactions; they enjoy being part of a peer group, and group therapy promotes this social aspect by allowing them to be with other children. Groups also meet children's developmental needs by being less intimidating and placing less pressure on children to interact with a therapist alone (Glass & Thompson, 2000).

Children who experience trauma feel isolated and uniquely different from their peers. Participation in traditional individual psychotherapy with a strange adult can be disquieting and intimidating for such children. In group therapy, this isolation is reduced because the child interacts with children who have similar issues. This interaction serves a normalizing function.

Children, and especially adolescents, are more positively reinforced by their peer group rather than by adults. Thus, the group format provides an opportunity, through peer feedback, to achieve change among this particular age group (Weinberg, 1990). Some adolescents isolate and become self-absorbed after a traumatic experience. Group therapy provides opportunities for these adolescents to focus on the external world as they give and receive support from their peers (Glass & Thompson, 2000).

Two theoretical models of group therapy have commonly been used with children: the integrated and the cognitive-behavioral therapy (CBT) models (Yule, 2001). Cognitive-behavioral approaches have shown the strongest empirical evidence for efficacy in resolving PTSD symptoms in children (Cohen, Berliner, & March, 2000). Several studies have evaluated the efficacy of CBT treatments for PTSD in children or adolescents (Cohen et al., 2000; Perrin, Smith, & Yule, 2000). These studies have focused on sexually abused children (Berliner & Saunders, 1996; Cohen & Mannarino, 1996, 1998; Deblinger, Lippmann, & Steer, 1996), children exposed to war (Saigh, 1987, 1989), adolescents exposed to a natural disaster (Goenjian, Karayan, & Pynoos, 1997), and adolescents exposed to a single stressor (March, Amaya-Jackson, Murray, & Schulte, 1998).

The integrated model uses techniques from several different theoretical traditions including CBT, while the CBT model focuses primarily on psycho-education, exposure therapy, and cognitive restructuring. In both models, participants meet weekly over 8 to 24 weeks. Group members are similar in terms of age and gender. To accommodate children's short attention span, groups are brief and focused (Glass & Thompson, 2000). Both the integrative and CBT group models report positive treatment results with children (Foy et al., 2001; Scheidlinger, 2004).

A growing number of studies are investigating crisis group interventions with school-age children (Brock, Lazarus, & Jimerson, 2002; Scheidlinger & Kahn, 2005; Zubenko & Capozzoli, 2002). Some of these group interventions have achieved successful outcomes (Stallard & Law, 1993). Children who participated in these interventions displayed fewer trauma symptoms compared to children who did not receive any post-trauma support (Stallard & Law, 1993; Thompson, 1993; Weinberg, 1990; Yule & Udwin, 1991).

However, time-limited trauma-focused group interventions may not always be effective, and some children may require longer-term therapy. For example, in a three-month follow-up study conducted among adolescent survivors of a minibus accident who participated in a trauma-focused crisis group, group members reported ongoing PTSD symptoms (Stallard & Law, 1993). These survivors had severe difficulties in concentration and displayed low academic performance. It was clear that they needed more intensive support and extensive intervention than a single group meeting allowed.

Trauma-Focused Groups for Children

Short-term crisis interventions may not provide children with enough support; they may need a more extended intervention (Silva et al., 2003). Short-term group therapies can be an alternative to crisis intervention. Brief trauma- and grief-focused psychotherapy groups conducted over several sessions significantly reduced stress symptoms of Armenian children exposed to a devastating earthquake (Goenjian et al., 1997). Structured and time-limited trauma groups (8 to 10 weeks) were effective in decreasing the rates of traumatic symptoms among inner-city African American youth who were survivors of homicide victims (Salloum, Avery, & McClain, 2001).

A school-based group therapy model extending over 18 sessions was effective in reducing trauma symptoms among children and adolescents exposed to a single trauma (March et al., 1998). The design of the group was cognitive-behavioral and focused on symptom reduction.

Similarly, Layne, Saltzmann, and Pynoos (1998) developed a school-based treatment manual for adolescents exposed to trauma and loss. All the students were diagnosed with PTSD. Group therapy, which extended over 20 sessions, was their primary therapeutic intervention. Trained group leaders focused on the following:

- Psycho-education, reconstruction, and reprocessing of trauma
- Coping with traumatic reminders
- Managing post-disaster stressors
- Loss and grief
- Facilitating normal developmental activities

Both school-based group models showed positive results in outcome studies (Silva, Alpert, Munoz, Singh, Matzner, & Dummit, 2000). Finally, a study was conducted with student survivors of a bus accident. The survivors met 11 times over a 6-week period (Turner, 2000). The core goals of the intervention were group building, developing coping skills, reconstructing the trauma narrative, and understanding loss and grief. A follow-up study found the majority of the group members were coping well and did not need further counseling. Overall, group treatment has positive results with children and adolescents. It is safe to conclude that group therapy may be a preferable intervention for this population.

I have used a CBT model to conduct groups with adolescent girls who have experienced sexual assault. The size of the group is limited to 8 to 10 members, and each session runs for 90 minutes for a period of 6 weeks. Ideally, this CBT group is co-led by therapists who provide support to each other before, during, and after each group session. The protocol below describes the steps followed in conducting these CBT groups.

A CBT Group With Adolescent Survivors of Sexual Assault

The goal of the cognitive-behavioral group is to increase adolescent survivors' understanding of trauma and its effects on the individual. Group members initially develop feelings of safety and mastery over traumatic material through psycho-educational exercises. Helplessness and a loss of control are common reactions to trauma; the information provided in the group informs members and helps them gain empowerment. Since trauma survivors often have difficulty regulating their feelings, the cognitive exercises practiced in the safety of the group help them achieve control over negative and unpleasant feelings. The capacity to trust is severely damaged after a sexual trauma. The group exercises and the format of the group helps restore confidence among survivors. Finally, normalization of reactions is important because survivors often feel alone in their pain and suffering. Being in the presence of other survivors can be self-validating.

Screening of Group Members

Co-facilitators screen group members. During this initial screening interview, group members are provided with a brief description of the group, its objectives, and other logistical details about meeting time and location.

Facilitators set the guidelines for eligibility. The following are some criteria to consider:

- Females between the ages of 12 and 16;
- Sexual assault occurred within the past year;
- No major trauma experienced prior to the current incident;
- Currently attending school;
- Not living in an unsafe home environment where the perpetrator may be present;
- Not taking any psychotropic medications;
- Does not have a major psychiatric disorder;
- Does not exhibit homicidal, suicidal, or para-suicidal behavior.

Group Design and Content

Each group session lasts 90 minutes because adolescents' attention span is shorter than that of adults. This shorter period also supports the goals of containment rather than exploration. An important goal of cognitive-behavioral group therapy is to focus on content rather than process. Each group therapy session is designed to include the six core elements outlined below:

1. Check–in occurs at the beginning of each group session and provides members with an opportunity to state how they are feeling, identify current problems and concerns, and generally establish a readiness to engage in the group process.

2. Group guidelines are established to maintain group safety and cohesion. These group rules will be reviewed at the beginning of each session so that members can become familiar with them.
   - Confidentiality and its limits.
   - Mutual respect. Members are asked to be respectful of each others' comments and not to judge the statements of other members, especially if they are different from one's own.
   - Openness. Members are encouraged to be open to new ideas and thoughts.
   - Self-focus. When making opinion statements, members are asked to maintain an "I" focus. Although members may feel strongly about something, it may not necessarily reflect the sentiment of the entire group.
   - Time. Because group time is limited, it is important for group members to share equally in the time. Co-leaders take responsibility to use a hand signal or any other agreed-upon signal to indicate when a particular group member takes too much time.

3. Relaxation exercises are taught and practiced in each session. These exercises help group members calm down when traumatic material threatens to overwhelm them.

4. Most of the group session is spent on a discussion of a specific topic. These topics are discussed in detail below.

5. Homework tasks are an important aspect of CBT groups and are assigned to bridge the time between group sessions. Group facilitators outline the rationale for these tasks and explore potential obstacles to their completion toward the end of each session.

6. All sessions end with a check-out, which provides group members with an opportunity to report on their reactions to the group session, to assist in the planning for the coming week, to calm distressed members, and to reinforce the individual changes that were observed in the group session.

Sample of a Six-Session Group

Session One

Co-leaders provide a brief overview of what group members can expect from participation in the group:

1. Cognitive framework for understanding trauma and its effects
2. Developing strategies for affect regulation (how we feel)
3. Developing strategies for managing negative thoughts
4. Exposure to stress or trauma through imagination/drawing/writing
5. Developing strategies for safety and self-care
6. Helping restore trust and connection with others

Traumatized adolescents are often hypervigilant and have difficulty relaxing physically and emotionally. There is substantial evidence that physical relaxation contributes to stress reduction (Foa & Zoellner, 1998). The following progressive muscle relaxation and deep breathing techniques are taught to help group members develop specific relaxation exercises.

Deep Breathing

This is a controlled breathing technique to help group members relax. They are asked to visualize the stomach as if it is a balloon. Taking in a deep breath, they begin to fill the balloon and the abdomen rises. Participants hold their breath for a count of 10 before exhaling slowly through the mouth as the balloon deflates and the abdomen falls. Group members complete 6 to 10 cycles of deep breathing (see also Appendix VI).

Muscle Relaxation

Group members sit comfortably in a chair with their feet flat on the ground and their hands in their laps. They are asked to gently close their eyes when ready or keep them open if it makes them uncomfortable. The co-leader explains that this exercise involves a series of muscle tensing and relaxing cycles in which participants are asked to tighten muscles in a specific area of the body (like making a tight fist) and then relax the muscles in that same area. They begin with the toes and progress up to the head. This exercise can take up to 10 to 15 minutes to complete. Group members practice this exercise during group sessions. They are encouraged to practice and use this exercise outside group sessions whenever they feel stress and anxiety (see also Appendix VII).

Group leaders assess which relaxation technique is preferred by group members and based on this information make a decision on which techniques to use in subsequent sessions.

Session Two

The major focus of this session is the symptom checklist and developing self-care strategies. Group leaders review the definition of trauma. They briefly describe how people respond to traumatic events and the broad range of responses that are dependent on an individual's personality, past experiences, and connection to the event (see Appendix I). Group leaders ask members to name some of the reactions they have noticed since the trauma occurred.

Using a flip chart, group leaders develop a list and teach that stress reactions fall into categories:

- Psychological: numbness, guilt, grief, helplessness, hopelessness, anger, rage, feeling unclean
- Physical: sleep problems, appetite increase or decrease, dizziness, sweating, rapid pulse
- Cognitive: confusion, difficulty remembering
- Behavioral: difficulty trusting, irritability, being critical of others, feeling isolated/alienated, feeling alone
- Spiritual: loss of faith, despair, feeling life is meaningless

Group leaders emphasize that there can be a wide range of reactions, but these are all normal reactions to trauma and stress. They predict that individuals will sometimes feel like they are on a roller coaster of reactions, feeling angry on one day and sad on another.

Next, group leaders ask members to brainstorm activities that have helped them reduce stress. Again, group leaders generate a list on a flip chart. They teach self-care strategies and emphasize the importance of engaging in activities that alleviate trauma and stress reactions. For example, if an individual isolates in response to stress, then she is encouraged to engage in social activities, like going to a movie or visiting a friend (see also Appendix II). Group members are encouraged to participate in self-care activities that are do-able and accomplished at minimal financial cost (e.g., visiting a friend in the next town may be more easily achieved than visiting someone in another state).

Group members are given a detailed handout that outlines common reactions and self-care strategies and an abbreviated handout that they can keep in their possession all the time. Group members are encouraged to refer to this abbreviated handout on a regular basis, to remind them that distressing reactions are to be expected and that self-care strategies reduce these reactions.

Group leaders ask members to complete a safety and self-care worksheet (see Appendix V). The following questions are included in the worksheet to encourage members to think about how they can both ensure safety and care for themselves:

- When have you felt safe? Describe.
- Describe three ways in which you take care of yourself.
- Describe ways in which you think you do not take care of yourself.
- I take good care of myself when I am feeling . . .
- I do not take care of myself when I am feeling . . .
- When I imagine myself feeling safe . . .

Session Three

The topic for Session Three is how to combat negative thoughts by using thought stopping and thought replacement.

This exercise enhances the individual's sense of control over unpleasant and negative thoughts. Group members are asked to think about what mechanism would best help them stop a thought (e.g., repeating a statement like "Stop!" or "Quit," looking at a picture that is always carried, wearing a rubber band that is snapped against the wrist when a negative thought surfaces).

Another method to control negative thoughts is to replace them with memories that are more positive. Group members are asked to think about a positive experience and to go over the details of the experience silently in their minds. They can keep doing this exercise until they have a clear picture of the pleasant/positive experience (e.g., walking along a beach, riding a bike in the park).

Group members are encouraged to use thought replacement when negative thoughts interfere with their daily activities. Sometimes they might find it helpful to write negative thoughts in a journal. This affords group members control over their thoughts, is experienced as empowering, and is less avoidant.

Session Four

One of the most profound consequences of a traumatic experience is the betrayal of trust. For this reason, the role of trust in recovery has to be explored. In rebuilding trust, group members are invited to talk about how their traumatic experience affects their ability to trust themselves and their world. Some may be distrustful of others while other clients may trust too quickly, out of fear of being alone. Sometimes, when the survivor is unable to recall all the details of the traumatic event, trust in one's own ability is eroded. Group therapy serves the role of restoring faith in self and others. Group leaders ask members to complete a worksheet on trust that answers the following questions:

- What do I understand by trust?
- How do I know I can trust someone?
- When does a person break my trust?
- How am I affected when someone breaks my trust?
- I trust others more when . . .
- Do I trust myself since the rape? Explain.

Session Five

The focus of Session Five is group members' traumatic memories. Exposure to stress or trauma can be achieved through imagination, drawing, and writing exercises. Group treatment that includes writing about traumatic memories has been shown to decrease trauma-related symptoms (Bradley & Follingstad, 2003). In cognitive-processing therapy, individuals elicit memories of an event by first writing about the trauma. This written account is later read to the group (Resick & Schnicke, 1992).

In their trauma narratives, members are encouraged to include sensory perceptions, thoughts, and emotional reactions that occurred during the incident. During this recounting of the traumatic experience, minimal prompts are given by the facilitators because the therapeutic objective is to encourage members to assume responsibility for their "self-exposure" (Foy et al., 2002). Group members are encouraged to continue this work by keeping a journal to record memories, thoughts, and reactions.

Session Six

The topic for this session is how to rebuild connections and support. Human interactions are a basic developmental need. Group members are invited to think about safe and supportive relationships and to name and discuss them. The following questions help group members think about relationships with others in ways that feel safe and secure.

- Who are the people in my life with whom I feel most supported and connected?
- When do I feel most comfortable socially?
- What things in a relationship make me feel uncomfortable?
- What change would I like to see in my relationships?
- What can I do to help myself become more comfortable in my relationships?
- Name someone I feel safe with and consider a support.
- How can I ask that person if she will be there for me?

Substantial time is spent on the closing discussion because it is the last session. Group members are given a list of resources for obtaining help once the group ends.

Conclusion

Several group models for trauma survivors have been reviewed. Groups provide individuals with opportunities that would take longer to achieve in individual therapy. Clients often find themselves confronted earlier and their denial questioned sooner by other group members, who may not be concerned about offending a fellow member.

By combining cultural practice with group therapy, it is possible to reach people who may not otherwise seek therapy. The use of these cultural practices serves a dual purpose of providing therapy in a manner that is culturally meaningful while benefiting those cultural groups for whom cultural preservation may be a concern. For children, a longer-term group therapy model is developmentally appropriate and more effective in helping them come to terms with traumas they experience.

References

Berliner, L., & Saunders, B. E. (1996). Treating fear and anxiety in sexually abused children: Results of a controlled 2-year follow-up study. *Child Maltreatment, 1,* 294–309.

Bradley, R. G., & Follingstad, D. R. (2003). Group therapy for incarcerated women who experienced interpersonal violence: A pilot study. *Journal of Traumatic Stress, 16*(4), 337–340.

Brock, S. E., Lazarus, P. J., & Jimerson, S. R. (Eds.). (2002). *Best practices in school crisis prevention and intervention.* Bethesda, MD: National Association of School Psychologists.

Chu, J. A. (1998). *Rebuilding shattered lives: The responsible treatment of complex post-traumatic and dissociative disorders.* New York: Wiley.

Cohen, J. A., Berliner, L., & March, J. S. (2000). Treatment of children and adolescents. In E. B. Foa, T. M. Keane, & M. J. Friedman (Eds.), *Effective treatments for PTSD* (pp. 330–332). New York: Guilford Press.

Cohen, J. A., & Mannarino, A. P. (1996). A treatment outcome study for sexually abused pre-school children: Initial findings. *Journal of the American Academy of Child & Adolescent Psychiatry, 35*(10), 1402–1410.

Cohen, J. A., & Mannarino, A. P. (1998). Interventions for sexually abused children: Initial treatment outcome findings. *Child Maltreatment, 3,* 17–26.

Deblinger, E., Lippman, J., & Steer, R. (1996). Sexually abused children suffering post-traumatic stress symptoms: Initial treatment outcome findings. *Child Maltreatment, 1,* 310–321.

Erikson, E. H. (1968). *Identity: Youth and crisis.* New York: Norton.

Foa, E. B., Keane, T. M., & Friedman, M. J. (2000). *Effective treatments for PTSD: Practice guidelines from the International Society for Traumatic Stress Studies.* New York: Guilford.

Foa, E. B., & Zoellner, L. A. (1998). Posttraumatic stress disorder in female victims of assault: Theory and treatment. In E. Sanavio (Ed.), *Behavior and cognitive therapy today: Essays in honor of Hans J. Eysenck* (pp. 87–101). Oxford: Elsevier Science.

Foy, D. W., Eriksson, C. B., & Trice, G. A. (2001). Introduction to group interventions for trauma survivors. *Group Dynamics: Theory, Research and Practice, 5*(4), 246–251.

Foy, D. W., Ruzek, J. I., Glynn, S. M., Riney, S. J., & Gusman, F. D. (2002). Trauma focus group therapy for combat-related PTSD: An update. *Psychotherapy in Practice, 58*(8), 907–918.

Glass, D., & Thompson, S. (2000). Therapeutic group work. In K. N. Dwivedi (Ed.), *Post-traumatic disorder in children and adolescents* (pp. 163–183). London/ Philadelphia: Whurr.

Goenjian, A. K., Karayan, I., & Pynoos, R. (1997). Outcome of psychotherapy among early adolescents after trauma. *American Journal of Psychiatry, 154*(4), 536–542.

Hanscom, K. L. (2001). Treating survivors of war trauma and torture. *American Psychologist, 56*(11), 1032–1039.

Hurdle, D. E. (2002). Native Hawaiian traditional healing: Culturally based interventions for social work practice. *Social Work, 47*(2), 183–192.

Jenkens, J. (1996). Culture emotion and PTSD. In A. J. Marsella, M. J. Friedman, E. T. Gerrity, & R. M. Scurfield (Eds.), *Ethnocultural aspects of posttraumatic stress disorder: Issues, research and clinical applications* (pp. 165–182). Washington, DC: American Psychological Association.

Johnson, D., & Lubin, H. (2000). Group therapy for the symptoms of posttraumatic stress disorder. In R. H. Klein & V. Schermer (Eds.), *Group psychotherapy for psychological trauma* (pp. 141–169). New York: Guilford.

Layne, C. M., Saltzmann, W. R., & Pynoos., R. S. (1998). A school-based mental health intervention program in Bosnia/Herzegovina: Preliminary findings. In R. S. Pynoos, *School-based mental health intervention with traumatized children and adolescents: Preliminary findings from programs in California and Bosnia/Herzegovina.* Symposium conducted at the meeting of the International Society for Traumatic Stress Studies, Washington, DC.

Loewy, M. I., Williams, D. T., & Keleta, A. (2002). Group counseling with traumatized East African refugee women in the United States: Using the Kaffa ceremony intervention. *Journal for Specialists in Group Work, 27*(2), 173–191.

Mapp, I., & Koch, D. (2004). Creation of a group mural to promote healing following a mass trauma. In N. B. Webb (Ed.), *Mass trauma and violence: Helping children and families cope* (pp. 100–119). New York: Guilford.

March J. S., Amaya-Jackson, L., Murray, M. C., & Schulte, A. (1998) Cognitive-behavioral psychotherapy for children and adolescents with posttraumatic stress disorder after a single incident stressor. *Journal of the American Academy of Child and Adolescent Psychiatry, 37,* 587–593.

Nader, K., Dubrow, N., & Stamm, B. H. (1999). *Honoring differences: Cultural issues in the treatment of trauma and loss.* Philadelphia, PA: Brunner/Mazel.

Pack-Brown, S. P., Whittington-Clark, L. E., & Parker, W. M. (1998). *Images of me.* Boston: Allyn & Bacon.

Perrin, S., Smith, P., & Yule, W. (2000). Practitioner review: The assessment and treatment of posttraumatic stress disorder in children and adolescents. *Journal of Child Psychology and Psychiatry and Allied Disciplines, 41,* 277–289.

Putnam, F. W. (1989). *The diagnosis and treatment of multiple personality disorder.* New York: Guilford.

Resick, P. A., & Schnicke, M. (1992). Cognitive processing therapy for sexual assault victims. *Journal of Consulting and Clinical Psychology, 60,* 748–756.

Saigh, P. A. (1987). In vitro flooding of an adolescent posttraumatic stress disorder. *Journal of Clinical Child Psychology, 16,* 147–150.

Saigh, P. A. (1989). The development and validation of the Children's Posttraumatic Stress Disorder Inventory. *International Journal of Special Education, 4,* 75–84.

Salloum, A., Avery, L., & McClain, R. P. (2001). Group psychotherapy for adolescent survivors of homicide victims: A pilot study. *Journal of the American Academy of Child and Adolescent Psychiatry, 40*(11), 1261–1267.

Scheidlinger, S. (2004). Group psychotherapy and related helping groups today: An overview. *American Journal of Psychotherapy, 58*(3), 265–280.

Scheidlinger, S., & Kahn, G. B. (2005). In the aftermath of September 11: Group interventions with children revisited. *International Journal of Group Psychotherapy, 55*(3), 335–354.

Silva, R. R., Alpert, M., Munoz, D. M., Singh, S., Matzner, F., & Dummit, S. (2000). Stress and vulnerability to post-traumatic stress disorder in children and adolescents. *American Journal of Orthopsychiatry, 157*(8), 1229–1235.

Silva, R. R., Cloitre, M., Davis, L., Levitt, J., Gomez, S., Ngai, I., et al. (2003). Early intervention with traumatized children. *Psychiatric Quarterly, 74*(4), 333–347.

Solomon, S. D., & Johnson, D. M. (2002). Psychosocial treatment of posttraumatic stress disorder: A practice-friendly review of outcome research. *Psychotherapy in Practice, 58*(8), 947–959.

Stallard, P., & Law, F. (1993). Screening and psychological debriefing of adolescent survivors of life threatening events. *British Journal of Psychiatry, 163*, 660–665.

Sue, D. W., & Sue, D. (2003). *Counseling the culturally different: Theory and practice* (4th ed.). New York: Wiley.

Thompson, R. A. (1993). Posttraumatic stress and posttraumatic loss debriefing: Brief strategic interventions for survivors of sudden loss. *The School Counselor, 41*, 16–22.

Turner, A. L. (2000). Group treatment of trauma survivors following a fatal bus accident: Integrating theory and practice. *Group Dynamics, Theory, Research and Practice, 4*(2), 139–149.

van der Kolk, B. A. (1993). Group psychotherapy with posttraumatic stress disorders. In H. I. Kaplan & B. J. Sadock (Eds.), *Comprehensive textbook of group psychotherapy* (pp. 550–560). Baltimore: Williams & Wilkins.

Washington, O. G. M., & Moxley, D. P. (2003). Promising group practices to empower low-income minority women coping with chemical dependency. *American Journal of Orthopsychiatry, 73*(1), 109–116.

Weeks, O. D. (2001, June). *Rituals.* Paper presented at the World Gathering on Bereavement, Columbus, OH.

Weinberg, R. B. (1990). Serving large numbers of adolescent victim-survivors: Group interventions following trauma at school. *Professional Psychology: Research and Practice, 21*(4), 271–278.

Wessells, M. G. (1999). Culture, power and community: Intercultural approaches to psychosocial assistance and healing. In K. Nader, N. Dubrow, & B. H. Stamm (Eds.), *Honoring differences: Cultural issues in the treatment of trauma and loss* (pp. 267–280). Philadelphia, PA: Brunner/Mazel.

Wilson, J. (1988). Treating the Vietnam veteran. In F. M. Ochberg (Ed.), *Posttraumatic therapy and victims of violence* (pp. 254–277). New York: Brunner/Mazel.

Yalom, I. D. (1995). *The theory and practice of group psychotherapy.* New York: Basic Books.

Yule, W. (2001). When disaster strikes—the need to be wise before the event: Crisis intervention with children. *Advances in Mind-Body Medicine, 17*(3), 191–196.

Yule, W., & Udwin, O. (1991). Screening child survivors for post traumatic stress disorders: Experiences from the "Jupiter" sinking. *British Journal of Clinical Psychology, 30*, 131–138.

Zubenko, W. N., & Capozzoli, J. A. (2002). *Children and disasters: A practical guide to healing and recovery.* New York: Oxford University Press.

7

Community Trauma and Working in the Schools

At 2:00 p.m. on a Tuesday afternoon in late September, a 911 call came from a high school in a Northeastern city. A sophomore was found slumped in the stairwell. Several attempts by EMT workers to revive the young man failed. He was taken to the hospital and later confirmed dead. The cause of his death was a heroin overdose. Two weeks earlier another student had suffered a similar death. Heroin abuse among young adults in the affected community was reaching epidemic proportions; the drug, at $4.00 a bag, was so potent that it was snorted instead of injected. Heroin overdose had become the leading causes of death among young adults in this close-knit community.

People in communities that lose children to tragic circumstances tend to bond together, and this community was no exception. In response to the crisis, concerned parents gathered at community meetings and at candlelight vigils. By collaborating with local mental health centers, parents were able to use these meetings to discuss their fears, vulnerabilities, and other emotional reactions. Substance abuse counselors provided information on addictive behaviors and resources for those who were willing to get help. In the company of people who had similar reactions, affected parents were slowly empowered to explore different strategies they could use to support their children. They were determined to discard their initial denial about their children's drug addiction. As a result of these meetings, a group of mothers with children addicted to heroin started a 24-hour hotline for families in need of help. The group finds treatment for those who seek it, sometimes driving people to their first appointment. For many young adults, they have become a lifeline.

The first half of this chapter focuses on different community approaches to healing in the aftermath of trauma. Guidelines for organizing and conducting community meetings, candlelight vigils, and town meetings are discussed. Particular attention is paid to making these interventions culturally appropriate. When an intervention is culturally appropriate, members of culturally diverse communities feel understood; they will have greater ownership of the intervention process. The psychotherapist is encouraged to focus on strengths and existing resources in the communities where the trauma occurred (Marotta, 2000).

The second half of the chapter covers effective approaches for working in school communities. Recently, in the wake of several major school-related traumas, schools have been encouraged to develop crisis protocols. Finally, the chapter concludes with a review of helpful strategies that can be incorporated in the construction of crisis protocols.

Types of Community Trauma

Communities offer individuals a sense of identity and belonging. Ecologically, the community serves as the interface between the individual and the larger society while providing members with knowledge, beliefs, traditions, and values. Through membership, communities support and unify people. The following are examples of incidents that can disrupt community cohesion:

- Incidents that occur in communities where people are strongly affiliated (e.g., the workplace, school, or neighborhood)
- Incidents that involve direct victims who hold a special position within the affected community (e.g., the violent death of a child or a well-known member of the community)
- Incidents that involve multiple direct victims and eyewitnesses
- Incidents that require numerous emergency or rescue workers
- Incidents that attract a great deal of media attention

Community Reactions to Trauma

Just as there are many possible ways an individual may respond to trauma, there are varied ways a community may respond to trauma as well. There is no universal reaction to a trauma. How a community responds to a trauma depends on many factors:

- The community's history of trauma. If a community has not experienced a traumatic event before, community members are apt to quickly mobilize their resources to deal with the traumatizing event.
- Whether the community has been traumatized on an ongoing basis. Chronically traumatized communities may withdraw in the face of a new stressor.
- The location of a community. Urban communities may have more access to resources than rural and outlying communities that find obtaining help challenging.
- Availability of resources within the community. Affluent communities offer members greater economic and psychological support.

Community reactions to trauma can be classified as psychological, behavioral, physical, spiritual, or relational.

Psychological. Psychological reactions that pervade a community are evident in tension, fear, and sadness among its members. Chronically traumatized communities often display these reactions. Similar reactions are evident in communities that experience an overwhelming trauma. For example, even if one was unaware that a terrorist attack had occurred in New York City on September 11, 2001, as one walked the streets or rode the subway on the days that followed, it would have become fairly obvious that something devastating had occurred.

Behavioral. Some communities become closed after a traumatic experience. This is evident in the drawn curtains and blinds that may cover the windows of houses in such neighborhoods. In closed communities, people appear preoccupied and hypervigilant. They may walk at a fast pace and hesitate to make eye contact with others. Individuals may be curt and dismissive when neighbors ask for help. Alternatively, some communities become more cohesive and inviting in the aftermath of a trauma. Members of such communities are likely to gather informally on the street, in schools, and in community centers.

Physical. Physical reactions to trauma are visible in communities that appear to be under "lockdown." Homes in these communities have sophisticated alarm systems, guard dogs, gates, and fences. Other communities are shabby and neglected. Garbage remains uncollected, homes dilapidated, and gardens unkempt. In contrast, some communities make concerted efforts to beautify and rehabilitate their physical surroundings. Flower beds are planted in public places and memorials are erected to honor losses incurred from the trauma.

Spiritual. Vigils, community prayers, memorials, healing rituals, and church attendance become more prevalent in some traumatized communities. Conversely, church attendance can decrease in a community after a trauma has occurred.

Relational. In some communities, a traumatic event results in community members' increased withdrawal from the outside world. A breakdown in trust between residents and local authorities develops. Overtures of help are frequently declined. Boundaries of some communities become hardened, especially those that are chronically traumatized. External help is viewed as intrusive, and community members possess little hope for the future. In contrast, communities with porous boundaries are open to receiving any offered help. Members of such communities are optimistic that their situation will improve. They make deliberate efforts to connect with the communities that surround them in order to maximize support.

Cultural Considerations in Community Responses

In assessing whether a group or individual intervention is appropriate, the intervenor must have familiarity with the community's cultural values. For example, Latino communities that are culturally grounded in a collectivist identity may favor a group intervention to trauma (Friedman & Marsella, 1996; Stamm & Stamm, 1999). Native American culture offers many useful examples of culturally appropriate community interventions to healing.

In 1990, the Big Foot Memorial Ride was organized in an effort to memorialize the 100-year anniversary of the massacre at Wounded Knee. Native people on horseback retraced steps taken from Standing Rock Reservation by Lakota Chief Si Tanka (Big Foot) after Tatanka Iyotake (Sitting Bull), the great spiritual leader, was killed. The Chief was intercepted by the U.S. Seventh Cavalry and escorted to Wounded Knee. In the battle that erupted, more than 250 Lakota men, women, and children were killed. The massacre destroyed the morale of the Plains Indians.

Despite the devastation experienced by the Plains Indians, the Memorial Ride successfully acknowledged and celebrated the fortitude and strength displayed by those who survived. Furthermore, it helped give closure to a 100-year period of the Native people's mourning. The Big Foot Memorial Ride has become an annual event to recognize the resilience of the Native people.

In the film *Carved from the Heart*, Stan Marsden is an Alaskan member of the Tsimshian tribe who describes the loss of his son: "A pain in my heart, it's hard to explain, a hurt and an ache, almost like a cramp." To commemorate the loss of his son, Marsden began carving a totem pole. Other community members soon participated in the project, viewing it as an opportunity to heal their own losses: a woman who suffered a miscarriage, a Vietnam veteran who had never spoken of his war trauma. The totem pole soon became a symbol of the community's healing and strength.

In Native American culture, traditional totem poles are sometimes carved to honor the death of a community leader or to memorialize a traumatic event. The ceremonious carving and raising of the totem pole helps community members express their grief. Amidst their losses, the community finds strength in a rich cultural tradition. Counselors are ethically responsible for identifying strengths inherent in a community to support culturally appropriate healing.

Traditional Native American healing practices are holistic. In contrast to Western approaches, which center on the individual, Native American practices focus on the emotional, spiritual, psychological, and cultural benefits of healing for the entire group (Dubrow & Nader, 1999). Sweat lodges are one example of a holistic healing practice. People from Native American communities sit in a sweat lodge to gain psychological healing. A ritual ceremony is performed while the individual endures extreme heat within the confined space of a sweat lodge. This practice has reportedly reduced negative reactions among trauma victims (Wilson, 1988).

Communities mourn in idiosyncratic ways, some of which are based on the developmental stage of their members. A state representative of a small town invited a local counseling agency to assist a grieving community by providing crisis support after the death of two teenagers in a "road rage" accident. Parents in this community were gravely concerned about how their teenage children would react to the incident. Would they engage in "copy cat" syndrome by recklessly driving? Would they respond with violence in order to avenge their friends' death?

Counselors found themselves standing on the sidewalk of a busy street with a group of teenagers. Wreaths, flowers, notes, cards, and personal items (including a plaid shirt and baseball cap of the deceased) were carefully placed on the growing memorial. The memorial was constructed hastily at the exact site of the accident that had cost these young boys their lives. The counselors spent several hours consoling upset young men and women; some cried uncontrollably, while others stared stoically. At the end of the day, counselors had to remind themselves that their presence was all the support the affected community needed at the time. The young people were not ready to talk that day, nor might they be in the future. For many, the fatal accident was the first experience of loss in their lives.

Important Principles in Community Trauma

History

Communities often have histories of trauma that influence future responses. The first step in designing community interventions is to establish the community's trauma history and understand its impact. Information regarding the success or failure of past interventions influences planning. Responses to the following points will build a historical account of a community's traumatic past.

- Dates of past traumatic incidents
- Description of events
- People involved
- Interventions planned
- Assessment of what worked and why it worked
- Assessment of what did not work and why it did not work

Reactions. In community trauma, individuals inevitably witness the reactions of others. Unlike individual trauma, community trauma offers individuals the opportunity to compare reactions and receive support from others who also experienced the event (Webb, 2004a). People react in a multitude of ways and at a varied pace. For some people, their own reactions may become prolonged or exacerbated as they observe the grief and loss of others entrenched in earlier stages of recovery. Children are particularly sensitive to the emotional climate that surrounds them. They are easily influenced by the mood of adults around them and may react with calm or panic, depending on the behavior of caregivers (Arroyo & Eth, 1996).

Boundaries. Traumatized communities struggle with boundaries. They often find themselves barraged by outsiders while they struggle to initiate their own coping strategies. The media, especially in high profile cases, presents significant challenges to vulnerable communities.

Fragmentation. Communities can become fragmented in the aftermath of trauma. The core organizing beliefs that may have served them well under normal circumstances may become strained and challenged under stress.

Cohesion. Traumatic events carry the potential to unite communities. When this happens, past differences fade or are cast aside as people focus on supporting each other. A traumatic event can be the glue that binds communities together.

Unpredictability. We cannot predict how a trauma will affect a particular community. In communities where shooting incidents are commonplace, a new incident may be viewed with apathy. However, an unusual trauma (e.g., the rape of an elderly woman) may evoke community outrage and indignation.

Legends. Violence can create legends. People make a permanent association between a community and a particular traumatic event. For example, the town of Littleton, Colorado, will always be associated with the Columbine School student shootings in 1999. Similarly, Waco, Texas, will always be remembered for the botched FBI attack on the home of a religious sect in 1993.

Community Interventions After Trauma

Community-based interventions call for a redefinition of the counselor's role to that of a consultant. This revised role is a facilitative rather than directive one. In the role of a consultant, the counselor brings valuable knowledge and expertise to a community. Simultaneously, community counselors collaborate with local leaders and agencies. Community members are viewed as experts regarding their own experiences, while the consultant assists in shaping community interventions. Communities are empowered when the consultant does the following:

- Remains in the background and takes an outsider role,
- Discourages dependency and encourages community leadership,
- Utilizes culturally appropriate practices,
- Advances the process of community change.

Different community interventions have been used in the aftermath of traumatic events: community debriefings, community meetings, and community information groups. Community meetings can support residents who feel helpless, thwart community outrage, and offer people a place to express their feelings of frustration. A community meeting can be organized as an immediate response, with local leaders and significant community members working closely with mental health providers to plan and conduct the meeting. Community members may hold opposing views, but community meetings can play an important role in bringing people with diverse opinions together to discuss these differences. In addition, community meetings play a valuable role in predicting and preparing community members for both short-term and long-term reactions. Guidelines on how to conduct a community meeting are outlined below. These guidelines are derived from my involvement in many diverse communities affected by violence. Pre-planning is a critical component of the model because careful planning will ultimately determine the success of an intervention.

Guidelines for Conducting Community Meetings

Pre-Planning

In the pre-planning stage of a community meeting, key community members (church leaders, mayor, local council members, and school superintendent) are identified and invited to all pre-planning gatherings. In some immigrant communities, local leaders from the dominant group may be perceived as not understanding the cultural needs of the community. Instead, local business leaders who share the community's culture may appropriately represent the community's interests. The goal is to use key community members to implement interventions. Additionally, the inclusion of significant community members is the first step toward empowering a community in crisis.

An understanding of a community's culture and history is gained through the help of community leaders. These leaders can also provide information on the success and challenges of past interventions. This understanding ultimately informs the planning of the next intervention. Determining how a community views change and receives outside help is both helpful and informative. Whether a community has open or closed boundaries provides information on whether the intervenor should proceed cautiously to prevent unnecessary community antagonism or proactively with subdued communities. Communities with open boundaries are generally receptive to outside help, while communities with closed boundaries may be suspicious of outsiders.

Knowing whether any hidden agendas (political, administrative, and personal) exist can be invaluable in building interventions. Sometimes an individual may request crisis services on behalf of a community in order to pursue a personal goal.

Several years ago, while intervening in a large, socioeconomically distressed housing development, my co-workers and I struggled to understand why this particular community was opposed to any suggestions that were discussed at pre-planning meetings. Later, while chatting informally with a community member, we learned that the community had a conflictual relationship with the housing manager who had requested our services. The community member stated that the manager was notorious for being inattentive to the community's needs. In the past, several petitions had been signed with the hope of discharging the housing manager from his duties. Since the traumatic incident attracted local and national attention, the housing manager was motivated to show strong investment in the psychological well-being of the residents, in order to enhance his own reputation. The community recognized his motivation as insincere. After learning this information, we decreased the housing manager's involvement. As a result, we made major progress with community members. For the first time, this community felt understood, and they were determined to make the intervention successful.

The community engaged the support of many of its members who were willing to share their skills and strengths with others. In the end, the community took credit for what was achieved and thus became an empowered community in which members felt they had contributed to their own healing. As consultants, we realized that we had initially neglected to ask an important question: Whose interests were being served by the intervention? We soon learned that a request for a community intervention can easily become a political ploy that serves the interests of some to the detriment of others.

An important goal of pre-planning a community meeting is to create a resource folder that is made available to all attendees. The folder includes the following information:

- Handouts that delineate trauma reactions, stages of grief, and trauma recovery, as well as culturally appropriate coping skills;
- Telephone numbers of important institutions that can provide help;
- Brochures from various mental health agencies that serve traumatized clients;
- Instructions on how to seek victim compensation.

A major challenge is to ensure that all community members are informed about the meeting. Community leaders can help with this challenge by providing valuable cultural information, such as which communication method would result in the most positive response from community members. Will flyers only be read if they are handed out personally, or would placing them in mailboxes be sufficient? Will distributing flyers be perceived as "too pushy" and repel people from the beginning? Community leaders can also help in designing and distributing flyers, which contributes to the success of the meeting. This also provides another opportunity to help community leaders feel empowered. The flyer should include maps, directions, and an agenda for the community meeting.

A community meeting can draw media attention. Designating a particular individual, or a group of people, to respond to reporters or journalists ensures that the information given to the media is consistent. This also protects community members from the intrusive glare of television cameras during moments of vulnerability. Although appearing on the national news may be glamorous for some, many may later regret such involvement.

Establishing a convenient time and location for the community meeting, with input from community leaders, ensures maximum community attendance. Locations should be accessible to both people who use public transportation and people with disabilities. Most communities view schools and places of worship as favorable locations for this type of meeting.

It is practical, though not always possible, to provide snacks and water for attendees, especially if the meeting is scheduled immediately after work hours. A suggestion box strategically placed at the back of the room allows participants to provide suggestions on improving future community meetings. Attendees should also be encouraged to place questions and comments not covered in the meeting in the suggestion box. An attendance list with contact information, for those comfortable disclosing this information, can be generated. This data is important if it becomes necessary to reach community members in the future.

Structure of Meeting

Ideally, community members open and end community meetings. This routine communicates the message that community members are in charge of the community's well-being. This is an empowering strategy that allows attendees to see a familiar face at both the beginning and the end of the meeting. Starting and ending the meeting on time is important; it shows respect for community members who may have made major sacrifices to obtain child care and time off work in order to attend the meeting.

The community leader begins with a brief welcome and introduction and then reviews the agenda (see Sample Community Meeting Agenda).

Sample Community Meeting Agenda

1. Welcome and introduction by Mr. Bill Matthews, local council member for the town of Plainville.

2. Review objectives of community meeting (sharing information, getting people together) and guidelines (confidentiality, time, respecting each other's opinions).

3. Statement by town mayor.

4. Police commissioner updates community on progress of investigation and addresses public safety concerns.

5. Mental health counselor reviews psychological impact of event, predictable traumatic reactions, and coping skills. Some guidelines on how to interact with media are provided.

6. Mr. Matthews resumes role and facilitates community discussion. Community members may have concerns about issues raised or other questions they would like to address.

7. Direct community members to suggestion box at the back of the room where they can drop off unanswered questions and sign the information sheet with their names and contact details.

8. The meeting is closed.

At this point, the community leader invites attendees to add agenda items before outlining the major objectives and guidelines of the meeting. Guidelines include a request for confidentiality, a request that people stay for the entire meeting, a request that people share the time (so that as many people as possible can participate), a request to respect and tolerate differing opinions, and a request that people refrain from interrupting when someone else speaks.

The town mayor is one of the first invited speakers whose role is to reassure the community and inform them about steps taken by local authorities to ensure the safety of the community. The police commissioner follows to provide a legal update. Information about whether an arrest has been made, how the criminal investigation is proceeding, and how the community will be informed about unfolding events is provided by this officer of the law.

The psycho-educational segment of the meeting which follows is conducted by a mental health professional. This individual discusses the concepts of primary and secondary trauma and its ripple effect; common reactions to trauma for both adults and children (psychological, behavioral, physical, cognitive, and spiritual) are reviewed. This is followed by a discussion of coping strategies. This segment ends with a brief statement on how to handle the media during a traumatic time (see Psycho-Educational Outline).

Psycho-Educational Outline

1. Definition of stress and trauma
2. Common reactions to trauma
3. Stages of grief and loss
4. Positive coping skills
5. Interacting with media
6. Further resources

Community members are encouraged to seek further support from sources provided in the resource folder. The primary objective of this psycho-educational segment is to communicate safety and support, to provide structure and predictability, and to direct individuals to places where they can receive more help.

The community leader resumes his or her role and facilitates an open discussion. After this segment, it may be useful to announce that if all issues and questions are not covered by the end of the meeting, attendees can make comments by using the suggestion box. Subcommittees can be established to continue working on important issues that are generated during the community meeting. The community leader should try to end on a positive note with a concrete plan of action.

Community meetings are a productive way to reach a large number of people simultaneously. The psycho-educational segment of the intervention may be all the help some people receive after a traumatic incident. Carefully conducted community interventions that include adequate preparation and community involvement can be empowering interventions for most communities.

Working With Large Groups in a School Setting

Working with a large number of students in a school setting requires a team of helpers. The team approach makes it possible to delegate the many tasks that emerge when working with a large and vulnerable group (Weinberg, 1990). The team can be involved in planning large school assemblies, facilitating small group meetings, and offering one-on-one sessions. School assemblies should have four primary objectives:

1. Describing and normalizing grief reactions

2. Identifying healthy coping responses

3. Identifying students who need further interventions

4. Decreasing the risk of suicide, especially following suicide deaths

If small group meetings are conducted, they should share similar goals. These groups allow group members to support each other and offer mutual assistance. Using groups to allow group members an opportunity to express their feelings may not be wise. Solely using a group for this purpose can actually increase anxiety and stress (Pynoos & Nader, 1993). Instead, the researchers suggest a constructive and therapeutic approach that promotes a child's sense of mastery and control while presenting new ways to problem-solve.

If psycho-educational groups are conducted in schools, Eth (1992) suggests that these groups should be conducted by both mental health professionals and teachers. A teacher can provide a group leader with information on a child's baseline functioning. This teacher can also continue to monitor the child once the group concludes. The mental health provider helps the teacher identify those children who may need further help (Yule, 1999). If a child continues to exhibit emotional and behavioral problems as a result of a traumatic event, caregivers are encouraged to seek professional help (Williams, 2004).

Planning Ahead in Schools

The increase in incidents of school violence (Barta, 2000) has led the federal government to pass legislation including the Safe Schools/Health Start Initiative (U.S. Department of Education, 2001) and No Child Left Behind Act of 2001. These acts require that all schools strive to be safe, violence-free environments that focus on the academic excellence of every student.

It is prudent for every school in the U.S. to follow these federal directives to create a climate that is conducive to learning.

Crises occurring in schools include bomb threats, gang activity, fights, natural disasters, youth suicide, and shooting incidents (Pitcher & Poland, 1992; Poland, 1994). In addition, schools may also be affected by community violence. When violence occurs in a community, the school becomes a practical location for meetings, interventions, and bringing members of a community together. Schools are an important element of a community because they are a place where young children spend a significant amount of time. School-based interventions are strongly recommended when a natural disaster (such as an earthquake or flood) causes a widespread disruption of service. When a child's environment becomes chaotic, as it is likely to become after a major disaster, attending school in the company of familiar peers and teachers can establish a sense of normalcy and predictability for the child (Yule, 2001a).

Schools are neutral settings that can accommodate a large number of people. Teachers play a significant role in monitoring children and assessing the progression of their recovery (Webb, 2004b). In addition, school administrators can identify anxious parents and refer them to appropriate resources. However, when traumatic events occur inside school walls, a special level of skill and expertise is required. The intervenor may be required to juggle several interventions simultaneously, based on the differing needs of students, teachers, administrators, and parents.

It is important to respond as soon as possible when children are victims of a trauma; responding quickly requires an intensive amount of pre-planning and foresight on the part of the intervenor. Planning does not cause a trauma, nor does it prevent it from happening. However, planning supports the intervention process when crises occur and some providers become immobilized. Institutions and organizations involved in the care of children are encouraged to plan ahead so that personnel are "wise before the event" (Yule, 2001b).

Each crisis that occurs in a school is unique. Even the most comprehensive plan cannot predict all the possibilities and anticipate all the consequences of crises in schools. However, crisis planning and preparedness can help address traumatic impact and provide short-term treatment for affected individuals. School personnel are usually people who know a school best; they should, therefore, take the lead in designing school-based interventions. Nevertheless, it may be necessary to create an alternate plan that includes outside support when school personnel are unable to assist.

An initial coordinating meeting with key administrators, school personnel, and representatives from local mental health agencies is necessary (Newgass & Schonfeld, 2000). This initial meeting achieves several purposes:

- It establishes a collaborative relationship from the beginning.
- It provides people who are feeling a loss of control an opportunity to re-establish it.
- It unites people in a positive, constructive context and prevents a duplication of efforts.
- It allows for a quick assessment and pooling of available resources so stronger support is provided to the affected community.
- A collaborative effort to resolve a problem ensures that little information is forgotten and the needs of all representative groups are met. In addition, group members have an opportunity to hold each other accountable.

After this initial meeting, mental health professionals can visit local schools and speak to the PTA/PTO (or other parent groups) about trauma and its stages of recovery. Responsibilities are delegated, tasks are assigned, and clear lines of communication are established at these meetings so that smooth coordination, collaboration, and communication evolves among various professional communities (Marshall & Suh, 2003).

Construction of Crisis Protocols

School personnel and administrators can better cope with crises if preparations have been made ahead of time (Yule, 2001b). The creation of crisis protocols is an important aspect of this preparation. The first step in creating a crisis protocol is to identify members of the crisis team. The creation of multidisciplinary teams is recommended (Knox & Roberts, 2005). Establish two teams, a core and an extended. The core team usually comprises the school principal (team leader), vice-principal, nurse, guidance counselor, psychologist, and a social worker. An extended team can include secretaries, traditional teachers (representative of each grade), special education teachers, bilingual/ESL teachers, chair of Parent-Teacher Organization, and the custodian (see Sample Crisis Protocol).

The core team should meet monthly to review protocol and procedures. The entire crisis team (both core and extended) should meet at least once a semester to review the crisis protocol. If any changes are made as a result of this review, all team members should be appropriately informed.

In the event of a crisis, the crisis team will have established guidelines for how they will convene. A primary contact list containing phone numbers and other additional details is generated for this purpose; creating a secondary list may be necessary. The first list delineates communication during school hours and includes alternative ways of communicating in the event that phone service is lost. A second list outlines how members can be contacted if the crisis occurs outside school hours.

Sample Crisis Protocol

1. Call main office. State nature of emergency, medical needs, location of incident.

2. Administrator (school principal) calls police, fire department, activates crisis team (telephone numbers listed here). Calls school district superintendent. Assigns staff to meet needs of situation.

3. Notification of staff, students, families (phone numbers listed here).

4. Provide safety for victims; designate areas for crisis assistance. Arrange additional staffing.

5. Identify and support most affected individuals. Communicate with and involve families as needed.

6. Follow-up with appropriate referrals; debriefing of crisis team. Write incident report.

Crisis protocol guidelines include how to appropriately inform the entire school population that a crisis has occurred. To prevent unnecessarily alarming students, teachers can establish a code that can be used in a crisis to communicate with each other. If telephone access is unavailable, other forms of communication should be readily available, such as a megaphone or bullhorn. Alternatively, designated staff could visit each class to inform them about the crisis.

The crisis protocol outlines "lock-down" (holding all students in one place), evacuation procedures, and evacuation sites. Nearby schools or community centers are identified as evacuation sites. If an evacuation site is distant, transportation guidelines are included in the crisis protocol.

It is important to develop a folder of resources to help parents, children, and teachers cope with a crisis. A brief list of telephone numbers for the local hospital, fire department, and police is helpful; this list can be posted in classrooms and other central areas, such as the lunchroom and gym. Most importantly, the list should be visible and accessible to all school staff.

Protocols are only as effective as the people who execute them. It is important to conduct ongoing training for team members who will become first responders should a traumatic event occur. Mock trials and practice sessions should be held regularly. Those who are included in a crisis team should preferably have previous experience in disaster work and bereavement.

The following are Internet resources for school crisis management:

- www.crisisinterventionnetwork.com
- www.schoolcrisisresponse.com
- www.aaets.com (The American Academy of Experts in Traumatic Stress)
- www.ncptsd.org (National Center for PTSD)
- www.ojp.usdoj.gov/ovc/inforces/crt/pdfwelc.htm (Community Crisis Response Team Training Manual from the U.S. Department of Justice, Office for Victims of Crime)

Dealing With Parents

Informing parents quickly and accurately is important in a trauma and crisis situation (Williams, 2004). Providing them with the facts helps prevent the spread of rumors. Information about the traumatic event is usually disseminated through notes or telephone calls made directly to parents and caregivers. The urgency of the incident dictates whether a call or note is a more timely method of communication.

Once parents are informed about an incident, school personnel can anticipate that they may also need support in managing their reactions. Parents or caregivers exposed to previous violence may experience numbness, fear, and depression that may prevent them from adequately helping their children (Osofsky, 2004). Stable and consistent adults play a central role in optimizing a child's ability to recover from a traumatic experience. Modeling calmness and composure serves as an effective emotional cue for children, who need reassurance that caregivers are in control of their responses.

It may be prudent for school personnel to prepare handouts ahead of time; these are distributed to parents in the event of a trauma. Handouts serve the following psycho-educational functions: They inform parents about trauma's effects, acknowledge that stress reactions are normal reactions to abnormal events, outline expected stress reactions, and offer effective coping skills for parents. Parents should be cautioned to carefully monitor the TV programs a child watches after a traumatic event has occurred; the media broadcast of the event may retraumatize the child.

Media

Reporters may attempt to interview parents, children, and school personnel after a traumatic event. Although school authorities cannot prevent parents and children from speaking with the press, it is nevertheless important to provide families with guidelines on how to handle the media and media reports. Traumatized individuals have a right to privacy, but they may forget this during a crisis. Schools that appoint a media liaison to address questions posed by the media can resolve many difficulties.

Funerals

Unfortunately, some crises result in a loss of lives. All schools should have a clear policy on students' attendance at funerals. In some cultures, the dead are buried within 24 hours, and the school may have a limited time to obtain parental permission for students to attend the funeral of a classmate. Additionally, parents may not want their children to observe particular religious practices used by some groups when they bury their dead. A consideration of these cultural differences makes establishing a clear policy imperative.

Children's traumatic reactions are amplified when they view the bodies of classmates (Dubrow & Nader, 1999). Some parents may not know how to explain the permanency of death to their children. Finally, children who experience the death of a friend or family member for the first time need a lot of support (see Appendix IV).

Memorializing

When a child dies, the ways in which the dead are remembered can become a major discussion. A common way to memorialize the loss of children is to create a scholarship fund. Cultural factors are a major consideration in discussing this issue. For instance, in a low-income community, contributing to a scholarship fund may be viewed as financially burdensome for families, whereas a bench or a plaque could be more affordable. When several children from a community are killed at once, there is the challenge of memorializing everyone equally.

If a student was killed in the past and nothing was done in remembrance, it may complicate current efforts. Some families may request the inclusion of cultural or other religious symbols to acknowledge their loss. These preferences and diverse beliefs can fracture an already vulnerable community. Chronically traumatized communities, in which apathy exists, may not want to be involved in the creation of a memorial. Instead, they may view such efforts as futile as they anticipate the next traumatic incident.

Conclusion

Violence challenges a community's ability to protect its members, especially children and the elderly, who tend to be the most vulnerable. In the aftermath of violence, carefully designed community interventions can potentially restore hope and trust among community members. Furthermore, community support can play a protective role in decreasing the level of risk faced by its members. However, community-wide responses are most effective when coordinated through one agency or program.

Both research and clinical data indicate that when it comes to children, interventions must take place quickly (Osofsky, 2004). Since children spend most of their time at school, it is imperative that schools play a major role in adequately planning for crisis and other traumatic incidents. When it comes to managing a traumatic event, a trained crisis team that has regularly practiced a crisis protocol is indispensable. With proper training, an organized plan, and a motivated team of intervenors who can provide an effective schoolwide intervention, positive consequences are not only possible, but quite likely.

References

Arroyo, W., & Eth, S. (1996). Posttraumatic stress disorder and other stress reactions. In R. J. Apfel & B. Simon (Eds.), *Minefields in their hearts: The mental health of children in war and communal violence* (pp. 52–74). New Haven, CT: Yale University Press.

Barta, M. T. (2000). Death in the classroom: Violence in the schools. In D. Capuzzi & D. R. Gross (Eds.), *Youth risk: A prevention resource for counselors, teachers, and parents* (3rd ed., pp. 385–408). Alexandria, VA: American Counseling Association.

Dubrow, N., & Nader K. (1999). Consultations amidst trauma and loss: Recognizing and honoring differences among cultures. In K. Nader, N. Dubrow, & B. H. Stamm (Eds.), *Honoring differences: Cultural issues in the treatment of trauma and loss* (pp. 1–18). Philadelphia, PA: Brunner/Mazel.

Eth, S. (1992). Clinical response to traumatized children. In L. S. Austin (Ed.), *Responding to disaster: A guide for mental health professionals* (pp. 101–123). Washington, DC: American Psychiatric Press.

Friedman, M. J., & Marsella, A. J. (1996). Posttraumatic stress disorder: An overview of the concept. In A. J. Maersella, H. J. Friedman, E. T. Gerrity, & R. M. Scurfield (Eds.), *Ethnocultural aspects of posttraumatic stress disorder* (pp. 11–32). Washington, DC: American Psychological Association.

Knox, K. S., & Roberts, A. R. (2005). Crisis intervention and crisis team models in schools. *Children & Schools, 27*(2), 93–100.

Marshall, R. D., & Suh, E. J. (2003). Contextualizing trauma: Using evidence-based treatments in a multicultural community after 9/11. *Psychiatric Quarterly, 74*(4), 401–419.

Marotta, S. (2000). Best practices for counselors who treat posttraumatic disorder. *Journal of Counseling & Development, 78*(4), 492–495.

Newgass, S., & Schonfeld, D. (2000). School crisis intervention, crisis prevention, and crisis response. In A. R. Roberts (Ed.), *Crisis intervention handbook: Assessment, treatment and research* (pp. 209–228). New York: Oxford University Press.

No Child Left Behind Act of 2001. Pub. L. No. 107-110, 115 Stat. 1425 (2002).

Osofsky, J. D. (2004). Community outreach for children exposed to violence. *Infant Mental Health, 25*(5), 478–487.

Pitcher, G., & Poland, S. (1992). *Crisis intervention in the schools.* New York: Guilford.

Poland, S. (1994). The role of school crisis intervention teams to prevent and reduce school violence and trauma. *School Psychology Review, 23,* 175–189.

Pynoos, R. S., & Nader, K. (1993). Issues in the treatment of posttraumatic stress in children and adolescents. In J. Wilson & B. Raphael (Eds.), *International handbook of traumatic stress syndromes.* New York: Plenum Press.

Stamm, B. H., & Stamm, H. E. (2003). Trauma and loss in Native North America: An ethnocultural perspective. In N. B. Webb (Ed.), *Mass trauma and violence: Helping children and families cope* (pp. 50–69). New York: Guilford.

U.S. Department of Education. (2001). *Safe schools/healthy students initiative* [Press release]. Retrieved August 12, 2005, from http://www.ed.gov/pressreleases/10-2001/100042001e.html

Webb, N. B. (2004a). The impact of traumatic stress and loss on children and families. In N. B. Webb (Ed.), *Mass trauma and violence: Helping children and families cope* (pp. 3–22). New York: Guilford.

Webb, N. B. (2004b). Ongoing issues and challenges for professionals. In N. B. Webb (Ed.), *Mass trauma and violence: Helping children and families cope* (pp. 347–359). New York: Guilford.

Weinberg, R. (1990). Serving large numbers of adolescent victim-survivors: Group interventions following trauma at school. *Professional Psychology: Research and Practice, 21,* 271–278.

Williams, M. B. (2004). How schools respond to traumatic events: Debriefing interventions and beyond. In N. B. Webb (Ed.), *Mass trauma and violence: Helping children and families cope* (pp. 120–141). New York: Guilford.

Wilson, J. (1988). Treating the Vietnam veteran. In F. Ochberg (Ed.), *Posttraumatic therapy and victims of violence* (pp. 254–277). New York: Brunner/Mazel.

Yule, W. (1999). Treatment of PTSD in children following road traffic accidents. In E. J. Hickling & E. B. Blanchard (Eds.), *International handbook of road traffic accidents & psychological trauma: Current understanding, treatment and law* (pp. 375–387). New York: Elsevier Science.

Yule, W. (2001a). Post-traumatic stress disorder in children and adolescents. *International Review of Psychiatry, 13,* 194–200.

Yule, W. (2001b). When disaster strikes—the need to be wise before the event: Crisis intervention with children. *Advances in Mind-Body Medicine, 17*(3), 191–196.

8

Traumatic Stress Debriefing With Adults

A local bank was robbed. The intruder had reportedly surveyed the premises earlier in the day and then entered the bank during a lull in business activities. He approached a teller and demanded that she give him all her large bills. He said that he had a gun and would use it if necessary. The petrified young woman, who had worked at the bank for three years, hurriedly did as told, and a few minutes later, the robber left the bank. The teller automatically pushed the panic button located below her counter before turning toward her colleagues. She began to shake uncontrollably.

The next day, six staff members attended a debriefing conducted by an Employee Assistance Program (EAP) counselor. The teller was part of the group. She disclosed that it took her about 20 minutes to enter the building that morning, and after she entered, she could barely go near her counter. The face of the robber had kept her awake all night. Many of the staff had been employed at the bank for several years. They were tearful as they talked about their feelings of anger, intrusion, and vulnerability. The women often nodded their heads in agreement as their colleagues described their traumatic reactions. The counselor allowed them to talk at length before brainstorming coping strategies. It was clear that the employees were a close-knit group; not surprisingly, most felt that their primary support would come from within the group. At the end of the session, visible differences were apparent in the demeanor of several employees. The manager later remarked that the teller who was robbed "looked much better coming out than going in."

This chapter reviews the background on debriefings and describes the various debriefing models used with adults. The debate on the efficacy of debriefings as a form of crisis intervention is examined. The chapter also introduces the community debriefing model that supports community empowerment. The mechanics of conducting this debriefing with adult clients are reviewed.

Types of Traumatizing Situations in a Community

The following are examples of single incidents of trauma, also referred to as critical incidents, that can overwhelm and severely test a community's coping mechanisms and result in widespread trauma:

- Incidents in communities that are strongly affiliated with each other (e.g., a homicide in a school, workplace, or neighborhood)
- Incidents involving multiple direct victims or eyewitnesses (e.g., a shooting in a shopping mall)
- Incidents in which the direct victims have a special significance to the affected community (e.g., rape of an elderly woman)
- Incidents that require numerous emergency or rescue workers or that attract a great deal of media attention (e.g., a nightclub fire)

Background on Debriefings

Debriefings were first conducted by the U.S. army. They were initiated 24 to 72 hours after military personnel experienced a traumatic event. The immediacy was intended to help soldiers rapidly "get over" negative reactions so that they could return to active duty. In 1983, an emergency medical technician (EMT) named Jeffrey Mitchell developed the critical incident stress debriefing (CISD) to help emergency service personnel cope with the secondary consequences of their vocation. Although both the military and Mitchell (1983) originally developed debriefings for specific populations, debriefings are now used with civilian groups affected by trauma.

Psychological debriefing, as a generic term, is defined by Devilly and Cotton (2003) as "immediate interventions following trauma (usually within 3 days) that seek to relieve stress with the hopeful intent of mitigating or preventing long-term pathology . . . [and] relies predominantly on ventilation/catharsis, normalization of distress, and psycho-education regarding presumed symptoms" (p. 145).

Models of Debriefing

A debriefing is a single-session, semi-structured crisis intervention designed to reduce and prevent the negative consequences of a trauma. The purpose of a debriefing is to offer clients an opportunity to review their reactions after a trauma. The group is used to emotionally process and vent feelings about a traumatic experience. A discussion of coping strategies prepares the group to overcome stress and prepares them for future incidents.

Critical Incident Stress Debriefing

The CISD model was first described by Mitchell (1983). It consists of a single session conducted by a mental health professional and a peer support person. CISD was originally conceived to help emergency personnel manage job-related stress. The single session typically takes place 24 to 72 hours after a critical incident. CISD consists of seven components:

1. Introduction to orient group members to the process;

2. Fact phase: Group members describe roles of people involved and provide facts about what occurred;

3. Thought phase: Group members are asked to remember first thoughts experienced during the traumatic incident;

4. Reaction phase: Members discuss the worst part of the experience and express their feelings;

5. Symptom phase: Members are asked to review physical, emotional, behavioral, and cognitive symptoms during and after the event;

6. Teaching phase: Group leaders provide information about normalcy of reactions and teach coping strategies;

7. Re-entry phase: Group leaders summarize and close the meeting. Recommendations are later provided to the individual who initiated the request for a CISD.

Participants are encouraged to describe their experience of the traumatic incident and any reactions they currently experience. A didactic overview of common stress reactions is the psycho-educational component of the debriefing. Guidelines on coping provide participants with ideas for managing stress.

CISD is an early intervention that provides opportunities for catharsis, group support, and peer support (Mitchell, 1983). The objective is to lessen the impact of stressful events and to help facilitate recovery at a pre-trauma level (Lane, 1993). In essence, it is a group meeting with the primary objective of diminishing the negative effects of a crisis by promoting group support and processing within the group.

Critical Incident Stress Management

In 1998, Mitchell and Everly expanded the idea of CISD and proposed critical incident stress management (CISM) as an integrated, comprehensive multi-component crisis intervention program. CISM spans the entire crisis continuum to include interventions at the pre-crisis, acute crisis, and post-crisis phase. Several components comprise this continuum: pre-crisis preparation, demobilizations and staff consultations, crisis management briefing, defusing, critical incident stress debriefing, individual crisis intervention, family CISM, community and organizational consultation, pastoral crisis intervention, and follow-up/referral (Everly & Mitchell, 1999).

The authors claim CISM is a crisis intervention that can be successfully used in a variety of settings. A meta-analysis of empirical studies on CISM have shown that it has positive clinical effects (Everly, Flannery, & Eyler, 2002).

Process Debriefing

The primary goal of process debriefing is to use the group process to restore functioning and enhance individual coping (Raphael & Wilson, 2000). Dyregov (1997) suggests that because the focus in process debriefing is the group, the leader's training, skills, and experience in group dynamics is important.

On-Scene Debriefing

On-scene debriefing emphasizes providing support to victims and responders while an incident is occurring (Paton, 1995).

Post-Incident Defusing

Post-incident defusing is intended to allow the release of feelings in the immediate aftermath of an incident. Administering psycho-education and providing information about post-traumatic stress is an additional goal.

Psychological Debriefing

Psychological debriefing increases participants' understanding of the traumatic reactions and its different phases.

All debriefing models share a basic design: a one-session intervention with a clear structure that places the responsibility on the facilitator to lead and shape the process. Debriefings are a combination of mutual help and support in which participants actively share experiences, provide information, and support each other (Schopler & Galinsky, 1993). Debriefings also serve the important purpose of identifying those individuals who require further help or follow-up services. Debriefings were originally designed as crisis interventions and not to replace psychotherapy; their purpose is to give members of an affected community some practical steps to support recovery.

Although debriefings are commonly used after crises, other support groups can be conducted following critical incidents (Wollman, 1993). Juhnke and Osborne (1997) describe the solution-focused debriefing group as an alternative to single-session debriefing. This group is designed for adult survivors of violence and meets once a week for a three-week period. Grief, mini-marathon, crisis, and ongoing debriefing groups can also provide support to those affected by a crisis (Terr, 1992).

Short-term cognitive-behavioral interventions show great promise as effective techniques post-crisis. Foa, Hearst-Ikeda, and Perry (1995) describe a therapeutic crisis intervention developed to prevent PTSD and restore resilience among female rape victims. The intervention consists of four two-hour therapy sessions. The research indicates that after two months, victims who participated in the cognitive-behavioral program had significantly fewer PTSD symptoms compared to a control group.

In another CBT study, 24 accident victims participated in either five sessions of CBT or received supportive counseling within two weeks of the trauma. The CBT treatment protocol consisted of relaxation training, cognitive restructuring, and imaginal exposure. The supportive counseling protocol included education about trauma, problem-solving skills, and social support. At post-treatment, only 8% of the CBT group met criteria for PTSD, compared to 83% of the supportive therapy group (Bryant, Harvey, Dang, Sackville, & Basten, 1998). Thus, research evidence shows that CBT interventions may be the most effective in reducing traumatic reactions.

The Debriefing Debate

A controversy has developed in recent years regarding the effectiveness of debriefings in preventing the negative psychological sequelae of trauma. As a form of intervention, debriefings have been heavily criticized as lacking in robustness and efficacy. Some research studies suggest discontinuing debriefing as a form of crisis intervention because of its harmful effects (Avery & Orner, 1998; Bisson, Jenkins, Alexander, & Bannister, 1997;

Rick & Briner, 2000). A meta-analysis of CISD conducted by Rose, Bisson, and Wessely (2003) found that single debriefing sessions did not reduce distress or prevent PTSD. In fact, this research found that those who participated in a debriefing showed higher rates of PTSD.

In another study, Rose, Brewin, Andrews, and Lirk (1999) did research among 157 victims of violent crime who participated in one-session debriefings. Follow-up data obtained six months later showed no evidence to support the efficacy of these brief interventions in preventing PTSD. Carlier, Voerman, and Gersons (2000) studied 243 police officers who received debriefings after violent experiences. They were also administered pre- and post-tests. These tests indicated no differences in the psychological morbidity of the debriefed officers at pretest, 24 hours, and 6 months later. In a study of British soldiers who fought in the Gulf War, those who had the responsibility of recovering and identifying bodies for burial were administered a psychological debriefing (Deahl, Gillham, Thomas, Searle, & Srinivasan, 1994). The debriefing did not appear to reduce their subsequent psychiatric morbidity.

Hytten and Hasle (1989) studied 115 firefighters involved in a major hotel fire they described as the worse experience of their lives. Thirty-nine of the firefighters participated in a debriefing. No significant differences were found between the firefighters who participated in the debriefing and those who simply talked with their peers. Evidence indicating that CISD/CISM maybe harmful to recipients of debriefings is derived from a study conducted by Snelgrove (1998).

Similarly, in their work with victims of road accidents, Hobbs, Mayou, Harrison, and Worlock (1996) found there was no evidence that participation in a debriefing had helped victims, who were described as "still too numbed or distressed to be receptive" (p. 1438). The psychiatric morbidity of victims was significant four months after the accident. The intervention was rated as irrelevant by those participants who expected a full recovery and too mild an intervention for those individuals who had major emotional problems.

Bisson, Jenkins, Alexander, and Bannister (1997) found that debriefings did not prevent psychological distress among victims of burn trauma. In some cases, they claim it may have even harmed recipients. Arendt and Elkit (2001) performed a narrative review of 25 studies that used debriefings. They found debriefings to have no preventive effect, although people were generally satisfied with their experience of participating in the debriefing.

Mitchell and Everly (1997) have criticized these studies for failing to demonstrate the efficacy of debriefings; they claim that these studies have several research flaws:

- Participants were self-selected.
- Interventions were done too quickly.
- The facilitators did not follow the format recommended by Mitchell (1983).

Attempts to assess the effectiveness of debriefings have been thwarted by the challenge of establishing a baseline on the nature, intensity, and duration of victims'/clients' traumatic event, history, and pre-morbid functioning. Another challenge for researchers is determining victims' capacity for resilience because this inevitably affects their reaction and ability to cope during and after the traumatic event. The challenge of lack of a control group has complicated researchers' ability to determine objective outcomes. Each debriefing session is unique to a particular community. Interventions that are helpful in one context may be counterproductive in another (Campfield & Hills, 2001). The challenge of maintaining uniformity in the context of the debriefing complicates an empirical understanding of its efficacy as a crisis intervention.

It is possible that early interventions may disturb the individual's psychological defenses against fear and distress, and instead may weaken one's ability to cope. Raphael, Meldrum, and McFarlane (1995) argue that although psychological debriefings are helpful to participants, debriefings are no different from informal discussions with colleagues.

Perhaps one of the problems with debriefings is that they were created for a specific population: those who are indirectly affected by a traumatic event, rather than those who are directly affected and who may remain in a state of shock during the first few days following an incident. Debriefings were originally designed to help firefighters and the military to contend with job-related stress responses. They were thus conceptualized as a collegial support system to release secondary stress accumulated from indirectly witnessing the pain and suffering of others.

The trauma literature shows that trauma victims often evidence numbness and shock in the immediate aftermath of a violent event. This may, therefore, not be the time when victims can be asked to organize their thoughts and process their experience in a coherent fashion, which is exactly what debriefings require. To participate effectively in a debriefings, an individual must be capable of both communicating and processing his or her traumatic reactions. People are not always cognitively ready to absorb the material outlined in debriefings, waiting for the shock to subside may be a logical option in such cases.

Why do we continue to use debriefings when this method has not adequately demonstrated prevention of post-traumatic symptoms? First, there are several studies that support debriefings as a form of intervention. For example, in a study done after a mass shooting in Killeen, Texas, 36 emergency medical workers were offered CISD 24 hours after the incident occurred (Jenkins, 1996). The mental health of participants who were involved in a CISD was compared with the mental health of those who were not. Those who participated in a debriefing reported decreased feelings of helplessness a week after the incident. They also reported that the debriefing helped them endure the experience because they felt socially supported. According to Bisson and Deahl (1994), psychological debriefings at best afford some protection against later-manifesting psychological sequelae, and at worst make no difference in the victim. The researchers concluded that the primary goal of debriefing is to identify individuals who are at risk for developing serious psychological distress because of the trauma.

Further support for the efficacy of CISD in the workplace is gleaned in a study that examined the effects of CISD in ameliorating the impact of work-related post-traumatic stress on direct care psychiatric workers (Matthews, 1998). The workers who were offered debriefings as a supportive intervention exhibited the lowest level of stress. Irving and Long (2001) conducted a study that asked women who experienced a traumatic event to participate in a CISD. In a six-month follow-up interview, all of the women indicated that the debriefing provided "a safe forum for them to explore their needs, process their experiences, and create constructive narratives" (p. 307). Although the study is criticized for having a small sample size, it provides qualitative support for CISD's success in preventing the development of PTSD.

When CISD is combined with CISM, it produces better results. For example, Richards (2001) compared victims of armed robberies in the United Kingdom who participated in CISD interventions with those who participated in a combined CISD/CISM protocol. Three days after the debriefing, the CISM/CISD group initially reported a marked reduction (66%) in clinically significant PTSD reactions. These positive results were sustained; the group showed decreased PTSD symptoms more than a month after the intervention. In contrast, the PTSD reactions in the group who only received a CISD intervention remained almost unchanged. The results of this study indicate the importance of using CISD within a CISM framework.

In a rigorously conducted study by Flannery (1998), the staff of several psychiatric hospitals participated in a CISD within a CISM framework. Flannery found a reduction in staff turnover, sick time, and worker's compensation claims in institutions where the CISD/CISM model was implemented to manage employee stress. This study provides further evidence that the CISD/CISM model may be more beneficial.

Despite controversial findings, CISD and other forms of debriefing are increasingly used by Employee Assistance Programs (EAPs) as the primary intervention in many workplace settings (Arthur, 2000; Sciegaj et al., 2001). The organizational rationale for supporting workplace stress interventions is the belief that it will result in improved productivity, reduced absenteeism, increased morale, and lower turnover (Kirk & Brown, 2003). Additionally, because debriefings are short-term interventions, they cause little disruption in participants' work schedules. They are also cost effective, a feature that most employers find attractive. When used in the workplace, debriefings are believed to serve several important purposes:

- They bring people together in a naturally supportive manner.
- They include people who may otherwise never seek help.
- They meet the needs of those not directly affected by a trauma to overcome a sense of helplessness.
- They provide those directly affected by a trauma with an additional opportunity to understand and gain control over the traumatic incident.
- They allow administrators an opportunity to demonstrate care and concern for their staff.

However, important questions must be asked about the provision of these services and whose needs are being met. Employers may be quick to offer debriefings to meet their own social and political needs but not necessarily to meet the needs of the victim. A discussion with employees ahead of time will clarify this question.

In light of the controversial findings regarding the efficacy of debriefings, Devilly and Cotton (2003) propose the following guidelines to maintain a healthy workforce:

1. Implement an organizational policy. An organization's critical incident management policy should be regularly updated; contracting with a recognized expert in the field can facilitate this process.

2. Facilitate access to immediate practical and social support. Organizations can offer practical assistance after a trauma (funeral arrangements, transportation, etc.). Contact with supervisors and managers and human resource officers can be supportive when employees are under stress.

3. Provide EAPs for those who request it. Providing access to appropriately qualified mental health service providers for face-to-face emotional support and follow-up is an important organizational gesture. This is regarded as a socially supportive intervention that also serves as an opportunity to screen individuals who may later require more substantive support.

4. Provide factual information and normalize reactions, not symptoms. Educating employees about reactions to stressors and providing them with information is important. This can be done by a telephone help line or via e-mail.

5. Promote proactive problem solving. This helps employees gain a sense of mastery over situations and increases their sense of self-efficacy. Coping strategies should correspond to the situation; no specific strategy should be mandated.

6. Monitor staff to identify at-risk individuals. Follow-up is important to check on how employees are faring. This can be achieved collaboratively when EAP providers, managers, and human resource professionals work together.

7. Provide access to early intervention for individuals who report ongoing distress. Specific and structured interventions that rely on cognitive-behavioral principles can mitigate long-term pathology. Effective delivery of these interventions requires specialized clinical training. EAP providers can usually provide these services.

8. Ensure appropriate organizational liaison and feedback. EAPs or other mental health professionals involved in service delivery should ensure that proper feedback is given to management. This should be done in a facilitative manner, without violating the privacy of individuals and with a careful differentiation between incident-related concerns and institutional flaws.

Finally, before we reach any firm conclusions about whether debriefings as a crisis intervention should be discontinued, we must assess whether researchers are evaluating the same model of debriefing. Additionally, when making comparisons, we have to make sure that facilitators have the same basic level of training and expertise. We can only draw firm conclusions about research findings once a similarity across participants' trauma and personal histories is established. Only once this is achieved can studies be assumed to be empirically valid. Thus, until such rigorous studies are possible, it is unwise to debunk the efficacy of debriefings. Instead, it may be more sensible to establish state and national standards for professional training and certification of counselors who conduct debriefings as a crisis intervention.

Community Trauma Debriefing

Robert was a 16-year-old Haitian male whose family immigrated to the United States when he was 4 years old. He attended an urban high school where he tried to avoid the many prevalent gangs. One afternoon on his way home from school, Robert was shot and fatally wounded by a stray bullet intended for a young man walking alongside him. His teachers, fellow students, the Haitian community, and members of his church were devastated by the incident; they are some of the groups who may benefit from a community trauma debriefing.

In my many years of working with traumatized communities, I have used a model of debriefing that I have named a community trauma debriefing (CTD) model. The model is culturally appropriate and attentive to the ecological framework of the people who participate in a debriefing. The CTD model incorporates components of both CISM and CISD. It also differs from them in several important ways. The CTD model, its process, and several stages within it emphasize the following:

- The pre-intervention consultation that is attentive to existing community resources
- A careful consideration of timing, with a recommendation for carefully planned, nonurgent meetings
- The importance of effective training for group facilitators
- The psycho-educational aspects of the debriefing, especially when working with chronically traumatized groups

Pre-Intervention Consultation

Pre-intervention consultation is viewed as a key component of the debriefing process because it ultimately determines the design of the CTD intervention and how community members may perceive it. An important goal of this phase is to involve significant community leaders in planning, designing, and conducting the debriefing. Every debriefing is viewed as unique and based on the specific cultural needs of the community.

Including community members in the planning of a CTD intervention is important for two reasons: first, it leaves them with the feeling that they have contributed significantly to their own recovery; it carries the potential to be an empowering intervention. Second, community consultation generates information on community strengths and resources. The skilled responder is then able to maximize these strengths and resources in designing the debriefing.

All community crisis efforts begin with a careful assessment of the community requesting the service and include the following:

- Existing community resources are identified.
- Other crisis response efforts that have occurred or are in the planning stages are considered so that a collaborative relationship is established.
- The community's response to past crises is reviewed. If crisis interventions were used, an evaluation of these interventions is necessary.

Since this consultation is the entry point into a community, establishing a good working relationship with community members helps the other elements of the intervention to unfold efficiently.

Timing

The timing of a debriefing is open to debate. There is little empirical evidence indicating the optimal time to conduct a debriefing; further studies are needed to establish when debriefings should occur (Amir, Weil, Kaplan, Tocker, & Witzum, 1998). Most existing models suggest that a debriefing should be planned soon after a crisis occurs. For example, Mitchell (1983) suggests that a debriefing should be conducted 24 to 72 hours after a crisis. However, in the aftermath of natural disasters, participation in a debriefing is only possible once physical stability and psychological readiness is achieved; this could take weeks or months.

Psychological readiness is an important aspect of debriefings; waiting for a client to be ready can influence a debriefing positively. For example, in a study of survivors of Hurricane Iniki in 1992, Chemtob, Tomas, Law, and Cremniter (1997) found that conducting a psychological intervention six to nine months after the event produced good results. In the time that elapsed between the natural disaster and the intervention, survivors gained physical stability and were receptive to the intervention. The results of this study show that a debriefing does not necessarily have to occur immediately.

However, the characteristics of the traumatic event should determine the time frame within which a debriefing is conducted. Campfield and Hills (2001) found that employees who participated in a CISD immediately after a noninjurious robbery displayed fewer symptoms of post-traumatic stress at each follow-up period when compared to groups whose debriefing was delayed. These findings were replicated in studies conducted by Raphael (1986) and Talbot (1990). Thus, research evidence is supportive of conducting debriefings in a timely manner after workplace trauma so that staff recovery can commence. Furthermore, a timely intervention serves to reassure employees that administrators are supportive and care about them.

In my own experience of conducting community debriefings within 24 hours in workplace settings (after incidents of physical assault, robbery, suicide, and car accidents), I have found that employees consistently view debriefings to be beneficial. Similar to the findings of Burns and Harm (1993), the reports from people I have worked with revealed that talking about the incident, realizing they are not alone, hearing others talk, participating in a group who experienced the same incident, and hearing how others handled stress were all elements that helped them in the healing process. I believe that professional judgment and experience should ultimately determine when a debriefing is conducted.

Training Debriefers

Because debriefing is used as a crisis intervention rather than a replacement for psychotherapy, it has become appealing as an intervention. However, trained personnel with background and experience in crisis intervention and counseling should conduct the intervention. Individuals with specialized training and experience are better able to effectively monitor the psychological well-being of a group, to make referrals, and to evaluate for suicidality and homicidality. When necessary, those with appropriate training and experience will also have the expertise to adjust the debriefing format to the needs of a particular community.

Mitchell and Everly (2003) cite several debriefing mistakes that can seriously harm participants. These mistakes include using untrained personnel in lieu of mental health professionals and attempting to turn a debriefing into a psychotherapy session.

Galinsky and Schopler (1980) describe negative experiences of debriefings that stem from problematic group processes that leaders fail to address. The short time frame of debriefings does not allow for proper screening of group members. Qualified and effective leadership becomes crucial to prevent harmful effects on group members (Dyregov, 1997). Leaders must quickly establish trust, motivate participation, and build cohesion and support within the group. At the same time, leaders must attend to the unattended, whether it is a particular group member or issues that have not been raised by the group (Aveline, 1993). A leader who can quickly engender trust and respect, who can effectively communicate, who demonstrates flexibility in style, and who can quickly troubleshoot will likely conduct effective debriefings.

Psycho-Education and Self-Care

For some communities, discussing private and personal information with strangers may be challenging. A debriefing that focuses on psycho-educational aspects provides useful information without compelling participants to disclose personal information. This style of debriefing is nonthreatening and allows participants to set their own pace. The psycho- educational aspect of a debriefing prevents participants from becoming overwhelmed while it provides useful coping suggestions. Although chronically traumatized communities who have experienced multiple incidents of trauma may be critical of the role of debriefing in ameliorating their difficulties, they may find the information imparted in debriefings helpful.

Klingman (2002) found that adapting a process debriefing model to focus on practical support and information was more realistic and contributed to the empowerment of participants. This approach also helped participants to develop optimistic expectations of both the situation and themselves; it can be perceived as therapy via group guidance rather than introspective counseling.

The self-care aspect of a debriefing is its most empowering characteristic. Self-care is an area in which most participants already possess skill and experience. Self-care potentially accomplishes the following:

- Helps identify effective behaviors
- Enhances personal control
- Strengthens self-confidence

Self-care strategies instill hope and the possibility that difficulties can be overcome. Encouraged by the success of past strategies, participants feel assured that these self-care strategies may also help in the future.

Mechanics of Conducting a Community Trauma Debriefing

Pre-Meeting Preparation

The room in which the debriefing takes place should contain a large table surrounded by enough chairs for participants. Water and a box of tissues should be placed on the table for participants to use. The facilitator should arrive on time so he or she can briefly meet with the contact person and attend to any last-minute details. When the debriefing is about to begin, the facilitator usually takes a position seated at the head of the table. The facilitator should have a good view of the entire room, to monitor participants who enter and exit the room. Additionally, making good eye contact with all participants is important. Dyregov (1999) maintains that the group's seating arrangement and the way each member is treated by the leader determines how willingly group members will discuss their trauma.

Ensuring that windows are covered and doors are closed maintains the privacy of participants. By turning off public address systems, cell phones, and pagers, interruptions are prevented. These conditions are negotiated with the community representative beforehand but should be restated upon arriving at the debriefing location. The time allotted for a debriefing should always include a buffer period of about 10 minutes at the conclusion of the debriefing. This 10-minute period allows participants to re-orient themselves before they leave the setting and resume their routine. Finally, participants should be provided with a list of helpful resources where they can receive further assistance. This list is prepared ahead of time with the help of the community representative.

Introducing the Debriefing

Objective: To introduce and set the stage for the debriefing.

The facilitator indicates that the debriefing will begin by greeting the group and introducing themselves, explaining the kind of work they do, and informing the group of the circumstances surrounding their invitation to conduct a debriefing. This introduction is followed by a brief outline of the structure of the debriefing. By sharing this information, the facilitator create safety and structure for participants, who are likely to become less anxious once they know what to expect. The Facilitator should maintain a slow pace at the beginning to orient participants and allow them to become comfortable in the room. When explaining the process of debriefings the facilitator should mention that community trauma, although similar to individual trauma, is more complicated because witnessing others' reactions may exacerbate one's own. Participants are reassured that their presence and participation is supportive to the rest of the group.

A review of group guidelines helps participants develop a common understanding of the group process. Participants usually acknowledge an acceptance of these guidelines by nodding their heads.

- Confidentiality and privacy are vital in a debriefing. The facilitator also outlines exceptions to maintaining privacy. For example, if concerns arise about the emotional and mental stability of a participant, at the end of a debriefing the facilitator may have to address this issue directly with the individual concerned.
- Participants are asked to stay for the duration of the debriefing. The debriefing is a process, and leaving before its conclusion may be unsettling for both the person who leaves and those who remain. The individual who departs before the debriefing ends fails to gain closure. Those who remain may feel that they contributed to the person's decision to leave.
- Participants are asked not to take notes or make recordings of the debriefing. The facilitator informs the group that some notes will be written on a flip chart; however, this material will be left with the group at the end of the debriefing.
- Participants are asked to respect each others' reactions. For example, they can be reminded that some people may feel the need to cry while others may not, but both reactions are acceptable.
- Participants are told that they can refrain from responding when asked a question. Their presence is more important to the group than their responses.
- The facilitator explains the role of other facilitators, if more than one is present.

Getting to the Facts and Thoughts

Objective: To initiate group participation at a comfortable level with a discussion of neutral facts.

This is the first cognitive stage of a debriefing. The expression of strong emotions and feelings in this phase is premature and is discouraged; if participants go into detail too quickly, they are gently redirected to answer the specific question posed by the facilitator. They are reminded that there will be time later in the debriefing to elaborate on details. The facilitator validates affective statements but always refocuses the group to answer relevant questions during this stage of the debriefing. Participants who might be involved in court proceedings participate in the debriefing but are cautioned not to say anything that might compromise their testimony in court.

Participants are informed that they will be asked a series of questions, which they can refrain from answering at any time. Going around the table, participants are asked to state their names and their connection to the setting (e.g., How long have you worked here? What is your position?). Once these questions have been answered by everyone, participants are asked to answer the following factual questions:

- Where were you when you first heard about the incident?
- Who did you talk to first?

Although participants may share some of their reactions to the event in this stage, the facilitator tries to keep the debriefing at a cognitive level. In the third and final round, participants are asked to answer the following questions:

- What was your first thought?
- What thoughts remain or have lingered?

At this point, participants will find themselves gently moving from the cognitive stage and entering the affective stage of the debriefing. Details of the traumatic event begin to dominate participants' recall. Individuals who may have to testify in legal proceedings are asked to answer these questions silently.

Discussing Affective Reactions

Objective: To facilitate a discussion of the full range of reactions.

The facilitator indicates that the debriefing is now open for participants to discuss their reactions. Typically, the facilitator begins this stage by asking, "What changes have you noticed since the incident occurred?" or "What is different this week compared to last week?"

As participants begin to discuss details of the traumatic event and their reactions to it, the facilitator scans the room to ensure that some statements are not overwhelming other members of the group. Group members' reactions must be constantly monitored; good facilitator must be able to make everyone feel included and to shift focus whenever necessary (Dyregov, 1999). While participants discuss their reactions, the facilitator records on a flip chart the participants' reactions in the following categories: cognitive, psychological, physical, spiritual, and behavioral.

Although according to Pennebaker (1990, 1993), long-term positive effects are gained by confronting negative affective reactions. However, the facilitator has to ensure that other participants are not unnecessarily traumatized by the vivid descriptions of some group members (Tehrani, 1998). When all participants have experienced the same event, the risk of contagion is reduced. However, when participants have different experiences of the event, the recollection of highly distressing memories by some participants places others at risk for harmful visualization. Facilitators with proper training, experience, and sensitivity ensure that all participants benefit equally from a debriefing; opportunities are not missed and situations are not mishandled. The following statements, when used appropriately, allow the discussion to proceed smoothly:

- Validating statements: "A lot of people have also said they . . ."
- Linking statements: "I noticed that when so and so said . . . , other people nodded."
- Supportive statements: "Often when any of us have gone through something traumatic, we notice changes in (give examples from a category of reactions that have not been mentioned yet). Has anyone noticed that?"

Once the facilitator feels that participants have spent sufficient time discussing their reactions, he or she redirects them to the next important segment of the debriefing: coping. To begin transitioning to this stage, note the amount of time remaining (usually 30 minutes) and indicate that there is still important work to be done and adequate time should be reserved for it. At this point in the debriefing, the co-facilitator (if one is available) assumes facilitation of the debriefing.

Psycho-Education: Reviewing Reactions

Objective: To gradually shift the group to the cognitive phase so participants can leave the debriefing feeling safe and comfortable.

The facilitator refers to the list of reactions recorded on the flip chart and emphasizes that much has been learned about the group. Reactions are reviewed, and if an important reaction has been omitted, it should be mentioned at this point. Key concepts emphasized by the facilitator include the following: reactions are normal reactions to stress, reactions are likely to change constantly (making participants sometimes feel as if they are on a rollercoaster), and participants may continue to notice these reactions in the following days and weeks. In addition, participants may notice some reactions returning around significant times such as special holidays, court appearances, trials, and anniversaries.

Strategies for Self-Care

Objective: To help participants move back to the cognitive level by reviewing their past and current self-care strategies.

Participants are invited to discuss self-care strategies they found helpful in the past. Turning the page on the flip chart, the facilitator begins to record participants' coping strategies. Participants are encouraged to list strategies that may seem small but are concrete and attainable. This segment is future-oriented and emphasizes practical approaches that participants have already found effective in stressful situations. Working with a participant's strengths and resources is a major focus of this phase.

Facilitators can suggest strategies they find personally helpful in times of distress. Self-care strategies usually fall into the following categories: exercise, rest, relaxation, healthy diet, and social and other physical activities. At the end of this phase, the facilitator should highlight the following:

- Coping should include activities that are relatively easy to accomplish (e.g., planning a weekend at a local country inn may be more cost effective and less stressful than planning an overseas vacation).
- Coping should be related to reactions experienced (e.g., if participants notice they tend to isolate in response to a trauma, an appropriate self-care strategy is to make a date with a friend).
- Participants are reminded that some self-care strategies can become problematic in the long term. (Drinking a glass of wine is acceptable occasionally, but if drinking wine is used as a coping strategy on a regular basis, it runs the risk of becoming problematic. There are positive and negative coping skills; alcohol can quickly fall into the realm of the negative.)

Wrapping up the Debriefing

Objective: To provide closure and to offer referral assistance.

The facilitator makes a note of the remaining time and informs participants that the debriefing will end soon. Participants are given a list of resource that outlines information on local mental health centers and other agencies that can provides assistance. The facilitator thanks participants for their attention, expresses appreciation for being invited to conduct a debriefing, and leaves the room. The group is encouraged to stay together for a few minutes before transitioning to scheduled activities.

Post-Meeting

The community representative is contacted, preferably within 24 hours of the debriefing. This gives the facilitator an opportunity to evaluate the debriefing, to assess whether further interventions are needed, and to discuss participants who may need further attention.

Conclusion

Debriefings are one form of group intervention used in the aftermath of a traumatic event. For some communities, it may be the most logical response, while for others it may be counterproductive.

Since the attacks on the World Trade Center and the Pentagon in September, 2001, the debate about psychological debriefing has intensified. Critics argue that debriefings offer no opportunity for follow-up treatment and may cause individuals unnecessary distress. Several studies show that debriefings have no effect in preventing psychological sequelae that accompany traumatic events. Other studies, conducted mostly with homogeneous groups, indicate that psychological debriefings are beneficial to participants.

In light of these findings, debriefings should be conducted with great caution and the guidelines discussed above should be observed. Until researchers can provide definitive data on the efficacy of debriefings, however, they should not be discontinued. Initially, it is important for the responder to assess the cultural needs and ecological resources of the community to establish whether a debriefing is the most appropriate intervention.

The community trauma debriefing (CTD) is proposed as a debriefing that is culturally and ecologically appropriate. Its emphasis on pre-intervention consultation includes a consideration of the existing strengths and resources in the community; this consideration makes CTD an empowering intervention because it provides the community with a sense of ownership over the trauma. By highlighting the psycho-educational aspects of the debriefing, the needs of chronically traumatized groups are served; they are provided with important information without being pressured to process complicated traumatic material.

A national body to provide standards and certification for individuals who conduct debriefings is long overdue; this body could institute uniform guidelines to enhance debriefings.

References

Amir, M., Weil, G., Kaplan, Z., Tocker, T., & Witzum, E. (1998). Debriefing with brief group psychotherapy in a homogenous group of non-injured victims of a terrorist attack: A prospective study. *Acta Psychiatrica Scandinavica, 98,* 237–241.

Arendt, A., & Elkit, A. (2001). Effectiveness of psychological debriefing. *Acta Psychiatrica Scandinavica, 104,* 423–437.

Arthur, A. R. (2000). Employee assistance programs: The emperor's new clothes of stress management? *British Journal of Guidance and Counseling, 28*(4), 549–559.

Aveline, M. O. (1993). Principles of leadership in brief training groups for mental health care professionals. *International Journal of Group Psychotherapy, 43,* 107–129.

Avery, A., & Orner, A. A. (1998). First report of psychological debriefing abandoned: The end of an era? *Traumatic Stress Points, 12,* 3–4.

Bisson, J. L., & Deahl, M. P. (1994). Psychological debriefing and prevention of post-traumatic stress: More research is needed. *British Journal of Psychiatry, 165,* 717–720.

Bisson, J. L., Jenkins, P. L., Alexander, J., & Bannister, C. (1997). Randomized controlled trial of psychological debriefing abandoned: The end of an era? *British Journal of Psychiatry, 171,* 78–81.

Bryant, R. A., Harvey, A. G., Dang, S. T., Sackville, T., & Basten, C. (1998). Treatment of acute stress disorder: A comparison of CBT and supportive counseling. *Journal of Consulting and Clinical Psychology, 66,* 862–866.

Burns, C., & Harm, N. J. (1993). Research emergency nurses' perceptions of critical incidents and stress debriefing. *Journal of Emergency Nursing, 9,* 431–436.

Campfield, K. M., & Hills, A. M. (2001). Effect of timing of critical incident stress debriefing on posttraumatic symptoms. *Journal of Traumatic Stress, 14*(2), 327–340.

Carlier, I. V. E, Voerman, A. E., & Gersons, B. P. R. (2000). The influence of occupational debriefing on posttraumatic stress symptomatology in traumatized police officers. *British Journal of Medical Psychology, 73,* 87–98.

Chemtob, C. M., Tomas, S., Law, W., & Cremniter, D. (1997). Post-disaster psychosocial intervention: A field study of the impact of debriefing on psychological distress. *American Journal of Psychiatry, 154*(3), 415–417.

Deahl, M. P., Gillham, A. B., Thomas, J., Searle, M. M., & Srinivasan, M. (1994). Psychological sequelae following the Gulf War: Factors associated with subsequent morbidity and the effectiveness of psychological debriefing. *British Journal of Psychiatry, 165,* 60–65.

Devilly, G. J., & Cotton, P. (2003). Psychological debriefing and the workplace: Defining a concept, controversies and guidelines for intervention. *Australian Psychologist, 38*(2), 144–150.

Dyregov, A. (1997). The process in psychological debriefing. *Journal of Traumatic Stress, 10,* 589–605.

Dyregov, A. (1999). *Helpful and hurtful aspects of psychological debriefing groups.* Paper presented at the Fifth World Conference on Stress, Trauma and Coping in the Emergency Services Professions, Baltimore, MD.

Everly, G. S., Flannery, R. B., & Eyler, V. (2002, September). Critical incident stress management: A statistical review of the literature. *Psychiatric Quarterly, 73*(3), 171–182.

Everly, G. S., & Mitchell, J. T. (1999). *Critical incident stress management: A new era and standard of care in crisis intervention* (2nd ed.). Ellicott City, MD: Chevron.

Flannery, R. B. (1998). *Assaulted staff action program.* Ellicott City, MD: Chevron.

Foa, E. B., Hearst-Ikeda, D., & Perry K. J. (1995). Evaluation of a brief cognitive-behavioral program for the prevention of chronic PTSD in recent assault victims. *Journal of Consulting and Clinical Psychology, 63,* 948–955.

Galinsky, M. J., & Schopler, J. H. (1980). Structuring co-leadership in social work training. *Social Work With Groups, 3,* 51–63.

Hobbs, M., Mayou, R., Harrison, B., & Worlock, P. (1996). A randomized controlled trial of psychological debriefing for victims of road traffic accidents. *British Medical Journal, 313,* 1438–1439.

Hytten, K., & Hasle, A. (1989). Fire fighters: a study of stress and coping. *Acta Psychiatrica Scandinavica, 80,* 50–56.

Irving, P., & Long, A. (2001). Critical incident stress debriefing following traumatic life experiences. *Journal of Psychiatric & Mental Health Nursing, 8*(4), 307–314.

Jenkins, S. R. (1996). Social support and debriefing efficacy among emergency medical workers after a mass shooting incident. *Journal of Social Behavior and Personality, 11*(3), 477–493.

Juhnke, G. A., & Osborne, W. L. (1997). The solution-focused debriefing group: An integrated post violence group intervention for adults. *The Journal for Specialists in Group Work, 22,* 66–76.

Kirk, A. K., & Brown, D. F. (2003). Employee assistance programs: A review of the management of stress and wellbeing through workplace counseling and consulting. *Australian Psychologist, 38*(2), 138–143.

Klingman, A. (2002). Children under stress of war. In A. M. La Greca, W. S. Silverman, E. M. Vernberg, & M. C. Roberts (Eds.), *Helping children cope with disasters and terrorism* (pp. 359–380). Washington, DC: American Psychological Association.

Lane, P. (1993). Critical incident stress debriefing for health care workers. *Omega, 28,* 301–315.

Matthews, L. R. (1998). Effect of staff debriefing on posttraumatic stress symptoms after assaults by community housing residents. *Psychiatric Services, 49,* 207–212.

Mitchell, J. T. (1983). When disaster strikes: The critical incident debriefing process. *Journal of Emergency Medical Services, 8,* 36–39.

Mitchell, J. T., & Everly, G. S. (1997). Scientific evidence for CISM. *Journal of Emergency Medical Services, 22,* 87–93.

Mitchell, J. T., & Everly, G. S. (1998). Critical stress management: A new era in crisis intervention. *Traumatic Stress Points, 2*(4), 6–11.

Mitchell, J. T., & Everly, G. S. (2003). Critical incident stress management: Basic group crisis intervention (3rd ed.). Ellicott City, MD: CISF.

Paton, D. (1995). *Dealing with traumatic incidents in the workplace: Management and organizational strategies for preparation and support.* Perth: Curtin University.

Pennebaker, J. W. (1990). *Opening up, the healing power of confiding in others.* New York: Morrow Co.

Pennebaker, J. W. (1993). Putting stress into words: Health, linguistic and therapeutic implications. *Behavior, Research, and Therapy, 31,* 539–548.

Raphael, B. (1986). *When disaster strikes.* New York: Basic Books.

Raphael, B., Meldrum, L., & McFarlane, A. (1995). Does debriefing after psychological trauma work? *British Medical Journal, 311,* 495–497.

Raphael, B., & Wilson, J. P. (2000). *Psychological debriefing: Theory, practice and evidence.* New York: Cambridge University Press.

Richards, D. (2001). A field study of critical incident stress debriefing versus critical incident stress management. *Journal of Mental Health, 10*(3), 351–362.

Rick, J., & Briner, R. (2000). *Trauma management vs. stress debriefing: What should responsible organizations do?* London: Institute of Employment Studies.

Rose, S., Bisson, J., & Wessely, S. (2003). Psychological debriefing for preventing posttraumatic stress disorder [Art. No. CD000560]. *The Cochrane Database of Systematic Reviews, 2.*

Rose, S., Brewin, C. R., Andrews, B., & Lirk, M. A. (1999). A randomized controlled trial of individual psychological debriefing for victims of violent crimes. *Psychological Medicine, 29,* 793–799.

Schopler, J. H., & Galinsky, M. J. (1993). Support groups as open systems: A model for practice and research. *Health and Social Work, 18,* 195–207.

Sciegaj, M., Garnick, D.W., Hogan, C. M., Merrick, E. L., Goldin, D., Urato, M. et al. (2001). Employee assistance programs among Fortune 500 firms. *Employee Assistance Quarterly, 16*(3), 24–35.

Snelgrove, T. (1998). Debriefing under fire. *Trauma Lines, 3*(2), 3–11.

Talbot, A. (1990). The importance of parallel process in debriefing crisis counselors. *Journal of Traumatic Stress, 3,* 265–277.

Tehrani. N. (1998). Debriefing: A safe way to defuse emotion. *The Therapist, 5,* 24–29.

Terr, L. C. (1992). Mini-marathon groups: Psychological "first aid" following disasters. *Bulletin of the Menninger Clinics, 56,* 76–86.

Wollman, D. (1993). Critical incident stress debriefing and crisis groups: A review of the literature. *Group, 12,* 70–83.

9

Children and Adolescents

When asked to draw a picture of her family, Keita chose a bright red crayon. She proceeded to draw strong horizontal lines, which filled the bottom of the page, with large squiggles occupying the upper half. She later told me the small squiggles were her with two large eyes, while the larger squiggles hovering over the smaller ones were an image of her mother. She said that her mother had no eyes.

Keita was four years old when referred for a sexual-abuse evaluation. Her mother reported that after she picked up Keita from a babysitter one afternoon (a male friend whom the mother had known for five years), she noticed her normally active and talkative daughter was unusually quiet and subdued. Additionally, Keita looked slightly disheveled; her sweater was haphazardly buttoned, and some of her braids were undone.

The child eventually told her mother that her "babysitter" put his fingers in her "coochie." In one evaluation session, Keita reenacted both her abuse and molestation. Afraid of losing custody of the child, her mother was determined to do the "right thing." She later handed me a note so that I would have an idea of her challenges at home. The note described her child as not listening, acting like a baby, not taking naps, and spanking her dolls. She also mentioned Keita's frequent temper tantrums. Keita was clearly displaying traumatic reactions to emotional difficulties. Keita exhibited these reactions through aggressive behavior and repetitive play. She often enacted themes or aspects of the trauma repeatedly, just as adult survivors of trauma replay intrusive thoughts. Her reenactment of the trauma through play paralleled the reenactment adult trauma survivors experience through flashbacks. Additionally, Keita suffered from anxiety and fear about sleeping.

This chapter begins with a discussion of background and research findings regarding children who experience trauma reactions, followed by an overview of the effects of chronic stress on children. Included is a section that describes potential responses to trauma by age group. Important clinical considerations for therapists who work with children are outlined. The chapter concludes with effective guidelines for helping traumatized children.

Background and Research Findings

Clinical descriptions of children's reactions to stress were first recorded in World War II. Freud and Burlingham (1943) reported children's reactions to war, including intrusive thoughts, fear of recurrent trauma, lack of concentration, anxiety, depression, psychosomatic disturbances, and other symptoms associated with post-traumatic stress. Years later, in 1987, Pynoos and colleagues conducted a study among children who witnessed a sniper shooting in a Los Angeles school yard. The researchers found children's reactions varied by the child's proximity to the shooting, how well he or she knew the deceased child, and whether he or she had previously experienced a traumatic event. Recent longitudinal studies indicate that several factors mediate the developmental difficulties of children in the aftermath of trauma. These are grouped into three broad categories (Pfefferbaum, 1997; Udwin, Boyle, Yule, Bolton, & O'Ryan, 2000; Winje & Ulvik, 1998):

1. The traumatic experience itself and the child's relationship to the event

2. The characteristics of the individual child (strengths and vulnerabilities, prior history)

3. The child's immediate post-trauma environment (which include family composition and social class)

There is statistical evidence that at least 50% of children who are affected by a major life-threatening incident later develop PTSD or other distressing disorders (Bolton O'Ryan, Udwin, Boyle, & Yule, 2000; Yule, Bolton, Udwin, Boyle, O'Ryan, & Nurrish, 2000). Research shows that witnessing school violence may explain the trauma symptoms and violent behavior of some elementary school children (Flannery, Wester, & Singer, 2004). When these children also become direct victims of violence at school or in the community, they display an increase in negative emotional and behavioral symptoms. However, the effects of exposure to violence are not limited to the development of emotional and behavioral difficulties among children; their worldview, expectations for future happiness, and moral development are also affected (Ney, Fung, & Wickett, 1994).

Although researchers agree that children exposed to violence suffer from a wide range of social and emotional problems, family support remains the single best predictor of a child's ability to recover from trauma (Bolton et al., 2000; Osofsky, 1998). Positive and stable familial and social support protects children from the debilitating effects of violence and trauma (Garmezy, 1988). However, not all families safeguard their children from the harmful consequences of psychological stress. For example, a National Institute of Mental Health (NIMH) study on community violence found that many parents from homes characterized by violence lack awareness of their children's traumatic reactions; these parents thus put their children at increased risk for developing maladaptive coping responses (Martinez & Richters, 1993). The study also found that exposure to violence is highly correlated with parents' level of education, with poorly educated parents tending to make unwise choices regarding the level of domestic and community violence their children witness.

Younger children and infants are not immune to the effects of environmental violence. Perceptions of distress in their caregivers are manifested in sleep disturbances, fear of being alone, and irritability, making them secondary victims of stress (Osofsky, 1998). Thus, the coping abilities of parents, primary caregivers, and other family members play an integral role in determining children's short- and long-term adaptation after violent incidents (Lyons, 1987; Udwin, Boyle & Yule, 2000; Winje & Ulvik, 1998).

Developmental age plays a significant role in children's responses to traumatic events, as was evident in Lenore Terr's (1981) groundbreaking work with a group of traumatized children. While on their way to summer camp in Chowchilla, the children were kidnapped and buried in a large pit. Rescuers found the children 16 hours later. The children's responses to the trauma differed, especially with regard to the chronological sequencing of events (Terr, 1981). Terr found that variances in age and cognitive level explained the differences in the children's responses.

Similarly, in another study that investigated the relationship between developmental factors and trauma, Sugar (1992) found that a child's ability to recall a traumatic memory depended on the child's age, cognitive ability, and language abilities at the time of the trauma. Children's pattern of psychopathology was investigated in a sample of 95 children (8 to 13 years old) who had experienced war in Bosnia (Papageorgiou, Frangou-Garunoviv, Iordanidou, Yule, Smith, & Vostanis, 2000). The researchers found that older children were more at risk of developing depressive symptoms. Their cognitive development and ability to inwardly conceptualize traumatic events, compared to younger children who might externalize the causes and consequences of events, may account for these findings (Thabet & Vostanis, 1998).

Children's proximity to traumatizing events contributes to the severity of their symptoms (Figley, 1993). In a study conducted after the *Challenger* shuttle disaster, Terr (1996) found that children who were more emotionally involved with the subject had more vivid and lasting memories of the disaster.

Children's and adolescents' reaction to traumatic events is a unique experience that includes what they see, what they hear, and the crisis reactions they witness in parents, teachers, neighbors, and other adults around them (Osofsky, 2004). As with adults, a child's distress can manifest in a number of specific ways, listed later in this chapter.

Effects of Chronic Stress

In the late 1980s and early 1990s, chronic or cumulative stress, and its effect on child development in terms of emotional and behavioral maladjustment, became a strong focus of research (Attar, Guerra, & Tolan, 1994; Compas, 1987). Chronic stress is prolonged or repeated exposure to stressors such as domestic or community violence or sexual, emotional, and physical abuse. Exposure to stressors immediately places children at risk for developing PTSD; repeated exposure to these stressors increases this risk (Silva et al., 2003).

Inhabiting disadvantaged urban neighborhoods exposes children to many stressors. Studies show that 60% to 70% of children and adolescents in high-risk environments are exposed to at least one stressor such as assault, stabbings, shootings, or other violent acts that may or may not be gang-related. At least one-quarter of those affected by urban violence develop PTSD (Fitzpatrick & Boldizar, 1992; Silva et al., 2003). The negative consequences of exposure to violence are illustrated in the findings of a major urban study that found that each of the 96 students surveyed experienced an average of 10 post-traumatic stress symptoms (Berman, Kurtines, Silverman, & Serafini, 1996).

Attar et al. (1994) examined the relationship between chronic exposure to violence and psychological maladjustment among African American and Hispanic children who displayed aggression, depression, and anxiety. The children attended elementary school and lived in disadvantaged communities.

The researchers found evidence of the following:

- Stressful life events in urban settings contribute significantly to children's aggressive behavior.
- Exposure to violence is predictive of both current and future aggressive behavior.
- Psychological adjustment does not vary based on gender, ethnicity, or school grade.
- Children who repeatedly witness violence are more likely to use violence as a problem-solving mechanism.
- Children avoided further victimization at all costs, even if it meant engaging in violent acts in order to do so.

In a similar study conducted in a metropolitan area, the single common variable associated with stress among 103 high school students was exposure to familial and community violence. Twenty-nine percent of the participants showed clinical levels of PTSD (Berton & Stab, 1996). More recently, children and adolescents at public schools in the New York City area were either direct or indirect witnesses of the September 11, 2001, terrorist attack on the World Trade Center and the Pentagon. However, this was not the first traumatic experience for many children in New York City. A Board of Education survey conducted six months after the terrorist attack found that 64% of these students had experienced at least one traumatic event before 9/11 (Applied Research and Consulting LLC, 2002). These traumatic experiences included witnessing the infliction of a serious injury or death (Silva et al., 2003). Clearly, these children were already at high risk for developing PTSD; 9/11 exacerbated their vulnerability.

Thompson, Norris, and Ruback (1998) point out that individuals who lose family members to homicide often live in highly stressful environments. This makes it difficult to establish whether the cause of their distress is the traumatic incident or the stressful environment they inhabit. In addition to being exposed to violence in their communities, children in chronically stressed communities tend to be exposed to the persistent stressor of poverty, with its accompanying stressors of unemployment, limited resources, substandard housing, violence, and crime. Poverty itself does not cause trauma, but the socioeconomic stressors that accompany it do. People of low socioeconomic status are also likely to witness violence, including murder and other similar events. Major epidemiological studies have consistently found low socioeconomic status to be a risk factor for developing mental health problems in adulthood (Blazer, Kessler, McGonagle, & Swartz, 1994; Robins & Regier, 1991). The stress of poverty also disproportionately affects minority communities, who are overrepresented in low socioeconomic groups. Thus, children who belong to such groups are likely to suffer the consequences of both racism and classism.

The effects of experiencing multiple stressors are not additive but multiplicative. Experiencing two risk factors does not double the likelihood of developing a psychiatric disorder; it quadruples the risk (Garmezy, 1987). Although the incidence of violence, witnessed or enacted, is higher among children and adolescents of low socioeconomic status, mental health services for this group remain scarce (Berman et al., 1996; Freeman, Shaffer, & Smith, 1996; Salloum, Avery, & McClain, 2001).

Adolescent Responses to Trauma

Developmentally, adolescence is a challenging time when teenagers struggle to establish their identities. Peer pressure and the appeal of experimentation are elements of adolescence that predispose this group to violence and other risk factors. Adolescents may be afraid that reactions they experience after a trauma are unusual or unacceptable; this fear of being negatively judged by others may push them to withdraw or become depressed. Psychosomatic reactions to trauma are common among this age group and may serve a defensive function.

Adolescents resent any disruption to their lives, social activities, and their contact with friends. Traumatic experiences are likely to disrupt their routine. Adolescents' resultant frustration, anger, or guilt might manifest in irresponsible behavior such as driving over the speed limit and abusing substances. Anxiety and tension can also manifest in adolescents' aggressive, rebellious, and withdrawn behaviors. Survivor guilt may also emerge in this age group.

Several studies have examined adolescent responses to trauma and disaster. A longitudinal study conducted among a group of teenagers who survived a shipping disaster found that over half the survivors had developed PTSD by the time they were young adults. Of those diagnosed, a third recovered within a year of onset, and half the remaining group recovered three to five years after the trauma. A quarter of the survivors recovered after five years, while a third were still symptomatic (Yule et al., 2000). The findings of this study indicate that following a major life-threatening trauma, adolescents face an increased risk of developing PTSD.

Another study conducted with the same group of survivors of a shipping disaster found that trauma in childhood or adolescence led to other forms of psychopathology (Bolton et al., 2000). Additionally, many developed co-morbid disorders: 80% of survivors suffered from depression, anxiety disorders, and PTSD. Concurrent disorders were found to be more prevalent among female survivors. In a significant number of cases, these co-morbid disorders (especially depression) occurred within one year of the trauma. The persistence of fear and an avoidance of situations resembling the traumatic event were also notable among survivors. Cross-culturally, these results are similar to those found in studies conducted among adolescent Cambodian refugees, who experienced major trauma as children and later suffered high rates of depression (Hubbard, Realmuto, Northwood, & Masten, 1995; Sack et al., 1994).

Witnessing violence is significantly associated with the development of trauma symptoms, while direct victimization accentuates them. In a study that investigated the relationship between children's and adolescents' exposure to school violence and psychological trauma and violent behavior, 9 out of 10 high school students reported witnessing a peer "hit, slapped, or punched" at school (Flannery et al., 2004, p. 569). Similarly, an earlier study found that youth who experienced high levels of victimization were more likely to display clinical levels of anger, depression, anxiety, and dissociation. These psychological reactions increased their risk for self-harming or aggressive behavior (Flannery, Singer, & Wester, 2001).

In another study, Harper and Ibrahim (1999) found that youth who were characterized as "quiet and withdrawn" often perpetrated violent acts and were driven by feelings of victimization, psychological hurt, and isolation. They wanted to hurt others as they had been hurt. Bullying in the classroom and playground can also significantly influence children's adjustment at school, placing them at risk for negative outcomes. Thus, it may be incumbent on school authorities to initiate programs that focus on curtailing bullying behavior in both the classroom and playground. For example, in a study that focused on combating bullying, DeRosier (2004) found that a school-based group intervention was successful in helping children build relationships and gain the support, skills, and coping mechanisms to withstand the negative influences of bullying. Schools are encouraged to adopt similar programs to reduce the social isolation and rejection often experienced by victims of bullying.

Children's Responses to Trauma

A child's reactions to trauma will vary greatly depending on age, development, culture, and ecosystem. Ecosystem includes a child's family, school, daycare, place of worship, and parent's workplace. Diagnostically, children's reactions differ from those of adults. Intense fear and helplessness are evident in traumatized adults, while children may show disorganized or agitated behavior. Younger children are cognitively unable to process intrusive and distressing recollections of the event. Instead, children may engage in repetitive play or enact themes or aspects of the trauma in an attempt to process distressing images. These reactions are similar to flashbacks or recurring traumatic images often evident in adult survivors. Similarly, while adults may have distressing dreams of a traumatic event, children may have frightening dreams with unrecognizable content.

Scheeringa, Zeanah, Drell, and Larrieu (1995) have developed criteria for diagnosing PTSD in infants and young children. *Re-experiencing* is manifested in post-traumatic play, reenactment of the trauma, recurrent recollection of the traumatic event, nightmares, flashbacks, or distress when exposed to reminders of the event. *Numbing* is manifested in constricted play, social isolation, restricted range of affect, and loss of previously acquired developmental skill. *Increased arousal* is noted in night terrors, difficulty falling asleep, night walking, decreased concentration, hypervigilance, or exaggerated startle response. *Fear* is present in separation anxiety, fear of the dark, and fear of being alone.

Eight-year-old Alex's maternal grandmother brought him for counseling. Alex and his four siblings were in the custody of their grandmother after the Department of Social Services removed them from the family home. His mother, in pursuit of drugs and a boyfriend, had abandoned the children. Alex and his siblings were unkempt and hungry. Like the children, the house was filthy and neglected.

Alex's grandmother informed the therapist that he was having "behavioral problems" at school. His teacher complained that he did not complete tasks and constantly fought with the other children in the classroom. The grandmother also stated that Alex often screamed or cried out in his sleep. In a therapy session, Alex eventually described his troubled sleep and terrifying dreams, the content of which was difficult to recognize. In one dream, Alex was asleep in a crib when the house caught on fire. He was alone, afraid that no one would rescue him and he would burn to death. The child visibly trembled as he recounted the dream. It was evident that Alex's abandonment by his mother was troubling him; it manifested in dreams in which he would die alone and forgotten.

As with adults, a child is likely to display distress in a number of different ways. Several investigators (Greenstone & Leviton, 2002; Klingman, 1987; Weaver, 1995) have described age-appropriate reactions of children exposed to trauma. According to these researchers, the following are some reactions displayed by children and adolescents of different age groups.

Preschool (Ages 2–6)

- Aggressive and hyperactive behavior
- Anxiety expressed when separated from parent/caregiver
- Silence, isolation, and withdrawal from others
- Regression: refusal to eat, dress, wash, lapse in toilet training, and/or bed-wetting
- Sleep disturbance, nightmares, fears of darkness, fears of "monsters," sleepwalking
- Loss of appetite, vomiting, diarrhea, tics
- Reenactment of trauma through play
- Inability to understand death and its permanency; child may discuss return of deceased

Early Childhood (Ages 6–10)

- Becoming quieter, showing an increase in lethargy/withdrawal, or becoming more active, irritable, and disobedient
- Fantasies about traumatic event with "savior" ending
- Regressive reactions including excessive clinging, crying, whimpering, wanting to be fed or dressed by caregiver
- Psychosomatic complaints may include headaches, stomachaches, and nausea, as well as persistent itching or scratching
- Sleep disturbance, nightmares, night terrors, bed-wetting
- School phobia, inability to concentrate, decreased school achievement
- Constant demand for attention and competition with siblings for parental attention
- Decreased trust in adults
- Displaced fears, for example, not feeling safe in a place where there is no immediate threat

Pre-Adolescence (Ages 11–14)

- Anger at unfairness of event
- More childlike in attitude
- Disruptive behavior, resistance to authority
- Increased difficulty relating to siblings, teachers, parents
- Loss of interest in peer activities
- Psychosomatic complaints: headaches, vague aches, stomachaches, bowel problems, skin disorders
- Sleep disturbances including excessive sleep
- Appetite disturbance: overeating or undereating
- Judgmental about own behavior, especially when in close connection to violence or trauma

- Antisocial behavior (e.g., stealing, lying, substance abuse)
- Sadness, depression, or possible belief that existence is meaningless
- Decrease in level of school performance, decrease in attendance
- High-risk behaviors (e.g., unprotected sex)

Adolescence (Ages 15–18)

- Accelerated entry into adult world in an effort to gain control over environment
- Feelings of anger, shame, and betrayal
- Feelings of inadequacy, depression, hopelessness, and/or helplessness
- Frustration manifested through rebellious behavior
- Judgmental of own behavior and/or behavior of others
- Antisocial behaviors (e.g., stealing, vandalism)
- Alcohol abuse, drug abuse, and/or general decrease in impulse control
- High-risk behaviors (including reckless driving and/or unprotected sex)
- Psychosomatic illness (including complaints of bowel and bladder symptoms, headaches, and/or skin disorders)
- Sleep (oversleeping, insomnia, nightmares)
- Eating disorders (marked loss or increase in appetite, weight loss)
- Painful menses or cessation of menses in females
- Isolation and/or withdrawal from peers and family
- Suicidal thoughts and/or gestures
- Revenge (desire to "get even")
- Marked increase or decrease in physical activity
- Marked decline in social interests and activities
- Foreboding of another tragedy, sense of a foreshortened future

Clinical Considerations and Guidelines for Helping

It is important to ascertain a child's pre-trauma functioning before beginning an intervention. With children this may be challenging, especially if they have not known a life without trauma; recovery from trauma may overlap with normal development. Thus, the therapist has to be careful that traumatic symptoms, and not normal processes, are being treated.

Assessment of PTSD in children depends upon careful clinical interviews with both the child and parents or caregivers. If a parent is the identified perpetrator of the child's trauma, the nonoffending parent or other caregiver should meet with the evaluator. It is helpful to interview non-offending parents and children separately.

The goal of this interview is to gather the following information:

- Family history (psychiatric illness, divorce, current living situation, siblings, etc.)
- Child's developmental history (milestones, prior trauma, school, peer relationships, etc.)
- Parental account of the trauma
- Treatment history, including what was done immediately after the trauma
- Child's current functioning and behaviors of concern
- Parental reactions and expectations

Parent or caregiver reports about a child's functioning should always be carefully weighed; some parents run the risk of minimizing a child's traumatic reactions, while others overdiagnose their children (Malmquist, 1986; Rigamer, 1986). Clinicians should not hesitate to ask children about their trauma because they do not want to offend a child or appear to be intrusive. Yule (2001) points out that "one must ask the children directly about their inner experiences and reactions, otherwise one risks missing the most important effects of traumatic events" (p. 200). Strong empirical evidence suggests that when adults avoid discussing trauma, children are less likely to be forthcoming about their symptoms (Almqvist & Brandell-Forsberg, 1997). Research has found that young children are able to provide graphic accounts of their traumatic distress (Sullivan, Saylor, & Foster, 1991). Clinicians are well advised to develop a solid understanding of children's development in order to assist them in expressing their inner distress.

In order to identify and plan interventions for children at risk of developing PTSD, therapists should gain as much information as possible about the traumatic experience. Several assessment instruments with empirical validity can help therapists make a thorough assessment (see also Appendix XI).

- PTSD Reaction Index (Pynoos et al., 1987)
- Post-traumatic Symptom Inventory for Children (Eisen, 1997)
- Checklist of Child Distress Symptoms (Martinez & Richters, 1993)
- The Trauma Symptom Checklist for Children (TSC-C) (Briere, 1995)

With younger children, careful observation of their play content can provide valuable diagnostic information (Almqvist & Brandell-Forsberg, 1997). Some children, in an attempt to relieve anxiety, compulsively repeat traumatic themes in post-traumatic play. Other children may replay the trauma less repetitively through play reenactment. Developmental age usually helps explain the variations in children's play content and trauma reactions.

Both traumatic play and traumatic reenactment provide insight into the effects of trauma on children.

When working with children who have experienced a traumatic event, responding swiftly is necessary for several reasons:

- Children show their distress physically, thus demanding immediate action.
- Children are dependent on adults to ensure safety.
- Schools and other institutions that are responsible for taking care of children for designated periods of time must act quickly if a child is traumatized while in their custody to avoid being sued for inaction.

Experts in the field, including Berliner (1997) and Friedrich (1995), concur that the following are essential in the treatment of children diagnosed with PTSD:

- A direct exploration of the trauma
- Utilization of specific stress management techniques
- Exploration and correction of inaccurate beliefs about the trauma
- Including parents and caregivers in treatment

Children need concrete, specific information regarding the traumatic event. This should be communicated in a manner appropriate to a child's age. When information is unclear, a child may fabricate details in an effort to understand and reduce the instability caused by a traumatic experience. Even when adults do not know all the details surrounding a traumatic incident, it is better to reassure children by sharing this limited knowledge rather than waiting for a full picture to emerge.

Research has found that children do not need to know a victim or be directly involved in a violent incident in order to experience its traumatic impact (Pynoos, Steinberg, & Goenjian, 1996). Hearing unanswered cries for help, smelling noxious odors, and simply being in the proximity of threats of violence can traumatize a child. Children tend to identify and connect easily with their external world. They may not understand why they feel "out of sorts" although they were not directly or personally involved in a violent incident. Explaining the indirect effects of trauma to children helps reduce their sense of confusion. It is also important to remember that memories of a traumatic event, rather than the event itself, can cause a child severe stress and anxiety (McFarlane, 1988).

Self-care activities are valuable in restoring children's sense of control. These should be activities over which the child has already gained some level of mastery and competence. Children find activities that are fun-filled appealing. Establishing and following a routine can provide a child with a safe structure that can ameliorate his or her feelings of disorganization.

In planning these self-care activities, it is imperative that the adults who have a caregiving role seek a child's feedback. Encouraging children to list activities that help them feel better can be an effective first step in restoring a child's sense of control and empowerment.

Children can engage in psychological interventions once physical safety is established. Physical safety is established by identifying and informing children about designated safe areas in the school, neighborhood, and community (if the school has to be evacuated). For emotional safety, children should be appropriately informed about the different people who may be available to support them.

"Talking therapy" does not help children who are in a state of shock and disbelief. Such help should be offered a week to 10 days after a traumatic incident, once parents or caregivers are adequately informed and their consent obtained. This waiting period also allows a child's natural coping mechanisms to emerge. Before proceeding with any therapeutic intervention, children must be appropriately screened for participation.

If counseling interventions are used in the early stages of recovery, a group rather than individual format is preferable for children. Individual interventions tend to further isolate children. In addition, spending time with a strange adult may be stressful for some children, while group activities can reduce these feelings of isolation. Most children are comfortable in the company of peers who experience similar reactions; this will also help normalize their experience.

Children's recovery from trauma takes time. They often require briefer but more frequent sessions because they have a limited attention span. They may need to return to a topic repeatedly as their minds attempt to assimilate a new and confusing experience. Supportive adults need to be patient. Because there is not enough empirical support for the use of medication for post-traumatic symptoms in children, if medication is used to help children cope, it should be done carefully and based on established practices (Perrin, Smith, & Yule, 2000). Medication should always be adjunctive to psychosocial treatments with children.

The treatment of children should be incorporated into broader programs that are familiar to children, such as schools and community agencies (Papageorgiou et al., 2000). When trauma affects a large number of children at once, a public health approach is required (Pynoos, Goenjian, & Steinberg, 1995). Planning ahead is necessary, and it is advisable to involve child and adolescent mental health services in this planning (Canterbury & Yule, 1999). Intervention programs that are offered in schools should address issues with perpetrators and victims, as well as those who witness threats, fights, and other violent incidents. Witnessing violence can negatively affect children's academic achievement, school behavior, and mental health, especially if the exposure is chronic (Flannery et al., 2004). In a study of Kuwaiti children who experienced the Gulf War, moderate to severe post-traumatic reactions were reported by 70% of the children (Nader, Pynoos, Fairbanks, Al-Ajeel, & Al-Asfour, 1993). Witnessing death and injury and viewing images of mutilation on television had the impact of increasing the severity of children's reactions.

Children who inhabit violent environments become hypervigilant to aggressive external stimuli, causing them to sometimes misinterpret environmental cues (Dodge, Lochman, Harnish, Bates, & Pettit, 1997). The direct effects of living in violent areas, such as war zones, are often compounded by other factors such as socioeconomic deprivation in the form of unemployment and overcrowding (Thabet & Vostanis, 1998). Family factors, particularly parents' responses to trauma, political persecution, and torture, may also exacerbate children's reactions (Allodi, 1989). Moreover, consistent and long-term exposure to violence carries the danger of socializing children to choose violence as an adaptive response (Corvo, 1999). Strategies to help children from different age groups cope with trauma are outlined below.

Preschool

Preschool-age children are particularly vulnerable to changes in their routine and the disruption of their previously secure environments. Because they generally lack the verbal and conceptual skills to deal with traumatic stress on their own, they become particularly dependent on family members and caregivers for comfort and support. If these family members or caregivers experience heightened post-trauma reactions, their children can be negatively affected; it is important for these adults to take care of their own reactions before proceeding to help children.

Self-care strategies for this age group should be geared toward comforting activities that provide the child with reassurance, reestablish routines, and provide opportunities for verbal and nonverbal expression of the child's feelings and responses. Providing children with physical affection and closeness on a regular basis can be ameliorative. Engaging children in play and drawing activities can be helpful in relieving feelings of stress and dissonance. Children may find it easier to share their anxieties and fears about a trauma through these active modalities.

Early Childhood

Regressive behaviors are especially common in early childhood, and children in this age group can often become withdrawn and/or aggressive.

Because children are especially affected by the loss of prized objects or pets, verbalization and play enactment of these losses should be encouraged. While routine expectations might be temporarily relaxed, the goal should be to resume normal functioning as soon as possible. Showing understanding and tolerance if the child becomes clingy and dependent will be experienced as comforting. This is not the time to set limits and reprimand a child. If questions are asked, adults should respond in a way that the child can understand, bearing in mind that developmental age plays a major role in cognitive processing.

Pre-Adolescence

Peer reactions are often important for pre-adolescents; acceptance from friends is equally important. An assurance that feelings of fear are a normal reaction to distress can be validating. Discussion with peers and adults in a group setting can fulfill both these needs. Additionally, participation in a group can reduce pre-adolescents' sense of isolation. Resuming routine activities and involving the pre-adolescent in physical activities helps reduce tension and relieve stress.

Adolescence

Most adolescent activities and interests revolve around a peer group. Traumatized adolescents should be encouraged to maintain contact with friends and resume athletic and social activities as soon as possible. Group discussion helps adolescents realize that others share similar reactions. Adolescents feel frustrated when not allowed to assume the full responsibility of their pre-trauma functioning. They can be empowered to participate in community activities to reduce their sense of frustration. Other strategies to facilitate recovery are encouraging adolescents to talk about what happened, acknowledging their fears and confusion without being judgmental, and reassuring them that others care and are concerned about their welfare.

Sexually Abused Children

Childhood sexual abuse is a pervasive trauma that affects children of all ethnic, racial, and socioeconomic backgrounds (Finkelhor & Browne, 1985). According to *Child Maltreatment 2004*, approximately 872,000 children were found to be victims of child abuse or neglect in calendar year 2004; the maltreatment rate was 11.9 per 1,000 children (U.S. Department of Health and Human Services, 2006). The U.S. Department of Health and Human Services (2005) reports that an estimated 206,000 children were removed from their homes because of a child abuse investigation or assessment in 2003.

Over the past 20 years, several models have been developed to understand and treat the effects of sexual abuse. The traumagenic factor model developed by Finkelhor and Browne (1985) identifies four significant factors in sexual abuse: betrayal, stigmatization, traumagenic sexualization, and powerlessness. The researchers explain these factors alter a child's "cognitive and emotional orientation to the world and create trauma by distorting children's self-concept, world view, and affective capacities" (p. 531).

In their information processing model, Hartman and Burgess (1988, 1993) describe several phases of sexual abuse treatment: the pre-trauma phase (previous experiences), the trauma encapsulation phase (the actual experience, memories, and coping), the disclosure phase (whether a child discloses or not), and the post-trauma phase (child's response). Friedrich's (1995) integrated contextual model considers the child's interpersonal, neurophysiological, behavioral, and cognitive reactions to trauma as they relate to self-development. Although each of these models is helpful, they tend to make the child the focus of change.

In contrast, Deblinger and Heflin (1996) present a time-limited cognitive behavioral approach to treating sexually abused children that considers the importance of the ecosystem by including non-offending parents in treatment. There are at least two advantages to such an approach: first, the child has another adult with whom he or she can discuss his or her abuse; second, the parent is given an opportunity to learn how to help the child in the future.

Deblinger and Heflin's model is based on the premise that cognitions, behaviors, and emotions are interconnected. Thus, interventions that target one area of human functioning are expected to indirectly affect other areas as well. According to Deblinger and Heflin (1996), cognitive-behavioral methods are appropriate for children because they offer a variety of techniques that can be explained. This culturally sensitive model is both attentive to the diverse backgrounds of children and attentive to the different developmental needs of children.

Therapists who use this model communicate to clients that their thoughts and responses are understandable; they normalize client experiences and enhance client self-confidence by focusing on client strengths and resources. Since parents and caregivers are required to work collaboratively with counselors, they participate in and are responsible for their child's therapy; thus, they can claim some credit for a child's progress. For parents who may feel disempowered by institutional involvement in their family life, this model can be restorative.

Conclusion

Traumatized children experience a plethora of negative psychological effects. Although *DSM-IV* acknowledges that major stressors cause serious morbidity and children may be plagued by post-traumatic reactions, the diagnosis remains adult-centric and much work remains to be done to clarify its applicability to children. There is no denying that the populations most developmentally vulnerable in our society are those deeply affected by trauma (Pynoos, Rodriguez, Steinberg, Stuber, & Frederick, 1998). When the psychological and developmental well-being of a victim is compromised, research indicates that many other high-risk behaviors may result (Jenkins & Bell, 1994).

Trauma has its most profound effect in the first decade of life (van der Kolk, 1996). It behooves helping professionals to intervene quickly and efficiently to ameliorate the deleterious effects of trauma on children. Interventions that are done early prevent distress from becoming a chronic disorder. Children respond positively to early therapeutic interventions; thus, schools and other institutions that serve them are encouraged to maintain a level of preparedness that allows for immediate support in the aftermath of violence (Pynoos & Nader, 1988; Yule & Udwin, 1991).

Often, helping adults may find themselves in a crisis in the aftermath of a traumatic incident. It is imperative that affected adults also seek support. This will be personally beneficial, increase their ability to support their children, and ensure that children are not exposed to the traumatic reactions of the adults around them.

For those who are involved in child-family assessment and intervention, it is essential to establish a foundation in developmental processes and systems theory. An interdisciplinary approach that includes cultural and linguistic competence (assessing for level of acculturation among family and community members involved in the care of the child or adolescent) should be embedded in this foundation.

References

Allodi, F. (1989). The children of victims of political persecution and torture: A psychological study of a Latin American refugee community. *International Journal of Mental Health, 18,* 3–15.

Almqvist K., & Brandell-Forsberg, M. (1997). Refugee children in Sweden: Post-traumatic stress disorder in Iranian preschool children exposed to organized violence. *Child Abuse & Neglect, 21*(4), 351–366.

Applied Research and Consulting, LLC. (2002). *Effects of the World Trade Center attack on NYC school children: Initial report to the New York City Board of Education*. New York: Columbia University Mailman School of Public Health and New York State Psychiatric Institute.

Attar, B. K., Guerra, N. G., & Tolan, P. H. (1994). Neighborhood disadvantage, stressful life events and adjustments in urban elementary school children. *Journal of Child Psychology, 23*, 391–400.

Berliner, L. (1997). Intervention with children who experience trauma. In D. Cicchetti & S. Toth (Eds.), *The effects of trauma and the developmental process* (pp. 491–514). New York: Wiley.

Berman, S. L., Kurtines, W. M., Silverman, W. K., & Serafini, L. T. (1996). The impact of exposure to crime and violence on urban youth. *American Journal of Orthopsychiatry, 66*, 329–336.

Berton, M. W., & Stab, S. (1996). Exposure to violence and posttraumatic stress disorder in urban adolescents. *Adolescence, 31*, 489–498.

Blazer, D. G., Kessler, R. C., McGonagle, K. A., & Swartz, M. S. (1994). The prevalence and distribution of major depression in a national community sample: The National Comorbidity Survey. *American Journal of Psychiatry, 151*, 979–986.

Bolton, D., O'Ryan, D., Udwin, O., Boyle, S., & Yule, W. (2000). The long-term effects of a disaster experienced in adolescence, II: General psychopathology. *Journal of Clinical Child Psychology and Psychiatry, 1*, 513–523.

Briere, J. (1995). *The trauma symptom checklist for children manual (TSC-C)*. Odessa, FL: Psychological Assessment Resources.

Canterbury, R., & Yule, W. (1999). Debriefing and crisis intervention. In W. Yule (Ed.), *Posttraumatic stress disorder* (pp. 221–238). Chichester, UK: Wiley.

Compas, B. E. (1987). Coping with stress during childhood and adolescence. *Psychological Bulletin, 101*, 393–403.

Corvo, R. E. (1999). Self-envy and intrapsychic interpretation. *Psychoanalytic Quarterly, 68*(2), 209–219.

Deblinger, E., & Heflin, A. H. (1996). *Treating sexually abused children and their nonoffending parents*. Thousand Oaks, CA: Sage.

DeRosier, M. E. (2004). Building relationships and combating bullying: Effectiveness of a school-based social skills group intervention. *Journal of Clinical Child and Adolescent Psychology, 33*(1), 196–201.

Dodge, K. A., Lochman, J. E., Harnish, J. D., Bates, J. E., & Pettit, G. S. (1997). Reactive and proactive aggression in school children and psychiatrically impaired chronically assaultive youth. *Journal of Abnormal Psychology, 106*(1), 37–51.

Eisen, M. (1997). Post-traumatic symptom inventory for children. In E. Carlson (Ed.), *Trauma assessments: A clinician's guide* (pp. 254–255). New York: Guilford.

Figley, C. R. (1993). Coping with stressors on the home front. *Journal of Social Issues, 40*(4), 51–71.

Finkelhor, D., & Browne, A. (1985). The traumatic impact of child sexual abuse: A conceptualization. *American Journal of Orthopsychiatry, 55*, 530–541.

Fitzpatrick, K. M., & Boldizar, J. P. (1992). The prevalence and consequences of exposure to violence among African-American youth. *Journal of the American Academy of Child and Adolescent Psychiatry, 32*(2), 424–430.

Flannery, D. J., Singer, M. I., & Wester, K. L. (2001). Violence exposure, psychological trauma, and suicide risk in a community sample of dangerously violent adolescents. *Journal of the American Academy of Child and Adolescent Psychiatry, 40,* 435–442.

Flannery, D., Wester, K. L., & Singer, M. I. (2004). Impact of exposure to violence in school on child and adolescent mental health and behavior. *Journal of Community Psychology, 32*(5), 559–573.

Freeman, L. N., Shaffer, D., & Smith, H. (1996). Neglected victims of homicide: The needs of young siblings of murder victims. *American Journal Orthopsychiatry, 66,* 337–345.

Freud, A., & Burlingham, D. T. (1943). *War and children.* London: Medical War Books.

Friedrich, W. N. (1995). *Psychotherapy with sexually abused boys: An integrated approach.* Thousand Oaks, CA: Sage.

Garmezy, N. (1987). Stress, competence and development: Continuities in the study of schizophrenic adults, children vulnerable to psychopathology and the search for stress-resistant children. *American Journal of Orthopsychiatry, 57,* 159–174.

Garmezy, N. (1988). Stressors of childhood. In N. Garmezy & M. Rutter (Eds.), *Stress coping and development in children* (pp. 43–84). Baltimore: Johns Hopkins University.

Greenstone, J. L., & Leviton, S. C. (2002). *Elements of crisis intervention: Crises and how to respond to them.* Belmont, CA: Brooks/Cole.

Harper, F. D., & Ibrahim, F. A. (1999). Violence and schools in the USA: Implications for counseling. *International Journal for the Advancement of Counseling, 21,* 349–366.

Hartman, C. R., & Burgess, A. W. (1988). Information processing of trauma: Case application of a model. *Journal of Interpersonal Violence, 3,* 443–457.

Hartman, C. R., & Burgess, A. W. (1993). Information processing of trauma. *Child Abuse & Neglect, 17,* 47–58.

Hubbard, J., Realmuto, G. M., Northwood, A. K., & Masten, A. S. (1995). Comorbidity of psychiatric diagnoses with posttraumatic stress disorder in survivors of childhood trauma. *Journal of the American Academy of Child and Adolescent Psychiatry, 34,* 1167–1173.

Jenkins, E. J., & Bell, C. (1994). Violence exposure, psychological distress, and high-risk behaviors among inner-city high school students. In S. Friedman (Ed.), *Anxiety disorders in African Americans* (pp. 76–88). New York: Springer.

Klingman, A. (1987). A school-based emergency crisis intervention in a mass school disaster. *Professional Psychology: Research and Practice, 18*(6), 604–612.

Lyons, J. A. (1987). Post-traumatic stress disorder in children and adolescents: A review of the literature. *Journal of Developmental Behavioral Pediatric, 8,* 349–356.

Malmquist, C. P. (1986). Children who witness parental murder: Posttraumatic aspects. *Journal of the American Academy of Child Psychiatry, 25,* 320–325.

Martinez, P., & Richters, J. E. (1993, February). The NIMH community violence project: Children's distress symptoms associated with violence exposure. *Psychiatry, Interpersonal and Biological Processes, 56*(1), 22–35.

McFarlane, A. C. (1988). The phenomenology of posttraumatic stress disorders following a natural disaster. *Journal of Nervous and Mental Disease, 176*(1), 22–29.

Nader, K., Pynoos, R., Fairbanks, L., Al-Ajeel, M., & Al-Asfour, A. (1993). A preliminary study of PTSD and grief among the children of Kuwait following the Gulf crisis. *British Journal of Clinical Psychology, 32,* 407–416.

Ney, P. G., Fung, T., & Wickett, A. R. (1994). The worst combinations of child abuse and neglect. *Child Abuse & Neglect, 18*(9), 705–714.

Osofsky, J. D. (1998). Children as invisible victims of domestic and community violence. In G. Holden & T. Geffner (Eds.), *Children exposed to marital violence: Theory, research and applied issues* (pp. 95–117). Washington, DC: American Psychological Association.

Osofsky, J. D. (2004). Community outreach for children exposed to violence. *Infant Mental Health, 25*(5), 478–487.

Papageorgiou, V., Frangou-Garunoviv, A., Iordanidou, R., Yule, W., Smith, P., & Vostanis, P. (2000). War trauma and psychopathology in Bosnian refugee children. *European Child & Adolescent Psychiatry, 9,* 84–90.

Perrin, S., Smith, P., & Yule, W. (2000). Practitioner review: The assessment and treatment of posttraumatic stress disorder in children and adolescents. *Journal of Child Psychology and Psychiatry, 41*(3), 277–289.

Pfefferbaum, B. (1997). Post-traumatic stress disorder in children: A review of the past 10 years. *Journal of the American Academy of Child and Adolescent Psychiatry, 36,* 1503–1511.

Pynoos, R. S., Frederick, C., Nader, K., Arroyo, W., Steinbergh, A., Eth, S., et al. (1987). Life threat and posttraumatic stress in school-age children. *Archives of General Psychiatry, 44,* 1057–1063.

Pynoos, R. S., Goenjian, A., & Steinberg, A. M. (1995). Strategies of disaster interventions for children and adolescents. In S. E. Hobfoll & M. Devries (Eds.), *Extreme stress and communities: Impact and interventions* (pp. 230–256). Dordrecht, NL: Kluwer.

Pynoos, R. S., & Nader, K. (1988). Psychological first aid and treatment approach for children exposed to community violence: Research implications. *Journal of Traumatic Stress, 1,* 243–267.

Pynoos, R. S., Rodriguez, N., Steinberg, A., Stuber, M., & Frederick, C. (1998). *The UCLA PTSD index for DSM-IV parent version.* Unpublished psychological instrument, UCLA. (Available from the National Child Traumatic Stress Network, www.nctsnet.org)

Pynoos, R., Steinberg, A., & Goenjian, A. (1996). Traumatic stress in childhood and adolescence: Recent developments and current controversies. In B. A. van der Kolk, A. C. McFarlane, & L. Weisaeth (Eds.), *Traumatic stress: The effects of overwhelming experience on mind, body and society* (pp. 331–358). New York: Guilford.

Rigamer, E. F. (1986). Psychological management of children in a national crisis. *Journal of American Academy of Child Psychiatry, 25,* 364–369.

Robins, L. N., & Regier, D. A. (Eds.). (1991). *Psychiatric disorders in America: The epidemiological catchments area study.* New York: Free Press.

Sack, W. H., McSharry, S., Clarke, H., Him, C., Kinney, R., Seeley, J., et al. (1994). The Khmer adolescent project, I. Epidemiologic findings in two generations of Cambodian refugees. *Journal of Nervous and Mental Disease, 182,* 387–395.

Salloum, A., Avery, L., & McClain, R. P. (2001). Group psychotherapy for adolescent survivors of homicide victims: A pilot study. *Journal of the American Academy of Child and Adolescent Psychiatry, 40*(11), 1261–1267.

Scheeringa, M. S., Zeanah, C. H., Drell, M. H., & Larrieu, J. A. (1995). Two approaches to the diagnosis of posttraumatic stress disorder in infancy and early childhood. *Journal of the American Academy of Child and Adolescent Psychiatry, 34,* 191–200.

Silva, R. R., Cloitre, M., Davis, L., Levitt, J., Gomez, S., Ngai, I., et al. (2003). Early intervention with traumatized children. *Psychiatric Quarterly, 74*(4) 333–347.

Sugar, M. (1992). Toddlers' traumatic memories. *Infant Mental Health Journal, 13*(3), 245–251.

Sullivan, M. A., Saylor, C. F., & Foster, K. Y. (1991). Post-hurricane adjustment of preschoolers and their families. *Advances in Behavior Research and Therapy, 13,* 163–171.

Terr, L. (1981). Psychic trauma in children: Observations following the Chowchilla school bus kidnapping. *American Journal of Psychiatry, 138*(1), 14–19.

Terr, L. (1996). Children's memories in the wake of Challenger. *American Journal of Psychiatry, 153*(5), 618–625.

Thabet, A. A., & Vostanis, P. (1998). Social adversities and anxiety disorders in the Gaza strip. *Archives of Disease in Childhood, 78,* 439–442.

Thompson, N., Norris, F., & Ruback, B. (1998). Comparative distress levels of inner-city family members of homicide victims. *Journal of Trauma Stress, 11,* 223–242.

Udwin, O., Boyle, S., Yule, W., Bolton, D., & O'Ryan, D. (2000). Risk factors for long-term psychological effects of a disaster experienced in adolescence: Predictors of post traumatic stress disorder. *Journal of Child Psychology and Psychiatry, 41*(8), 969–979.

U.S. Department of Health and Human Services, Administration on Children, Youth, and Families. (2005). *Child maltreatment 2003.* Washington, DC: U.S. Government Printing Office. Retrieved April 5, 2005, from http://www.acf.hhs.gov/programs/cb/pubs/cm03/index.htm

U.S. Department of Health and Human Services, Administration on Children, Youth, and Families. (2006). *Child maltreatment 2004.* Washington, DC: U.S. Government Printing Office.

van der Kolk, B. A. (1996). Trauma and memory. In B. A. van der Kolk, A. C. McFarlane, & L. Weisaeth (Eds.), *Traumatic stress* (pp. 279–302). New York: Guilford.

Warner, B. S., & Weist, M. D. (1996). *Urban youth as witnesses to violence: Beginning assessment and treatment efforts.* Dordrecht, NL: Kluwer.

Weaver, J. D. (1995). *Disasters: Mental health interventions.* Sarasota, FL: Professional Resource Press.

Winje, D., & Ulvik, A. (1998). Long–term outcomes of trauma in children: The psychological consequences of a bus accident. *Journal of Child Psychology and Psychiatry, 39,* 635–642.

Yule, W. (2001). Post-traumatic stress disorder in children and adolescents. *International Review of Psychiatry, 13,* 194–200.

Yule, W., Bolton, D., Udwin, O., Boyle, S., O'Ryan, D., & Nurrish, J. (2000). The long-term psychological effects of a disaster experienced in adolescence: The incidence and course of PTSD. *Journal of Child Psychology and Psychiatry, 41*(4), 503–511.

Yule, W., & Udwin, O. (1991). Screening child survivors for post-traumatic stress disorders: Experiences from the "Jupiter" sinking. *British Journal of Clinical Psychology, 30*(2), 131–138.

10

Treating Interpersonal Violence

Karen, a 35-year-old white female, sought treatment after experiencing symptoms related to a rape that had occurred when she was a sophomore in college. She described recurrent thoughts, hypervigilance, and other intense emotional reactions. Her difficulties sleeping and concentrating were affecting her performance at work. At the time of the rape, Karen attended a prestigious Catholic university. One night she accompanied a friend to a fraternity party, where she had too much to drink. She found herself in the room of a male student the next morning. When she returned to her dorm room, the full impact of her rape and molestation hit her, and she immediately called campus security.

Consumed by shame and guilt, Karen felt that she could have stopped the rape. These emotions, combined with her loss of confidence in the criminal justice system, ultimately led to her dropping the charges and transferring to another university. Karen's recent engagement to her boyfriend of three years triggered her current difficulties. Since her confidence in the trustworthiness of others had been broken, a therapeutic model that focused on relationship building was utilized. Additionally, her therapy included cognitive-behavioral techniques to help her manage self-defeating cognitions and anxiety. After six months, Karen reported she had minimal symptoms, was performing well at her job, and was busy with wedding plans.

This chapter covers two forms of interpersonal violence that commonly occur in society: rape and domestic violence. The chapter begins with a sociocultural construction of rape and reviews treatment options for rape survivors. This section is followed by a discussion of domestic violence and an exploration of ecological interventions (individual, community, and political) used with its survivors. A discussion of children who witness violence describes an ecological approach to helping those most vulnerable in our society. Finally, the chapter ends with a review of programs for men who batter.

Sociocultural Constructions of Rape

Although this chapter focuses on female victims, this does not mean that interpersonal violence is limited to women as victims. However, gender is a powerful predictor of interpersonal violence and aggression; women tend to be the most prevalent victims, while men tend to be the most prevalent perpetrators (Rozee & Koss, 2001). The U.S. Department of Justice reports that 99% of all persons arrested for rape are men (Rozee & Koss, 2001). Although men are sometimes rape victims, they are more frequently perpetrators of rape. Fear of male violence is cited as a primary safety issue for women (Rozee, 2000; Stanko, 1998). This fear acts as a barrier to women's full participation in society and limits their rights as citizens (Rozee & Koss, 2001).

The feminist movement has made major contributions to reframing the definition of rape over the past 30 years. First, feminists have challenged the sociocultural and legal meaning of rape so that we no longer talk about the subject in the same manner as we did prior to the 1970s (Best, 1999; Bourque, 1989). Feminist activism has also made a major contribution in transforming society's attitude about violence against women. The perception of women as seductresses who entice perpetrators has begun to change, and male perpetrators are required to take more responsibility for their actions. Second, the feminist movement has provided an alternative framework for defining and interpreting sexual violence by placing more emphasis on how rape is socially constructed, rather than primarily blaming the victim (Brownmiller, 1975; Matthews, 1994). This has resulted in the reframing of rape within the larger pattern of gender inequality, women's oppression, and men's abuse of power (Clark & Lewis, 1977; Lloyd & Emery, 2000).

The feminist movement defined rape as any situation of coercive sex, regardless of the behavior or characteristics of the people involved. This definition met with backlash from those who claimed that feminists eraggerated the rape pandemic (Bourque, 1989; Rozee & Koss, 2001). Three main tenets exemplify the feminist definition of rape: any woman can be a rape victim, any man can be a rapist, and rape occurs in many relationships. Types of rape include acquaintance, date, and marital rape (Brownmiller, 1975).

- The prevalence of completed rape over a lifetime is 15% among women and 2.1% among men (Tjaden & Thoennes, 1998).
- Over half a million rapes and sexual assaults are reported by women annually (Bachman & Salzman, 1995).
- Women are twice as likely to develop post-traumatic stress disorder following traumas such as rape compared to other traumas (Bachman & Salzman, 1995).
- Worldwide, at least one woman in three has experienced some form of male violence (Heise, Ellsberg, & Gottemoeller, 1999).
- Intimate violence is the leading cause of injury for women between the ages of 15 and 44 (Tjaden & Thoennes, 1998).
- Rape and other forms of violence against women are the most pervasive but least recognized of all global human rights issues (Rozee, 2000).

Rape survivors are most affected by social and cultural attitudes. As Lebowitz and Roth (1994) contend, "living in a culture which tolerates and promotes a negative, rape-conducive construction of gender makes it difficult for a survivor to achieve a view of reality which encompasses both positive and negative perspectives" (p. 384). Others have concluded that the United States has a "rape culture," where the act of rape becomes a normative and a condoned behavior (Koss, Heise, & Russo, 1994; Rozee & Koss, 2001). As themes of rape in the U.S. media abound (in crime narratives, made-for-TV movies, and soap operas), rape has increased to the point where viewing interpersonal violence becomes acceptable (Brooks, 1997). Not surprisingly, this distorted media portrayal of rape complicates victims' struggle to see rape in the broader normative pattern of male-female relationships.

Several factors have contributed to the structural integration of rape into all levels of current society. One factor is the patriarchal values and socialization practices that view males as tough, competitive, and aggressive, while women are viewed as demure and weak. A second factor is the political, familial, social, and economic systems that bestow special advantage and privilege on men. Third, criminal justice systems that fail to protect women contribute to the structural integration of rape. Research supports the important role that cultural beliefs play in rape victims' understanding of trauma. Rape can illuminate aspects of the sociocultural system that previously went unnoticed (Lebowitz & Roth, 1994). Self-blame, a common reaction among rape victims, is often influenced by the sociocultural context they inhabit (Lefley, Scott, Llabre, & Hicks, 1993). For example, in many Hispanic communities, females are enculturated to accept "marianismo," or female chastity, as highly important. Women raped in these communities may view themselves as tainted and unworthy (Lefley et al., 1993).

It is imperative to integrate psychological and sociocultural factors when treating rape survivors. Otherwise, the blame for abusive incidents may fall solely on individual functioning rather than the ecological context that contributed to the trauma. A multiculturally competent and effective therapist who treats rape survivors makes a comprehensive assessment of sociocultural factors. Such therapists will not be later accused of colluding with the pervading social discourse. However, as these sociocultural factors are explored, the realization that they live in an unsupportive environment that may have contributed to their trauma may lead to increased feelings of disappointment and alienation among some clients. These feelings, unfortunately, may become an additional weight for an already burdened person.

Some cultural practices encourage retribution against the perpetrator by the victim's family. This retribution reportedly honors and protects the family name (Lefley et al., 1993). When a therapist suspects retribution, the family of the rape survivor should immediately be contacted to prevent the commission of another crime. The police should always be involved in cases in which threats of violence are made.

In communities with strong cultural identities, the well-being of the victim within the context of her community is a priority. The victim should be seen as a person of strength who possesses inner resources, while the community should be viewed as a valuable source of ongoing care and support. The therapist who focuses on a rape as an act of violation helps a community depend on the criminal justice system rather than themselves for resolution of a crime.

Some rape victims benefit from group treatment, especially those from group-oriented cultures whose members derive self-definition from cultural norms. For example, African American rape survivors prefer support groups provided by community mental health centers and churches rather than individual therapy (Lefley et al., 1993). As the following case vignette illustrates, all interventions should first be discussed with clients.

Shelly, who had recently relocated from a Midwestern state to the East Coast, sought treatment after she was raped by a friend of her adult son. The client reported that on the day she was raped, she had finished packing her belongings and was ready to move the following day. When she heard a knock late at night on the door of her apartment, she opened it tentatively. She felt reassured to see that it was her son's friend. After he entered her apartment, Shelly recalled that the man acted strangely, and she surmised he had been using drugs. Her alarm turned into horror when he then presented a knife and ordered her to get into bed. She vaguely remembered being repeatedly raped until the early hours of the morning before the rapist eventually left the apartment.

Feeling defiled, shocked, and in great pain, Shelly stated, "I did not want to talk to anyone about it; I felt so embarrassed." Shelly did not press charges against her perpetrator. She left town the next morning as she had originally planned. Several days later, she sought therapy in her new location. At the end of the evaluation, hoping to give the client as much support as possible, I proposed the idea of a rape survivors' group. Shelly was feeling isolated and alone, and I believed that a group would help her to receive support from other survivors. I became alarmed at her outrage. Shelly was raised in a conservative Irish Catholic family. "We never talked about our stuff in public." The very idea of discussing her rape with people whom she did not know was horrifying to her. In treating Shelly, I had failed to make an adequate cultural assessment of the client and I had also failed to adequately consult with her.

I reassured the client that she could continue with individual therapy and that I respected her decision to decline group therapy. I was relieved and pleased that my alliance with Shelly was not completely destroyed when she appeared for the next session. Shelly continued to show up regularly for individual therapy. Ten weeks later, she inquired about attending a rape survivors' group because she was feeling stronger and less vulnerable; she wanted to meet other survivors. We discussed the possibility of Shelly attending a group and evaluated options. What was important was that Shelly felt empowered to eventually take charge of her treatment according to her own timetable. I applauded Shelly's strength.

Treatment Options for Rape Survivors

The rape survivor seeks therapy after her world has been torn asunder, when all that was familiar is no longer trusted. This can be an intensely vulnerable position. Establishing a safe and trusting therapeutic relationship is a foundational step in restoring trust. This creates a framework within which clinical techniques become effective and recovery begins. The safety and protection of the therapeutic relationship should permeate all the other systems that surround the rape survivor: the medical, legal, and criminal justice systems. Unfortunately this does not always happen. It is not unusual for rape victims to feel doubly shamed by the insensitive response of judicial institutions. Motivated by self-protection, they may retract their charges against the perpetrator.

Cognitive-Behavioral Therapy for Rape Survivors

CBT has been the most studied and effective approach in reducing PTSD reactions in rape survivors (Foa, Dancu, Hembree, Jaycox, Meadows, & Street, 1999; Foa & Jaycox, 1999; Foa & Meadows, 1997; Foa & Riggs, 1993; Jaycox, Zoellner, & Foa, 2002). In a study using CBT techniques of imaginal exposure and cognitive restructuring in the context of an empathetic and supportive therapeutic relationship, clients felt safe to discuss their rape (Foa & Meadows,1997). They were also helped to correct erroneous cognitions and irrational beliefs.

Jaycox et al. (2002) describe a treatment program for rape survivors that is used at the Center for Treatment and Study of Anxiety in Philadelphia (Foa & Rothbaum, 1998). Conducted within a caring therapeutic environment, the program involves four components: breathing retraining, PTSD education, imaginal exposure to trauma and confrontation of feared situations, and cognitive restructuring. The full treatment extends over 12 sessions and includes the completion of homework assignments. The treatment has been successful in reducing symptoms of both PTSD and depression. Clients were found to retain these therapeutic gains in a one-year follow-up study. Specific CBT techniques used with rape survivors are outlined below.

Imaginal Exposure to Trauma

It is normal for rape survivors to reduce distress by repressing memories of their trauma. Before beginning imaginal exposure, the client is taught relaxation techniques to reduce any anxiety that may arise when traumatic memories are recalled. As the client is encouraged to repeatedly confront the feared situation, habituation is achieved. The traumatic memory becomes less harmful when it is remembered without the experience of overwhelming anxiety and thought disruption. This new sense of control over traumatic images can be empowering for a client. When used together, relaxation training and imaginal exposure are found to be effective in reducing anxiety in rape victims (Foa & Riggs, 1994). Since imaginal exposure does not directly address the victim's self-schemas and perception of the rape, the next step in the treatment is to address this limitation through cognitive restructuring.

Cognitive Restructuring

Once victims are able to see trauma memories as distinct rather than overwhelming memories, they can begin to make sense of their traumatic experience.

In cognitive restructuring, clients adjust past schemas to incorporate new experiences. This adjustment is only possible once self-control is established and when clients have the capacity to discriminate between danger and safety. A trauma survivor's ability to make meaning of trauma is strongly influenced by his or her sociocultural context (cultural beliefs, practices, and institutions). If sociocultural values demonize the rape victim, these values must be addressed immediately. Rape survivors commonly hold unrealistic assumptions that the world is unsafe; they often believe they are unable to cope with stress. The primary goal of cognitive restructuring is to reduce anxiety by having clients identify, evaluate, and modify negative thoughts.

The first step in cognitive restructuring is assessing the strength of a trauma-related thought. Clients are asked to keep a chart, which is referred to as a subjective unit of distress (SUD) chart. Situations, thoughts, and feelings as well as their accompanying level of intensity are recorded on this chart on a continuum of 1 to 10. In therapy, these irrational beliefs and cognitive distortions are examined and challenged until the client realizes the futility of these irrational beliefs; he or she then becomes motivated to replace them.

Rape Prevention Education

Through the efforts of feminist activists, the number of rape crisis centers to support rape victims continues to grow. Rape prevention education is an important aspect of these programs. However, this psycho-education has had little effect on the rate of rape prevalence, which has not varied for the past 25 years (Bachar & Koss, 2001; Breitenbecher, 2000). Programs that focus on teaching women avoidance behaviors or precautions they can take with strangers are ineffective for two reasons: first, women already practice these behaviors, and second, most rapes are committed by known assailants (Rozee & Koss, 2001). Given the failure of rape prevention programs to yield positive results, new ways of thinking about how to prevent rape have been considered. One of these is resistance training.

Self-Defense and Resistance Training

Resistance training programs focus on making women agents of their destiny. These programs view self-defense as a matter of technique rather than strength and physical size (Rozee & Koss, 2001). Such programs assume that women who receive coaching on how to overcome physical threats with physical resistance will successfully confront rapists. Self-defense programs also teach students early warning signs and pre-rape behaviors, which include sexual entitlement, power, control, hostility, anger, and acceptance of interpersonal violence (Malamuth, Linz, Heavey, Barnes, & Acker, 1995).

Empirical evidence has shown the efficacy of self-defense programs (Rozee, 2000; Ullman, 1997). Self-defense has several advantages: it is empowering, it fosters a positive attitude towards self, it enhances control and coping, and it decreases vulnerability as well as negative thinking and anxiety about safety (Ozer & Bandura, 1990; Wade, 1997). It may be worthwhile to use the Internet to identify several local self-defense and resistance training programs. Therapists can refer their clients to these programs.

Social Organizing and Commonality

In the process of recovery, survivors need to find ways to "deconstruct blaming and degrading constructions of women and sexuality" (Lebowitz & Roth, 1994, p. 388). This process begins in therapy and continues through involvement with groups outside of treatment that are committed to ending violence. Rape survivors gain a sense of empowerment by becoming members of such groups. "Take Back the Night" is an example of a group that empowers survivors of rape to march near local pornography shops. The goal of this group is to protest the sexualized and demeaning images of women that this industry relies upon.

Domestic Violence

Domestic violence is also referred to as spousal abuse, partner violence, family violence, intimate partner violence, wife beating, and wife battering. It describes any act of interpersonal violence between or among family members. As previously mentioned, acts or threats of violence by men against women dominate the field. As a group, battered women comprise one of the largest traumatized populations in North America (Council on Scientific Affairs, American Medical Association, 1992). Domestic violence pervades most cultural and socioeconomic groups; few communities are free of it. While it is understood that battering is also perpetrated by females and can occur between same-sex partners, this chapter focuses on female and child survivors of domestic violence who are often victims of domestic violence. The U.S. Department of Justice estimates that one in four women will be subjected to domestic abuse during her lifetime, and women are up to eight times more likely to be victimized by an intimate partner than are men (1998).

Background

In a historical account that explored the evolution of domestic violence, Linda Gordon (1988) analyzed 1,500 cases of child abuse and neglect. These cases were recorded by social service agencies in the Boston area between 1880 and 1960. The records indicated that in these cases, originally opened for reported child abuse, one-third of the fathers who abused their children were also husbands who abused their wives. In interviewing the women involved in these cases, it became clear that although the women sought help for their children, they did not report their own abuse. English common law prevailed during this era; according to this law, women and children were regarded as wards or property of the husbands, and the abuse of women was not perceived as criminal behavior. This may account for the low reports of domestic violence at the time.

After World War II, the women's movement grew steadily and gained momentum in the 1960s. Through the efforts of the women's movement, domestic violence was, for the first time, viewed as a societal issue rather than an interpersonal problem. Thus, the women's movement laid the groundwork for the emergence of the battered women's movement in the 1970s. In this decade, as a result of the efforts of the battered women's movement, marital violence was clearly defined as an abuse of power.

Although the occurrence of domestic violence is universal, efforts at exposing its negative effects have primarily taken place in Western countries. Limited economic resources, a lack of political will, and lack of structural support are some of the factors that may have contributed to slow efforts in non-Western communities to publicize the negative effects of domestic violence (Krane, 1996).

When domestic violence is viewed through an ecological lens, it is not seen as an isolated issue, but instead is enmeshed with other forms of oppression that promote the power and privilege of some and diminish the value of others. The social acceptance of violence as a means to an end contributes to the promotion of violence in social and intimate relationships. Schools are not exempt from this acceptance of violence. Many children are plagued by bullying on the school playground (DeRosier, 2004). The media is part of the ecosystem that plays a significant role in popularizing and sensationalizing violence so that it becomes an acceptable facet of life.

The diagnosis of PTSD is much higher among battered women than in the general population. The prevalence rate of PTSD among battered women falls in the range of 45% to 84% (Kubany, Abueg, Owens, Brennan, Kaplan, & Watson, 1995). The following statistics illuminate the extent to which domestic violence permeates homes, schools, communities, and society:

- It is estimated that every year 960,000 to three million women are physically abused by their husbands or boyfriends (U.S. Department of Justice, 1998).
- Around the world, at least one in every three women has been beaten, coerced into sex, or otherwise abused during her lifetime (Heise, Ellberg, et al., 1999).
- Only about 1/7 of all domestic assaults receive police attention (U.S. Department of Justice, 2002).
- Women who obtain a permanent civil protection order experience an 80% reduction in their risk of police-reported physical violence (Holt, Kernic, & Wolf, 2003).
- Women who are separated are 3 times more likely than divorced women, and 25 times more likely than married women, to become victims of violence at the hands of intimate partners (Bachman & Salzman, 2000).
- Approximately one-third of all female murder victims were killed by an intimate partner (U.S. Department of Justice, 2001).
- Although domestic violence occurs across all socioeconomic groups, the rate of intimate partner violence increases as household income decreases (Rennison & Welchan, 2002).
- Asian/Pacific Islander women have the lowest reports of intimate partner violence. African American and American Indian/Alaska Native women have the highest reports of intimate partner violence (Tjaden & Thoennes, 2000).

Intervention With Survivors of Domestic Violence

In reviewing the literature on domestic violence, Kubany and Watson (2002) identified several issues faced by battered women:

- Overwhelming feelings of guilt and shame
- Experiences of prolonged or repeated trauma by past partners
- Histories of interpersonal violence, especially childhood sexual abuse
- Enmeshed relationships with the abuser
- The risk of revictimization by subsequent partners

An intervention with survivors of domestic violence must occur within an ecological framework. Such a framework places the responsibility on the individual survivor as well as the community and the political system. An ecological approach also emphasizes and ensures that batterers can and will obtain necessary help to take responsibility for their violent behavior.

Individual Level

Domestic violence involves the abuse of power by one partner against another. Interventions that focus on self-advocacy, self-efficacy, and empowerment are the most beneficial. As a first step, the therapist must carefully assess the strengths, needs, and available resources of the client. This careful assessment will inform the pacing of therapy and prevent the client from becoming overwhelmed by strategies that may be implemented prematurely.

CBT is an effective treatment model for battered women. In one of the first treatment-outcome studies using cognitive trauma therapy with battered women, Kubany et al. (2004) found that at the end of treatment, 87% of women no longer met the diagnostic criteria for PTSD. In three- and six-month follow-up studies, they showed a corresponding reduction in depression, guilt, and shame and a significant increase in self-esteem.

More importantly, studies have shown that cognitive treatments are effective for both ethnically and educationally diverse women (Cloitre, Koenen, Cohen, & Han, 2002; Resick, Nishith, Weaver, Astin, & Feuer, 2002). Therapists who possessed no formal training in psychotherapy achieved many of these positive results; this has important implications for victim services in this country and underdeveloped communities globally. It demonstrates that the services of paraprofessionals can produce good outcomes. In addition, the study found that male psychotherapists did not have any detrimental effects on client treatment outcomes, suggesting that gender may not always hinder the therapeutic process.

Community Level

Informal interventions that take place at the community level effectively discourage domestic violence and reveal batterers to all community members. Churches, schools, and employers can help curtail violent behavior (Campbell, 1992). Female solidarity groups can contribute to a reduction in battering behavior. For example, in some English working class communities, women draw attention to the perpetrator's violent actions by banging pots and pans outside a house where a woman is battered (Levinson, 1989). The actions of these women have led to a drastic reduction in the occurrence of domestic violence in their communities.

In large immigrant and refugee communities, it is important to publicize programs that raise awareness about women's rights. Many women in these communities may be unaware of the rights to which they are entitled by living in the U.S. Additional ways to end domestic violence include developing educational material and programs for children who witness violence, increasing information about male batterer groups, and enforcing legislation against battering. It is unfortunate that many women are forced to remain in abusive relationships for economic reasons. The provision of incentives and other resources may encourage some women to leave an abusive partner. Food, clothing, social support, health care, transportation, child care, and legal aid are some of the resources battered women may be afraid to relinquish.

Political Level

Efforts to eradicate domestic violence at the political level are crucial. It is important to advocate for legislation mandating tougher consequences for those who use violence and abuse as a means of control in intimate relationships. While all states mandate the reporting of child abuse, few states have a similar mandate for domestic violence (Lamberg, 2000). Lobbying in these states is one way to end domestic violence nationally.

The Model Code on Domestic and Family Violence (American Bar Association, 1994) provides comprehensive details on anti-violence legislation guidelines that all states can employ.

- The Code views domestic and family violence as a crime.
- The Code emphasizes the safety of victims (including children) and full accountability by the batterer.
- The Code offers procedures for comprehensive victim protection orders.
- The Code outlines guidelines for state and community coordination in identifying, intervening, and preventing domestic violence.

Many states have passed legislation to reflect these guidelines. However, formal sanctions, judicial proceedings, and the payment of compensation to discourage domestic violence are not always stringently enforced. This lack of enforcement compromises the safety of both victims of domestic violence and their children.

Shelters to meet the immediate needs of women who try to escape domestic violence are an important social service that requires continued state and federal funding. Once a woman makes the decision to leave an abusive relationship, she must be assured of a safe and accessible shelter. Waiting lists and other bureaucratic hurdles that arise from limited resources ultimately discourage battered women from seeking help. Furthermore, increased private, state, and federal funding ensures continued research on interpersonal violence. This research will enhance our current knowledge and update us on best practices in treating survivors of domestic violence.

Safety Planning

The safety of battered women should be a primary concern for those in the helping professions because abuse is likely to escalate over time and become especially volatile when battered women attempt to separate from their abusers. Battered women are twice as likely to be killed when they leave their abusers than when they choose to remain in abusive relationships (Wilson, Johnson, & Daly, 1995). Thus, the construction of a safety plan becomes crucial for battered women who want to take steps to protect themselves and their children. Several safety plans may be necessary, depending on the situation of each survivor:

- Personal safety while living with the abuser
- Guidelines on leaving an abusive relationship
- Safety after leaving an abusive relationship

Sample Personal Safety Plan (Living With Abuser)

- Keep important phone numbers (police, battered women's shelters, friends, and family members who are aware of your situation) in as many places as possible (bedroom, purse, and car). Call a domestic violence hotline periodically to assess your options and get support.
- Avoid abusive situations by leaving. Keep a list of at least four places that you can go to if you decide to leave.
- Leave extra money, a spare set of car keys, clothes, and copies of important documents (driver's license, list of credit cards, information about bank accounts, citizenship documents, and medical information) in a small bag that is kept in an undisclosed but accessible place.
- Identify safe areas in your home where there are no weapons and easy access to an exit. If arguments occur, try to move to those areas. Avoid running toward the children because your partner may hurt them as well.
- Practice how to safely escape; your escape plan should be practiced with your children as well. Think about how you will explain yourself if your children tell your partner about your plan or your partner discovers it.
- Always keep potential weapons, like guns and knives, locked up or inaccessible.
- Make sure that your car is always fueled and the doors are unlocked for a quick escape.
- Teach children that violence is never a solution to conflict, even when someone they love is being violent. Reassure them that neither you nor they are to blame for the violence in the home. Identify a safe place for them (a room with a lock or a friend's house where they can go for help). Reassure them that their job is to stay safe themselves, not to protect you.
- Teach your children not to get involved in the violence between you and your partner. However, you can plan a code word to signal them when they should get help or leave the house.
- Devise a code word to use with family and friends when you need them to call the police.

Every woman's safety plan is unique. It should be concise and written on a small piece of paper that can be folded and easily tucked into a pocket or the side of a bag. Safety plans should be reviewed and updated on a regular basis.

Additional Resources for Battered Women

National Domestic Violence Hotline

(800) 799-SAFE (7233)

(800) 787–3224 (TTY)

National Coalition Against Domestic Violence

P.O. Box 18749

Denver, CO 80218

(303) 839–1852

National Resource Center on Domestic Violence

Pennsylvania Coalition Against Domestic Violence

6400 Flank Drive

Suite #1300

Harrisburg, PA 17112

(800) 537–2238

National Council on Child Abuse and Family Violence

1155 Connecticut Ave., NW

Suite #400

Washington, DC 20036

(800) 222–2000

Children Who Witness Domestic Violence

Domestic violence, or the violence that occurs between adult caregivers, is the most "toxic form of exposure that children witness" (Groves, 2002, p. 50).

Children of battered women who see and hear conjugal conflict are the innocent bystanders of such violence. Witnessing violence that threatens life or inflicts injuries adversely affects children's functioning and predisposes them to post-traumatic disorder (McCloskey, Figueredo, & Koss, 1995). Disabling responses experienced by children who witness domestic violence include the following (*DSM-IV*):

- Re-experiencing events of trauma in the form of memories or flashbacks, with psychological and physiological distress (arousal) when exposed to reminders of trauma
- Avoidance of stimuli that are related to the trauma or periods of emotional detachment
- Physiological arousal characterized by such problems as hypervigilance, sleep disorders, or inappropriate anger

In a study done among 50 battered mothers and children, Chemtob and Carlson (2004) documented a 40% rate of PTSD among their children. PTSD symptoms were still evident two years after the abusive relationship had ended. In a similar study, witnessing domestic violence, and especially a mother's distressed reaction to the violence, had multiplicative effects on children (Silva, Alpert, Munoz, Singh, Matzner, & Dummit, 2000). Dissociative symptoms observed among their children correlated with depression in mothers (Chemtob & Carlson, 2004). Although this defense mechanism possibly helped children cope with the violence at home, dissociative behavior became problematic at school, where attention and concentration are important.

The Child Witness to Violence Project at the Boston Medical Center in Boston, Massachusetts, is described as a program that began as a service for children exposed to community violence (Groves, 2002). Inundated with referrals for children who witnessed domestic violence, the focus of the program quickly shifted to providing services for these children. This shift was based on findings that children are more likely to be exposed to violence in their homes than in the community (Groves, 2002). Many children learn their first lessons in violence from their parents. Although the impact of community violence cannot be minimized, exposure to domestic violence has more damaging consequences. Groves (2002) points out that the effects of domestic violence on children tend to be long term for the following reasons:

- Both people involved in the violent event are people the child loves
- Taking sides can trigger emotional and cognitive dissonance for the child
- Domestic violence is seldom a single occurrence but tends to happen repeatedly, making it a chronic or Type II trauma

- Strong societal taboo disallows a discussion of intimate violence
- Children quickly learn that they cannot talk about the violence they witness
- Children are sometimes threatened by parents to "keep it a secret," and this compounds their feelings of guilt

In the 1990s, two factors resulted in the growth of services for the children of battered women. First, the research on the devastating impact of environmental trauma on children and the impact of early experiences on brain development began to flourish (Garbarino, 1987; Terr, 1981). Second, the Violence Against Women Act, 1994, was passed. This legislation provided one billion dollars to fund services for battered women and mental health services for their children.

Of all the abuses children may face, domestic violence is the most harmful. In a study that examined the stressors most strongly correlated with a diagnosis of PTSD among children, witnessing domestic violence was found to be more harmful than being a direct victim of child abuse (Famularo, Fenton, & Kinscherff, 1993). Physical exposure to any violent event threatens a child's well-being, but a child's close involvement as witness in situations of domestic violence heightens his or her reactions. These reactions become intensified when children also perceive themselves to be in danger. Children's feelings of helplessness intensify when they sense that a caregiver's life may be in danger.

Another disturbing research finding is the evidence that fathers who batter their partners are more likely to abuse their children (McCloskey et al., 1995). Moreover, even when support from siblings and a nonabusive parent is available, children who witness domestic violence do not take advantage of this support (McCloskey et al., 1995). Thus, environmental support may not always buffer the psychologically harmful effects of family violence. Children as young as 20 months are reported to show reactions of distress and increased aggression with their playmates after witnessing verbal arguments between parents at home (Cummings & Davies, 1994). In addition, the researchers found that repeated exposure to parental conflict did not desensitize children or diminish their reactions to distress; instead, it increased their anxiety and aggression.

Parental Stress

It is inevitable that the psychological and physical abuse of women negatively affects their interactions with their children. According to a comprehensive review done by Van Horn and Lieberman (2004), women who have been exposed to violence show elevated levels of parenting stress.

Further research indicates that maternal and parental stress is higher in families where domestic violence is prevalent; domestic violence is also a significant predictor of behavior problems in children (Holden & Ritchie, 1991; Levendosky & Graham-Bermann, 2000).

In a review of the effects of domestic violence, Margolin (1998) noted that 45% to 70% of children exposed to domestic violence were also victims of physical abuse. Additionally, children of battered women are at increased risk for sexual abuse (McCloskey et al., 1995). Another disturbing finding is that children who witness domestic violence tend to identify with and adopt characteristics of the aggressor by interacting in a hostile and emotionally aggressive manner with their abused mothers (Levendosky & Graham-Bermann, 2000). Early intervention with children in homes where domestic violence occurs is essential to prevent children from assuming that aggression is an acceptable behavior.

An Ecological Approach to Helping Children Who Witness Violence

The widespread use of violence in international relations, in the popular media, and in families runs the risks of normalizing coercion, aggression, and violence. Once we admit that domestic violence is a socially created problem, we can look at the ecological environment that surrounds both the child and the abused parent to seek possible resolutions. Resolving the issue of domestic violence begins with those closest to the child: parents and caregivers.

Parents and Caregivers

Experiences of abuse sometimes results in battered women adopting a laissez-faire parenting style with their children. An important step in the healing of battered mothers is, therefore, to initiate empowering parenting interventions that help them have authority in their homes and control over their children (Levendosky & Graham-Bermann, 2000). Such parental authority can be severely undermined, however, if the batterer remains in the home. It is important that the victimized parent be allowed to hone her parenting skills without criticism in a nonjudgmental parenting environment. Before psychological interventions begin, one of the first issues to raise with a survivor of domestic violence is whether the home is safe (Osofsky, 2004). Public policy that mandates dire consequences for men who do not adhere to court orders is one way of supporting the efforts of battered women to make their homes safer.

Groves (2002) emphasizes the importance of reassuring parents that although they could not have prevented a child's exposure to trauma, they can always help the child gain a sense of equilibrium by doing the following:

- Reestablish order and routine
- Spend more time with children
- Participate in reassuring and soothing activities
- Depending on the child's developmental stage, provide a clear explanation of what happened
- Reassure the child that it was not his or her fault
- Respond to the child with honesty

Sometimes parents avoid reassuring a child that the violence will end because they themselves do not have this guarantee. However, admitting this to a child can be comforting and reduce his or her sense of helplessness. A referral for counseling should always be considered as an option for children who may need further help. The decision to make a referral for counseling is always based on the severity of symptoms, the severity of the violence witnessed, and the severity of ongoing risk to the child.

When a child is referred for psychotherapy, the first session should include spending some time with the nonoffending parent to determine background and current information. When children observe caregivers interacting favorably with therapists, they are likely to feel comfortable disclosing abuse in the home. Finally, developing a safety plan for children in homes where domestic violence is prevalent is critical. Such plans include strategies to locate a shelter, teaching children the telephone numbers of the nearest emergency room and police department, and teaching them how to dial 911.

Schools and Teachers

Children who are raised in violent homes experience the structure and predictability of the classroom as unfamiliar, uncomfortable, and anxiety provoking. These experiences often manifest in behavioral problems in the classroom, problems which teachers find frustrating. Although it is sometimes difficult to notice a child's underlying vulnerability amidst his or her negative behavior, teachers may be the first to observe changes in a child and identify problems in a child's home. Teachers who are attuned to these changes can effectively assist the child by reporting any negligent parental behavior.

Teachers who create an atmosphere of acceptance and show a willingness to listen give children permission to talk. In this way, the teacher plays an active role as a child advocate. Teachers who provide emotional and practical support contribute to a child's adjustment; they buffer the negative effects of stress (Hawkins, Farrington, & Catalano, 1998).

School administrators may find it useful to organize workshops and training on child development on a regular basis, to better equip their staff to deal with children who come from violent homes. Topics that can be covered include the effects of violence on children and how to help children cope with stress. Children need safe places. When the home is unable to fulfill this need, then the school and other community settings can serve as surrogates (Noddings, 1996). Positive school environments can be a crucial resource for children at risk.

Community

Several community-based institutions are used by battered women, including hospitals and police departments. However, research indicates that although battered women visit physicians for isolated injuries, multiple somatic complaints, chemical dependency, depression, and other problems, physicians often prescribe psychoactive and analgesic drugs without exploring the underlying causes of complaints (Lamberg, 2000). This failure to ask relevant questions increases the battered woman's level of despair and isolation.

Physicians can benefit from learning how to ask battered women questions in a supportive and nonthreatening manner. Displaying resources where victims of domestic violence can seek help is beneficial because it conveys concern for the well-being of the battered woman. Emergency rooms, police departments, and other public service organizations are some places where battered women and children first seek help. Staff members of these organizations should be well informed about the harmful effects of domestic violence on children.

Since police officers are the first to respond to crime scenes, they are in a good position to identify children exposed to violence. Early identification and referral of child witnesses to violence can ensure that they receive the help they need. Osofsky (2004) describes an innovative program that attempts to reach traumatized children as quickly as possible. The Violence Intervention Program, first established in New Orleans, Louisiana, is a partnership among psychologists, social workers, teachers, the police department, and community representatives. A key component of the program is educating police officers about the effects of violence on children to increase their knowledge and sensitivity. The police officers, who respond to homes where domestic violence is suspected, are trained to refer family members to a 24-hour hotline that provides immediate help for affected families.

In some communities, the church plays an integral role in the welfare of its members. The church minister may be the first person approached by a battered woman. How clergy respond to domestic violence becomes significant in these communities. Some religious communities have made concerted attempts to eradicate domestic violence in their community while others have not supported domestic violence or done anything to condone it. A church minister can play a key role in convincing both a victim and a perpetrator to seek assistance.

Community programs are also helpful in supporting children who are negatively affected by violence. For example, Farrell and Bruce (1997) found that a midnight basketball league helped 96 delinquent youths to transform their lives in positive directions. Tierney and Grossman (2000) found that a mentoring program conducted through Big Brother/Big Sister contributed to improved family relationships of youth participants.

Programs for Men Who Batter

Although the battered women's movement initially defined domestic violence as a crime against women, men were strongly encouraged to participate in efforts to end abuse. Legislative and social initiatives emphasized the importance of ending domestic violence for both men and women. The goal was to encourage men to become better informed about the negative consequences of violence and to take responsibility for it.

The nation's first program for men who batter women, Emerge (Adams & Cayouette, 2002), was established in 1977 based on the following philosophy:

- Battering includes a range of coercive behaviors that serve to undermine a victim's self-esteem and independence.
- Battering is purposeful, intentional behavior aimed at gaining and maintaining control in relationships.
- Battering is learned through modeling and positive reinforcement.

Batterer programs have since grown substantially and include cultural competence in the provision of services. Many programs have group facilitators who come from the local community and who are familiar with its culture. Groups are also conducted by facilitators who are fluent in local languages such as Spanish, Vietnamese, or Khmer. Outreach workers and staff who are responsible for evaluation are often culturally competent. Since this is usually a batterer's first interaction with the helping profession, it is important to make the interaction as supportive as possible. Culturally specific batterer groups give batterers the option of participating in a homogenous group setting (e.g., African American and Asian batterer groups).

Conclusion

The effects of interpersonal violence persist long after the abuse ends. The more severe the abuse, the worse its impact. Moreover, experiencing multiple episodes of abuse over time evokes cumulative effects. When children are the innocent bystanders of interpersonal violence, they are placed at developmental risk for long-term consequences.

An ecological approach is the most effective approach to help children who witness domestic violence. Parents are an important part of the child's ecosystem and a valuable resource. They provide children with an emotional buffer, and children tend to handle stress better when parents are involved in helping interventions. Before batterers are reunited with their families, they need to be educated about the detrimental consequences of their behaviors on their children. Empowering nonoffending parents to become better role models by fulfilling their caregiver responsibilities creates a safer environment for children. The initial call of the battered women's movement highlighted violence against women as a human rights violation. This movement made a major contribution in publicizing the challenges faced by survivors of domestic violence. We should always remember this call and heed it in the battle to end all forms of violence.

References

Adams, D., & Cayouette, S. (2002). Emerge: A group education model for abusers. In E. Aldarondo & F. Mederos (Eds.), *Programs for men who batter: Interventions and prevention strategies in a diverse society* (pp. 4-1–4-35). New York: Civic Research.

American Bar Association. (1994). *Model code on domestic and family violence.* Retrieved August 15, 2005, from http://www.abanet.org/domviol/attorneys.html

American Psychiatric Association. (1994). *Diagnostic and statistical manual of mental disorders* (4th ed.). Washington, DC: Author.

Bachar, K., & Koss, M. P. (2001). From prevalence to prevention: Closing the gap between what we know about rape and what we do. In C. M. Renzetti, J. L. Edelson, & R. K. Bergen (Eds.), *Sourcebook on violence against women* (pp. 117–142). Thousand Oaks, CA: Sage.

Bachman, R., & Salzman, L. E. (1995). *Violence against women: Estimates from the redesigned survey.* Washington, DC: U.S. Dept. of Justice.

Bachman, R., & Salzman, L. (2000). *Violence against women: Estimates from the redesigned survey.* Washington, DC: U.S. Dept. of Justice.

Best, J. (1999). *Random violence: How we talk about new crimes and new victims.* Berkeley: University of California Press.

Bourque, L. B. (1989). *Defining rape.* Durham, NC: Duke University Press.

Breitenbecher, K. H. (2000). Sexual assault on college campuses: Is an ounce of prevention enough? *Applied and Preventive Psychology, 9,* 23–52.

Brooks, D. L. (1997). Rape on soaps: The legal angle. In M. A. Fineman & M. T. McCluskey (Eds.), *Feminism, media and the law* (pp. 104–119). New York: Bantam Books.

Brownmiller, S. (1975). *Against our will: Men, women, and rape.* New York: Bantam Books.

Campbell, J. (1992). Prevention of wife battering: Insights from cultural analysis. *Response to the Victimization of Women and Children, 14*(3), 18–24.

Chemtob, C. M., & Carlson, J. G. (2004). Psychological effects of domestic violence: Children and mothers. *International Journal of Stress Management, 11*(3), 209–226.

Clark, L. M. G., & Lewis, D. J. (1977). *Rape: The price of coercive sexuality.* Toronto: Canadian Women's University Press.

Cloitre, M., Koenen, K. C., Cohen, L. R., & Han, H. (2002). A phase-based treatment for PTSD related to child abuse. *Journal of Consulting and Clinical Psychology, 70,* 1067–1074.

Council on Scientific Affairs, American Medical Association. (1992). Violence against women: Relevance for medical practitioners. *JAMA, 267,* 3184–3189.

Cummings, E. M., & Davies, P. (1994). *Children and marital conflict: The impact of family dispute and resolution.* New York: Guilford.

DeRosier, M. E. (2004). Building relationships and combating bullying: Effectiveness of a school-based social skills group intervention. *Journal of Clinical Child and Adolescent Psychology, 33,* 196–201.

Famularo, R., Fenton, T., & Kinscherff, R. (1993). Child maltreatment and the development of post-traumatic stress disorder. *American Journal of Diseases of Children, 147,* 755–759.

Farrell, A. D., & Bruce, S. E. (1997). Impact of exposure to community violence on violent behavior and emotional distress among urban adolescents. *Journal of Clinical Child Psychology, 26*(1), 2–14.

Foa, E. B., Dancu, C. V., Hembree, E. A., Jaycox, L. H, Meadows, E. A., & Street, G. P. (1999). A comparison of exposure therapy, stress inoculation training and their combination for reducing posttraumatic stress disorder in female assault victims. *Journal of Consulting and Clinical Psychology, 67*(2), 194–200.

Foa, E. B., & Jaycox, L. H. (1999). Cognitive-behavior theory and treatment of post-traumatic stress disorder. In D. Spiegel (Ed.), *Efficacy and cost-effectiveness of psychotherapy* (pp. 23–61). Washington, DC: American Psychiatry Press.

Foa, E. B., & Meadows, E. A. (1997). Psychosocial treatments for posttraumatic disorder: A critical review. *Annual Review of Psychology, 48*(1), 449–481.

Foa, E. B., & Riggs, D. S. (1993). Post-traumatic stress disorder in rape victims. In J. Oldham, M. B. Riba, & A. Tasman (Eds.), *American Psychiatric Press review of psychiatry* (pp. 273–303). Washington, DC: American Psychiatric Press.

Foa, E. B., & Riggs, D. S. (1994). Posttraumatic stress disorder and rape. In R. S. Pynoos (Ed.), *Posttraumatic stress disorder: A clinical review* (pp. 133–163). Baltimore, MD: Sidran Press.

Foa, E. B., & Rothbaum, B.O. (1998). *Treating the trauma of rape: Cognitive behavioral therapy for PTSD.* New York: Guilford.

Garbarino, J. (1987). What can the school do on behalf of the maltreated child and the community. *School Psychology Review, 16*(2), 181–187.

Gordon, L. (1988). *Heroes of their own lives: The politics and history of family violence: Boston 1880–1960.* New York: Viking Press.

Groves, B. M. (2002). *Children who see too much.* Boston, MA: Beacon Press.

Hawkins, J. D., Farrington, D. P., & Catalano, R. F. (1998). Reducing violence through the schools. In D. S. Elliott & B. A. Hamburg (Eds.), *Violence in American schools: A new perspective* (pp. 188–216). New York: Cambridge University Press.

Heise, L., Ellsberg, M., & Gottemoeller, M. (1999). Ending violence against women. *Population Reports, 27,* 1–43.

Holden, G. W., & Ritchie, K. L. (1991). Linking extreme marital discord, child rearing, and child behavior problems: Evidence from battered women. *Child Development, 62*(2), 311–327.

Holt, V. L., Kernic, M. A., & Wolf, M. E. (2003). Do protection orders affect the likelihood of future partner violence and injury? *American Journal of Preventative Medicine, 24*(1), 16–21.

Jaycox, L. H., Zoellner, L., & Foa, E. B. (2002). Cognitive-behavior therapy for PTSD in rape survivors. *Journal of Clinical Psychology, 58*(8), 891–906.

Koss, M. P., Heise, L., & Russo, N. F. (1994). The global health burden of rape. *Psychology of Women Quarterly, 18,* 509–537.

Krane, J. E. (1996). Violence against women in intimate relations: Insights from cross-cultural analyses. *Transcultural Psychiatric Review, 33,* 435–465.

Kubany, E. S., Abueg, F. R., Owens, J. A., Brennan, J. M., Kaplan, A., & Watson, S. (1995). Initial examination of a multidimensional model of guilt: Applications to combat veterans and battered women. *Journal of Psychopathology and Behavioral Assessment, 17,* 353–376.

Kubany, E. S., Hill, E. E., Owens, J. A., Iannce-Spencer, C., McCaig, M. A., Tremayne, K. J., et al. (2004). Cognitive trauma therapy for battered women with PTSD (CTT-BW). *Journal of Consulting and Clinical Psychology, 72*(1), 3–18.

Kubany, E. S., & Watson, S. B. (2002). Cognitive trauma therapy for formerly battered women with PTSD (CTT-BW): Conceptual bases and treatment outlines. *Cognitive and Behavioral Practice, 9,* 111–127.

Lamberg, L. (2000). Domestic violence: What to ask, what to do. *JAMA, 284*(5), 554–556.

Lebowitz, L., & Roth, S. (1994). "I felt like a slut": The cultural context and women's response to being raped. *Journal of Traumatic Stress, 7*(3), 363–390.

Lefley, H. P., Scott, C. S., Llabre, M., & Hicks, D. (1993). Cultural beliefs about rape and victims' response in three ethnic groups. *American Journal of Orthopsychiatry, 63*(4), 623–632.

Levendosky, A. A., & Graham-Bermann, S. A. (2000). Behavioral observations of parenting in battered women. *Journal of Family Psychology, 14*(1), 80–94.

Levinson, D. (1989). *Family violence in cross-cultural perspective.* Newbury Park, CA: Sage.

Lloyd, S. A., & Emery, B. C. (2000). *The dark side of courtship: Physical and sexual aggression.* Thousand Oaks, CA: Sage.

Malamuth, N. M., Linz, D., & Heavey, C. L., Barnes, G., & Acker, M. (1995). Using the confluence model of sexual aggression to predict men's conflict with women: A 10-year follow-up study. *Journal of Personality and Social Psychology, 69*(2), 353–369.

Margolin, G. (1998). Effects of domestic violence on children. In P. K. Trickett & C. J. Schellenbach (Eds.), *Violence against children in the family and the community* (pp. 57–101). Washington, DC: American Psychological Association.

Matthews, N. A. (1994). *Confronting rape: The feminist anti-rape movement and the state.* London: Routledge.

McCloskey, L. A., Figueredo, A. J., & Koss, M. P. (1995). The effects of systemic family violence on children's mental health. *Child Development, 66*(5), 1239– 1261.

Noddings, N. (1996). Stories and effect in teacher education. *Cambridge Journal of Education, 26*(3), 435–447.

Osofsky, J. (2004). *Young children and trauma: Intervention and treatment.* New York: Guilford.

Ozer, E. M., & Bandura, A. (1990). Mechanisms governing empowerment effects: A self-efficacy analysis. *Journal of Personality and Social Psychology, 58*(3), 472–486.

Rennison, C. M., & Welchan, S. (2002). *Bureau of Justice statistics: Intimate partner violence.* Washington, DC: U.S. Department of Justice.

Resick, P. A., Nishith, P., Weaver, T. L., Astin, M. C., & Feuer, C. A. (2002). A comparison of cognitive processing therapy with prolonged exposure for the treatment of posttraumatic stress disorder in female rape victims. *Journal of Consulting and Clinical Psychology, 70,* 867–879.

Rozee, P. D. (2000). Sexual victimization. In M. Biaggio & M. Hersen (Eds.), *Issues in the psychology of women* (pp. 93–113). New York: Kluwer Academic/Plenum.

Rozee, P. D., & Koss, M. P. (2001). Rape: A century of resistance. *Psychology of Women Quarterly, 25,* 295–311.

Silva, R. R., Alpert, M., Munoz, D. M., Singh, S., Matzner, F., & Dummit, S. (2000). Stress and vulnerability to post-traumatic stress disorder in children and adolescents. *American Journal of Orthopsychiatry, 157*(8), 1229–1235.

Stanko, E. (1998). Warnings to women: Police advice and women's safety in Britain. In S. Miller (Ed.), *Crime, control and women: Feminist implications of criminal justice policy* (pp. 52–71). Thousand Oaks, CA: Sage.

Terr, L. (1981). Psychic trauma in children: Observations following the Chowchilla school bus kidnapping. *American Journal of Psychiatry, 138*(1), 14–19.

Tierney, J., & Grossman, J. B. (2000). What works in promoting positive youth development: Mentoring. In M. P. Kluger & G. Alexander (Eds.), *What works in child welfare* (pp. 323–328). Washington, DC: Child Welfare League of America.

Tjaden, P., & Thoennes, N. (1998). *Prevalence, incidence and consequences of violence against women: Findings from the National Violence Against Women Survey* [Research brief]. Washington, DC: National Institute of Justice, Centers for Disease Control and Prevention.

Tjaden, P., & Thoennes, N. (2000). *Prevalence, incidence and consequences of violence against women: Findings from the National Violence Against Women Survey.* Washington, DC: U.S. Department of Justice, Office of Justice Programs.

Ullman, S. E. (1997). Review and critique of empirical studies of rape avoidance. *Criminal Justice and Behavior, 24,* 177–204.

U.S. Department of Justice. (1998). *Violence by intimates: Analysis of data on crimes by current or former spouses, boyfriends, and girlfriends.* Washington, DC: Author.

U.S. Department of Justice. (2001). *Bureau of Justice statistics: Homicide trends in the United States.* Washington, DC: Author.

U.S. Department of Justice. (2002). *Bureau of Justice statistics: Rape and sexual assault: Reporting to police and medical attention 1992–2000.* Washington, DC: Author.

Van Horn, O., & Lieberman, A. F. (2004). *Domestic violence and parenting: A review of the literature.* Unpublished manuscript.

Wade, A. (1997). Small acts of living: Everyday resistance to violence and other forms of oppression. *Contemporary Family Therapy, 19,* 23–39.

Wilson, M., Johnson, H., & Daly, M. (1995). Lethal and non-lethal violence against wives. *Canadian Journal of Criminology, 37*(3), 331–362.

11

Treating Political Refugees

Elleni is a 45-year-old Ethiopian woman who has lived in the U.S. for more than 10 years. As a younger woman in Ethiopia, she was detained and imprisoned on several occasions because of her membership and political involvement with a democratic party, which was organizing the overthrow of the ruling military regime. Elleni endured interrogation and torture with each imprisonment.

Elleni described how a military official escorted her to an empty room and then proceeded to tie her to a chair with her hands behind her back and her feet shackled before torturing and interrogating her. The officer asked her questions about her party affiliation. When Elleni refused to answer, she was tortured by the infliction of cigarette burns, electric shocks, and rape threats. Sometimes the pain was so intense she would lose consciousness. Elleni showed the therapist conducting her evaluation for a political asylum application the scars on her body from these experiences.

She also reported frequent intrusive nightmares in which she is tortured. These distressing dreams cause her to remain awake for the rest of the night. She barely sustains three or four hours of sleep each night. During Elleni's waking hours, intrusive recollections of her experiences in prison flood her with terror. When speaking about her torture, Elleni displayed a limited range of emotion. It was clear that she was trying to hold herself together. Although many of her symptoms have diminished in intensity since she has lived in the United States, Elleni is unable to focus. Unexpected noises throw her into a panic, and she is afraid to leave her apartment.

Victims of political trauma are forced to seek refuge by fleeing their native country. After undergoing the long and arduous U.S. visa process known as "political asylum," they ultimately create a new home here. This chapter focuses on survivors of political trauma and violations of human rights. Common refugee reactions and the challenges involved in accurately assessing their difficulties are reviewed. The chapter concludes with a description of a multiculturally and ecologically competent torture treatment center, as well as further resources to help those interested in continuing to work with this special population of trauma survivors.

Background and Research Evidence

Article 5 of the United Nations Universal Declaration of Human Rights states "No one shall be subjected to torture or to cruel, inhuman, or degrading treatment or punishment" (United Nations General Assembly, 1948). Yet, the systematic torture of human beings occurs in more than 110 countries throughout the world (Asad, 1997). Over 20 years ago, the U.S. Congress passed the Refugee Act of 1980, which standardized resettlement services for all refugees admitted to the United States. This act incorporates the definition of "refugee" used in U.N. Protocol; it defines refugees as people outside their country of nationality who are unable or unwilling to return to their country because of persecution or a well-founded fear of persecution due to race, religion, nationality, or membership in a particular social or political group. Representatives of the U.S. Immigration and Naturalization Service (INS) travel to conduct interviews with individuals who have fled persecution; they are ultimately responsible for determining refugee status. Once individuals are given refugee status, they are admitted to the United States where voluntary agencies initiate programs to assist them with resettlement.

Since 1975, the U.S. has resettled 2.4 million refugees. Nearly 77% of these refugees are either Indochinese or citizens of the former Soviet Union, two groups in which the U.S. has had particularly strong humanitarian and foreign policy interests. Since the enactment of the Refugee Act of 1980, annual admission figures have ranged from 61,000 in 1983 to 207,000 in 1980. The average number of refugees admitted annually since 1980 is 98,000 (U.S. Department of Health and Human Services, 2005).

Asylees are individuals who travel on their own to the United States and apply for asylum. They do not enter the United States as refugees, but instead may enter as students, tourists, or businesspersons. Alternatively, they may be individuals who simply enter the U.S. without papers. Once asylees arrive in the United States (land or port entry), they apply to the INS for asylum, which is a status acknowledging that they meet the criteria for the definition of a refugee. More importantly, receiving this status allows refugees to remain in the United States. Asylees have no immigration status until the Department of Homeland Security (the Federal department responsible for supervising immigration) declares them to be refugees; often this status is not attained until the asylee has participated in months or even years of judicial hearings.

These individuals often possess limited initial financial resources because they may have decided to forfeit all material possessions when escaping an oppressive government. Since September 11, 2001, the number of political asylees detained in prison facilities across the U.S. has increased steadily. In 2004 alone, 235,247 asylum seekers were detained by the Department of Homeland Security (Feinberg, 2006). As a result of the surplus of detainees, official detention centers are overburdened. Many asylees are without political representation, and only a handful of organizations are willing to provide pro bono services. Asylees are only eligible for legal assistance once they have been granted asylum status. Although many asylees have not committed crimes, they share cellblocks with convicted inmates. As if sharing a cellblock with a convicted inmate were not enough, incarcerated convicts have access to work programs and educational opportunities, whereas detainees do not (Feinberg, 2006).

Research in refugee mental health began with post–WWII studies of Jewish and many Southeast Asian (Vietnamese, Cambodian, and Laotian) refugees who later sought asylum in this country. Given the horrific atrocities and incomprehensible pain and suffering they endured before relocating to the U.S., refugees are likely to experience many psychological consequences. A 50% prevalence rate of PTSD was found among Southeast Asian refugee patients from multi-ethnic groups (Mollica, Wyshak, & Lavelle, 1987). Among Cambodian refugees, 86% met criteria for PTSD (Carlson & Rosser-Hogan, 1991). Several factors predispose refugees to developing PTSD, including the loss of higher socioeconomic status in their home country, being a single female head of household, advanced age, female gender, and co-morbidity with depression. These factors correlate with a higher prevalence rate of PTSD in refugee populations (Kinzie, Boehlein, Leung, Moore, Riley, & Smith, 1990; Lin, Tazuma, & Masuda, 1979; Sack, McSharry, Clarke, Kinney, Seeley, & Lewinsohn, 1994; Vignes & Hall, 1979).

The severity of traumatic experiences influences the refugees' ability to recover and adjust to a new environment. Many PTSD symptoms among political refugees have been found to be tenacious, debilitating, and treatment-resistant (Boehnlein & Kinzie, 1995). Such qualities produce a downward spiral that can severely compromise recovery. Research has consistently discovered chronic symptoms of fear, paranoia, and mistrust among refugee clients (Mattusek, 1975). Longitudinal studies find that depression, anxiety, and somatic symptoms impair social adjustment and contribute to a fatalistic outlook among survivors of political trauma (Chodoff, 1975).

Frankl (1969) has written extensively on survivorship among Jewish concentration camp refugees. A concentration camp survivor himself, Frankl found that individuals who could create meaning out of their concentration camp experience were also able to triumph over their misfortunes. However, this ability to glean meaning from suffering may not be an attainable objective for all groups. For example, a study conducted among former political prisoners by Ehlers (2000) compared those who developed PTSD with those who did not. She found that the prisoners who did not develop PTSD lacked the resiliency described by Frankl (1985) but continued to see their situation as hopeless and failed to see "meaning in suffering" (p. 53).

Common Reactions Among Refugees

Refugees who endure the atrocities of torture and forced resettlement suffer prolonged, multiple, and repeated traumatization (Weine & Laub, 1995). It is this type of traumatic experience that Herman (1992) labels "disorders of extreme stress" (DESNOS). The specific issues faced by refugees are different from issues suffered by other trauma survivors:

- Relocation to another country and a loss of original home means that all that was considered familiar instantly changes. From the outset, adjustment is traumatic. Connections are disrupted with significant contexts, that include land, language, customs, families, and social networks (Marsella, 1994; Rechtman, 1992).
- Loss of employment and dwindling financial resources increase refugees' socioeconomic stressors (Boehnlein & Kinzie, 1995).
- Loss of former social roles and status affects family structure (Miller, Worthington, Muzurovic, Tipping, & Goldman, 2002).
- Language and cultural challenges are inevitable during the process of adjusting to a new country. Therapists must be sensitive to the refugees' culture and the degree to which they may be experiencing cultural loss, acculturation stress, and cultural prejudice in their new surroundings (Pope & Garcia-Peltoniemi, 1991).
- When significant dissonance exists between traditional sociocultural values and those of the new host country, mourning the loss of a culture to which refugees may feel strongly connected becomes a challenge (Boehnlein, 1987).
- Intergenerational change and conflict are inevitable for those who may have emigrated with their families (Nguyen & Williams, 1989).

Besides facing these challenging issues of adjustment in a new country, refugees from countries that are severely fragmented by war or ravaged by conflict may have memories of extraordinary trauma. These memories may result in insomnia, nightmares, emotional numbing, startle reactions, memory impairment, and other common psychological reactions to trauma. The following symptoms are heightened in this group:

- Fear and anxiety is often evident among refugee clients (Pope & Garcia-Peltoniemi, 1991). Formal settings (such as office or hospital waiting rooms) may act as traumatic reminders, especially if refugees were tortured in institutional settings. Some victims may fear they are still in danger, and others may constantly fear deportation.
- Sleeplessness due to anxiety becomes pervasive. Inadequate sleep and insomnia diminishes alertness and concentration.
- Cognitive impairment is typical among refugee clients. Concentration and memory difficulties interfere with language acquisition and refugees' ability to pursue an education or keep a job (Pope & Garcia-Peltoniemi, 1991). Forgetfulness and disorientation resulting from the traumatic experience may contribute to refugees' apparent absentmindedness.
- Flashbacks, intrusive thoughts, and traumatic memories may impede refugees' normal functioning and interfere with their ability to adjust to a new environment.
- Physical reactions of headaches, stomachaches, and other somatic concerns may become dominant at the beginning of a therapeutic relationship. Culturally, for some it may be easier to discuss physical complaints than psychological complaints. A depressed immune system increases refugees' susceptibility to illness.
- Psychological and behavioral reactions of anger, denial, grief, isolation, emotional numbing, helplessness, panic, shame, and survivor guilt can overwhelm their daily functioning.

Assessment Considerations

One of the historical problems in refugee treatment has been a lack of appropriate assessment of groups that are culturally different from the dominant U.S. population, the population on which the diagnostic criteria for the *DSM-IV* were established. The use of the *DSM-IV* with cross-cultural groups has always been an area of considerable controversy (Kinzie et al., 1990; Sack et al., 1994), with some authors claiming that the diagnostic manual is ethnocentric and "culturally encapsulated" (Kress, Eriksen, Rayle, & Ford, 2005). The concept of "cultural bereavement" has been suggested as a more appropriate and normalizing term that captures the traumatic experience of refugees (Eisenbruch, 1991, 1992). In addition, reducing the human pain and suffering of a political trauma to a psychiatric diagnosis of depression and PTSD downplays the legitimacy of refugees' trauma. According to Kleinman and Kleinman (1991), this reductionist approach erroneously converts the pain and suffering of refugees into a "moral conceptualization" rather than a legitimate experience.

Clinicians who conduct evaluations of torture survivors should take a neutral stance. However, neutrality must be carefully expressed because clients may incorrectly perceive a clinician's neutrality as disbelief and skepticism. This may contribute to a disconnection with the therapist, and clients may provide incorrect information simply to end the session quickly. The work of Mollica and his colleagues with Indochinese refugees provides research evidence that skepticism and disbelief are toxic to torture victims and others who have suffered interpersonal violence (Mollica, Caspi-Yavin, Bollini, Truong, Tor, & Lavelle, 1992).

In a compelling account of a Hmong family seeking health services in California, Fadiman (1997) recounts how well-meaning health care professionals culturally humiliate a young female patient and her family. Cultural incompetence by health care providers can contribute to the additional difficulties endured by politically traumatized clients.

Cultural factors can affect the information a refugee client is willing to provide during a therapeutic interaction. Refugees from Central and South America are described as frequently displaying somatic rather than psychological reactions, for example. Fear of dishonoring their home country and shame regarding the actions perpetrated by fellow citizens make this group reluctant to discuss past traumas (Lopez, Boccellari, & Hall, 1988). This reluctance to disclose details of a trauma becomes a challenge for those counselors mandated to complete political asylum evaluations; they may not be able to get the evidence they need to write a supportive report.

Cultural beliefs play a major role in determining whether or not an individual seeks help. Many individuals who belong to cultures that view suffering as an inevitable part of life may not seek treatment (Gorman, 2001). Even when therapy is sought, cultural beliefs may continue to exert a strong influence over the client's cognitive processes and the authenticity of material disclosed. A client's hesitation in disclosure may be perceived as resistance by the therapist. Traumatic reactions of dysphoria and neurological arousal may also influence whether refugee clients seek psychotherapy (Yehuda & McFarlane, 1995). The therapist thus has to struggle to differentiate between culture-bound reactions and those that are a consequence of a trauma (Gorman, 2001).

Early clinical work with refugees neglected to make a correct assessment of a refugee client's functioning. The tendency was to assess refugees as suffering from schizophrenia, depression, and anxiety rather than viewing their functioning as normal cognitive and behavioral reactions to trauma. The severity of symptoms experienced may dilute a refugee's ability to coherently recall traumatic details. Unfortunately, such difficulties may lead some therapists to misinterpret and unnecessarily pathologize a client.

One of the refugee's first interactions with his or her new country's culture is likely to occur within the medical and mental health system. Ong (1995) cautions health professionals to ensure that "medical acculturation does not invalidate a cultural understanding" (p. 1243). Understanding the larger sociocultural milieu of a client is one way for clinicians to distinguish between psychopathology and culture-bound beliefs and behaviors (Westermeyer, 1987). Successful therapy with politically traumatized clients is conducted in an environment that avoids dichotomization and instead views trauma treatment as comprehensive and interactive. Such an environment allows individuals to "participate in culturally sanctioned activities that enhance the grieving and recovery process" (Boehnlein & Kinzie 1995, p. 242.)

Given concerns about the *DSM-IV*'s usefulness for understanding the difficulties of refugees from cross-cultural populations, it is prudent to use the *DSM-IV* criteria as markers or scaffolding upon which the clinician builds a framework. A biopsychosocially informed approach, rather than one based solely on *DSM-IV* criteria, benefits a client. A solid therapeutic relationship, allows the traumatized refugee's unique experience a chance of being more fully understood.

Neurological Functioning and Traumatic Brain Injury

Traumatic Brain Injury (TBI) and PTSD overlap in attention and memory functioning (Jacobs & Iacopino, 2001). Refugees who are survivors of political torture often complain about difficulties in cognitive functioning. It is therefore important (especially if refugees were physically tortured) that refugees are neurologically examined (Jacobs & Iacopino, 2001). These examinations can inform assessment, explain behavioral problems, and guide treatment or rehabilitation.

It may be necessary to use assessment instruments to ascertain the neurological functioning of a political refugee. However, using such instruments on a cross-cultural group can present challenges. First, clients may not be familiar with the language used in assessment instruments. Even if instruments are translated, some refugees may not be literate in their own native language. Second, in general, tests require an ability to focus. Since many refugees are wrought with anxiety, they often find it challenging to achieve such focus. Third, the test may not have been standardized for the refugees' particular cultural group. Additionally, some clients may feel that they are simply being used as research subjects rather than clients; formal assessment may be experienced as invasive to their sense of privacy and alien to their culture (Pope & Garcia-Peltoniemi, 1991). Finally, refugees may feel stress when a therapist requests them to "do their best" while under observation. The time constraints of standardized tests may also be problematic for some clients. Furthermore, placing a client in a evaluation situation may evoke memories of his or her torture experiences. Given these challenges, if testing is done, the client must adequately understand the goals and the purposes for which the testing may be used (Pope & Vasquez, 1991). Clients must always freely consent to assessment. However, it is advisable to use an assessment tool only after a trusting relationship has been established with the client. It is necessary to create a comfortable atmosphere in which clients are encouraged to take frequent breaks or reassured that they can stop the testing at any time.

Neurological assessments are always case-specific and sensitive to cross-cultural differences (Jacobs & Iacopino, 2001). An overreliance on testing is discouraged. Although qualitative assessments (which include acquiring personal histories and making observations) lack the rigor of rating instruments, they can produce equally valuable information.

Special Therapeutic Factors in Counseling Refugees

An Ecological Approach

Refugees from non-Western cultures may find talking to a stranger, especially one perceived as an authority figure, challenging. In addition, a refugee may experience the mental health process, with its focus on the individual, as intrusive and oppressive. Some refugees may correctly perceive the perpetrator or a dysfunctional environment as problematic rather than themselves (Hernandez, 2002). These are understandable and expected reactions to political repression.

Outreach is an effective way to increase understanding of refugee clients and establish contact with their ecological environment. Unlike traditional therapy where the therapist maintains a social distance from the client, outreach requires the therapist to become a familiar figure in the refugee's community. Outreach requires the therapist to visit individuals' homes, communities, and recreation centers. Such outreach can quickly foster trust between a client and a therapist. However, under these circumstances, confidentiality must be carefully negotiated, especially in cases where the client insists that the whole family participate in an interview.

Refugees should be involved in creating safe therapeutic environments in which they feel comfortable. The following case vignette illustrates the importance of including the client in the creation of a comfortable therapeutic space.

When Hamad entered the therapist's office for a political asylum evaluation, he displayed many traumatic symptoms. He fidgeted incessantly, crossed and uncrossed his legs, his eyes darted across the room, and occasionally stared at the ceiling. His forehead seemed sweaty. A member of his community with whom he was currently living accompanied Hamad, who spoke little English. It was clear that Hamad brought a friend along because he did not want to be alone with a female therapist. His religious faith forbade him to share the company of a strange woman.

Halfway through the interview, his friend tentatively outlined Hamad's fears of being in confined spaces. He claimed that Hamad chose to sleep in a living room since he preferred the large windows and French doors. Furthermore, his friend stated, Hamad spent much of his time outdoors, even when it was cold. Upon hearing this information, the therapist understood why Hamad appeared to be so agitated: the therapist's office had no windows, and she had closed the door to ensure privacy. Grateful for this new data, she promptly asked Hamad whether the office was comfortable. The therapist almost jumped when Hamad retorted that the room reminded him of his torture experience.

Apologizing for not having asked the question earlier, she negotiated to meet in a coffee shop nearby for the next session. After several weeks, Hamad began to feel more comfortable in the therapeutic relationship. He agreed to continue therapy, but this time the sessions took place in the conference room, which was the largest room at the mental health agency. The therapist who engages the client in decision making ensures that the client's comfort is a primary consideration in therapy.

The Role of Family

The family is an important part of the ecosystem of a politically traumatized client and the primary social unit for many refugees. The therapist who asks the refugee client questions about family members has to be open to different definitions of family structure (McGoldrick, Giordano, & Garcia-Preto, 2005). Family members may be valuable in providing information on the refugee's pre-morbid and pre-trauma functioning, especially if the client currently has severe impairments in functioning. Family members can also provide salient information on the culture of the refugee's native country. However, when material is gleaned from a third party or family member, it is always done with the client's permission.

Parenting can become a significant cultural issue for refugees who flee their home countries accompanied by their children. Previously conceived ideas on parenting and disciplining children may not be acceptable in the host country. While parents continue to uphold traditional values from their past, adolescents who may have more contact with the host culture may develop a different understanding about parent-child relationships. Intergenerational conflicts are likely to result in these cases, adding to the challenges of resettlement.

Parents' traditional expectations of children's behavior can conflict with their dependence on children to translate language and complete other tasks. During a counseling session, a Chinese adolescent client once disclosed that his father waited for his return from school so they could buy hamburgers together at McDonald's. The older man could not understand English, and the large and detailed menu overwhelmed him.

A refugee's distress is heightened when family members are left behind in his or her native country, where a repressive regime may still be in power (Fabri, 2001). Feelings of guilt and abandonment become pervasive, especially if those left behind are children. The therapist can expect major setbacks in treatment when refugees receive distressing communication from family members in their native countries.

The Role of Interpreters

Language interpretation can be a challenge when linguistically and culturally competent therapists are not available. Miller and his colleagues identify two factors that distinguish political refugees from other clients for whom language is a barrier. First, political refugees come from an environment where they may have experienced extreme violence and deprivation. Second, victims of political trauma may have experienced multiple losses because of their forcible displacement (Miller, Martell, Pazdirek, Caruth, & Lopez, 2005).

Thus, interpreters who work with refugee clients risk intense secondary traumatization and emotional involvement as they translate traumatic material. They hear stories that may echo their own experiences. Many formal interpreter training models used in counseling are based on those used by medical and legal interpreters. These models do not include the ongoing relational aspects of psychotherapy or the effects of listening to emotionally charged material on an ongoing basis. In addition, the inclusion of interpreters significantly alters the dyadic relationship of psychotherapy. Some clients may form a strong attachment to an interpreter, which may negatively influence the client-therapist dynamic. After all, it is the interpreter and not the therapist who speaks the client's language (Miller et al., 2005).

When the interpreter comes from the same community as the refugee client, the therapist can anticipate strong emotional reactions from both the client and the interpreter (Kinzie, 1986). Ethnic conflicts may also have occurred in such communities. These similarities or differences can cause intense volatility in the therapeutic interaction. Therapists must recognize the interpreters' multiple roles while accepting the meaningful relationships that develop between interpreters and their clients (Miller et al., 2005). When therapists use interpreters, the following guidelines are suggested (Jacobs & Iacopino, 2001; Paniagua, 1998; Westermeyer, 1989):

- Hire certified and qualified interpreters.
- Identify mental health workers who speak the language of survivors and identify with the survivor's culture.
- Determine the survivor's dialect before asking for an interpreter.
- Match the level of acculturation of the interpreter with that of the survivor to ensure effective communication.
- Interpreters should be part of the assessment team.
- The interpreter and counselor should meet before a session with a client.
- The survivor and the interpreter should be introduced and allowed to informally converse before beginning a session.
- After a session, a follow-up or debriefing should take place with the interpreter in an effort to prevent secondary traumatization.

Sometimes refugees who are fearful of strangers may insist on using family members to interpret on their behalf. In these cases, it is imperative for the therapist to discuss issues of confidentiality and therapeutic boundaries. Therapists should fully expect cultural differences to emerge in interpreting these sensitive issues. Counselors are cautioned against enlisting children as translators because children are not developmentally capable of managing discussions that involve traumatic material; they may, in fact, be severely harmed by it (U.S. Department of Health and Human Services, 2000).

The Client as Authority

The conventional therapeutic stance is one of neutrality and emotional detachment. This stance may be interpreted by clients as disconnection. In contrast, constant questioning by the therapist may be perceived as a form of interrogation. The therapist should constantly monitor the client's reactions to the therapeutic relationship and make adjustments when necessary. A collaborative therapeutic relationship combines the expertise and psychological training of a therapist with refugees' fund of knowledge regarding their personal experience. The survivor who is allowed to assume responsibility and control in the clinical setting will feel empowered; the helpless nature of the refugee experience thus diminishes. In cultures where the belief that support should be sought within one's own family or community is prominent, counseling may not be considered helpful. A strong therapeutic alliance can mitigate this perception.

Therapeutic Trust and Unconditional Acceptance

Refugees who have suffered unspeakable violence inevitably experience a profound destruction of trust. Encounters with medical, psychological, and other authority figures can remind them of the abusers' authority. These encounters also carry the potential for triggering distress and re-traumatization. Assessment and treatment should strive to create a trusting atmosphere. Therapists who explain each step of treatment to clients and seek their permission when necessary can achieve this. The client should not be confronted with any surprises. For someone who has occupied a powerless position in the past, being asked for permission can be a restorative experience.

Traumatic events are often viewed within moral and social parameters, especially when the trauma is politically based. Therapeutic moral neutrality is impossible when injustices occur and human rights are violated. Refugees may need to know where a therapist stands in terms of moral and political beliefs (Hernandez, 2002). The United Nations Convention Against Torture and Other Cruel, Inhuman, or Degrading Treatment or Punishment (United Nations, 1987) and the Geneva Convention Relative to the Treatment of Prisoners of War (1950) are helpful documents for counselors who may want to familiarize themselves with essential human rights. Clinicians cannot allow their own political beliefs to interfere with the provision of appropriate client services. On the other hand, therapists should not risk attending "only to a political agenda at the expense of the client's individual wants and needs" in an attempt to create political solidarity with clients (Pope & Garcia-Peltoniemi, 1991, p. 270).

The Guidelines on Multicultural Education, Training, Research, Practice, and Organizational Change for Psychologists (American Psychological Association, 2003) describes the role of counselors as agents of change. To fulfill this role effectively, counselors who are involved in cases of political trauma must be culturally proficient and appropriately informed about the refugee's native country. Aggressors may have told survivors that no one will believe their story (Fabri, 2001). Therapy becomes a refuge where this myth can be effectively discredited. By believing the survivor, the therapist can validate his or her experience.

The therapist who counsels refugees who have been politically tortured must be prepared to hear the most unusual experiences. Suspending one's own values and beliefs may be necessary so that the client can be accurately heard; the therapist's feelings and responses of counter-transference should not interfere with the provision of clinical services. Therapists who have difficulty listening severely traumatizing stories should seek supervision or consultation in order to manage their vicarious reactions (Pope & Garcia-Peltoniemi, 1991).

Well-intentioned therapists can develop a reserve of cultural knowledge by reading about a client's cultural background. Although gaining such information can be beneficial for both therapist and client, merely reading about a client's culture does not make a therapist an authority on a client's culture. Additionally, the therapist must be careful not to engage in ethnic stereotyping but must continue to recognize intercultural and intra-group variability (Ishisaka, Nguyen, & Okimoto, 1985; Pope & Garcia Peltoniemi, 1991).

Therapeutic Power

The therapist may be perceived as an authority or power figure by refugees, especially those who depend on the therapist for political asylum. This perception may not be far from the truth. The INS requires psychological information about a political refugee to be provided in a timely manner. This requirement forces the therapist to take a more assertive role in gathering information.

It is the responsibility of therapists to outline their role and what may be required of them. Clients need reassurance that therapists are working on their behalf. Therapists who accompany their clients to legal hearings show therapeutic support and care (Fabri, 2001). By constantly seeking client feedback, the therapist assesses the client's comfort level and ensures that the therapist does not inadvertently trigger distress in a client. Because many refugees are unfamiliar with psychotherapy, they may need some information about its structure and goals.

Finally, it is crucial for the therapist to monitor and maintain a safe therapeutic relationship to prevent an unconscious reenactment of the destructive relationship between torturer and victim (Pope & Garcia-Peltoniemi, 1991).

Gender Issues

A therapist's gender may be a challenging issue for some clients, especially those whose torture included sexual assault and violation. Cultural beliefs may not favor intimate conversations between members of the opposite sex. Clients who find themselves in uncomfortable settings may not be willing to discuss their traumatic experiences. Establishing at the outset whether a client is comfortable working with a therapist is important because it may mean that the therapist will have to make a gender-appropriate referral.

Interventions With Political Refugees

In planning interventions for any individual or group, it is important to examine the sociocultural framework, family, social structure, religion, other beliefs, and political environment. When working with political refugees, such an examination becomes especially salient. Political and social patterns of authority that were previously familiar may no longer be viable. This change can cause tremendous identity confusion and uncertainty in the refugee. The therapist should be knowledgeable about the refugee's past social patterns. This information can aid the therapist in supporting the refugee's adjustment (Williams & Berry, 1991).

To facilitate this process, a trauma counselor working with refugees must adopt a flexible approach that includes both multicultural and trauma recovery principles (Gorman, 2001). When a therapist is unable to acquire sufficient information regarding a client's distinct historical, spiritual, and sociopolitical background, others (including the client's family and community members) should be consulted as possible resources.

Multiculturally competent therapists adapt their style to the differing needs of diverse cultural groups. Members of some cultural groups may need additional time to establish trust before they feel comfortable disclosing personal information. Treatment should be sensitively paced to match a client's needs. Clinical material is explored only when the client is ready. A multicultural approach focuses on the client's strengths and takes advantage of the resources the client already possesses. An appreciation of a client's culture is central.

Several trauma recovery models were outlined earlier in this book. The therapist can opt to use any of these models with refugees who have experienced political trauma. For example, Herman's (1992) three-stage model of trauma recovery (which includes safety, reconstruction, and reconnection) can help the refugee forge a new and resilient identity. First, the client achieves stability. Second, the client is encouraged to re-tell his or her story. The therapist helps survivors regain their voice through compassionate exploration and empathetic reassurance. This process destabilizes the dominant messages of fear instilled by the aggressor and facilitates the telling of a new story. It is important in a client's healing that a story is fully presented and authentically received. Third, the client mourns the loss of his or her past. Finally, the client is encouraged to rely on his or her own resilient aspects, which helped him or her to survive the ordeal of political trauma.

Refugee Treatment Centers

In the mid-1980s, the U.S. began treating survivors of torture. Treatment centers providing specialized services for political trauma survivors soon developed. In 1997, these centers organized into a consortium of trauma treatment centers to provide ongoing training and to share new ideas as well as innovative approaches. Today, more than 30 similar programs exist across the country. The Oregon Indochinese Psychiatric Program is one treatment center with over 16 years of success in the treatment of over 1,000 patients (Boehnlein & Kinzie, 1995). The treatment model adopted by this program is outlined below.

Oregon Indochinese Psychiatric Program

This program emphasizes diagnosis and assessment, which integrates ethnocultural factors (language, metaphors, and symbols), an awareness of acculturation pressures, and long-term supportive treatment. Treatment is not time-limited; this can be reassuring for clients who may be at risk for social isolation.

The following are the basic elements of the treatment model:

- Education: A psycho-educational approach that informs clients about the effects of trauma and helps them with normalization and acceptance.
- Co-morbid disorders: Depression often co-occurs with PTSD. Tricyclic antidepressants and Serotonin Reuptake Inhibitors are prescribed to reduce depression.
- Reduction of intrusive symptoms: Clonidine is prescribed as a medication that greatly reduces irritability, startle reactions, and nightmares.
- Reduction of other stressors: Clients are provided with adequate physical resources and support in securing housing, clothing, and medical care. These resources provide security and reduce the basic concerns that refugees often face.
- Supportive psychotherapy: Empathetic, reality-based, ongoing psychotherapy with a psychiatrist from the host culture (U.S.) is a central focus of treatment.

This serves to introduce refugees to their new country. The client is encouraged to engage in therapeutic processing of past and current experiences. Medication is usually discussed in these sessions, which family members can attend.

- Socialization Groups: Group activities are led by a mental health counselor from the client's culture. These activities provide clients with a sense of community and shared experience. Groups are bi-cultural and incorporate activities from both the native and host country. Group members' skills are used as a resource in the creation and development of group activities.
- Indochinese Socialization Center: Refugee clients are given an opportunity for increased social involvement at these separate centers. Additional centers have been created to provide vocational rehabilitation and job training.

Resources

This section lists contact information for a few of the approximately 32 torture treatment centers that exist throughout the U.S. Those interested in centers located in other countries may obtain information from Amnesty International or the Internet.

Intercultural Psychiatric Program

Tel: (503) 494-4222

Fax: (503) 494-6143

Department of Psychiatry (UHN88)

Oregon Health and Science University

3181 SW Sam Jackson Park Road

Portland, OR 97201

rileyc@ohsu.edu

Boston Center for Refugee Health and Human Rights

Tel: (617) 414–4794

Fax: (617) 414–4796

Boston Medical Center

1 Boston Medical Center Place

Boston, MA 02118

www.bcrhhr.org

Minnesota Center for Victims of Torture

Tel: (612) 436–4800

Fax: (612) 436–2600

717 East River Road

Minneapolis, MN 55455

cvt@cvt.org; www.cvt.org

Bellevue/NYU Program for Survivors of Torture

Tel: (212) 994–7159

Fax: (212) 263–8234

462 First Ave, Bellevue Hospital Center, C&D 7th Floor, Room 710

New York City, NY 10016

www.survivorsoftorture.org

Harvard Program in Refugee Trauma

Tel: (617) 876–7879

Fax: (617) 876–2360

22 Putnam Avenue

Cambridge, MA 02139

www.hprt-cambridge.org

Additional Resources for Refugees

United Nations Voluntary Fund for Victims of Torture

In 1981, the UN General Assembly established the United Nations Voluntary Fund to receive voluntary contributions from governments, nongovernmental organizations, and individuals. This fund distributes aid to nongovernmental organizations that provide humanitarian assistance to victims of torture and members of their family (http://www.unhchr.ch/html/menu2/9/vftortur.htm).

Amnesty International

Amnesty International's site contains more than 10,000 documents pertaining to human rights. Amnesty International is also a world leader in the fight to eradicate torture (http://www.amnesty.org/).

Derechos Human Rights

Derechos Human Rights, the first Internet-based human rights organization, strives to promote respect for human rights all over the world and works against impunity for human rights violators (http://www.derechos.org/).

Doctors of the World

Doctors of the World, founded in 1980, is the autonomous U.S. affiliate of the French medical relief organization Médecins du Monde. The organization is part of an international network of 12 Doctors of the World/Médecins du Monde delegations in Europe and the Americas, whose joint aim is to provide medical assistance to the world's most vulnerable populations (http://www.doctorsoftheworld.org/).

Human Rights Internet

Human Rights Internet (HRI), founded in 1976, is a leader in the exchange of information within the worldwide human rights community. HRI's headquarters are located in Ottawa, Canada. From Ottawa, HRI communicates by phone, fax, mail, and the Internet and includes more than 5,000 organizations and individuals around the world working for the advancement of human rights (http://www.hri.ca/index.aspx).

Human Rights Watch

Human Rights Watch (HRW) investigates and exposes global human rights violations. Their Web site provides an extensive listing of country reports documenting human rights abuse (http://www.hrw.org/).

International Committee of the Red Cross

The International Committee of the Red Cross (ICRC) is an impartial, neutral, and independent organization whose exclusively humanitarian mission is to protect the lives and dignity of victims of war and internal violence and to provide them with assistance (http://www.icrc.org/eng).

Conclusion

The world of the refugee is usually one that has been torn asunder. Refugees may have experienced heinous and incomprehensible acts of torture aimed at crushing their will and destroying community cohesion. Refugee women may have experienced rape, which is often used by the perpetrator to inflict pain, shame, and fear.

Silence and amnesia are two of the methods victims employ to manage their trauma; unfortunately, these coping mechanisms can also prevent them from seeking the help they need. Working with refugees requires expertise in trauma treatment, multicultural competence, and a preparedness to work outside of one's usual comfort zone. The therapeutic relationship has to be caring and compassionate, and one that is neutral, especially if the therapist has the responsibility of completing a political asylum evaluation.

Issues of counter-transference always threaten the therapeutic relationship with refugee clients; a therapist's moral beliefs are often tested. Consequently, the therapist is encouraged to receive adequate supervision and support so that he or she can always remain open to serving the best interests of the client.

It cannot be assumed that all victims of torture will benefit from the same type of intervention; refugee clients suffer in infinite ways and adopt diverse survival and recovery techniques. Rather, a therapist should consider what works best for each individual client; effective interventions are those that the client helps shape. These successful interventions often include multicultural, ecological, and empowering principles.

Work with refugees can be immensely rewarding; the therapist is given an opportunity to witness the resilience of the human spirit as normal, healthy people defy the challenges imposed by a dysfunctional environment.

Financial support to establish treatment centers for torture survivors must continue. Funding of research studies that document the prevalence of torture and evaluate effective treatment techniques are also important. Such research will help illuminate the reality of torture, preventing us from becoming complicit through silence.

Finally, education programs must address the reality of torture. The United Nations Declaration of Human Rights urges "every individual and every organ of society, keeping this Declaration constantly in mind, shall strive by teaching and education to promote respect for these rights and freedoms and by progressive measures . . . secure their universal and effective recognition" (United Nations General Assembly, 1948, p. 2). Programs that train mental health professionals to meet the needs of refugee clients must heed this call.

References

American Psychological Association. (2003). Guidelines on multicultural education, training, research, practice, and organizational change for psychologists. *American Psychologist, 58,* 377–402.

Asad, T. (1997). On torture, or cruel, inhuman, and degrading treatment. In A. Kleinman & M. Lock (Eds.), *Social suffering* (pp. 285–308). Los Angeles: University of California Press.

Boehnlein, J. K. (1987). Clinical relevance of grief and mourning among Cambodian refugees. *Social Science and Medicine, 25,* 765–772.

Boehnlein, J. K., & Kinzie, J. D. (1995). Refugee trauma. *Transcultural Psychiatry Review, 32,* 223–252.

Carlson E. B., & Rosser-Hogan, R. (1991). Trauma experiences, post-traumatic stress, dissociation, and depression in Cambodian refugees. *American Journal of Psychiatry, 148,* 1548–1551.

Chodoff, P. (1975). Psychiatric aspects of the Nazi persecution. In S. Arieti (Ed.), *American handbook of psychiatry* (pp. 932–946). New York: Basic Books.

Ehlers, A. (2000). Posttraumatic stress disorder following political imprisonment: The role of mental defeat, alienation, and perceived permanent change. *Journal of Abnormal Psychology, 109*(1), 45–55.

Eisenbruch, M. (1991). From post-traumatic stress disorder to cultural bereavement: Diagnosis of Southeast Asian refugees. *Social Science and Medicine, 33,* 673–680.

Eisenbruch, M. (1992). Toward a culturally sensitive DSM: Cultural bereavement in Cambodian refugees and the traditional healer as taxonomist. *Journal of Nervous and Mental Disease, 180,* 8–10.

Fabri, M. R. (2001). Reconstructing safety: Adjustments to the therapeutic frame in the treatment of survivors of political torture. *Professional Psychology: Research and Practice, 32,* 452–457.

Fadiman, A. (1997). *The spirit catches you and you fall down: A Hmong child, her American doctors, and the collision of two cultures.* New York: Farrar, Straus, & Giroux.

Feinberg, C. (2006, Spring). Staying here. *Boston College Magazine,* 25–33.

Frankl, V. E. (1969). *Man's search for meaning.* New York: Washington Square Press.

Frankl, V. E. (1985). *Man's search for meaning.* New York: Washington Square Press.

Geneva Convention Relative to the Treatment of Prisoners of War. (1950). New York: United Nations Office of the High Commissioner for Human Rights.

Gorman, W. (2001). Refugee survivors of torture: Trauma and treatment. *Professional Practice: Research and Practice, 32*(5), 443–451.

Herman, J. L. (1992). *Trauma and recovery.* New York: Basic Books.

Hernandez, P. (2002). Trauma in war and political persecution: Expanding the concept. *American Journal of Orthopsychiatry, 72*(1), 16–25.

Ishisaka, H. S., Nguyen, Q. T., & Okimoto, J. T. (1985). The role of culture in the mental health treatment of Indochinese refugees. In T. C. Owan (Ed.), *Southeast*

Asian mental health: Treatment, prevention, services, training and research (pp. 41–63). Washington, DC: National Institute of Mental Health.

Jacobs, U., & Iacopino, V. (2001). Torture and its consequences: A challenge to clinical neuropsychology. *Professional Psychology: Research and Practice, 32*(5), 458–464.

Kinzie, D. (1986). The establishment of outpatient mental health series for Southeast Asian refugees. In C. Williams & J. Westermeyer (Eds.), *Refugee mental health in resettlement countries* (pp. 61–73). Washington, DC: Hemisphere.

Kinzie, J. D., Boehlein, J. K., Leung, P., Moore, L., Riley, C., & Smith, D. (1990). The high prevalence rate of PTSD and its clinical significance among Southeast Asian refugees. *American Journal of Psychiatry, 147,* 913–917.

Kleinman, A., & Kleinman, J. (1991). Suffering and its professional transformation: Toward an ethnography of interpersonal experience. *Culture, Medicine, and Psychiatry, 15,* 275–301.

Kress, V. E. W., Eriksen, K. P., Rayle, A. D., & Ford, S. J. W. (2005). The DSM-TR and culture: Consideration for counselors. *Journal of Counseling & Development, 83,* 97–104.

Lin, K. M., Tazuma, L., & Masuda, M. (1979). Adaptational problems of Vietnamese refugees, part I: Health and mental health status. *Archives of General Psychiatry, 36,* 955–961.

Lopez, A., Boccellari, A., & Hall, K. (1988). Post–traumatic stress disorder in a Central American refugee. *Hospital and Community Psychiatry, 39,* 1309–1311.

Marsella, A. J. (1994). Ethnocultural diversity and international refugees: Challenges for the global community. In A. J. Marsella, T. Bornemann, S. Ekblad, & J. Orley (Eds.), *Amidst peril and pain: The mental health well-being of the world's refugees* (pp. 341–364). Washington, DC: American Psychological Association.

Mattusek, P. (1975). *Internment in concentration camps and their consequences.* New York: Springer.

McGoldrick, M., Giordano, J., & Garcia-Preto, N. (Eds.), (2005). *Ethnicity and family therapy* (3rd ed.). New York: Guilford Press.

Miller, K. E., Martell, Z. L., Pazdirek, L., Caruth, M., & Lopez, D. (2005). The role of interpreters in psychotherapy with refugees: An exploratory study. *American Journal of Orthopsychiatry, 75*(1), 27–39.

Miller, K., Worthington, G., Muzurovic, J., Tipping, S., & Goldman, A. (2002). Bosnian refugees and the stressors of exile: A narrative study. *American Journal of Orthopsychiatry, 72,* 341–354.

Mollica, R. F., Caspi-Yavin, Y., Bollini, P., Truong, T., Tor, S., & Lavelle, J. (1992). The Harvard Trauma Questionnaire: Validating a cross-cultural instrument for measuring torture, trauma and posttraumatic stress disorder in Indochinese refugees. *Journal of Nervous and Mental Disease, 180,* 111–116.

Mollica, R. F., Wyshak, G., & Lavelle, J. (1987). The psychosocial impact of war: Trauma and torture on Southeast Asian refugees. *American Journal of Psychiatry, 144,* 1567–1574.

Nguyen, N. A., & Williams, H. L. (1989). Transition from east to west: Vietnamese adolescents and their parents. *Journal of the American Academy of Child and Adolescent Psychiatry, 28,* 505–515.

Ong, A. (1995). Making the biopolitical subject: Cambodian, immigrants, refugee medicine and cultural citizenship in California. *Social Science and Medicine, 40,* 1243–1257.

Paniagua, F. (1998). *Assessing and treating culturally diverse clients.* Thousand Oaks, CA: Sage.

Pope, K. S., & Garcia-Peltoniemi, R. E. (1991). Responding to victims of torture: Clinical issues, professional responsibilities, and useful resources. *Professional Psychology: Research and Practice, 22*(4), 269–276.

Pope, K. S., & Vasquez, M. J. T. (1991). *Ethics in psychotherapy and counseling: A practical guide for psychologists.* San Francisco: Jossey-Bass.

Rechtman, R. (1992). The appearance of ancestors and the deceased in traumatic experiences: Introduction of clinical ethnography in Cambodian refugees in Paris. *Cahiers d'Anthropologie et Biometrie Humaine, 10,* 1–19.

Sack, W. H., McSharry, S., Clarke, G. N., Kinney, R., Seeley, J., & Lewinsohn, P. (1994). The Khmer adolescent project: I. Epidemiologic findings in two generations of Cambodian refugees. *Journal of Nervous and Mental Disease, 182,* 387–395.

United Nations. (1987, June 26). *Convention against torture and other cruel, inhuman or degrading treatment or punishment.* Retrieved April 6, 2005, from http://www.unhchr.ch/html/menu3/b/h_cat39.htm

United Nations General Assembly. (1948, December 10). *Universal declaration of human rights.* New York: Author.

U.S. Department of Health and Human Services. (2000). Psychosocial issues for children and adolescents in disasters (2nd ed.; Pub. No. ADM 86–1070R). Rockville, MD: U.S. Department of Health and Human Services, Substance Abuse and Mental Health Services Administration, Center for Mental Health Services.

U.S. Department of Health and Human Services. (2005). *Office of Refugee Resettlement archives.* Retrieved April 6, 2005, from http://www.acf.hhs.gov/programs/orr/archives/index.htm

Vignes, A. J., & Hall, R. C. W. (1979). Adjustment of a group of Vietnamese people in the United States. *American Journal of Psychiatry, 136,* 442–444.

Weine, S., & Laub, D. (1995). Narrative constructions of historical realities in testimony with Bosnian survivors of ethnic cleansing. *Psychiatry, 58,* 246–260.

Westermeyer, J. (1987). DSM-III psychiatric disorders among Hmong refugees in the United States: A point prevalence study. *American Journal of Psychiatry, 145,* 197–202.

Westermeyer, J. (1989). Cross-cultural care for PTSD: Research, training, and service needs for the future. *Journal of Traumatic Stress, 2,* 515–536.

Williams, C. L., & Berry, J. W. (1991). Primary prevention of acculturative stress among refugees: Application of psychological theory and practice. *American Psychologist, 46*(6), 632–641.

Yehuda, R., & McFarlane, A. C. (1995). Conflict between current knowledge about posttraumatic stress disorder and its original conceptual basis. *American Journal of Psychiatry, 152*(12), 1705–1713.

12

Terrorism

On September 17, 2001, I was in a conference room on the 22nd floor of a skyscraper in midtown Manhattan conducting a crisis group for employees of a large financial institution. The group intervention allowed everyone an opportunity to process the unfathomable act of terror that struck New York on a balmy fall day in September, a day that would forever be remembered as 9/11. With the World Trade Center still smoldering in the distance, we settled into groups of 30 in an effort to begin processing the horror, fear, and disbelief that such an unthinkable atrocity had become a reality. We all struggled with the intense anxiety that a terrorist act could, in fact, happen again.

In this crisis group, the average age of those sitting around the table was 25. They shook their heads in anguish, and many wore a pained, puzzled look. "Our parents did not prepare us for something like this," said a young account executive. "Nothing bad ever happened to me before," remarked a 20-something female financial analyst. "This must be a nightmare... I know my roommate will come home. She must have just lost her way," were some of the other remarks made by the traumatized group. Equally distressed, the administrators fluctuated between numbness and shock. However, they were determined to support their staff. They showed resolve by encouraging staff members to take frequent breaks and providing them with food and beverages. A common space was designated for people to congregate and discuss the terrorist attack.

On my way into New York that morning, I took a quick look at the hundreds of photographs of the missing and dead victims that were plastered on the walls of Grand Central Station. Some frantic relatives lined the sidewalks, thrusting pictures into the faces of those who passed by. The relative would say, "Have you *seen this person?" Many were not fluent in English. I wondered whether their loved ones were some of the undocumented immigrants working at the World Trade Center on that fateful morning. Could they even go to the police to inquire about a mom, dad, or sister? Or would they be forced to wait and wonder if the missing would ever return home? What resources were available for them? Would they seek help if they needed it?*

This chapter provides a background on terrorism by exploring some of the terrorist activities that have occurred over the years. Currently, Americans live in a country where terror alerts, airport security checks, and surveillance cameras attempt to deter the next terrorist attack. A primary objective of this chapter is to provide an explanation of individual reactions to terrorism and to describe steps to consider when responding in the immediate aftermath of a terrorist attack. Working with family members of victims killed in a terrorist attack is challenging; some useful strategies to assist the long term recovery of families and communities are offered.

Background

Terrorism, especially international terrorism, became a prominent global issue in the 1970s. The movie *Hijacked* was an example of the fear instilled by terrorism. Hauntingly, it was a harbinger of what was to later unfold in real life. In 1972, 30 people were killed in Northern Ireland after the IRA set off 22 bombs in an incident that became known as Black Friday. Later that year at the Olympic Games, 11 Israeli athletes were held hostage and were subsequently killed by a terrorist group called Black September. U.S. citizens were directly affected by the Pan Am Flight 103 crash in Lockerbie, Scotland, that killed 270 people, including 189 Americans, on December 21, 1988. It is often described as the worst act of terrorism against the United States prior to September 11, 2001. The World Trade Center bombing in 1993 killed six people and injured over 1,000. The Oklahoma City bombing in 1995 killed 168 people, 19 of whom were children. These terrorist attacks that occurred on U.S. soil elicited the outrage of the American public.

Terrorism has been an ongoing travail of life for many people in other parts of the world, including Northern Ireland and Israel. Because of the September 11, 2001, attack on the World Trade Center in New York and the Pentagon in Washington, DC, many Americans have an abiding fear of terrorism. This human-engineered catastrophe yielded devastating consequences. For the first time, it forced Americans to seriously pay attention to the destructive consequences of terrorism. In addition to increased attention to terrorist activities, literature on the subject burgeoned. Counselors began to familiarize themselves with interventions they could use to help large numbers of people affected by the trauma of a terrorist attack. Responding to this type of trauma requires specialized skill and expertise.

Terrorism is derived from the Latin word *terrere,* which means "to frighten." The primary goal of perpetrators of terrorism is to instill terror and fear in an entire population by targeting a specific group. In a 2001 executive order, the U.S. government defines terrorism as an intentional act designed to intimidate or coerce a civilian population. This intimidation is usually accomplished by an action that evokes fear and stress among a group of people who become both directly and indirectly affected by terrorism (Combs, 1997). Terrorism is also a psychological attack on a nation's social capital; in this way, it is different from other traumatic events (Stein et al., 2004).

After an act of terrorism, the distress symptoms among survivors tend to be broad and prolonged, achieving the terrorist's goal which is to evoke a chronic sense of unease, uncertainty, and anxiety in an entire population. Kastenbaum (2001) states, "Terrorism changes the way a society thinks about itself" (p. 236). Terrorists seek to harm individuals so that they become afraid to live in ways they once knew. Threats, harassment, and instilling an atmosphere of fear are the strategies used by terrorists to achieve a desired behavior. Many of us can recall President Bush's plea to U.S. citizenry in the days after September 11, 2001, asking U.S. citizens to maintain daily routines and other scheduled activities in defiance of the terrorists' goals.

Hills (2002) states that the destruction caused by terrorist acts is usually an end in itself; these acts have the features of criminal assaults and acts of war. Similarly, the epidemiologists Susser, Bresnahan, and Link (2002) maintain that terrorism is a form of psychological warfare. Terrorists tend to have an intense and fanatical loyalty to the mission of their organization. It is this loyalty that motivates them to commit otherwise unthinkable acts that may include taking their own life in the process. This fearlessness makes potential victims, who have a higher regard for life, extremely wary of the violent steps terrorists are prepared to take in the name of their cause (Moghadam, 2003; Schbley, 2003).

In the *DSM-IV,* witnessing terrorism meets Criterion A of PTSD. Terrorism combines elements of malevolent intent with actual or threatened extreme harm. Additionally, terrorism evokes an unending fear of the future, of injury or threat to self or others, as well as "the experience of intense fear, helplessness, or horror" (*DSM-IV,* p. 428). After their work with survivors of the 1993 World Trade Center bombing, Difede, Apeldorf, Cloitre, Spielman, and Perry (1997) described how survivors found themselves with shattered fundamental beliefs about themselves, their environment, and others. Anger, isolation, and existential questions haunted many, while those who had suffered previous traumas began to re-experience symptoms from past events.

Short-Term Reactions to Terrorism

The following reactions also occur in the aftermath of other traumas but tend to be more prevalent after terrorist attacks.

Increased Vulnerability. Survivors of terrorist attacks experience a heightened sense of vulnerability. Many of us can probably recall warily turning our heads toward the sky each time a plane flew overhead in the days that followed 9/11.

Preoccupation With Unanticipated Loss. The sudden loss of a loved one can be the most unsettling aspect of terrorism because it challenges survivors to live with the memory that a loved one was viciously murdered. Family members typically become preoccupied with the final moments of a loved one's life. They question the nature of the victim's injuries, whether the death was painless, and the victim's level of suffering just before death occurred.

Anger. Survivors may be seized by an impulse to "do something." They may want to take action in an effort to ameliorate the pain of what happened. Anger develops quickly and can consume survivors emotionally. Even when the terrorists are arrested and convicted, a survivor's feelings of rage may persist. It is common for survivors to obsessively ruminate about ways to exact revenge.

Fear. A pervasive sense of fear is more common than anger and constantly looms over survivors. A heightened sense of vulnerability may spur them to change their daily routines, to install house and car alarms, to carry weapons, to avoid leaving the house after dark, and to avoid certain areas. In the aftermath of September 11, 2001, for example, many people bypassed tall buildings and avoided using elevators. Similarly, train travel in London subways decreased after train bombings occurred in the city on July 7, 2005. A phobic elusion of anything trauma-related, including people and places, is to be expected.

Guilt. Survivor grief is often compounded by guilt. Survivors erroneously believe they could have foreseen the terrorist attack or done more to keep a loved one safe.

Family Closeness. Many survivors possess a strong need to surround themselves with family members. They have an urge to draw family members together and ensure that family members are in close proximity. They want immediate access should something happen in the future (Sprang & McNeil, 1995).

Idealization. Surviving relatives often idealize the dead. When the loved one is killed by terrorism, this idealization tends to be even stronger. Media attention and news reports about the act of terrorism increase survivors' idealization of their loved one. This idealization is sometimes accompanied by overidentification (wearing the deceased's clothes, ordering food that the loved one liked, etc.). Survivors report experiencing frequent nightmares in which the horrifying death of the loved one is imagined; they also report experiencing a proliferation of dreams in which they try to protect or rescue their loved one (Sprang & McNeil, 1995).

Physical Symptoms. Common psycho-physiological disorders in the aftermath of a terrorist attack include an increase or decrease in appetite, sleep disturbances, gastrointestinal problems, cardiovascular disorders, and a lowered immune system. Psychosomatic reactions, such as headaches and migraines, stomachaches, and body pain may also occur.

Steps in Crisis Intervention

After a terrorist attack, first responders usually come from law enforcement, emergency medical services, the National Guard, and mental health agencies. The following guidelines are helpful for mental health responders who find themselves in the highly volatile aftermath of a terrorist attack. Initial contact with victims and survivors is likely to occur at the site of the impact, which may be a bombed building or a plane crash. Counselors can anticipate a wide range of reactions among victims and survivors. These reactions may extend from numbed unresponsiveness to raw panic.

- Introduce yourself to the victims and bystanders and, if necessary, show an identification card that indicates the organization you represent. This personal introduction provides a context for clients, even if they may be too distraught to absorb much of what is said. Be prepared for rejection by those survivors who may be too shocked and too distraught to accept help. Child victims who may have been traumatized by adults may consider introduction to a new adult too anxiety-provoking.
- Always offer support in a manner that is direct, nonjudgmental, and practical: "We are here to get you to a safe place," "I can understand why you're so upset," or "What can I do to help?" are good examples of statements to use in this situation.
- Try to involve victims in the decision-making process and always explain what you plan to do next. For example, "Is it okay for me to hold your arm as we

walk toward the van?" or "We are going to the local hospital. Is that okay with you?" These simple acts help restore control in individuals who may otherwise feel helpless and disoriented. It encourages them to participate in their own recovery and helps them transition from feelings of vulnerability and powerlessness to feelings of empowerment.

- If victims show an inclination to discuss what just happened, support this process by allowing them to control the conversation. Listen actively and empathetically by nodding your head and making encouraging statements. Victims can be tangential or repetitive in an attempt to "get it all out." Encourage them to engage in this process by asking open-ended questions. Avoid asking questions that can be potentially re-traumatizing, particularly questions that delve into the details of the traumatizing incident.

- It is useful to consider Maslow's hierarchy of needs during this phase of the response. Providing a survivor with basic needs might be the only psychological help that can be provided in this early phase of trauma recovery. Establishing safety and stability by providing nourishment, medical care, shelter, and protection are the primary goals of acute crisis intervention (Ursano, Fullerton, & Norwood, 1995).

- Once victims are free from immediate danger, they usually search for the reasons something happened to them. Survivors who are provided with accurate information about the nature and consequences of the terrorist attack, as well as the progress of any ongoing relief efforts, will feel supported.

- Psycho-education plays an important role in early intervention. Victims of terrorism benefit from basic information about the onset and course of post-traumatic symptoms. It is essential to normalize the traumatic stress experience by giving survivors information on what to expect next in a manner that promotes safety rather than alarm.

- Finally, those at risk for suicidal or homicidal ideation should be identified immediately, and steps must be taken to ensure their safety.

The Media: A Mixed Blessing

The media can play a useful role in relief efforts. Newspapers, official bulletins, television, the Internet, cell phones, and radio can provide practical information and emotional support. Rumors can add to a victim's level of distress; accurate communication of information can prevent this from happening. The general public can be offered guidance and information on where to seek help.

Technological advances provide people with news instantly. These advances have increased our ability to circulate information rather dramatically, which can be useful. It also carries the potential to unnecessarily raise our sense of fear and vulnerability. Broadcasting traumatic news is a mixed blessing. Although it can help in alerting the public to potential risk and danger, it can also traumatize those individuals who may not have experienced the trauma and re-traumatize those with a history of trauma. Several authors (Keinan, Sadeh, & Rosen, 2003; Kingston, 1995; Nacos, 1994) have noted the interdependence between the media and terrorism.

The extent to which the public should be exposed to the gruesome details of a terrorist act has been a controversial subject since the September 11, 2001, terrorist attacks in the U.S. The argument in favor of detailed coverage is that democratic principles favor the public being appropriately informed, and neither the government nor the media has a right to deny the public access to information (Keinan et al., 2003). Defenders of selective coverage propose that exposure to extensive media reporting on terrorism has adverse effects on mental health (Dougall, Hayward, & Baum, 2005). They found that after the September 11 terrorist attacks, the viewing of media images of the attack affected the psychological functioning and post-traumatic stress reactions of people living far from the focal points of the attack.

Similar studies found that television viewing after 9/11 was associated with increased distress and clinical disorders (such as PTSD and depression) in samples across the U.S. and as far away as Italy (Galea et al., 2002; Schuster et al., 2001). Although many people may have watched television as a coping strategy, research indicates that it was ineffective. Instead, it decreased adjustment and increased distress well beyond direct exposure (Schlenger et al., 2002; Schuster et al., 2001).

Media coverage of violence has been found to produce adverse reactions in children as well as adults. Parents reported that their children exhibited reactions of distress, sleep disturbances, and nightmares in response to television coverage of the Gulf War (Cantor, Mares, & Oliver, 1993). Additionally, a positive correlation exists between media violence and aggression among children (Bushman & Anderson, 2001). In an earlier study, Bushman (1995) found that media violence is more likely to elicit aggressive affect and behavior in high trait-aggressive individuals than in low trait-aggressive individuals. There were no sex differences in susceptibility to media violence (Bushman, 1995). He concluded that habitual exposure to television violence might partially account for the susceptibility of high trait-aggressive individuals to the effects of media violence.

Most people rarely encounter terrorism in their personal lives; the convergence between terrorism and the wider public occurs through the images filtered by mass media (Montiel & Anuar, 2002). Consequently, the media has the capacity to subjectively influence public understanding through selective attention and endorsement of particular beliefs. This can take the form of promoting dominant political messages and stereotypes about different racial groups. When communicated during periods of high arousal, which is what occurred after September 11, 2001, these messages are likely to shape and influence public opinion in powerful ways (Montiel & Anuar, 2002).

Heldring (2004) describes effective and objective media reporting as possessing the following characteristics:

- It is credible and trustworthy
- It conveys specific information about risk
- It relates specific information regarding ongoing efforts to reduce risk
- It clearly defines steps people can take toward recovery
- It acknowledges apprehension and validates individuals' reactions

While it is important for the media to provide factual information, it is also important to do so in a discreet and tactful manner so that the public is protected from unnecessarily viewing extremely violent details (Ferguson, 1999). In order to limit the risk of harming the public's mental health, Keinan et al. (2003) suggest the formulation of a set of clear guidelines to "ensure restrained and cautious coverage" of violence (p. 161).

Coping With Death

An unrelenting exposure to death because of the presence of dead bodies and mutilated remains is another aspect of terrorism that makes it a particularly atrocious trauma. The sights, smells, and sounds of the dying and the dead can overwhelm the survivor with a tenacious dread. Victims directly exposed to dead bodies have been found to subsequently avoid eating meat and often engaging in compulsive hand-washing (Ursano et al., 1995).

It may be distressing for surviving friends or family to identify a victim's body. However the finality of identifying a loved one's remains can be bittersweet: It can be a confirmation that a loved one's suffering is over, yet it can also put an end to any hope of the person still being alive. Although viewing the body of the deceased reduces the duration of denial, survivors should be able to choose whether or not they want to take this painful step (Sprang & McNeil, 1995). If involving the family in the identification process is forensically necessary, adequate support should be provided. The family should be appropriately notified whether or not there is a chance of recovering the remains of a lost one. Next of kin should also be informed about future identification procedures, which may include swabbing for DNA samples and matching dental records (Spungen, 1998).

We have learned from the September 11, 2001, terrorist attacks how important it is for survivors to gain some form of physical confirmation that their loved one is dead. Rings, driver's licenses, and other mementoes become personally revered and can allow survivors to finally "let go" (Boss, 2002). When no definitive remains are found, symbolic remains may be substituted. For example, those families of 9/11 victims whose remains were never found were given an urn of ashes from Ground Zero, the site of the victims' death.

Individual Counseling

Survivors of terrorism often require extensive and long-term counseling. The challenge of dealing with painful memories may cause many survivors to delay getting help, while others may never seek it. Re-experiencing traumatic reactions around the anniversary of the trauma may motivate some survivors to seek therapy. An event like 9/11 can exacerbate the symptoms of those with histories of trauma, thus forcing them to seek therapy. The negative effects of family dissolution or loss of employment resulting from the trauma may provide others with the impetus to seek therapy. The counselor must carefully assess clients' presenting issues before embarking on a course of treatment that best serves their needs.

Stabilization. Stabilization of the individual's emotional, social, and physical environment is always a priority in the early stages of individual counseling. The therapist challenges a client's defenses cautiously; defense mechanisms may be serving a self-protective function. Some client defenses (e.g., avoidance of the site of trauma) may actually require strengthening to prevent clients from decompensating psychologically.

Normalization. Normalization of a client's reactions is an important step in the early stages of recovery. Empathetic support and validation of the client's reactions are the other foci of treatment during this phase. As in all therapies, the goal is to establish trust, develop rapport, and maintain a positive therapeutic alliance.

Self-Care. Self-care activities are encouraged for two primary reasons: They help clients manage their symptoms and take control of their lives. Those individuals who adapt well to stressful experiences typically possess a wide range of coping strategies and resources. Being equipped with a repertoire of self-care skills permits the individual to practice greater flexibility when facing his or her traumatic memories in therapy. A history of trauma may compound a person's ability to recover from a new trauma, especially if the individual has not dealt with the prior event.

Although individuals should be encouraged to engage in activities that make them feel better, they should be forewarned that some self-care activities may be unhealthy and lead to further problems. For example, in a recent study, Kalb (2002) found that 11% of New Yorkers showed symptoms of PTSD two months after the 9/11 attack. Their degree of distress was strongly correlated with how much television they watched. It can be deduced that these individuals may have used television viewing as a coping mechanism; unfortunately, they were maintaining the very symptoms they were trying to eradicate.

Grief Work. Grief work is a necessary treatment for clients mourning the loss of their loved ones. This type of work may also be used to grieve the loss of a time and a place that felt safe and stable. For example, we all mourn the era when air travel was easier, when aircraft safety and physical safety was not a major concern, and when flight delays were largely weather-related.

Once survivors achieve a comfortable level in their recovery, they may want to participate in a group with similarly affected individuals. For example, various support groups developed in response to 9/11: groups for widows of 9/11 victims, groups for mothers of 9/11 victims, groups for children of 9/11 victims, and groups for the families of firefighter victims. Some survivors of similar traumas may be motivated to co-lead a group. Co-leading is a role that can serve several purposes. First, the survivor attains a sense of fulfillment from helping others. Second, the opportunity to assist those who were recently affected can be empowering; the individual realizes how much he or she may have recovered. Finally, co-leading a trauma group can help individuals gain mastery over their own traumatic material (De Fauw & Andriessen, 2003).

Cognitive Distortions. A basic goal of trauma therapy is to reduce cognitive distortions and curtail self-destructive thought patterns perpetuated by traumatic memories. Constructing meaning from adverse experiences is a process that positively affects recovery and restores a client's sense of control; it is a dynamic process that changes along with the individual and his or her psychosocial environment. Meaning is always shaped by the ecological context that a client inhabits—a context that interacts with an individual's history, present life circumstances, and unique interpretation of the traumatic event.

Telling the Story. At some point in therapy, all victims must tell the story of their traumatic experience. Asking questions about what was heard, touched, smelled, and tasted is one way to elicit a full narrative of the trauma. The client experiences catharsis or abreaction by telling the trauma story. Catharsis is an important aspect of trauma recovery (Foy et al., 2003). It gives clients an opportunity to gain authority over a traumatic memory so it no longer dominates their lives. Clients can then, with the help of the therapist, integrate their loss into current functioning.

Providing Resources. Therapists should provide clients affected by terrorism with potential resources:

- American Red Cross (www.redcross.org)
- National Organization for Victim Assistance (www.trynova.org)
- Crime Victim Compensation Fund (www.nacvcb.org)
- Employee Assistance Programs (www.eap-sap.com)

Family Therapy

The trauma of a terrorist attack can affect a family in myriad ways. For some families, relationships become tighter. For others, underlying issues in the family may become more prominent. The varied effect of terror on families can either lead to a family's unification or its dissolution. Mutual support within families, under stressful conditions, can be paradoxical. The family that one uses as a source of support can also be a source of tension (Figley, 1988).

When a family loses a primary breadwinner, the loss can be both emotionally and economically devastating. This loss is multiplied if more than one family member is killed. With survivors of a terrorist attack, the goal of family therapy is to help the family adjust to the new dynamic within the family. The family therapist helps family members gain a perspective on any rage and guilt they may feel. Grief reactions are examined and sources of support are explored during family therapy sessions. Sharing reactions with other family members helps each family member process and accept his or her own reactions. It can be normalizing for family members to observe other family members experiencing similar traumatic reactions. However, sharing reactions with each other also carries an inherent danger of heightening an individual family member's reactions or re-traumatizing him or her (Miller, 2003).

A new family structure may have to be established to accommodate the loss of a family member. Some members may have to adopt new roles and responsibilities in an effort to attain family stability. The family therapist's task is to ensure that the family returns to a cohesive level of functioning despite the loss of one or more of its members. Family therapy for terrorist bereavement may need to address past unresolved issues that become highlighted after the trauma. These issues may be related to school or employment, marital conflict, or substance abuse. The therapist has to prioritize which issue to address first. The therapeutic intervention should serve the role of lessening the effects of trauma, increasing the self-esteem of family members, and altering the family's functioning so the impact of the traumatic event becomes more manageable (Sprang & McNeil, 1995).

Although discussing family losses in therapy is important, this process should not be required. Rather, discussion of family loss should only be initiated when the family is ready. At that point, each individual family member's perception of death can be examined. This examination helps family members gain insight into each other's belief systems. Family therapy that includes children should be adjusted to accommodate for their specific developmental needs. The focus should always be on family members collaborating together in activities, rituals, and projects that help them make meaning of their loss (Spungen, 1998). For example, family members can create a scrapbook of pictures to symbolically memorialize their loss.

By including children in these activities, adults promote their own recovery as well as the recovery of children. Children usually have the skills to complete these activities; which are developmentally engaging and help children feel included in the recovery process.

Community Responses

In a national longitudinal study conducted two months after 9/11, researchers found that a significant number of adults in the U.S. continued to experience terrorism-related distress and disruption in their lives; this qualified them for a PTSD diagnosis (Stein et al., 2004). Although many affected individuals turned to family and friends for support, just as many individuals felt uncomfortable doing so because they did not want to burden those close to them. The highest rates of distress were seen in groups of adults who were previously at risk for trauma-related symptoms, namely women and minority groups. Both these groups rarely sought mental health services to reduce their distress. This may be a wake-up call for health care providers and policy makers to explore ways such groups can view the health care system more positively. A community approach may be the answer.

Community organizing promotes a more coordinated response after a terrorist attack. Community interventions work best when collaborative relationships exist among police, mental health professionals, school teachers and administrators, business managers and executives, health professionals, and religious leaders. These relationships must be established prior to an event occurring. The mental health provider can act as a resource in building collaborative relationships in a community.

Community leaders play a vital role in offering support and increasing social morale in a time of distress. Helping professionals who consult with these leaders maximize the efficacy of a community response and increase their own understanding of what needs to be done. Community leaders can be instrumental in modeling how to express grief and loss in a healthy and positive way (Ursano et al., 1995).

Outreach programs can be used to reach those individuals who may not normally seek traditional mental health services. Identifying and reaching out to high-risk groups should be a first step for outreach programs; the next step is knowing which community members can keep the community informed about the different resources available to them.

Memorials

Memorials to the victims of a terrorist disaster are part of the healing process. Helping professionals should encourage community members' participation in this process of community recovery. Communities have culturally diverse ways of expressing loss. Candlelight vigils, prayer services, healing ceremonies, and protest marches are some ways communities strive to heal.

Acknowledgments

The timely acknowledgment of a disaster by an authority figure who is representative of the larger ecosystem (governor or president) is important to the healing and recovery of a community. When a distressed community is acknowledged in this way, its members feel less isolated.

National and International Responses

According to the United Nations Commission on Crime Prevention and Criminal Justice, a comprehensive victim services program must include

1. immediate crisis intervention, short-term counseling, longer-term counseling;

2. victim advocacy, protection, support (especially during the investigation and the prosecution of terrorist and other violent crimes);

3. adequate education and/or training on victim issues for allied professionals;

4. violence prevention strategies, intervention strategies, and public awareness (Kratcoski, Edelbacher, & Das, 2001).

In cases of mass terrorism, interventions organized by professionals in the mental health community must involve international coordination and cooperation (Kratcoski et al., 2001). At a national level, the following organizations currently offer coordinated support in the aftermath of a terrorist attack:

- American Red Cross
- Federal Emergency and Medical Administration
- National Organization of Victim Assistance

Conclusion

Over the past 30 years, international terrorism has claimed an increasingly prominent position on the public agenda. Its fanatical roots inspire terrorists to send a violent message to politicians, governments, and entire nations. Tragically, that message can result in the decimation of families, personal property, and entire communities. On a larger scale, the psychological well-being of society is severely compromised by these acts of violence. The terrorist acts of 9/11, the Bali bombings, the Madrid bombings, the 7/7 attacks in the UK, and the beheading of journalists, as well as countless other terrorist acts, have kept the world on edge.

Adequate public communication is valuable in promoting resilience and in helping people stay healthy during extremely stressful times. However, such communication can also create confusion and heighten public anxiety. News that includes tragic personal events should be carefully reported so that an individual's right to privacy is fully respected. Sensitive reporters provide assistance and support to viewers rather than vicariously traumatizing them.

The skilled trauma practitioner is essential in helping people recover and establishing psychological well-being in the aftermath of a terrorist attack. Empowering individuals, groups, and communities to regain control of their lives may go far in deterring the goals of those who promote violence. By encouraging people to speak openly about their fears, anger, hatred, and vulnerabilities, efforts can be made to mitigate these reactions. Only when this happens will individuals, communities, and nations fully recover from acts of violence.

References

American Psychiatric Association. (1994). *Diagnostic and statistical manual of mental disorders* (4th ed.). Washington, DC: Author.

Bolz, F., Dudonis, K. J., & Schultz, D. P. (1996). *The counter-terrorism handbook: Tactics, procedures, and techniques.* Boca Raton, FL: CRC Press.

Boss, P. G. (2002). Ambiguous loss: Working with families of the missing. *Family Process, 41,* 14–17.

Bushman, B. J. (1995). Moderating role of trait aggressiveness in the effects of violent media on aggression. *Journal of Personality and Social Psychology, 69,* 950–960.

Bushman, B. J., & Anderson, C. A. (2001). Media violence and the American public. *American Psychologist,* 477–489.

Cantor, J., Mares, M. L., & Oliver M. B. (1993). Parents' and children's emotional reactions to TV coverage of the Gulf War. In B. S. Greenberg & W. Gantz (Eds.), *Desert Storm and mass media* (pp. 325–340). Cresskill, NJ: Hampton Press.

Combs, C. C. (1997). *Terrorism in the twenty-first century.* Upper Saddle River, NJ: Prentice Hall.

De Fauw, N., & Andriessen, K. (2003). Networking to support suicide survivors. *Crisis: The Journal of Crisis Intervention and Suicide Prevention, 24*(1), 29–31.

Difede, J., Apfeldorf, W. J., Cloitre, M., Spielman, L. A., & Perry, S. W. (1997). Acute psychiatric responses to the explosion at the World Trade Center: A case series. *Journal of Nervous and Mental Disease, 186,* 519–522.

Dougall, L. A., Hayward, M. C., & Baum, A. (2005). Media exposure to bioterrorism stress and the anthrax attacks. *Psychiatry, 68*(1), 28–42.

Ferguson, C. (1999). Television news. In S. Harrison (Ed.), *Disasters and the media: Managing crisis communications* (pp. 36–45). London: Macmillan.

Figley, C. R. (1988). Post-traumatic family therapy. In F. M. Ochberg (Ed.), *Post traumatic therapy and victims of violence* (pp. 83–109). New York: Brunner/Mazel.

Foy, D. W., Glynn, S. M., Schnurr, P. P., Weiss, D. S., Wattenberg, M. S., Marmar, C. R., et al. (2003). Group psychotherapy for posttraumatic stress disorder. In E. B. Foa, T. M. Keane, & M. J. Friedman (Eds.), *Effective treatment for PTSD: Practice guidelines from the International Society for Stress Studies* (pp. 153–175). New York: Guilford.

Galea, S., Ahern, J., Resnick, H., Kilpatrick, D., Bucuvalas, M., Gold, J., et al. (2002). Psychological sequelae of the September 11 terrorist attacks in New York City. *New England Journal of Medicine, 346,* 982–987.

Heldring, M. (2004). Talking to the public about terrorism: Promoting health and resilience. *Families, Systems and Health, 22*(1), 67–71.

Hills, A. (2002). Responding to catastrophic terrorism. *Studies in Conflict and Terrorism, 25,* 245–261.

Kalb, C. (2002, August 19). How are we doing? *Newsweek,* p. 53.

Kastenbaum, R. J. (2001). *Death, society and human experience* (7th ed.). Boston: Allyn & Bacon.

Keinan, G., Sadeh, A., & Rosen, S. (2003). Attitudes and reactions to media coverage of terrorist acts. *Journal of Community Psychology, 31*(2), 149–165.

Kingston, S. (1995). Terrorism, the media, and the Northern Ireland conflict. *Studies in Conflict and Terrorism, 18*(3), 203–231.

Kratcoski, P. C., Edelbacher, M., & Das, D. K. (2001). Terrorist victimization: Prevention, control, and recovery. *International Review of Victimology, 8,* 257–268.

Miller, L. (2003). Family therapy of terroristic trauma: Psychological syndromes and treatment strategies. *American Journal of Family Therapy, 31,* 257–280.

Moghadam, A. (2003). Palestinian suicide terrorism in the second Intifada: Motivations and organizational aspects. *Studies in Conflict & Terrorism, 26,* 65–92.

Montiel, C. J., & Anuar, M. K. (2002). Other terrorisms, psychology and media. *Peace and Conflict: Journal of Peace Psychology, 8*(3), 201–206.

Nacos, B. L. (1994). *Terrorism and the media.* New York: Columbia University Press.

Schbley, A. (2003). Defining religious terrorism: A causal and anthological profile. *Studies in Conflict & Terrorism, 26,* 105–134.

Schlenger, W. E., Caddell, J. M., Ebert, L., Jordan, B. K., Rorke, K. M., Wilson D., et al. (2002). Psychological reactions to terrorist attacks: Findings from the national study of Americans' reactions to September 11. *Journal of the American Medical Association, 288,* 581–588.

Schuster, M. A., Stein, B. D., Jaycox, L. H., Collins, R. L., Marshall, G. N., Elliott, M., et al. (2001). A national survey of stress reactions after the September 11, 2001, terrorist attacks. *New England Journal of Medicine, 345,* 1507–1512.

Sprang, G., & McNeil, J. (1995). *The many faces of bereavement: The nature and treatment of natural, traumatic, and stigmatized grief.* New York: Brunner/Mazel.

Spungen, D. (1998). *Homicide: The hidden victims. A guide for professionals.* Thousand Oaks, CA: Sage.

Stein, B. D., Elliott, M. N., Jaycox, L. H., Collins, R. L., Berry, S. H., Klein, D. J., et al. (2004). A national longitudinal study of the psychological consequences of the September 11, 2001 terrorist attacks: Reactions, impairment, and help-seeking. *Psychiatry, 67*(2), 105–117.

Susser, E., Bresnahan, M., & Link, B. (2002). Peering into the future of psychiatric epidemiology. In M. Tsuang & M. Tohen (Eds.), *Textbook in psychiatric epidemiology* (2nd ed., pp. 195–211). New York: Wiley-Liss.

Ursano, R. J., Fullerton, C. S., & Norwood, A. E. (1995). Psychiatric dimensions of disaster: Patient care, community consultation, and preventive medicine. *Harvard Review of Psychiatry, 3,* 196–209.

13

Natural Disasters

On September 6, 2005, the day after Labor Day, the American Red Cross deployed me to Baton Rouge, Louisiana. Hurricane Katrina had devastated the Gulf Coast. The nation's largest natural disaster, it severely affected Louisiana and Mississippi. The words I read in the morning's newspaper reverberated in my mind: "Ignore the bodies; we want the living." I was filled with both dread and anticipation. A day later, I picked up my Red Cross card at a shelter outside Baton Rouge and was assigned a clientele of 2,500 men, women, and children. I worked at this shelter for more than 18 hours a day, trying to eat and sleep during the remaining time. Stories of my experiences in this place of extreme loss, pain, and suffering are endless. The lack of a coordinated multicultural approach to helping victims of disaster was clear; more than 95% of the people in the shelter were African American and indigent.

The disproportionate degree to which African Americans bore the brunt of the suffering and loss is unquestionably due to the economic and social stratification that existed in New Orleans before Hurricane Katrina. The discrepancy was always there, but it became undeniably evident after Hurricane Katrina magnified economic and social disparities in New Orleans, making them obvious to the entire world. The underlying and insidious effects of exclusion from society's resources along with the ongoing stigmatization in the form of a delayed governmental response were evidenced in the rapid loss of hope among many of the survivors I worked with after the storm.

While walking around the shelter, I was constantly assailed by anxious individuals inquiring about financial reparations so that they could take an initial step toward healing. Many survivors were unaware of the whereabouts of some *family members; the formidable task of locating loved ones filled them with helplessness and anxiety. In an attempt to offer help, a cell phone company had established a booth allowing people to make free calls. Many had stored their friends' and family's telephone numbers in their cell phones and could no longer remember them. As crisis workers know, remembering mundane information after a disaster is stressful. On my trip back home two weeks later, I stared vacantly out the window of the plane; I would continue to feel that sense of emptiness for several days. It was hard to shake off the images of devastation I witnessed.*

The primary objective of disaster response is the stabilization of injury and illness and the preservation of life. The priority of those responding to a disaster is to attend to the physical and psychological needs of survivors. Counselors who provide psychological services in the aftermath of natural disasters must be adequately prepared. This chapter begins by reviewing the background on disaster response, followed by a discussion of important ecological and cultural considerations for disaster responders as well as common reactions observed among survivors of a disaster. Important principles and guidelines to bear in mind when addressing the psychological needs of survivors are outlined. This is followed by a discussion of some specific interventions and different steps in disaster counseling. The chapter concludes with an exploration of the challenges facing disaster responders.

Background

Within minutes, a natural disaster can rip apart a community, changing people's lives forever. Hurricane Katrina showed us the devastation disasters are capable of inflicting and how quickly communities can be obliterated. The destruction can be immeasurable: serious physical injuries, the loss of loved ones, destruction of property and familiar possessions. Sometimes natural disasters, depending on the level of severity, become national disasters. This occurred with Hurricane Katrina.

Although there is no explicit definition of a disaster, there is agreement that it is sudden, unpredictable, uncontrollable, threatening to lives and property, and disruptive (Canterbury & Yule, 1999). Natural disasters are environmental stressors that affect the lives of thousands of people each year.

For 2004, the National Weather Service (2005) reported the following statistics on disasters:

- There were 369 weather-related fatalities.
- The biggest weather threat to life was flooding.
- September was the deadliest month with 72 fatalities, most of which were caused by a series of strong hurricanes that pounded the southeastern states.
- Severe weather caused $25.3 billion in property damage.
- Florida was the hardest hit by wind and rain from three major hurricanes. Losses from crop damage totaled $19.3 billion.

The Federal Emergency Management Agency (FEMA) reports that in the past 20 years, national disasters have increased from an average of 27 to 47 per year (FEMA, 2003). FEMA has three categories for disasters:

1. Natural (hurricanes, floods, mudslides, avalanches)

2. Accidental disasters (fires, explosions, motor vehicle accidents)

3. Human-made or technological disasters (bombings, industrial accidents)

All disasters cause immediate threat to individuals, families, and communities, changing lives forever. Causes differ, and not all disasters can be prevented; the unexpectedness of disasters makes it difficult to assess premorbid functioning and to obtain baseline information on affected individuals (Canino, Bravo, & Rubio-Stipec, 1990; Phifer & Norris, 1989). Natural disasters include hurricanes, floods, earthquakes, typhoons, tsunamis, volcanic eruptions, wildfires, and blizzards. We expect natural disasters to occur because we have no control over nature.

Technological disasters, often the result of technological malfunctioning or human error, can sometimes produce more devastating results than natural disasters. The nuclear disaster that occurred at the Chernobyl plant in the former USSR (now Ukraine) in 1986, for example, is described as the world's worst nuclear power accident (OECD Nuclear Energy Agency, 1995). A flawed reactor design that was operated by inadequately trained personnel and without proper regard for safety resulted in a steam explosion and fire releasing at least 5% of the radioactive reactor core into the atmosphere. Twenty-eight people died within four months from radiation or thermal burns, 19 have subsequently died, and there have been about 9 deaths from thyroid cancer apparently caused by the accident—a total of 56 fatalities as of 2004 (Jaworowski, 2004). Since we have control over technology, we expect to have control over technological disasters (Baum, Fleming, & Davidson, 1983).

Silent technological disasters that are not immediately detectable include radiation leaks, groundwater contamination, chemical spills, and chemical toxin exposure. It may be hard to assess the damage of silent disasters because their effects may not be experienced immediately; cancer, birth defects, and other diseases may develop later. An example of a silent disaster is the 1979 nuclear leak at Three Mile Island, a nuclear power plant near Middletown, Pennsylvania. This leak caused the evacuation of thousands of residents who were relocated to other communities.

The nuclear accident caused concerns about the possibility of radiation predisposing residents in the area surrounding the plant to cancer. As a result of these concerns, the Pennsylvania Department of Health maintained, for 18 years, a registry of more than 30,000 people who lived within five miles of Three Mile Island at the time of the accident. The state's registry was discontinued in 1997 without any evidence of unusual health trends in the area. The only notable effect was psychological stress during and shortly after the accident (GPU Nuclear Corp., 1999).

All disasters, no matter what their cause, have a detrimental long-term effect on mental health. This is evidenced through higher lifetime rates of depression, anxiety, and PTSD (Baum, Schaeffer, Lake, Fleming, & Collins 1986; Shore, Tatum, & Vollmer, 1986). The long-term mental effects of disasters, both natural and man-made, may be minimized by ecological and cultural community support.

Ecological and Cultural Considerations in Disaster Response

The individual's psychological reactions to disaster cannot be assessed without an ecological consideration of his or her political, cultural, environmental, and social realities (Kaniasty & Norris, 1999). Researchers Beaver and Miller (1992) differentiate between formal and informal networks of support within communities, arguing that they are equally important in disaster recovery. Formal support networks consist of services offered by governmental and nongovernmental organizations (NGOs). Family, friends, and other community members provide informal support networks. Adults 65 and older receive over 80% of their primary support from informal support networks after disasters (Bowie, 2003). For instance, in the 1990s, older adult survivors of the Midwest flood who had secure social support systems experienced fewer depressive symptoms compared to those with minimal support (Tyler, 2000).

Parental response and the home atmosphere mediate children's reactions to disasters (Green, et al., 1991; McFarlane, Policansky, & Irwin, 1987). Although close family ties are usually supportive, this may not be the case for all family members. For instance, women who may be the primary source of emotional support within their family can find themselves overextended in disaster situations (Shumaker & Brownell, 1984). A 1987 study on women in the workplace found that women with close spousal relationships demonstrated greater pathology than single women during a disaster (Solomon, Smith, & Robins, 1987). The stress of simultaneously working, maintaining a household, and supporting a spouse appeared to overwhelm participants in this study. In contrast, the same study found that male participants with close spousal relationships displayed fewer stress responses. Apparently, the support they received from their spouses helped them cope with the consequences of the disaster. When making an ecological assessment, it may be important for the disaster responder to consider the specific roles and responsibilities of individual members of a household.

A family breadwinner whose role is disrupted is likely to experience a disaster as debilitating. A cross-national study that included the U.S. Virgin Islands, Puerto Rico, and the Dominican Republic investigated the psychological functioning of survivors of a hurricane (Sattler, Preston, Kaiser, Olivera, Valdez, & Schlueter, 2002). Loss of economic resources and social support were two factors that caused participants significant stress. The researchers found that developing informal neighborhood groups was an effective strategy for helping distressed householders.

Research has found that victims of a natural disaster should remain in familiar surroundings in order to maintain family cohesion and preserve a sense of community (Galante & Foa, 1986). This allows survivors an opportunity to participate in recovery and reconstruction efforts. A study that investigated survivors' recovery from disaster found that women who relocated to another town after an earthquake in Armenia did not do as well as those women who remained close to the affected area (Najarian, Goenjian, Pelcovitz, Mandel, & Najarian, 2001). The women who were relocated displayed symptoms of depression and challenges in adjusting to their new environment; the women who remained in the disaster-affected community appeared to be recovering much better. The researchers concluded that a loss of community and sense of connection compromised the recovery of those who relocated.

Conversely, those who remained resumed responsibilities as soon as things settled down. In a similar study conducted among older adults forced to relocate after a natural disaster, participants reported experiencing feelings of numbness, anxiety, grief, and despair along with impaired sleeping patterns and decision-making skills (Gerrity & Steinglass, 1994).

However, direct victims are not the only ones in need of support after a disaster; counselors who enroll as first responders in large-scale disasters also need support.

As physical proximity to the crisis increases, the responder risks witnessing gruesome and painful events. For example, seeing dead and victimized children can overwhelm and impair the first responder's coping and problem-solving capacities. This vulnerability increases when responders themselves inhabit disaster-affected communities (Shumaker & Brownell, 1984; Solomon, 1986). Going to work can be a distraction for most individuals; however, this is not the case for human services personnel from disaster-affected communities. Stories of loss and suffering are likely to proliferate their lives both at home and at work.

Secondary traumatization affects many others besides those directly involved in disaster response. In the immediate aftermath of a disaster, the media presents details indiscriminately to the viewing audience. As graphic images of the disaster are continuously shown on television and in newspapers, the general public may find it increasingly difficult to shake off images of death and destruction. Society as a whole soon becomes an indirectly affected group. For individuals with histories of loss and trauma, these images can be profoundly distressing, yet their needs may go unattended because of their distance from the disaster.

When natural disasters occur, everyone in a community is affected, albeit not equally. The commonality of the experience provides opportunities for community sharing and increased understanding. Community interventions are well suited to maximizing the use of community resources while increasing well-being. Psychosocial interventions that are locally available and culturally appropriate strengthen disaster-affected communities. Community leaders and local healers, empowered through the consultation and support they receive, take the lead in developing community interventions (Reyes & Elhai, 2004).

Sometimes community interventions make up for the physical losses individuals encounter in a disaster (Golec, 1983). When the Teton Dam of Wyoming collapsed in 1976, 70% of homes were destroyed. Despite substantial material loss, the recovery of residents was increased through several community interventions that fostered a cohesive and integrated community. In the aftermath of this disaster, local responses were effective in maintaining social networks, providing financial compensation, and supplying adequate resources.

The cultural needs of communities is an important consideration when intervening in disasters. Culturally sensitive disaster responders are attentive to religion, language, and other communication and interpersonal styles of victims. A community's willingness to share information with strangers, style of grieving, and assumptions about causality of death are respected, along with any other cultural variables that may present themselves.

The following case vignette illuminates the importance of culturally appropriate support in the aftermath of a disaster.

Several Latino families occupied almost half the floor of a shelter after Hurricane Katrina. On my routine daily walk through each floor, many individuals asked questions, and I found myself shaking my head helplessly to indicate that I did not speak Spanish. I have never regretted not learning Spanish as much as I did in those two awful weeks when I felt as powerless as the people I had come to serve. I saw fear in the eyes of those who were undocumented; they were too afraid to approach anyone for help.

A young Latino man was suicidal. He had lost both his wife and two children in the floods caused by Hurricane Katrina. He haltingly described in broken English how their bodies were found by the local sheriff, tied to their beds so that they could at least die together and not float away. He cherished the water-blemished note written by his wife as she made the final plans for her family's demise. His sense of grief was tangible and his earnest quest was to see their bodies. He desperately needed to give them a respectable burial, but it would take several weeks for that to happen. He was experiencing immeasurable anguish expressed in sleepless nights and a lack of appetite. Talking to a strange woman about his intimate feelings of loss was humiliating. Doing so in English, a language that failed to capture his pain, exacerbated his helplessness. Quickly gauging his discomfort, I connected him to other Spanish-speaking families. They swiftly surrounded him with a warm bond of friendship. Days later, observing him animatedly talking in this new circle of friends brought a rare smile to my lips.

Although national disaster response organizations, like the American Red Cross and FEMA, are trained to respond in a timely manner, this rapid response comes at the expense of adequate cultural planning. This was clearly reflected in disaster response efforts undertaken with survivors of Hurricane Katrina. For example, there was little consideration of those who did not speak English. As a result, a large number of survivors did not have access to information about resources or professionals they could talk to about their losses. The sacrifice of rapid responding is that disaster responders do not have the time to explore how the crisis response interfaces with the needs and existing resources of affected communities. The World Health Organization (2003) cautions disaster response organizations to make every effort to collaborate with local resources, including local and traditional healers, when responding to disasters. It behooves relief organizations to make these efforts, while bearing in mind that at the time of a disaster the culture of a victim intersects with the culture of responders to produce an emergent disaster culture:

Victim's culture—→ emergent disaster culture ←—Responder's culture

Community members can assist in planning culturally appropriate relief efforts and designing interventions. They possess knowledge of the unique needs of their communities and, as direct survivors, have the authority of experience. For affected communities, the major benefit of such collaboration is empowerment and the feeling that they contributed to their own healing. The crisis can then be experienced as an opportunity to grow and change, rather than as a danger or loss.

Throughout a disaster, victims experience many common reactions.

Some Common Responses to Disasters

Shock. It is common for survivors to experience emotional shock, numbness, and a sense of "nothingness." Survivors may experience "freezing" during and after the disaster. This shock may translate behaviorally into an inability to walk or move around; some may have difficulty leaving the site of the disaster.

Denial. Denial serves as a coping mechanism that prevents people from becoming overwhelmed. Survivors may believe that what they are currently experiencing is just a bad dream and their old life will resume. As smoke rose out of the World Trade Center three days after the terrorist attack, a young financial trader was convinced that her roommate would be found alive. It was obviously too overwhelming for this young woman to accept what may have happened to her friend.

Panic. Feelings of extreme anxiety, nervousness, and an inability to settle down increase steadily. An exaggerated startle response is common among survivors.

Flashbacks. Replaying the events repeatedly in the mind is the survivor's attempt to make sense of the traumatic experience. These intense and recurring traumatic memories cause individuals to feel as if they are in a dangerous situation again. Flashbacks include the behavioral and sensory aspects of the disaster, terrifying the survivor experiencing them.

Guilt. Guilt is commonly felt among survivors, especially if a spouse and children are among the loved ones killed. Survivors often question their own survival and have a foreshortened sense of the future. They commonly feel guilt for outcomes that they could not possibly have controlled.

Fight or Flight Mode. This is a basic survival mode activated by the right brain. Once the left side of the brain (thinking) regains control, individuals process and label traumatic events; stability is established and recovery resumes.

Impaired Thinking. Survivors' ability to concentrate and focus is severely compromised; simple decision making becomes an effort. Recalling mundane information like a previous address or a relative's telephone number may be challenging.

Hypervigilance. An increased or exaggerated startle response is common among survivors; they become excessively watchful, cautious, nervous, and wary. Hyperarousal is usually accompanied by hypervigilance, in which the survivor feels the need to be constantly on guard, constantly scanning and appraising the environment.

Behavior. Some people become withdrawn and noncommunicative after a traumatic event. Others become impulsive and energetic. It is common for victims to avoid reminders of the event (thoughts, feelings, conversations, activities, people, and places). Survivors may minimize interactions with the outside world and prefer isolation; this, however, reduces opportunities for new and gratifying experiences.

Physical Changes. Survivors experience many physical changes, such as headaches, muscle aches, and stomachaches. Those who have difficulty breathing or who experience chest pains, palpitations, or other serous physical reactions should seek medical help immediately. Changes in sleep patterns and disturbing dreams are likely to occur. Survivors can have difficulty getting to sleep and may have difficulty remaining asleep. Some survivors relive the traumatic experience in sleep, nightmares and night sweats. Without a good night of rest, survivors may feel tired and lethargic in the morning. Loss of appetite and changes in eating patterns are also possible. Some individuals may lack any appetite; if a loved one was killed in the disaster, the survivor may not feel the need to live and food can become distasteful. Others may develop voracious appetites especially for "junk food,"; this may be an attempt to nurture themselves.

Responders communicate to survivors that their reactions are expected and that others who experienced a disaster felt similarly. However, this should be done in a manner that does not minimize the survivor's own suffering.

Addressing the Psychological Needs of Survivors

There can be enormous differences in psychosocial distress and survivor needs following a disaster. These differences are influenced by the characteristics of each affected group (primary victims, families, rescue workers, community members) and the resources that may be available to each of them. It can be a formidable task for mental health professionals to reach the inordinate number of people directly and indirectly affected by a natural disaster. Psychosocial interventions should be comprehensive and flexible to meet the diverse needs of survivors; a multi-modal approach is the most effective.

The media (e.g., radio, television, and newspapers) can also play an indirect and integral role in the recovery process. The media can be used to offer the viewing audience practical information on managing the crisis and seeking resources. Information provided can include the location of available shelters, food banks, economic resources, and emergency telephone numbers. The media can also update the general public on rescues and relief efforts currently underway. Communities that are widely dispersed in rural or outlying locations benefit greatly from the information transmitted through the media.

The way in which an individual responds to a natural disaster is based upon a number of variables:

- Pre-trauma factors—an individual's history of mental illness, prior traumatic exposure, substance abuse, and so on
- Characteristics of the traumatic event—the severity of the event, extent of damage to life and property, and level of individuals' exposure to the event (primary or secondary victims)
- Post-trauma factors—the medical and psychological help that is available in the immediate aftermath of an event, support from friends and family members, degree of financial and social losses, and so on
- Personal meaning that an individual makes of the disaster, which is usually dependent on individual characteristics
- Extent of community disruption and the proportion of community members affected
- Physical environment—rural versus urban setting
- A community's response to stress, which will influence how individual members respond to a disaster (solidarity and cohesion vs. conflict and fragmentation)

Noji (2000) identifies the following as the overall objectives of disaster management:

- Assessing the needs of disaster-affected populations
- Matching available resources with needs
- Preventing further adverse health effects by implementing disease control strategies
- Evaluating disaster relief programs on a regular basis with the goal of improvement

In addition, Noji (2000) emphasizes a consideration of the following before addressing psychological needs of survivors:

- Time constraints and the intensity of an individual's reactions will influence the type of intervention that is planned.
- Interventions may not follow a neat progression.
- Responders will need to be flexible in their interventions; adhering to a strict protocol may not work in a disaster situation.
- Psychological interventions should be planned only once physical safety has been established.
- If possible, remove people from the location of the trauma in order to eliminate further risk of traumatic exposure.
- Evaluate whether the survivor is alert and responsive to verbal stimuli.
- Recognize that psychological shock may be adaptive in the short-term by preventing the individual from experiencing the full impact of the event too quickly.
- It is critical that trained emergency medical personnel provide medical intervention; life-threatening illness and injury are addressed before psychological needs.
- Since children spend a great deal of time at school, school administrators and teachers should take a central role in planning a psychosocial response.

Disaster Counseling in the Acute Phase

The mental health counselor who responds in the immediate aftermath of a disaster has to make an accurate and timely assessment. A multi-method assessment of functioning includes a detailed assessment of the nature and severity of the stressors, individual factors that affect post-trauma processing of the event, and elements in the recovery environment that impede or enhance recovery (Green, 1991).

The responder should be familiar with the emotional, cognitive, behavioral, and physical reactions of traumatic stress. Survivors who rapidly fluctuate between shock and hyper-arousal are unable to benefit from psychological interventions; in this acute phase of the disaster, they require a sympathetic listener and assistance in contacting loved ones. Professional help should not undermine an individual's natural coping responses. Responders cannot assume, based on an initial observation of survivors, that they will or will not require help in the future (Canterbury & Yule, 1999).

The First Step

As a first step in helping, responders introduce themselves as individuals who specialize in providing support. Acknowledge and name the event, recognize that it is upsetting and distressing, and communicate that a wide range of reactions is expected. Responders explain that their purpose is to provide information and resources; they attempt to develop rapport with survivors by showing understanding and empathetic listening.

Responders should communicate competence and compassion by inquiring how people are doing and allowing for voluntary expressions of affect. A simple question such as "How are you doing?" can be a comfortable way to engage distressed individuals. Appropriate nonverbal communication, such as making eye contact and attempting a gentle touch with body turned toward a survivor, are other ways to effectively connect with survivors. Always strive to provide a safe, structured, and supportive environment that validates participants' thoughts, feelings, and reactions.

Individual reactions are likely to extend over a continuum from totally detached, withdrawn reactions to more intense displays of emotion that include uncontrollable crying, screaming, panic, anger, and fear. Individuals also have culturally different ways of reacting to a stressful event and "understanding the socio-cultural milieu is crucial for distinguishing psychopathology from culture-bound beliefs or behavior" (Westermeyer, 1987, p. 160). For example, Mexican Americans, who perceive loss as both an emotional and a physical process, tend to display more somatic reactions to stress than Anglo Americans (Candelaria & Adkins, 1994; Kolody, Vega, Meinhardt, & Bensussen, 1986).

Providing Facts

Once a connection is established with survivors, responders can provide them with facts and updates of the disaster. These details include information on how many people were affected, what help is forthcoming, and what next steps are being planned. This information helps orient the survivor to the moment; it keeps the interaction on a cognitive level and forces an attention to current circumstances. Thus, the survivor's tendency to replay the events repeatedly is disrupted.

Focusing on the Here and Now

Although expressions of emotion are not completely discouraged, the responder attempts to keep the focus on the here and now. This allows the individual to become slowly aware of the reality of his or her situation. Responders who encourage individuals to tell their story by describing what was seen, heard, and smelled permit an emotional and cognitive release.

Empathetic Understanding

It is important to establish and maintain an empathetic helping environment by understanding and respecting the uniqueness of individual thoughts and feelings. An overwhelming sense of being alone in their pain contributes to some individuals withdrawing into their own world. Every effort should be made to respectfully enter this world by reassuring victims that they are not alone. However, individuals should not be talked out of important feelings. Communicating an appreciation and understanding of the uniqueness of an individual's experiences conveys empathy.

Normalizing

Normalizing is important when intervening with people who have been exposed to a disaster. Experiencing new and conflicting emotions may cause some individuals to feel as if they are "losing it" and "going crazy." Normalizing and validating an experience reassures individuals who are attempting to deal with an abnormal event and promotes resiliency. An important aspect of the normalization process is educating affected individuals about typical emotional, cognitive, behavioral, and physiological responses to traumatic events while emphasizing the normalcy of these reactions. Such understanding can be comforting for survivors; it restores some of the control taken away by the disaster. Immediate interventions in the acute phase of a disaster should not resemble psychotherapy, but aim at helping individuals resume normal functioning. They provide basic stress management techniques and information on how to access additional support. A transition to a future focus is achieved by referring individuals to appropriate resources in their communities.

Children

Interventions with children must be attentive to their developmental level. Offering children more information than they are cognitively able to manage may do more harm than good. Younger children are generally unable to express their feelings verbally; instead, they are more likely to convey their feelings through their behaviors and actions. It is developmentally more appropriate to provide younger children with opportunities to express their feelings through drawing rather than talking. Drawings provide a glimpse into the inner world of the child and helps identify those children who need additional support.

I am reminded of an incident that occurred one night after dinner in the shelter where I worked after Hurricane Katrina. A young girl I will call "Dina" came over to speak to me. She and I were soon engrossed in the earnest task of coloring pictures in her coloring book. At the same time, she talked about the "fight between Jesus and the Devil" that happened on the night of the storm. Thinking quickly, I chose the picture of a fairy to color in the coloring book.

Several children soon asked to join our activity. I asked each newcomer to request permission from Dina before joining our group. She beamed radiantly as I said this; clearly, a simple acknowledgment made her feel valued. As the children and I sat in a circle, the lights went out for a brief period; another rainstorm had begun. I quickly instructed the children to take each other's hands; in this way, we offered each other support during the minute or so it took for the generators to restore electricity. Dina quickly informed me that the "Devil" was back again. We continued drawing and talking about what had just happened. When it was time for the children to go to bed, I gave Dina the picture of the fairy that I hoped would comfort her in the coming days. The children asked me to come back the next night.

Physical contact may be necessary when supporting young children who survive a disaster. This is always done without violating their boundaries. Because children take their cues from the adults around them, it may be necessary to separate them from emotionally overwhelmed adults.

The Elderly

The vulnerability of elderly individuals increases after a natural disaster, especially if they have weakened social networks (loss of a spouse and/or children), co-morbid disorders, limited financial resources, or a history of chronic stress that may have eroded their coping capacities (Kohn, Leva, Garcia, Machuca, & Tamasiro, 2005). These factors place them at risk for developing emotional disorders. A study conducted after an earthquake in Taiwan found more psychological distress and post-traumatic symptoms in the elderly rather than younger disaster survivors (Yang et al., 2003). A year after the crash of Pan Am 103, 84% of elderly residents of Lockerbie, Scotland, met the criteria for a PTSD diagnosis and 51% had a coexisting major depression. However, three years later only 16% continued to have PTSD symptoms (Jenike, 1995).

Two studies report resiliency among elderly survivors of disasters. After a flood in Kentucky, elderly residents (55 years and older) demonstrated several psychological reactions (anxiety, depression, somatic symptoms), but the reactions of the older subset (64–75) were mild compared to the younger people in the group (Phifer, 1990). Kato, Asukai, and Miyake (1996) found that eight weeks after an earthquake in Japan the elderly experienced fewer traumatic reactions compared to a younger group. The authors concluded that extensive social networks and previous disaster experiences may have inoculated the elderly against the negative sequelae of trauma.

In contrast, in a study conducted after a hurricane struck a Central American country, researchers confirmed that the elderly were at risk for post-traumatic stress and were equally as affected by disasters as younger adults (Kohn, Leva, & Garcia, 2005). The researchers suggested that the elderly should be included in reconstruction efforts; access to medical and mental health support is mandatory for the elderly. Like all groups, the elderly are at risk for psychological morbidity if they do not get the appropriate help before, during, and after disasters; responders have to ensure that this vulnerable group, which tends to suffer quietly, does not have a lower priority in disaster situations (Raphael, 1986). Disaster recovery efforts should include the personal involvement of elderly survivors, if possible, to support feelings of empowerment. The elderly survivors are best served by elderly volunteers; training such volunteers to respond to the needs of their peers is invaluable when a disaster strikes (Fernandez et al., 2002).

Specific Disaster Interventions

Some of the most common interventions used in disaster situations follow:

Crisis Intervention

The counselor who responds in a disaster must have crisis intervention skills. The sheer breadth of emotional pain, the multiplicity and diversity of victims involved, and the extensive destruction to property suffered by disaster survivors is what sets them apart from other trauma survivors. Crisis intervention skills require an attention to the following issues:

- Interventions have to occur rapidly. Timing is one of the elements that differentiate crisis intervention from psychotherapy.
- The responder needs to take an active and directive role in helping a survivor. There may be little time to explore and discuss alternatives, as normally occurs in psychotherapy.
- The initial goal of crisis intervention is palliative; the ultimate goal is to refer individuals to appropriate local service providers for ongoing services.

Psycho-Education

Confusion tends to proliferate in the aftermath of a disaster because affected individuals do not know what to expect next. Survivors who are educated about the recovery process regain some control over their chaotic feelings. Psycho-education is a way of empowering survivors and providing them with much-needed information. Handouts that outline the stages of recovery, the common reactions to trauma, effective coping strategies, the stages of grief, and ways parents can help children assist survivors to regain control of their lives.

Psycho-education is a component of traditional supportive interventions; it is the least controversial and most often recommended early intervention in the mental health field (Raphael, 1986). A key strategy in early intervention efforts is outreach; most disaster survivors do not actively seek mental health services. NIMH (2002) suggests accomplishing psycho-education through outreach as follows:

- Offer information and education by walking around the area where survivors congregate.
- Frequent community centers, places of worship, and schools.
- Distribute flyers and host Web sites.

Institutions that are unaffected by the disaster, such as schools, emergency rooms, and social service agencies, can also distribute handouts, make referrals, and communicate important messages. Psycho-educational information should be communicated clearly and simply, without jargon. Survivors need reassurance that they are not going crazy and the reactions they are experiencing are normal reactions to an abnormal event, or ordinary reactions to an extraordinary event. Counselors may not be able to predict how long reactions will last, but they can assure survivors that their symptoms will decline over time.

The media can be used to broadcast appropriate information, including where to access resources. The media can also be used to conduct interviews and programs and distribute media releases. Counselors can also help survivors contend with the media; survivors may feel an obligation to respond to questions posed by the media, only to later regret their participation. In the aftermath of Hurricane Katrina, one of the lessons we learned was how the media can misconstrue and misinterpret actions taken by survivors. Counselors can play an integral role in educating survivors about the advantages and disadvantages of dealing with the media.

Debriefing

Debriefing is a crisis intervention technique that, despite controversy, continues to be used widely in the aftermath of disasters. Critical incident stress debriefing (CISD), a specific model of debriefing developed by Jeffrey Mitchell (1983), consists of seven phases that unfold as a structured group discussion. This model is usually offered 24 to 72 hours after a critical incident. As a semi-structured group intervention, debriefings are designed to alleviate initial distress and prevent the development of PTSD following exposure to traumatic events. The reviewing of facts and the sharing of emotions in a group format validates individual experiences of trauma. Survivors learn coping skills that help them manage short-term reactions to stress.

Although some controlled studies of CISD has shown that most survivors perceive it as beneficial, other studies indicate that CISD was not effective in preventing PTSD. In fact, CISD was found to have long-term negative effects and increased trauma reactions (Yehuda, 2002).

Planning

The final phase of disaster intervention involves planning; disaster survivors have evolving needs. Communities are inundated with offers of services in the immediate aftermath of a disaster. However, many of these services may not be around when survivors are ready to take advantage of them weeks or even months after the disaster.

The principles of trauma recovery inform us that affected communities must be monitored long after a disaster has occurred. Relief organizations should leave individuals with clear guidelines on how to locate and access resources in the future. Information about victim self-help groups tailored to specific populations—such as parents, children, and single women—can be especially helpful. When people are feeling depressed, they lack the initiative to look for telephone numbers and to ask for help. A brief handout distributed to survivors at the outset and clearly listing counseling and other resources can be invaluable.

Informal social networks can also monitor the well-being of individual members of a community. Bartenders and merchants sometimes serve as non–mental health caregivers; they are apt to notice markedly unusual behaviors in their customers. Religious and other community leaders who have ongoing contact with community members are also in a position to identify and refer individuals who are in need of help. This is especially the case for elderly survivors of a disaster. Traditional healers and indigenous workers are another group that may be in a position to identify and refer survivors for assistance.

Immigrant populations tend to congregate in areas where they conduct business and shop for food. Ensuring that merchants in these areas are knowledgeable about how to direct individuals to relevant resources is crucial in a disaster response. Finally, ethnic newspapers, television, and radio stations play an invaluable role in keeping people of all cultural backgrounds effectively informed.

Social support is promoted by self-help efforts in which families, neighbors, and others in a community come together to help each other. These activities help survivors resume feelings of control, increase self-worth, and overcome feelings of helplessness. They also re-establish social support networks, develop new support networks, and offer an opportunity to share disaster-related experiences (Sattler et al., 2002).

The Challenges of Disaster Mental Health

The setting and structure of interventions in disaster situations can present the counselor with unique challenges. Before entering a disaster-affected area, first responders should have an awareness of these challenges to prevent unnecessary hardship and potential burnout.

Setting

Temporary mass shelters, backyards, parking lots, and other unusual settings often become the "office" of the disaster mental health responder. Home visits are normal if survivors are able to remain in their homes; the responder is expected to meet the survivor in places where he or she feels safe. The responder may be required to work in unfamiliar sociocultural settings and communities he or she may otherwise avoid.

Rural communities may lose electricity and water supply in disaster conditions. Additionally, these communities may be underserved and lacking in the resources of social services, mental health providers, and community centers that are available in more urban settings. This can present challenges of extreme hardship for counselors working in disaster situations; the motivation to help may diminish rapidly under such circumstances.

Structure

The client-counselor relationship assumes a different structure under conditions of acute disaster. The relationship is intentionally short-term and emotionally supportive with pragmatic underpinnings. Since helping may take place in public settings, there should be a concerted effort toward maintaining boundaries. The ethical codes of the counseling profession and licensing regulations are never sacrificed, even under disaster conditions.

Command centers are often set up in the aftermath of a disaster. These centers are usually responsible for directing responders and delegating duties. For counselors who are used to working independently, following orders from individuals whose style and training may be different can be challenging. However, working cooperatively and collaboratively should take precedence over individual professional needs in a disaster setting. The disaster counselor must be prepared to be flexible and willing to adapt to the demands of a situation.

Self-Care for Disaster Responders

Working under disaster conditions can be extremely stressful for disaster responders and can take a toll in terms of professional performance and personal functioning. Recognizing the occupational hazards of the work is a first step. The next is making a conscious and sustained effort to remedy vicarious traumatization. This is accomplished through self-care activities, which are covered in more detail in the next chapter. A few activities that specifically relate to disaster responders are outlined below:

- Participating in regular supervision
- Maintaining boundaries between personal and professional activities
- Taking time off when instructed to do so
- Leaving the site of the disaster, if possible, to take a break, relax, or have a meal
- Working as a team or with a partner, rather than individually
- Maintaining contact with friends and family at home

Additional Disaster Resources: Federal Government Organizations

Federal Emergency Management Agency (FEMA)

FEMA coordinates with other state and federal agencies to respond to individuals and businesses after presidentially declared disasters.

www.fema.gov

Center for Mental Health Services (CMHS)

CMHS provides FEMA with consultation and technical assistance for crisis counseling and training.

www.samhsa.gov

Substance Abuse and Mental Health Services Administration (SAMHSA)

SAMHSA provides publications and videotapes on disaster responses.

www.mentalhealth.samhsa.gov

Federal Communications Commission (FCC)

The FCC is an independent U.S. government agency charged with regulating interstate and international communications by radio, television, wire, satellite, and cable.

www.fcc.gov

Health Resources and Services Administration (HRSA)

The HRSA, an agency of the U.S. Department of Health and Human Services (HHS), is the primary federal agency for improving access to health care services for people who are uninsured, isolated, or medically vulnerable.

www.hrsa.gov

Indian Health Service (IHS)

The IHS upholds the federal government's obligation to promote healthy American Indian and Alaska Native people by raising the physical, mental, social, and spiritual health of American Indians and Alaska Natives to the highest level.

www.ihs.gov

Office for Civil Rights (OCR)

The OCR promotes and ensures that people have equal access to and opportunity to participate in and receive services from all HHS programs without facing unlawful discrimination, and that the privacy of their health information is protected while ensuring access to care. OCR helps HHS carry out its overall mission of improving the health and well-being of all people affected by its many programs.

www.hhs.gov/ocr/mission.html

U.S. Dept. of Health and Human Services (HHS)

HHS is the U.S. government's principal agency for protecting the health of all Americans and providing essential human services, especially for those who are least able to help themselves.

www.hhs.gov/ocr

Office of Public Health and Science (OPHS)

The OPHS, under the direction of the Assistant Secretary for Health, serves as the Secretary's primary advisor on matters involving the nation's public health and oversees the U.S. Public Health Service for the Secretary.

http://www.osophs.dhhs.gov/ophs

U.S. Office of Minority Health Resource Center (OMH)

The OMH was established by HHS to improve and protect the health of racial and ethnic minority populations through the development of health policies and programs that will eliminate health disparities.

www.omhrc.gov

Rural Information Center Health Service (RIC)

The RIC provides information and referral services to local, tribal, state, and federal government officials; community organizations; libraries;

businesses; and citizens working to maintain the vitality of America's rural areas.

www.nal.usda.gov/ric

National Organizations

American Red Cross (ARC)

The ARC has chapters in most large cities and is responsible for disaster readiness and response. The ARC helps families with basic needs (food, clothing, and shelter) and support in the immediate aftermath of a disaster.

www.redcross.org

Professional Organizations

American Psychological Association (APA)

The APA is a scientific and professional organization that represents psychology in the United States. With 150,000 members, the APA is the largest association of psychologists worldwide.

www.apa.org

Cross Cultural Health Care Program

The mission of the Cross Cultural Health Care Program is to serve as a bridge between communities and health care institutions to ensure full access to quality health care that is culturally and linguistically appropriate.

www.xculture.org

National Alliance for Hispanic Health

The National Alliance for Hispanic Health works to improve the health and well-being of Hispanics. It is the premier organization focusing on Hispanic health. Members reach over 14 million Hispanic consumers throughout the U.S. and are dedicated to community-based solutions.

www.hispanichealth.org

National Asian American and Pacific Islander Mental Health Association (NAAPIHMA)

NAAPIHMA advocates on behalf of AAPI mental health issues and serves as a forum for effective collaboration of community-based organizations, consumers, family members, service providers, program developers, researchers, evaluators, and policy makers to develop comprehensive, culturally competent services to meet the needs of AAPI communities.

www.naapimha.org

National Association for Rural Mental Health (NARMH)

NARMH develops and enhances rural mental health and substance abuse services and supports mental health providers in rural areas. Members work proactively to develop and support initiatives that strengthen the voices of rural consumers and their families.

www.narmh.org

National Association of Social Workers (NASW)

NASW is the largest membership organization of professional social workers in the world, with 150,000 members. NASW works to enhance the professional growth and development of its members, to create and maintain professional standards, and to advance sound social policies.

www.naswdc.org

National Indian Health Board (NIHB)

NIHB is a nonprofit organization representing tribal governments operating their own health care delivery systems. NIHB presents the tribal perspective and conducts research, policy analysis, program assessment, and development for tribes, area health boards, tribal organizations, federal agencies, and private foundations.

www.nihb.org

State and Local Government Agencies

Departments of Mental Health

Contact the state agency responsible for mental health services in a particular state. The main office is located in each state's capital city.

Emergency Services

The emergency services agency is the lead agency delegated by the state's governor to manage an emergency within a state. The Office of Emergency Services is located in each state's capital city.

Conclusion

Disasters, which rob survivors of a sense of power and control, can strike anyone regardless of race, ethnicity, and culture. No one who experiences a disaster remains untouched by its destruction. Effective disaster responses are attentive to the mental health needs of all disaster survivors by considering the unique experiences, beliefs, norms, values, traditions, customs, and language of all affected individuals.

In the aftermath of a natural disaster, it is common for counselors to volunteer their services to help address the devastating loss of life and destruction. Some authors caution that expertise in treating trauma-related disorders may not be sufficient preparation for conducting disaster intervention (Reyes & Elhai, 2004). What sets a disaster apart is the breadth of its impact and the extent of emerging needs. Given the complex challenges of disaster mental health, it is important that counselors who are interested in disaster relief work are involved with organizations mandated to provide such services.

The American Psychological Association, American Red Cross, International Critical Stress Foundation, Federal Emergency Management Association, and National Organization for Victim Assistance are such organizations. Familiarity with these organizations before a disaster occurs is prudent. These organizations often require service providers to be trained and certified prior to deployment to a disaster site.

Finally, it is clear that humanitarian aid should provide survivors with food, shelter, and medical and psychological aid. Efforts should always be made to keep survivors in familiar environments; this has been proven to expedite the process of reconstruction.

References

Baum, A., Fleming, R., & Davidson, L. (1983). Natural disaster and technological catastrophe. *Environment and Behavior, 15*, 333–354.

Baum, A., Schaeffer, M., Lake, R., Fleming, R., & Collins, D. (1986). Psychological and endocrinological correlates of chronic stress at Three Mile Island. *Perspectives on Behavioral Medicine, 2*, 201–217.

Beaver, M. L., & Miller, D. A. (1992). *Clinical social work practice with the elderly: Primary, secondary and tertiary intervention* (2nd ed.). Belmont, CA: Wadsworth.

Bowie, S. L. (2003). Post-disaster crisis intervention with older adults in public housing communities. *Crisis Intervention and Time Limited Treatment, 6*(3), 171–184.

Candelaria, E., & Adkins, E. (1994). A Mexican-American perspective on death and the grief process. *The Forum, 20*(5), 7–8.

Canino, G. J., Bravo, M., & Rubio-Stipec, M. (1990). The impact of disaster on mental health: Prospective and retrospective analysis. *International Journal of Mental Health, 19*(1), 51–69.

Canterbury, R., & Yule, W. (1999). Debriefing and crisis intervention. In W. Yule (Ed.), *Post-traumatic stress disorder concepts and therapy* (pp. 221–238). Chichester: Wiley.

Federal Emergency Management Agency. (2003). *Total major disaster declarations.* Retrieved August 12, 2005, from http//www.fema.gov/library/drcys.shtm

Fernandez, L. S., Byard, D., Chien-Chih, L., Benson, S., & Barbera, J. A. (2002). Frail elderly as disaster victims: Emergency management strategies. *Prehospital and Disaster Medicine, 17*(2), 67–74.

Galante, R., & Foa, A. (1986). An epidemiological study of psychic trauma and treatment effectiveness for children after a natural disaster. *Journal of the American Academy of Child and Adolescent Psychiatry, 25,* 357–363.

Gerrity, E. T., & Steinglass, P. (1994). Relocation stress following natural disasters. In R. J. Ursano, B. G. McCaughey, & C. S. Fullerton (Eds.), *Individual and community response to trauma and disaster: The structure of human chaos* (pp. 220–247). Cambridge, UK: Cambridge University Press.

Golec, A. (1983). A contextual approach to the social psychological study of disaster recovery. *International Journal of Mass Emergencies and Disasters, 1*(2), 255–276.

GPU Nuclear Corp. (1999). *Ten briefing papers.* Retrieved September 9, 2006, from http://www.uic.com.au/nip48.htm

Green, B. L. (1991). Evaluating the effects of disasters. *Psychological Assessment, 3*(4), 538–546.

Green, B. L., Korol, M., Grace, M. C., Vary, M. G., Leonard, A. C., Gleser, G. C., et al. (1991). Children and disaster: Age, gender, and parental effects on PTSD symptoms. *Journal of the American Academy of Child and Adolescent Psychiatry, 30,* 945–951.

Jaworowski, Z. (2004, April). Lessons of Chernobyl, with particular reference to thyroid cancer. *Australasian Radiation Protection Society Newsletter, 30.*

Jenike, M. A. (1995). Posttraumatic stress disorder in the elderly: A three-year follow up of the Lockerbie disaster. *Journal of Geriatric Psychiatry and Neurology, 8*(2), 137.

Kaniasty, K., & Norris, F. (1999). The experience of disaster: Individuals and communities sharing trauma. In R. Grist & B. Lubin (Eds.), *Response to disaster: Psychosocial, community and ecological approaches* (pp. 25–62). Philadelphia, PA: Brunner/Mazel.

Kato, H., Asukai, N., & Miyake, Y. (1996). Posttraumatic symptoms among younger and elderly evacuees in the early stages following the 1995 Hanshin-Awaji earthquake in Japan. *Acta Psychiatrica Scandinavica, 93*(6), 477–481.

Kohn, R., Levav, I., Garcia, I. D., Machuca, M. E., Tamasiro, R. (2005). Prevalence, risk factors and aging vulnerability for psychopathology following a natural disaster in a developing country. *International Journal of Geriatric Psychiatry, 20,* 835–841.

Kolody, B., Vega, W., Meinhardt, K., & Bensussen, G. (1986). The correspondence of health complaints and depressive symptoms among Anglos and Mexican-Americans. *Journal of Nervous and Mental Disease, 174*(4), 221–228.

McFarlane, A., Policansky, S., & Irwin, C. (1987). A longitudinal study of the psychological morbidity in children due to natural disaster. *Psychological Medicine, 17,* 727–738.

Mitchell, J. T. (1983). When disaster strikes: The critical incident debriefing process. *Journal of Emergency Medical Services, 8,* 36–39.

Najarian, L. M., Goenjian, A. K., Pelcovitz, D., Mandel, F., & Najarian, B. (2001). The effect of relocation after a natural disaster. *Journal of Traumatic Stress, 14,* (3), 511–526.

National Weather Service. (2005). *Summary of natural hazard statistics for 2004 in the United States.* Retrieved May 16, 2006, from http://www.nws.noaa.gov/om/severe_weather/sum04.pdf

NIMH. (2002). *Mental health and mass violence: Evidence-based early psychological intervention for victims/survivors of mass violence. A workshop to reach consensus on best practices* [NIH Publication No. 02-5138]. Washington, DC: Government Printing Office.

Noji, E. K. (2000). The public health consequences of disasters. *Prehospital and Disaster Medicine, 15*(1), 32–53.

OECD Nuclear Energy Agency. (1995). *Chernobyl ten years on, radiological and health impact.* Paris: Author.

Phifer, J. F. (1990). Psychological distress and somatic symptoms after natural disaster: Differential vulnerability among older adults. *Psychology and Aging, 5,* 412–420.

Phifer, J. F., & Norris, F. H. (1989). Psychological symptoms in older adults following natural disaster: Nature, timing, duration and course. *Journal of Gerontology, 44*(6), 207–217.

Raphael, B. (1986). *When disaster strikes: How individuals and communities cope with catastrophe.* New York: Basic Books.

Reyes, G., & Elhai, G. (2004). Psychosocial interventions in the early phases of disasters. *Psychotherapy Theory Research Practice Training, 41*(4), 399–411.

Sattler, D. N., Preston, A. J., Kaiser, C. F., Olivera, V. E., Valdez, J., & Schlueter, S. (2002). Hurricane Georges: A cross-national study examining preparedness, resource loss, and psychological distress in the U.S. Virgin Islands, Puerto Rico, Dominican Republic, and the United States. *Journal of Traumatic Stress, 15*(5), 339–350.

Shore, J., Tatum, E., & Vollmer, W. (1986). Psychiatric reactions to disaster: The Mount St. Helens experience. *American Journal of Psychiatry, 143,* 590–595.

Shumaker, S. A., & Brownell, A. (1984). Toward a theory of social support: Closing conceptual gaps. *Journal of Social Issues, 40*(4), 11–36.

Solomon, S. D., Smith E. M., & Robins, L. N. (1987). Social involvement as a mediator of disaster-induced stress. *Journal of Applied Social Psychology, 17*(12), 1092–1112.

Solomon, Z. (1986). Three Mile Island: Social support and affective disorders among mothers. In S. E. Hobfoll (Ed.), *Stress, social support, and women* (pp. 85–97). Washington, DC: Hemisphere.

Tyler, K. A. (2000). The effects of an acute stressor on depressive symptoms among older adults. *Research on Aging, 22,* 143–165.

Westermeyer, J. (1987). Clinical considerations in cross-cultural diagnosis. *Hospital and Community Psychiatry, 38,* 160–166.

World Health Organization. (2003). *Mental health policy and service guidance package: Organization of services for mental health.* Switzerland: Author.

Yang. Y. K., Yeh, T. L., Chen C. C., Lee, C. K., Lee, I. H., Lee, L., et al. (2003). Psychiatric morbidity and posttraumatic symptoms among earthquake victims in primary care clinics. *General Hospital Psychiatry, 25,* 253–261.

Yehuda, R. (Ed.). (2002). *Treating trauma survivors with PTSD: Bridging the gap between intervention, research and practice.* Washington, DC: American Psychiatric Press.

14

Helping the Helper

Secondary Trauma

It has been three years since Rosario graduated from college. Shortly after gradua-
tion, she began working as a mental health counselor in a program for battered
Latina women. Her supervisor describes her as a hard worker who goes beyond the
call of duty. Rosario wanted to do mental health counseling since she was a child.
When she was seven, she would watch from a crack in the door as her parents
fought violently. As they yelled and screamed at each other, her father would some-
times pummel her mother with his large fists. Eventually the shouting stopped, and
her father would slam the front door behind him as he went off to a local bar.
Rosario's mother was left whimpering in pain, her head buried in her arms at the
kitchen table. Rosario would find her there in a helpless state. She gently comforted
her mother, saying that things would soon get better. Nowadays, she frequently
finds herself telling her clients in the battered women's program the same thing.

Lately, Rosario has been getting frequent headaches and feels exhausted at the
end of each workday. She finds little time and energy for other activities. She often
makes excuses not to socialize with her boyfriend. Rosario's case is not unusual;
as a child witness to domestic violence, she may have unaddressed issues around
trauma. If these issues are left unattended, vicarious trauma and burnout will
soon follow.

Mental health counselors are not immune to the potential stress and burnout that accompany working in the field of trauma. This is especially true for practitioners who have their own histories of trauma. Counselors must be knowledgeable about the emotional risks they face in treating trauma survivors. Most counselors entering this specialized field possess altruism and compassion, which are critical characteristics in working with trauma survivors. However, these characteristics also contain the hidden risk of increased personal vulnerability.

This chapter begins with a discussion of the concepts of countertransference, secondary trauma, vicarious trauma, compassion fatigue, and burnout. These concepts comprise the areas in which counselors may find themselves personally affected when engaging in trauma work. This chapter also discusses useful strategies for maintaining health and well-being, providing practitioners with an understanding of the challenges of working with trauma survivors in ways that will not compromise their own performance. Not surprisingly, the demand for secondary trauma and self-care workshops has increased along with the use of trauma services. The mechanics of conducting a secondary trauma workshop are outlined as well. Finally, the chapter concludes with strategies for institutions to create a supportive environment for trauma service workers.

A Matter of Definitions

The *DSM-IV* indicates that the trauma response can be produced by direct and by indirect exposure to a traumatic event. Terr (1989) describes trauma as "a pebble thrown into a pool: just as the circles of water spread further and further to the perimeter of the pool, the anxiety generated by a traumatic event can have a rippling effect on families, on communities, and even on future generations" (p. 15). Trauma counselors are one of the inevitable circles that surround a trauma survivor. In listening to the shocking images that traumatized clients bring to therapy, trauma counselors become an extremely vulnerable group.

Working for an extended period with a traumatized population can result in a conflict in counselors' cognitive beliefs about whether the world is safe and can be trusted (McCann & Pearlman, 1990). Several other symptoms of PTSD, including intrusive thoughts and hypervigilance, may begin to increase. Even the routine task of walking to a car at night can become one filled with anxiety and uneasiness. The terms countertransference, secondary trauma, vicarious trauma, compassion fatigue, and burnout describe the adverse effects of exposure to a client's trauma history on the counselor (Sexton, 1999). An explanation of each follows.

Countertransference is a psychoanalytic term, first described by Freud (1957) as a therapist's unconscious reaction to a patient's transference. He believed that it is important for the therapist and the supervisor to identify and work through countertransference. Counselors have since come to understand the concept as a normal emotional reaction to a client and a reflection of the counselor's personal life experiences (Figley, 1995). Countertransference refers to the feelings and reactions that therapists have toward their clients as a result of a therapeutic relationship (McCann & Pearlman, 1990). These feelings and reactions are produced by the therapist's personal and professional experiences and are capable of influencing the therapist's attitude and behavior toward a client (Dass-Brailsford, 2003). The counselor's negative feelings are due to resolved and unresolved conflicts within the clinician (McCann & Pearlman, 1990). Awareness of these feelings is an important first step; discussing them in supervision is a necessary second step to prevent countertransference from having a deleterious effect on the client. If countertransference is left unattended, it can contribute to a counselor's vulnerability to secondary or vicarious trauma. Counselors who are unaware of the effects of secondary trauma may lose their sense of optimism and overidentify with clients.

Vicarious trauma or secondary traumatic stress reaction is defined as the change that occurs within the therapist as a result of empathetic engagement with a client's trauma experiences (Pearlman & MacIan, 1995); it describes a counselor's reactions to exposure to a client's traumatic experience (Tripanny, White Kress, & Wicoxon, 2004). The concepts of secondary trauma and vicarious trauma are used interchangeably. Vicarious trauma is the "negative transformation of a therapist's inner experience as a result of empathetic engagement with traumatized clients" (Saakvitne, 2003, p. 143). Changes in the therapist's self-image and disruptions in identity, memory, and belief systems are likely to occur (Pearlman & Saakvitne, 1995). Vicarious trauma is an occupational hazard for those who work in the trauma field (Munroe, 1995).

The repeated exposure to a client's traumatic experience can negatively affect a therapist's core beliefs about the world. Practitioners who see a large number of traumatized clients fall into a high-risk group. Additional characteristics that might influence vicarious trauma include a therapist's personal trauma history, the meaning attached to traumatic life events, psychological and interpersonal style, current stressors, and support systems (Pearlman & MacIan, 1995). Research has found that counselors who work with sexually abused clients, for example, experience profound and disruptive psychological effects that persist months and years after working with this particular client group (Cunningham, 2004).

However, secondary or vicarious trauma should not be perceived as a pathological reaction to the inherent stress of working with traumatized clients (Cunningham, 2004). Pearlman and Saakvitne (1995) believe that it reflects neither pathology on the part of the therapist nor intentionality on the part of the survivor. Rather, it is a consequence of a sensitive therapeutic interaction; it occurs when counselors engage empathetically with a client's traumatic material. While issues of countertransference and other unresolved personal factors may complicate the therapeutic process, vicarious reactions are expected, just as post-traumatic stress reactions are expected reactions to abusive environments (Pearlman & Saakvitne, 1995).

Untreated secondary or vicarious trauma can be deleterious to the psychological well-being of a counselor, and the earliest signs require swift attention. As long as we engage empathetically with trauma survivors and feel a strong sense of responsibility to help others, we increase our vulnerability to developing secondary trauma (Pearlman, 1995). However, vicarious traumatic reactions can develop into burnout.

In September, 2005, I was deployed with a disaster team to provide mental health services to those affected by Hurricane Katrina on the Gulf Coast. After spending two weeks at a shelter near Baton Rouge, LA, I looked forward to returning to the familiar surroundings of my home, family, friends, and work. Yet, I found it difficult to engage in activities that previously gave me such joy. It was equally hard to return to work. My regular life suddenly felt dull, empty, and colorless. I would find myself often staring vacantly; questions of how I could enjoy life when others were suffering constantly filled my mind. The simple task of grocery shopping and surveying the different varieties of available food brought back memories of the long lines that would grow at meal times at the shelter in Louisiana; there was little opportunity to be selective about what to eat there. Despite many years of conducting secondary trauma workshops (I was well aware of the negative reactions of stress), my own vicarious trauma came as a huge surprise. This awareness was the first step in my recovery. Eventually, with the help and support of colleagues, family, and friends, the heaviness that loomed over me slowly dissipated and I developed a renewed interest in my old lifestyle.

Compassion fatigue is a term that was first proposed by Figley (1995) and is viewed as a normative occupational hazard of working with traumatized clients. Compassion fatigue is a consequence of listening to a client's traumatic history and the negative reactions that derive from such empathetic contact. When counselors are unable to maintain a psychological distance from clients' traumatic material, they may feel as if the trauma were happening directly to them. In effect, the counselor takes on the clients' trauma as his or her own.

Figley (1995) suggests that because the symptoms of compassion fatigue parallel the symptoms of post-traumatic stress syndrome, the term *secondary traumatic stress disorder* (STSD) is more appropriate. STSD meets the diagnostic Criterion A, or "the event" criterion of PTSD (*DSM-IV*), with the counselor affected by "hearing about" rather than "directly experiencing" a traumatic event (Figley, 1995). Compassion fatigue, however, tends to be the more "user-friendly" term commonly used in the trauma field (Figley, 1995). Although compassion fatigue can show up suddenly with very little warning, recovery is possible, and affected counselors overcome compassion fatigue much faster than burnout (Figley, 1995). The following case vignette is illustrative of an individual who experiences compassion fatigue.

> *Jenny decided to spend a year working at a refugee camp in Rwanda after her third year in college. She had a rewarding experience working as a lay counselor in a camp specially designated for children and found it hard to leave once her year was over. She referred herself to our program within a few weeks of returning to the U.S. Jenny was having great difficulty sleeping. Nightmares would often wake her from sporadic sleep. She also described notable weight loss; A her favorite foods were no longer appealing.*
>
> *Her thoughts and feelings remained intricately connected to the children in Rwanda. The traumatic stories she had heard "were all in my head and I cannot get them out; I need to be there again." Through stage-oriented trauma-focused therapy, Jenny was able to first practice relaxation and self-care strategies. Once she was able to acquire a state of mental and emotional calmness, she was able to talk about the guilt she felt about being "safe" in the U.S. while the children she worked with in Rwanda continued to experience instability. Over several months of weekly therapy, her compassion fatigue diminished and she was able to resume her regular routine.*

Burnout is described as a general malaise, psychological stress, and a "chronic tedium in the workplace" (Jenkins & Baird, 2002, p. 425). Burnout, due to psychological depletion, is accompanied by feelings of physical exhaustion, helplessness, hopelessness, disillusionment, negative self-concept, and negative attitudes toward work, people, and life itself (James & Gilliland, 2005; see also Appendix VIII).

Some of the other danger signs of burnout are difficulty leaving home in the morning, frequent clock watching, an inability to concentrate or focus on tasks, high absenteeism, increased pessimism, and cynicism about the workplace. A sense of being overloaded and overextended dominates the counselor's reactions. Feelings of burnout tend to develop gradually over an extended period and do not derive from a specific or identifiable incident; rather, the stress of working under unrelenting pressure and with little support appears to have a cumulative effect. The slow progression of burnout eludes early detection. Most counselors who work with traumatized clients carry the dual risk of experiencing both vicarious trauma and burnout; chronic vicarious trauma is a significant cause of counselor burnout (Figley, 1995).

The concepts of countertransference, secondary trauma, compassion fatigue, and burnout have similarities and differences. While the development of burnout is gradual, the onset of vicarious or secondary trauma and compassion fatigue is sudden and identifiable. Burnout is usually related to external factors such as large client caseloads, a lack of adequate supervision, isolation in doing trauma work, and other institutional and bureaucratic factors. In contrast, countertransference stems from issues that reside within the counselor.

Vicarious trauma and compassion fatigue are the result of the interaction between a counselor's worldview and the client's traumatic material. Thus, compassion fatigue and secondary trauma give us a fuller understanding of the ripple effect of trauma (McCann & Pearlman, 1990; Pearlman & Saakvitne, 1995).

Countertransference is distinct from vicarious trauma in that a specific aspect of a client or a client's experience triggers resolved or unresolved issues in a counselor's own life. In contrast, vicarious or secondary trauma reactions develop from simply hearing about a client's traumatic experience. Saakvitne (2003) makes an important distinction between vicarious or secondary trauma and countertransference by pointing out that countertransference refers to the response the therapist has to a particular client, while vicarious and secondary trauma is the cumulative effect of counseling traumatized clients.

Secondary traumatic stress (STS) is the most comprehensive and commonly used term that can be interchangeably used to describe vicarious trauma, countertransference, compassion fatigue, and burnout. STS is generally conceptualized as "reactions to the emotional demands on the therapist—from exposure to a trauma survivor's terrifying, horrifying, and shocking images" (Jenkins & Baird, 2002, p. 423). It is a form of "work-induced post-traumatic stress disorder" (Bell, 2003, p. 514). Throughout the rest of this chapter, secondary trauma is the term used to refer to the counselor's reactions to working with traumatized clients.

Supervision as a Self-Care Strategy

There are inevitable costs of caring (Figley, 1995). Despite these costs, most practitioners describe their work as rewarding. In a qualitative study investigating secondary trauma among counselors working with battered women, Bell (2003) found that 40% of the participants felt their work had the positive effect of making them more compassionate, grateful, and less judgmental, while only 10% described any negative effects of their work (p. 516).

Agencies that employ counselors who provide services to traumatized clients play a large role in counselor job satisfaction. Most importantly, the agency has a responsibility to provide counselors with adequate supervision in order to maintain work satisfaction and to decrease the effects of secondary trauma. Education, support, and administration are three salient functions of supervision; effective supervisors perform these functions in a positive therapist-supervisor relationship. The supervisory relationship can be the first place to detect countertransference, secondary trauma, and burnout. When counselors "are suffering, there is likely to be a consequent detrimental effect on the organizations within which they work" (Sexton, 1999, p. 397). Supervision carries the potential to provide trauma counselors with both a perspective on an issue and guidance on a challenge (Yassen, 1995).

Just as counselors seek to empower their clients to develop physical and psychological health, supervisors can encourage trauma counselors to expand their self-care strategies to deal with the stress of their work. Supervision can be one such self-care strategy: It is a place where counselors can be authentically heard, guided toward maintaining clinical boundaries, and supported when caseloads become overwhelming and homogenous with trauma clients. Supervisees should choose a supervisor who understands them, whom they feel they can trust, and with whom they can develop an alliance. Supervisors who have expertise in doing trauma work have an awareness of the challenges of the field; this reduces the possibility of supervisors inadvertently shaming counselors who share honest reactions (Cunningham, 2004).

Although multicultural competence is often gained through formal college coursework, a supervised clinical experience is critical in translating multicultural training into culturally sensitive practice. Supervisors play a salient role in facilitating this process (Inman, 2006). Cultural factors play a significant role in the development of trauma reactions; an understanding of these factors is critical for the development of a positive client-therapist relationship. Studies have found that supervisors who are open and attentive to cultural factors and who process cultural issues within the supervision relationship have a strong working alliance with supervisees; supervisees perceive such supervisors positively (Inman, 2006; Killian, 2001). This positive relationship has a ripple effect on the client.

Power is an important element in the supervisory relationship; it has to be addressed to maintain healthy supervisor-supervisee interaction (Vallance, 2004). Supervisors must be candid about the inherent power of their role to prevent it from being unconsciously played out in the supervisory relationship. Supervisors who make efforts to share power within the supervisory relationship can mislead supervises. Supervisory relationships are not structurally egalitarian, and any pretense to make them so merely submerges structural power so that it becomes a hidden force (Hewson, 1999).

In addition to improving counseling skills, another important goal of supervision is to safeguard the well-being of the client and the quality of the therapeutic relationship. Parallel processing is a valid phenomenon (Morrissey & Tribe, 2001). Supervisor-supervisee relationships are likely to replicate themselves at the client-therapist level (Williams, 1997). Skilled supervisors who strive to empower their supervisees increase the possibility of replicating this relationship at the client-therapist level. Conversely, supervisors who demonstrate disempowering behaviors risk a duplication of these harmful interactions by supervisees in their own therapeutic relationships. Such negative supervisory relationships indirectly victimize clients. The counselor's ultimate goal, which is to deliver the best possible services to the client, is therefore achieved through good supervision. Supervisors who do not meet professional and ethical standards of responsibility should be held accountable by their supervisees (Vallance, 2004).

The supportive function of supervision is evident in supervisory relationships that communicate a sense of worth, trust, and security similarly found in positive therapeutic interactions (Cearley, 2004). Good supervision affirms supervisees; it increases their self-confidence, self-esteem, and self-awareness. Supervisees who have positive relationships with their supervisors are likely to have an accurate and sensitive understanding of their clients (Constantine, 2001).

Peer supervision is an important resource for counselors (Catherall, 1995). Counselors who feel a sense of connection with other counselors are less likely to report secondary trauma responses (Pearlman & Saakvitne, 1995). When counselors share their reactions to a client's traumatic material with a peer counselor, they initiate potential support. This sharing permits a normalization of the counselor's reactions and a reduction of secondary trauma; it allows the counselor to continue with the important task of meeting the best interests of the client.

Secondary trauma workshops are one way of reminding counselors about the value of self-care. Such workshops encourage health and wellness, and provide peer support. Counselors' regular participation in secondary trauma workshops helps them maintain a positive attitude toward their work. Although such workshops may not completely impede the occurrence of work-related stress, they can serve as a protection against it.

Below is a model for conducting secondary trauma workshops that I have used over the years when working with community agencies that serve traumatized clients. It is based on the premise that in order to continue working with trauma survivors, counselors' first responsibility is to take care of themselves.

How to Conduct a Secondary Trauma Workshop

Preparation

A secondary trauma or self-care workshop is conducted with a homogenous group of participants (people who have a common purpose, usually work-related) for several reasons. Participation in a workshop often creates a sense of community and support. For this support to continue, workshop participants need to have ongoing contact with each other.

Workshop participants ensure full participation in a workshop by informing all concerned parties that they cannot be interrupted during the workshop. Since workshop leaders assure participants of privacy during the workshop, it is important to discuss the effects of administrative and supervisory relationships ahead of time so that the secondary trauma workshop does not become an arena for power dynamics.

If participants are provided with food, it should be consumed either before or after the workshop. People are allowed to bring beverages. The ideal set up for a workshop includes a room set up in a conference style, with a large table for people to sit around; water and a box of tissues is made available for participants. These conditions are usually arranged ahead of time with the person who requested the workshop, but should be checked before the workshop begins.

The time allotted for the workshop should always include a "buffer" period of 10 minutes at the end. This provides participants with an opportunity to transitional before resuming their routine activities. Finally, a flip chart and markers should be available and set up in an area that is easily accessible to the individual conducting the workshop.

Introduction and Guidelines

I usually begin the workshop by introducing myself and inviting participants to do the same by stating their names, the position they hold in the agency or company, and how long they may have worked or volunteered there. I then move on to the next segment of the workshop by reviewing a few important guidelines. These guidelines provide participants with structure and safety:

- *Confidentiality.* Participants are requested to keep any disclosure of personal information made in the workshop confidential so that everyone in the group can feel safe. The complexity of holding dual roles (employed in a professional setting and being personally affected by a client's trauma narratives) is highlighted. Participants are reminded that under stress, boundaries often become confused. There are, however, some exceptions to confidentiality. If at the end of the workshop there are concerns about the well-being of a group participant, I will initially address this concern directly with the individual and later with a supervisor if necessary.
- *Attendance.* Participants are encouraged to attend the entire workshop. Leaving prematurely can result in unresolved feelings; group members left behind may wonder whether something they said caused a participant to leave. However, if at any point in the workshop participants feel overwhelmed by the issues raised, they can choose to leave the room with the understanding that they will rejoin the group once they feel better.
- *Mutual Respect.* Participants are requested to respect each others' reactions and reminded that individuals have different ways of expressing intense emotions. By being nonjudgmental and open to others' reactions, they create an atmosphere of mutual respect.
- *Pass Rule.* Participants can choose to refrain from speaking. Their presence in the workshop and support provided by this presence is considered more important. This guideline offers those individuals who may be anxious about speaking in a group the choice of participating at their own pace.

Finally, participants are asked whether they have any guidelines they would like to include. Group participants are usually knowledgeable about the cultural dynamics of their group; they may have a particular guideline they would like to bring to the facilitator's attention.

Getting Everyone on the Same Page

The primary goal of the workshop is to look at the effects working with trauma survivors have on professional functioning. Since it is important for everyone to have a common understanding before beginning the workshop, it is helpful to review the following definitions with the group before proceeding:

Psychological trauma is defined as "the direct personal experience of an event that involves actual or threat of death or serious injury or threat to the physical integrity of another person or learning about unexpected or violent death, serious harm, or threat of death, or injury experienced by a family member or other close associates" (*DSM-IV*).

Countertransference occurs when a counselor's history interferes with his or her relationship with a client. Sometimes the past issue may be an unresolved one that causes the helper to become subjectively involved with a client's issues. Participants are reminded that when countertransference is left unattended or unresolved it can eventually lead to burnout, which is exemplified by days when counselors find themselves dragging their feet to work and having difficulty getting up in the morning.

Identifying Red Flags

Participants are asked to think about a time when they felt severely stressed and to visualize a particular signal or object that indicated that they were overwhelmed. Stressor signals usually reported include feelings of irritability, uncontrolled crying, and difficulty with concentration. These signals are important markers because they play the role of raising "red flags" that challenge affected individuals to stop and review their situation.

I often share the story of my cat, who acts as my "red flag." He usually rushes to the door to greet me when I arrive home at the end of the day. When I am feeling particularly stressed, I notice myself not returning his warm welcome and sometimes even disregarding his presence at the door. I soon enough realize my errant ways and acknowledge that the stressors of the day have plagued me. Attention to my self-care needs becomes critical at this point. It is important to have a red flag that is tangible or identifiable. External indicators quickly alert individuals to the need for self-care.

Common Response to Trauma

In this segment of the workshop, I ask participants to reflect on difficulties or challenges they may have experienced when working with traumatized clients. Participants are asked to comment on any personal changes they noticed physically, emotionally, and behaviorally. As participants discuss their responses, I record words and phrases on a flip chart; either direct or summarized participant statements are recorded. The list generated may resemble the list on the next page.

Common Reactions to Trauma

Physical Responses

Change in sleep patterns	Changes in appetite
Shallow, rapid breathing	Dizziness
Headaches	Pain or tension in body
Increased heart rate	Stomach upset
Fatigue	Sweating/rapid pulse
Chest palpitations	Nightmares/night terrors

Inability to remove oneself from event (emotionally or physically)

Tearful and crying for no apparent reason

Psychological/Emotional Responses

Shock or numbness	Anxiety
Feelings of fear/terror/disbelief	Anger toward others involved
	Depression
Guilt/Frustration	Sadness
Feeling unsafe/vulnerable	Loneliness
Helpless/hopeless	Powerless/worthless
Anger/rage	Emotional rollercoaster
Fear of what others think	Fear of ongoing victimization

Cognitive Responses

Confusion	Difficulty concentrating
Lapses in memory	Difficulty making decisions
Distorted thoughts	Too many thoughts at once
Slowed thinking	Thinking the world is unsafe
Thoughts about dying	Flashbacks
Intrusive images	Replaying the event repeatedly

Behavioral Responses

Easily startled	Increased conflict with others
Jumpiness	Withdrawal from others
Angry outbursts	Nervous energy/hyperactivity
Crying	Tendency to overwork
Fear of being alone	Difficulty trusting
Conflict in relationship	False generalizations about others
Critical of others	Doubts about relationships

Irritability	Strong reactions to small change
Clinging to people	Inability to perform easy tasks
Decreased energy	Changes in sexual activity
Sense of aloneness	Disruption of daily routine
Alienation	Increased use of alcohol or
Avoidance of places that	medications
evoke the event	Lower productivity

Spiritual Responses

Loss of faith	Spiritual doubts
Questioning old beliefs	Despair
Life is meaningless	Withdrawal from church or
Sense of the world	community
being changed	

Once participants have substantively shared their reactions, I use the group-generated list to highlight common reactions to stress and place them in physical, psychological, cognitive, behavioral, or spiritual categories. This is the psycho-educational segment of the workshop, which informs participants of expected reactions to secondary trauma. In addition, the following points are emphasized:

- Reactions are expected responses to a traumatic event.
- Reactions may come and go (a rollercoaster effect).
- Accompanying a traumatized client to court, although necessary, may exacerbate or trigger these reactions.

It is important to note that although these trauma reactions are likely to occur, how one copes with these reactions is more important. Turning to a fresh page on the flip chart, participants are redirected to consider the most important segment of the workshop: self-care.

Self-Care

For practitioners who counsel traumatized clients, finding ways to release stress is critical if they plan to continue working in the field. In this segment, participants are asked to brainstorm and share strategies they find helpful when they feel overwhelmed. The facilitator records these strategies on the flip chart. The goal is to have participants identify specific activities they find supportive and rewarding.

In conducting several secondary trauma workshops over the years, I have been impressed by the diversity of strategies people use to reduce stress in their lives: these include house cleaning, mowing the lawn, jogging, and taking long walks. Workshop participants tend to become quite animated during this segment of the workshop. After the earlier intense discussion of trauma reactions, this can be a refreshing change and a comfortable segue to the conclusion of the workshop.

It is important to remember that self-care strategies are culture-specific and often determined by financial and other resources. It is common for participants to list alcohol and smoking as possible self-care strategies. In some communities, visiting relatives or cooking a dinner for a large family are perceived as comforting activities. I recall a workshop participant relating to a group of co-workers that her self-care was going home at the end of the day and doing a load of laundry. Perhaps for this participant, doing her laundry was a symbolic act of cleansing and a release of heavy feelings.

Self-care strategies should pay attention to the following:

- Eating healthy meals by avoiding stimulants such as caffeine, chocolate, and nicotine and depressants (such as alcohol) is important. A poor diet increases stress levels (Andrews, Creamer, & Crino, 2003).
- Exercise is effective in managing stress. Walking, jogging, swimming, and cycling on a regular basis are good ways to exercise.
- Sleep is important in rejuvenating and re-energizing the body. Getting into the habit of doing something relaxing before sleep, such as listening to music, reading, or taking a bath, helps increase one's readiness for bed.
- Comfortable, familiar surroundings are stress-reducing. Trauma counselors should avoid spending too much time alone; instead, they should strive to spend time with people, but avoid a discussion of trauma. The support of family and friends is encouraged. Boundaries are set with people who have not been helpful in the past. Communicate your feelings clearly. Others may not know how to respond to you appropriately. Let them know which responses are helpful and which are not.
- Talking with trained helpers is beneficial. By sharing thoughts and feelings with those who are supportive and helpful, secondary trauma can be avoided. Seeking help if reactions are interfering with job responsibilities is critical.

- Engaging in fun activities can be stress-releasing. Laughing is a good way to increase good feelings and discharge tension. Norman Cousins (1991) describes laughter and humor as "internal jogging."

In summarizing the self-care segment of the workshop, the following points are emphasized:

- Self-care strategies should be attainable; focus on concrete, easily achievable tasks. For example, choosing to go to a bed-and-breakfast as a weekend getaway may be more practical and financially realistic than planning a vacation to a Caribbean island. The completion and control of activities is encouraged. Adequate time should be set aside to accomplish self-care activities; they should not become an additional task for an already stressed individual.
- Self-care strategies should be connected to the reactions a participant already experiences. For example, if individuals isolate themselves as a reaction to stress, then self-care strategies should include making a date with a friend, visiting a family member, or other social activities.
- Recognize that some self-care strategies may lead to further problems. For example, participants may identify having a glass of wine as a form of stress release. Remind them that alcohol is an addictive substance and one should be cautious about the self-care choices one makes.
- Participants should practice strategies that are comforting, healing, and restorative. These may include mindful self-care strategies that balance work and personal life and allow the individual to become present, conscious, and focused in the moment (Kabat-Zinn, 1994). Mindful activities are reminders of the importance of living each moment to the fullest (Cunningham, 2004).

Secondary trauma workshops do not immunize counselors against the vicarious effects of working in the trauma field. However, at the very least, those who participate in self-care workshops become better informed about the risks of the profession. With this awareness, participants may be motivated to do something at the first signs of secondary trauma.

Secondary trauma is intrinsic to the discipline of trauma counseling. However, a workplace that confers trust, safety, and support can protect its members from the damaging effects of secondary trauma. A cohesive workplace community in which members constantly remind each other to practice self-care contributes to the prevention of secondary trauma. Finally, the act of conducting secondary trauma workshops can be fulfilling for facilitators and remind them to practice their own self-care.

Besides the supervision and the support that is offered through secondary trauma workshops, other organizational changes can support those in the trauma profession.

Supportive Organizational Strategies

A supportive organizational environment mitigates the secondary stress experienced by trauma workers. Therapists who received empathetic support from co-workers following the Oklahoma City bombing, for example, had lowered levels of secondary trauma and psychological distress (Batten & Orsillo, 2002). An institution can support its workers in several ways. Some guidelines on achieving a supportive institutional environment are outlined below:

- Lowered clinical caseloads reduce a counselor's exposure to traumatized clients. In addition, smaller caseloads give practitioners more time (between clients) to process their clinical experience and complete administrative tasks. In contrast, larger caseloads are strongly associated with disruptions in cognitive schemas, increased PTSD symptoms, and secondary trauma among counselors (Schauben & Frazier, 1995). Ethical and practice guidelines from professional organizations such as the American Psychological Association (APA) and the American Counseling Association (ACA) provide procedures for maintaining manageable caseloads (Pearlman, 1995).
- Clear limits on actual work time should be established. Counselors should not be allowed to work more than 40 hours per week. If a clinical situation demands that a counselor work beyond an agreed schedule, he or she should be encouraged to take compensatory time after the situation is over. Lunch breaks should be viewed as important personal time. The delineations between work and personal time should be clear; counselors should be given adequate vacation, sick, and family leave time (Munroe, 1995).
- Offering in-service education on a continuous basis updates counselors on innovative and best practices in the field (Neumann & Gamble, 1995). In-service training serves as an opportunity to combine professional development, skill building, and organizational issues. In addition, it can identify administrative or clinical problems and explore possible solutions (East, James, & Keim, 2001).
- Time should be set aside for formal structured support groups, which serve a problem-solving function and build a sense of competency. A team approach provides opportunities to consult with colleagues or debrief difficult cases in a supportive collegial environment. Encouraging counselors to ask for assistance and to bring unresolved cases to a team reduces individual blame (Catherall, 1995).
- Work areas and therapy rooms should be clean, well lit, and cheerfully decorated. A well-stocked resource area includes books, videos, and reference

materials. Supplies should be adequate and readily available. All staff should have offices, phones, computers, and other equipment to achieve optimal performance. Safety procedures should be taught to all employees and constantly reinforced. Adequate office and administrative support prevents counselors from becoming overwhelmed with paperwork (East et al., 2001).

- Counselors should receive positive feedback on a consistent basis; successes should be shared and celebrated. This feedback indirectly helps counselors understand the importance of empowerment; they are likely to replicate this behavior with their clients (Galant, Trivette, & Dunst, 1999).

- The psychological well-being of counselors should be a priority. Access to professional mental health care, in the form of an Employee Assistance Program (EAP), should be part of a benefits package. Counselors should be able to seek help in a way that does not lead to stigmatization in a work setting. EAPs also provide counselors with opportunities to manage other stressors that may affect their ability to work effectively (Catherall, 1995).

Institutions that observe the guidelines outlined above create harmonious working environments, which sustain trauma counselors in the field.

Conclusion

Counselors who choose to specialize in the field of trauma counseling face many challenges. Primary among them is the transformation of a counselor's inner self as a result of compassionate engagement with a traumatized client—and the risk of secondary trauma that can result. Trauma counselors should be aware of the inherent risks in doing trauma work.

However, this awareness does not mitigate the effects of their work; it merely acknowledges that trauma work is stressful. Knowledge about secondary trauma can provide a framework for understanding the costs that accompany listening to the pain and suffering of trauma survivors. Most importantly, it increases the counselors' awareness so that when secondary trauma reactions arise, they can make efforts to address them. Counselors who use active coping skills will not hesitate to seek social support and other effective self-care strategies.

These strategies should be enjoyable, nurturing, and strive to produce psychosocial balance. They are likely to keep trauma counselors emotionally, psychologically, and physically healthy to withstand the emotional toll of helping the traumatized. Developing a sense of community with other trauma counselors reduces the isolation of doing trauma work.

A counselor's ability to play an integral role in a client's healing process can be immensely fulfilling and overshadow the negative aspects of secondary trauma. The strength, resilience, and fortitude that many traumatized clients exhibit during the recovery process is encouraging and professionally transformative. Finally, trauma therapists have an ethical responsibility to pay attention to self-care for two reasons: first, to shield themselves professionally; second, to ensure that their clients continue to receive high-quality services.

An important clinical implication related to the prevention of secondary trauma is training in trauma therapy. Trauma therapy involves the building of therapeutic relationships that demand the very best of counselors. This level of expertise requires adequate training and support. Trauma therapists should receive professional support provided by supervisors with expertise and experience in the trauma field. A core function of such supervision should be to both support and empower counselors so that they can similarly empower their clients.

The perspective taken in this book is that psychological and behavioral adaptations to trauma are expressions of pain and efforts to cope with unacceptable environmental demands and stressors. Traumatic reactions are, therefore, not always pathological, but are often grounded in cultural systems of meaning-making. It is the trauma counselor's responsibility to locate and utilize the inherent strength and resilience within individuals, families, and communities to empower them toward healing and recovery.

To this end, we have looked at trauma from a multicultural, historical context. We have explored interventions on multiple levels: individual, group, community, and national. The common theme throughout has been that traumatized individuals, groups, and communities can, ultimately, be empowered to overcome their trauma through effective therapy.

To work effectively with clients, clinicians must acknowledge that trauma is prevalent; it exists in all socioeconomic groups and in all families. Further, effective trauma therapy involves an understanding that trauma reactions are culture-bound, and trauma can have damaging long-term negative consequences. Using this paradigm, trauma can be viewed as an interaction between an individual's personality, psychological needs, and coping styles; the salient aspects of the traumatic event; and the social and cultural variables that shape psychological responses.

When doing trauma work, a loss of faith in humanity and a decrease in the idealism and enthusiasm with which counselors initially entered the field of trauma counseling is possible. Clinicians, like survivors, may be thrust into a grieving process when their beliefs are shattered. But with appropriate supervision and the practice of self-care, counselors can overcome the malaise of their work. Although their beliefs may change, trauma counselors are encouraged to remain steadfast in their values (see Appendix IX). One of these is an acknowledgment of the resiliency and essential goodness in every human being.

Resiliency provides the hope and trust that recovery is possible. As altruistic beings, counselors join the profession to make a difference; they have a commitment to be part of a client's healing. This is a noble calling and its fundamental purpose should always be remembered.

References

American Psychiatric Association. (1994). *Diagnostic and statistical manual of mental disorders* (4th ed.). Washington, DC: Author.

Andrews, G., Creamer, M., & Crino, R. (2003). The treatment of anxiety disorders: Clinician's guides and patient manual (2nd ed.). New York: Cambridge University Press.

Batten, S. V., & Orsillo, S. M. (2002). Therapist reactions in the context of collective trauma. *Behavior Therapist, 25,* 36–40.

Bell, H. (2003). Strengths and secondary trauma in family violence work. *Social Work, 48*(4), 514–522.

Catherall, D. R. (1995). Coping with secondary traumatic stress: The impotence of the therapist's professional peer group. In B. H. Stamm (Ed.), *Secondary traumatic stress: Self-care issues for clinicians, researchers and educators* (pp. 80–94). Lutherville, MD: Sidran Press.

Cearley, S. (2004). The power of supervision in child welfare services. *Child & Youth Care Forum, 33*(5), 313–327.

Constantine, M. G. (2001). Multiculturally-focused counseling supervision: Its relationship to trainees' multicultural counseling self-efficacy. *The Clinical Supervisor, 20,* 87–98.

Cousins, N. (1991). *The celebration of life: A dialogue on hope, spirit and the immortality of the soul.* New York: Bantam Books.

Cunningham, M. (2004). Avoiding vicarious traumatization. In N. B. Webb (Ed.), *Mass trauma and violence* (pp. 327–346). New York: Guilford.

Dass-Brailsford, P. (2003). A golden opportunity in supervision: Talking about countertransference. *Journal of Psychological Practice, 8*(1), 56–64.

East, T. W., James, R. K., & Keim, J. (2001). *The best little vicarious trauma intervention program in Tennessee.* Paper presented at the 25th Annual Convening of Crisis Intervention Personnel, Chicago.

Figley, C. R. (1995). Compassion fatigue: Toward a new understanding of the costs of caring. In B. H. Stamm (Ed.), *Secondary traumatic stress: Self-care issues for clinicians researchers and educators* (2nd ed., pp. 3–28). Lutherville, MD: Sidran Press.

Freud, S. (1957). *Introductory lectures on psychoanalysis.* New York: Liveright.

Galant, K. R., Trivette, C. M., & Dunst, D. J. (1999). The meaning and implications of empowerment. In G. G. Bear, K. M. Minke, & A. Thomas (Eds.), *Children's needs II: Development problems and alternatives* (pp. 681–688). Bethesda, MD: National Association of School Psychologists.

Hewson, D. M. (1999). Empowerment in supervision. *Feminism and Psychology*, 9(4),406–410.

Inman, A. G. (2006). Supervisor multicultural competence and its relation to supervisory process and outcome. *Journal of Marital and Family Therapy*, 32(1), 73–85.

James, R. K., & Gilliland, B. E. (2005). *Crisis intervention strategies* (5th ed.). Belmont, CA: Thomson Brooks/Cole.

Jenkins, S. R., & Baird, S. (2002). Secondary traumatic stress and vicarious trauma: A validational study. *Journal of Traumatic Stress*, 15(5), 423–432.

Kabat-Zinn, J. (1994). *Wherever you go, there you are: Mindfulness meditation in everyday life*. New York: Hyperion.

Killian, K. D. (2001). Differences making a difference: Cross–cultural interactions in supervisory relationships. *Journal of Feminist Family Therapy*, 12, 61–103.

McCann, I. L., & Pearlman, L. A. (1990). Vicarious traumatization: A framework for understanding the psychological effects of working with victims. *Journal of Traumatic Stress*, 3, 131–149.

Morrissey, J., & Tribe, R. (2001). Parallel process in supervision. *Counseling Psychology Quarterly*, 14, 103–110.

Munroe, J. (1995). Ethical issues associated with secondary trauma in therapists. In B. H. Stamm (Ed.), *Secondary traumatic stress* (2nd ed., pp. 211–229). Baltimore, MD: Sidran Press.

Neumann, D. A., & Gamble, S. J. (1995). Issues in the professional development of psychotherapists: Countertransference and vicarious traumatization in the new trauma therapist. *Psychotherapy: Theory, Research, Practice, Training*, 32(2), 341–347.

Pearlman, L. A. (1995). Self-care for trauma therapists: Ameliorating vicarious traumatization. In B. Hudnall Stamm (Ed.), *Secondary traumatic stress* (2nd ed., pp. 51–64). Baltimore, MD: Sidran Press.

Pearlman, L. A., & MacIan, P. S. (1995). Vicarious traumatization: An empirical study of the effects of trauma work on trauma therapists. *Professional Psychology: Research and Practice*, 26(6), 558–565.

Pearlman, L. A., & Saakvitne, K. W. (1995). Treating therapists with vicarious traumatization and secondary traumatic stress disorders. In C. R. Figley (Ed.), *Compassion fatigue: Coping with secondary traumatic stress disorder in those who treat the traumatized* (pp. 150–177). Bristol, PA: Brunner/Mazel.

Saakvitne, K. W. (2003). Holding hope and humanity in the face of trauma's legacy: The daunting challenge for group therapists. *International Journal of Group Psychotherapy*, 55(1), 137–148.

Schauben, L. J., & Frazier, P. A. (1995). Vicarious trauma: The effects on female counselors working with sexual violence survivors. *Psychology of Women Quarterly*, 19, 49–64.

Sexton, L. (1999). Vicarious traumatization of counselors and effects on their workplaces. *British Journal of Guidance and Counseling*, 27(3), 393–403.

Terr, L. C. (1989). Family anxiety after traumatic events. *Journal of Clinical Psychiatry*, 50(11, Supp.), 15–19.

Tripanny, R. L., White Kress, V. E., & Wicoxon, S. A. (2004). Preventing vicarious trauma: What counselors should know when working with trauma survivors, *Journal of Counseling and Development, 82,* 31–37.

Vallance, K. (2004). Exploring counselor perceptions of the impact of counseling supervision on clients. *British Journal of Guidance and Counseling, 32*(4), 559–573.

Williams, A. B. (1997). On parallel process in social work supervision. *Clinical Social Work Journal, 25,* 425–435.

Yassen, J. (1995). Preventing secondary traumatic stress disorder. In C. Figley (Ed.), *Compassion fatigue: Secondary traumatic stress disorder from treating the traumatized* (pp. 178–207). New York: Brunner/Mazel.

Appendix I

Common Reactions to Trauma

Physical Responses

Change in appetite	Increased heart rate
Change in sleep patterns	Muscle tension
Chest palpitations	Nightmares/Night terrors
Dizziness	Shallow, rapid breathing
Fatigue	Stomach upset
Headaches	Sweating/rapid pulse

Psychological/Emotional Responses

Anger toward others involved	Feeling helpless/hopeless
Anger/rage	Feeling powerless/worthless
Depression	Feeling unsafe/vulnerable
Emotional rollercoaster	Guilt/Frustration
Fear	Loneliness
Fear of ongoing victimization	Sadness
Fearing what others think	Shock or numbness

Cognitive Responses

Confusion

Difficulty concentrating

Difficulty making decisions

Difficulty remembering

Distorted thoughts

Flashbacks

Intrusive images

Role-playing the event

Slowed thinking

Thinking the world is unsafe

Thoughts about dying

Too many thoughts at once

Behavioral Responses

Alienation from family/friends

Angry outbursts

Changes in sexual activity

Clinging to people

Conflict in relationship

Critical of others

Crying

Decreased energy

Difficulty trusting

Disruption of daily routine

Doubts about relationships

False generalizations about others

Fear of being alone

Inability to perform easy tasks

Increased use of alcohol or medication

Irritability

Sense of aloneness

Strong reactions to small change

Withdrawal from others

Spiritual Responses

Despair

Feeling life is meaningless

Loss of faith

Questioning old beliefs

Sense of the world being changed

Spiritual doubts

Withdrawal from church or community

Appendix II

Coping With Trauma

- Care for yourself by eating well, exercising, and resting when necessary.
- Avoid stimulants such as caffeine, chocolate, and nicotine and depressants such as alcohol.
- Seek comfortable, familiar surroundings and avoid spending too much time alone.
- Share thoughts and feelings with those who are supportive and helpful—don't try to block recollections. It helps to talk. Feel free to set boundaries with people who have not been helpful in the past.
- Don't be anxious if reactions from past traumas re-emerge even though you felt those issues were resolved.
- Give yourself time to recover. Difficulties with concentration, memory, or decision-making are common; they are usually short-term reactions.
- Seek help if reactions are interfering with job responsibilities. Focus on concrete and achievable tasks.
- Remember that difficulty sleeping, nightmares, flashbacks, and hyper-alertness are common reactions and will diminish with time.
- Avoid personalizing or taking responsibility for how others respond to the traumatic event. Do not compare or measure your reactions to those of other people—each individual's experience is unique and personal.
- Communicate your feelings clearly. Others may not know how to respond to you appropriately. Let them know which responses are helpful and which are not.
- Know that anniversary dates or a specific holiday may trigger feelings related to the trauma.
- Seek help from a professional counselor if reactions persist.

Appendix III

Coping With Grief and Loss

G rief occurs in response to the loss of a loved one, a job, or a role (e.g., retirement, child leaves for college). It can be sudden or expected. However, each individual's experience of loss is unique. Grieving is a natural healing process. For most people, grieving proceeds through several stages, as outlined below. These stages are not hierarchical, and individuals may find themselves cycling through earlier stages as they attempt to come to terms with their loss.

Acknowledging and understanding grief reactions promotes the healing process and helps affected individuals know when to get additional support. Individuals respond to loss in many ways; some are healthy coping mechanisms and others hinder the grieving process.

Stages of Grief

Denial, Numbness, and Shock

- Denial protects the individual from experiencing the intensity of the loss.
- Numbness to experience is a normal reaction to loss and should not be viewed as a lack of care.
- Emotional paralysis causes the mind to exclude painful feelings of loss.
- Denial and disbelief will diminish as the individual slowly acknowledges the impact of loss and accompanying feelings.

Bargaining

- Individuals may ruminate about what they could have done to prevent the loss.
- Individuals may become preoccupied with the ways things could have been; they imagine all the things that will never happen.
- If not properly resolved, intense feelings of remorse or guilt may hinder the healing process.

Depression

- Once individuals realize the extent of their loss, they may experience depressive symptoms.
- Disturbances in sleep and appetite, lack of energy and concentration, and frequent crying and tearfulness are typical symptoms of this stage.
- Feelings of loneliness, emptiness, isolation, and self-pity may become prevalent.
- For some individuals, this phase must be experienced before they can begin reorganizing their lives.

Anger

- Feelings of anger surface when individuals feel helpless and powerless.
- Anger may also result from feelings of abandonment because of the loss.
- Feelings of resentment toward a higher power for the injustice of loss may surface.
- Once an individual acknowledges anger, feelings of guilt may surface.
- All feelings are natural and should be acknowledged and honored.

Acceptance

- Time helps individuals to resolve their feelings.
- Healing occurs when individuals integrate the loss into their lives.
- It is not unusual to return to earlier feelings of loss.
- The grieving process has no time limit; each individual's healing process is unique.

Guidelines to Help Resolve Grief

- Give yourself time to express feelings openly. Crying offers a release; allow yourself to experience thoughts and feelings of loss.
- Acknowledge and accept both positive and negative feelings. Anger is an acceptable emotion, but how one deals with it is important.
- Try to maintain schedules and routines.
- Rest, sleep, and try to relax as much as possible.
- Journaling assists in the healing process.

- Confide in a trusted individual; telling the story of loss can promote recovery.
- Identify unresolved feelings and find ways to settle them.
- Bereavement groups provide opportunities to share grief with others who have similar experiences.
- Seek professional help when the grieving process becomes overwhelming or suicidal feelings emerge.
- Avoid minimization of one's emotions (e.g., by overworking).
- Avoid self-medicating with alcohol or drugs.

Further Reading

Kubler-Ross, E. (1969). *On death and dying.* New York: MacMillan.

Kubler-Ross, E. (1975). *The final stage of growth.* Englewood Cliffs, NJ: Prentice Hall.

Appendix IV

Helping Children Cope With Loss and Grief

D eath and loss can be quite confusing to children. The following guidelines can help make this challenging task a little easier.

Tell your child about a death or loss as soon as possible to prevent the child from
hearing about it from someone else.

- Choose a quiet, familiar setting with few distractions.
- Be direct and accurate in your communication and avoid words that could be
  misinterpreted (e.g., "We lost Uncle David" could be interpreted literally by
  your child that Uncle David could be found). Depending on their age, children
  may see death as reversible.
- Listen carefully, ask your child if he or she has any questions, and allow for
  silence.
- Talk about your own feelings without burdening the child. Expressing your
  own grief and sadness is appropriate.
- Offer your child reassurance and show your love. The recent loss may engender
  fears of losing you as well.
- Children may ask the same questions repeatedly as they struggle to come to
  terms with their loss; try to be patient.
- Children may question whether they are to blame for the loss of a loved one and
  may need reassurance in this area.
- For the first time, children may realize they could also die and may need reassurance that people usually die when they are older.

- Funerals can help children accept the reality of death, but children's attendance at a funeral should only occur if they appear ready for it; they should always be given a choice.
- If children attend a funeral, they should be informed about what to expect. Explain the purposes of a service and prepare some activities (e.g., coloring book and crayons) to occupy them should they get bored.
- Monitor the child carefully for behavioral changes and seek professional help if necessary.

Some Children's Books on Death and Loss

Thomas, P., & Harker, L. (2000). *I miss you: A first look at death.* Hauppauge, NY: Barron's Educational Series.

Helps children understand that death is a natural part of life and that grief and a sense of loss are normal feelings. The story is direct and simple and easy to understand. Full-color illustrations attract children's attention (Ages 4–7).

Eldon, A. (2002). *Angel catcher for kids: A journal to help you remember the person you love who died.* San Francisco, CA: Chronicle Books.

Angel Catcher for Kids helps children cope with the painful and confusing process of grieving. This book helps children overcome the loss of a loved one by recording their special memories of the person who has died (Ages 7–12).

Kidd, D. (1993). *Onion tears.* New York: Orchard Books.

Through this tale of Nam-Huong, a refugee child who wants to adjust to her new life in Australia, children learn how to deal with the loss of home and familiar people. Nam-Huong slowly develops trust and is able to love again with the help of her foster mother and her teacher (Ages 5–8).

Palmer, P., & O'Quinn Burke, D. (2000). *I wish I could hold your hand: A child's guide to grief and loss.* Atascadero, CA: Impact.

This book helps grieving children identify and express feelings of loss. Uplifting and cheerful illustrations and accessible writing helps children accept that loss is a natural part of life (Ages 9–12).

Schriver, M., & Speidel, S. (1999). *What's heaven?* New York: Golden Books.

In this touching tale, a young girl tries to understand the loss of her great-grandmother. Reassuring explanations help children understand that death and grieving are a normal part of life (Pre-K).

Buscaglia L., & Buscaglia L. F. (2000). *The fall of Freddie the leaf: A story of life for all ages.* New York: Holt, Rinehart & Winston.

In this story, Freddie experiences the changing seasons along with his companion leaves who change with the passing seasons, finally falling to the ground with a winter's snow. This inspiring story illustrates the delicate balance between life and death (Ages 4–8).

Alley, R. W. (1998). *Sad isn't bad: A good-grief guidebook for kids dealing with loss.* St. Meinrad, IN: Abbey Press.

This guidebook teaches children how to deal with loss. It is filled with positive, life-affirming advice on how to cope with loss as a child; the world is seen as safe, life is seen as good, and hurt hearts are able to recover (Ages 4–8).

Appendix V

Client Safety and
Self-Care Worksheet

T he following questions can help you think about your ability to keep yourself safe and care for yourself.

1. When have you felt safe? Describe.

   _____

   _____

   _____

   _____

2. Describe three ways in which you take care of yourself.

   _____

   _____

   _____

   _____

3. Describe ways in which you think you do not take care of yourself.

_____

_____

_____

_____

4. I take good care of myself when I am feeling . . .

_____

_____

_____

_____

5. I do not take care of myself when I am feeling . . .

_____

_____

_____

_____

6. When I imagine myself feeling safe . . .

_____

_____

_____

_____

Appendix VI

Deep/Diaphragmatic Breathing

D iaphragmatic breathing makes use of the muscles of the diaphragm (a strong dome-shaped muscle) located under the ribs and above the stomach. When we breathe in, we push the muscle down, and our tummy moves forward. When we breathe out, the diaphragmatic muscle moves back to resting position and our tummy moves back in. There is little or no upper chest movement during diaphragmatic breathing.

When you first learn the diaphragmatic breathing technique, it may be easier to follow the instructions while lying down. As you gain more practice, you can try the diaphragmatic breathing technique while sitting in a chair (described below). To begin this exercise, lie on your back on a flat surface or in bed with your knees bent and your head supported. You can use a pillow under your knees to support your legs. Place one hand on your upper chest and the other just below your rib cage. This will allow you to feel your diaphragm move as you breathe.

Breathe in slowly through your nose so that your stomach moves out against your hand. The hand on your chest should remain as still as possible. Tighten your stomach muscles, letting them fall inward as you exhale through pursed lips. The hand on your upper chest remains as still as possible.

To perform this exercise while sitting in a chair,

- Sit comfortably, with your knees bent and your shoulders, head, and neck relaxed.
- Place one hand on your upper chest and the other just below your rib cage. This will allow you to feel your diaphragm move as you breathe.

- Tighten your stomach muscles, letting them fall inward as you exhale through pursed lips. The hand on your upper chest remains as still as possible.

You may notice an increased effort is needed to practice diaphragmatic breathing correctly. At first, the exercise may be exhausting. With continued practice, however, diaphragmatic breathing will become easy and automatic.

Practice this exercise for 5 to 10 minutes about 3 or 4 times per day in the beginning. Gradually increase the amount of time you spend doing this exercise; the effort of doing the exercise can be increased by placing a book on your abdomen.

Appendix VII

Progressive Muscle Relaxation

P rogressive muscle relaxation (PMR) is a simple, easy-to-learn technique for relaxation. In PMR, the client is taught to relax his or her muscles through a two-step process: first deliberately applying tension to certain muscle groups and then releasing the tension and noticing how the muscles relax and the tension dissipates. With practice, clients quickly learn to distinguish between tense muscles and relaxed muscles. With this simple knowledge, they can induce physical muscular relaxation at the first signs of tension and anxiety. Mental calmness usually follows physical relaxation.

Suggestions for Practice

- Practice PMR twice a day for about a week before moving on to the shortened form (also outlined below).
- Begin practicing full PMR in a quiet place, without distractions or background sounds (music).
- Remove shoes and wear loose clothing.
- Sit in a comfortable chair, if possible. You may practice lying down, but this increases the likelihood of falling asleep.
- Begin by focusing on the muscles of your right foot; inhale and squeeze the muscles as hard as you can for about eight seconds. This may feel slightly uncomfortable. After eight seconds, quickly release the muscles and let the tightness flow out as you simultaneously exhale. Feel the muscles relax and become limp while the tension flows away. Allow yourself to notice the difference between tension and relaxation.
- Systematically repeat this process with the lower right leg and the entire right leg before moving to the left foot, lower left leg, and entire left leg. Tense and

relax the right hand, forearm, and entire arm; then do the same with the left side. Next, tense and relax muscles in the abdomen, chest, shoulders, neck, and face. This is a full PMR procedure, which provides a deep sense of relaxation.

- When you finish a session, relax and sit with your eyes closed for a few seconds before getting up slowly. Some people count backwards from five while breathing deeply before allowing themselves to become fully alert.

PMR (Short Form)

The shortened form of PMR is often used in therapy sessions after clients have practiced the full PMR at home or on their own time. The focus is on a group of muscles rather than individual muscles:

- Lower limbs
- Abdomen and chest
- Arms, shoulders, and neck
- Face

The individual focuses on both legs and feet at once, rather than each individually. The shortened form should be practiced under similar environmental conditions to full PMR, twice daily for a week, to gain proficiency.

Finally, as a word of caution, individuals with a history of serious injuries, muscle spasms, or back problems should consult a physician. Deliberate tensing of muscles, as is required in PMR, can exacerbate pre-existing conditions.

Appendix VIII

Stages of Burnout

Stress Arousal Stage (Evidenced by Two of the Following)

- Persistent irritability
- Persistent anxiety
- Insomnia
- Forgetfulness
- Heart palpitations
- Inability to concentrate
- Headaches
- Bruxism (grinding teeth in sleep)

Conservation Stage (Evidenced by Two of the Following)

- Procrastination
- Frequent clock watching at work
- Difficulty going to work/showing up late for work
- Decreased sexual desire
- Tiredness in mornings
- Social withdrawal
- Cynical attitudes
- Resentfulness
- Increased alcohol consumption
- Increased tea, coffee, and soda consumption
- Loss of interest in work
- Need for three-day weekends

Fatigue Stage (Evidenced by Two of the Following)

- Chronic sadness/depression
- Stomach or bowel problems; frequent colds and flu

- Chronic mental fatigue
- Migraines and headaches
- Extreme physical fatigue at end of workday
- Social withdrawal and loss of interest
- Isolation and withdrawal from friends, family, and co-workers
- Desire to commit suicide
- Decrease in compassion for victims
- High absenteeism
- Excessive drug use

Appendix IX

Counselor Self-Care

Beliefs, Conflicts, and Rewards

1. Identify all the ways you are caring and providing services for others:

   At work:
   In your family:
   For colleagues:
   For friends:
   For your community:
   Any other ways:

2. How long have you been doing this?

3. What did your family of origin teach you about altruism and caring?

4. What are your beliefs about caring for others?

5. What are your difficulties/conflicts/challenges in caring?

6. What are the rewards of being a caregiver?

7. Who/what are your sources of inspiration?

8. What was your original purpose for becoming a volunteer/human service provider?

Appendix X

Trauma Assessment Tools for Adults

S everal tools have been developed to assess a trauma survivor's level of functioning. These tools are briefly outlined below.

Before using any assessment tool, Kulka et al. (1991) cautions the counselor to keep in mind the following variables:

- What can be accomplished by using an assessment tool?
- What evidence supports its use?
- How long does it take to complete?
- How might gender, ethnicity, and cross-cultural differences influence the results?
- How might translations, which are not always psychometrically equivalent to the original instruments, impact assessment?
- How are multiple measures incorporated, given that their use is strongly recommended in assessing PTSD?

The counselor should always remember the goal of assessment is not to simply acquire a test score, but rather to improve a practitioner's understanding of how a trauma has affected a client. All assessment measures are fallible to some degree; combining methods helps reduce diagnostic errors (Weathers & Keane, 1999).

Trauma Symptom Inventory

The Trauma Symptom Inventory (TSI) is a test containing 100 items that measures post-traumatic stress and psychological sequelae of traumatic events. The TSI was devised to assess symptoms of acute and chronic traumas such as rape, physical assault, spouse abuse, major accidents, combat trauma, and natural disasters. Additionally, the TSI assesses the enduring effects of abuse and trauma that may have occurred in childhood (Briere, 1995).

Clinician-Administered PTSD Scale

The Clinician-Administered PTSD Scale (CAPS) is a structured, comprehensive interview designed to assess PTSD among adults. The CAPS scale evaluates 17 symptoms of PTSD listed in *DSM-IV*. Additionally, the CAPS includes the following five features associated with PTSD: guilt, dissociation, derealization, depersonalization, and reduction in awareness of surroundings. Initially developed by the National Center for PTSD (Blake et al., 1990), the CAPS scale evaluates

- self-reports of exposure to potential Criterion A events.
- current and/or lifetime *DSM-IV* diagnoses of PTSD,
- the frequency and intensity of each symptom,
- the impact of the 17 PTSD symptoms on social and occupational functioning,
- the overall severity of PTSD.

Impact of Events Scale

The Impact of Events Scale (IES) is a 15-item questionnaire devised by Horowitz, Wilner, and Alvarez (1979) to measure subjective distress as it relates to a specific event. The IES is one of the earliest self-report measures of post-traumatic disturbance, and it has displayed the ability to discriminate a variety of traumatized groups from nontraumatized groups (Briere, 1997). This scale's sensitivity to change renders it useful for monitoring a client's progress in therapy (Corcoran & Fischer, 1994).

Measured by the IES, the intrusion and avoidance scales are two major response sets that show good internal consistency. However, Briere (1997) found that the IES is racially sensitive; he recommends that interpretations of results from the IES should include a consideration of racial factors.

Dissociative Experience Scale

The Dissociative Experience Scale (DES; Bernstein & Putnam, 1986) is a 28-item self-report instrument that can be completed in 10 minutes and scored in less than 5 minutes. The questionnaire is easy to understand, and the questions are framed in a manner that does not stigmatize the respondent who responds positively. A typical DES question reads, "Some people have the experience of finding new things among their belongings that they do not remember buying. Mark the line to show what percentage of the time this happens to you." The DES outlines a variety of dissociative experiences, many of which can be considered normal.

References

Bernstein, E. M., & Putnam, F. W. (1986). Development, reliability and validity of a dissociation scale. *Journal of Nervous and Mental Disease, 174*(12), 727–735.

Blake, D. D., Weathers, F. W., Nagy, L. M., Kaloupek, D. G., Kluaminzer, G., Charney, D. S., et al. (1990). A clinician rating scale for assessing current and lifetime PTSD: The CAPS-1. *Behavior Therapist, 13,* 187–188.

Briere, J. (1995). *Trauma symptom inventory: Professional manual.* Odessa, FL: Psychological Assessment Resources.

Briere, J. (1997). *Psychological assessment of adult posttraumatic states.* Washington, DC: American Psychological Association.

Corcoran, K., & Fischer, J. (1994). *Measures for clinical practice: A sourcebook* (3rd ed., Vol. 2). New York: The Free Press.

Horowitz, M., Wilner, M., & Alvarez, W. (1979). Impact of event scale: A measure of subjective stress. *Psychosomatic Medicine, 41,* 209–218.

Kulka, R. A., Schlenger, W. E., Fairbank, J. A., Hough, R. L., Jordan, B. K., Marmar, C. R., et al. (1991). Assessment of posttraumatic stress disorder in the community prospects and pitfalls from recent studies of Vietnam veterans. *Psychological Assessment, 3,* 547–560.

Weathers, F. W., & Keane, T. M. (1999). Psychological assessment of traumatized adults. In P. A. Saigh & J. D. Bremner (Eds.), *Posttraumatic stress disorder: A comprehensive text.* Boston: Allyn & Bacon.

Appendix XI

Trauma Assessment Tools for Children and Adolescents

Trauma Symptom Checklist for Children

Although several multi-scale tests exist that assess childhood post-traumatic symptoms, none were standardized on a large sample of children in the general population. This deficit was addressed in 1996 when Briere designed the Trauma Symptom Checklist for Children (TSCC). The TSCC evaluates children's responses to unspecified traumatic events in different symptom domains. Additionally, the TSCC is standardized on a large sample of racially and economically diverse children from a variety of living conditions. This checklist also includes norms for age and gender; it is suitable for both individual and group administration (Briere, 1996).

Child and Adolescent Version of the Clinician-Administered PTSD Scale

The Child and Adolescent version of the Clinician-Administered PTSD Scale (CAPS-CA) is a structured clinical interview that can be developmentally adjusted for use with children and adolescents. The CAPS-CA evaluates self-reports of exposure to potential Criterion A events; current and/or lifetime diagnosis of PTSD; the frequency and intensity of each symptom; the impact of the 17 PTSD symptoms on developmental, social, and scholastic functioning; and the overall severity of PTSD.

To increase the utility of this assessment tool with children, there are additional features of the CAPS-CA:

- Iconic representations of the rating scales
- Opportunities to practice the format prior to questioning
- A standard procedure for identification of the critical one-month time frame for current symptoms

Traumatic Events Screening Inventory—Child

The Traumatic Events Screening Inventory—Child (TESI-C) is a guide for clinical and/or research interviewing that screens for children's history of exposure to potentially traumatic experiences. The protocol is designed to help clinicians systematically focus on the primary domains of child trauma. These primary domains include direct exposure/witness to severe accidents, illness, or disaster; family or community conflict or violence; and sexual molestation.

The questions gradually lead up to the most intimate traumatic experiences; this assists children to tolerate the distress of disclosing a trauma. As a result, sexual trauma is only discussed at the end of the interview. Furthermore, the inventory is structured to foster the child's recollection not only of physical harm or violence but also threats of harm and the witnessing of trauma. Since this protocol merely provides hypotheses, findings should be corroborated with information gained from other independent sources (Ribbe, 1996).

Child Dissociative Checklist

The Child Dissociative Checklist (CDC) is an easily administered scale designed to assess dissociative symptoms in sexually abused children. There are 20 items, which assess the following symptoms:

- Dissociation
- Spontaneous trance states
- Hallucinations
- Alterations in identity
- Aggressive and sexual behavior
- Rapid shifts in mood and cognition (Putnam, 1988)

References

Briere, J. (1996). *Trauma symptom checklist for children: Professional manual.* Odessa, FL: Psychological Assessment Resources.

Putnam, F. W. (1988). *Child dissociative checklist.* Bethesda, MD: Author.

Ribbe, D. (1996). Psychometric review of traumatic event screening instrument for children (TESI-C). In Stamm, B. H. (Ed.), *Measurement of stress, trauma and adaptations* (pp. 386–387). Lutherville, MD: Sidran Press.

Index

Brain:
  effects of PTSD, 32–34
  Traumatic Brain Injury (TBI),
    231–232
Brand, S., 76
Brandell-Forsberg, M., 187
Brandsma, J. M., 58
Brave Heart, M.Y.H., 7, 9
Bravo, M., 265
Breitenbecher, K. H., 205
Bremner, A., 32
Bremner, J. D., 32, 33
Brennan, J. M., 207
Brent, D. A., 110
Bresnahan, M., 249
Brewin, C. R., 36, 37, 160
Brief psychodynamic
  psychotherapy, 53
Briere, J., 39, 61, 62, 67, 77, 187
Briner, R., 160
Brock, S. E., 105, 106, 123
Bromet, E., 40
Bronfenbrenner, U., 75, 76
Brooks, D. L., 201
Brown, D. F., 45, 163
Brown, P. J., 41
Brown-Cheatham, M., 78
Browne, A., 191, 192
Browne, C., 80
Brownell, A., 267, 268
Brownmiller, S., 200, 201
Bruce, S. E., 218
Brunet, A., 3
Bryant, P., 32
Bryant, R. A., 31, 36, 37, 159
Buit, B., 30
Bunce, S. C., 30
Bureau of Indian Affairs, 9
Burgess, A. W., 192
Burgess, P. M., 40
Burlingham, D. T., 178
Burnout, 295–297
Burns, C., 166
Burton, K. B., 53, 86
Bush, G. W., 249
Bushman, B. J., 253
Bybee, D., 76
Bybee, R. F., 96

Caddell, J. M., 55
Cambodian refugees, 227
Campbell, J., 209
Campfield, K. M., 161, 166

Candelaria, E., 270, 274
Canino, G. J., 265
Canterbury, R., 189, 264, 270, 274
Cantor, J., 253
Caplan, G., 94, 95
Capozzoli, J. A., 123
Carlier, I. V. E., 160
Carlson, E. B., 43
Carlson E. B., 227
Carlson, J. G., 213
Carroll, K., 40
Carson, M. A., 32
Caruth, M., 234
Carved from the Heart (film), 139
Caspi-Yavin, Y., 230
Castillo, R. J., 79
Catalano, R. F., 217
Catharsis, 256
Catherall, D. R., 298, 306, 307
Cayouette, S., 218
CBT (cognitive-behavioral therapy):
  adolescent survivors of sexual
    assault, 125–131
  anxiety management, 56
  battered women, 209
  exposure therapy, 55, 57
  techniques, 55
  accident victims, 159
  group therapy model, 120, 123
  rape survivors, 204–205
  stress inoculation therapy (SIT), 56
  systematic desensitization, 55–56
CBT groups (adolescent sexual
  assault survivors):
  group design and content, 126–127
  sample group, 127–131
  screening, 125–126
Cearley, S., 298
Center for Mental Health Services
  (CMHS), 282
Center for Research on Rape, 4
Certificate of Indian Blood, 9
Challenger shuttle disaster, 180
Chattarji, S., 32
Chemtob, C. M., 58, 166, 213
Cheng, W.J.Y., 15
Chernobyl plant disaster (1986), 265
Child abuse:
  domestic violence, 214, 215
  See also Sexual child abuse
Child Maltreatment 2004, 191
Child Witness to Violence
  Project (Boston), 213

About the Author

Dr. Priscilla Dass-Brailsford is an Associate Professor in the Division of Counseling and Psychology at Lesley University in Cambridge, MA. She has over 18 years of clinical experience working with the underserved and chronically traumatized. She has worked in child advocacy and conducted court-ordered sexual abuse evaluations.

For several years, Dr. Dass-Brailsford coordinated a state crisis team, the first of its kind at its inception. In this role, she responded to high profile incidents of violence and helped affected communities in their healing.

Dr. Dass-Brailsford's research has focused on resiliency in the aftermath of political trauma and socioeconomic stress. She also has a multicultural research project that examines racial identity development. Through her consulting practice, Dr. Dass-Brailsford conducts crisis interventions in corporations and financial institutions. She was a first responder in New York after the terrorist attack in 2001 and was deployed to New Orleans after Hurricane Katrina devastated the Gulf Coast in 2005. Dr. Dass-Brailsford has assisted several school districts to develop crisis protocols.

This book is a culmination of her clinical experience and dual expertise in trauma and multicultural work that she hopes will inspire and empower psychotherapists who engage in the challenging and rewarding work of trauma therapy.